THE REED SMOOT HEARINGS

The
REED SMOOT
HEARINGS

The Investigation of a Mormon Senator and
the Transformation of an American Religion

EDITED BY

Michael Harold Paulos and Konden Smith Hansen

UTAH STATE UNIVERSITY PRESS

Logan

Published by Utah State University Press
An imprint of University Press of Colorado
245 Century Circle, Suite 202
Louisville, Colorado 80027

First paperback edition 2022
Manufactured in the United States of America.

The University Press of Colorado is a proud member of
the Association of University Presses.

ASSOCIATION
of UNIVERSITY
PRESSES

The University Press of Colorado is a cooperative publishing enterprise supported, in part, by
Adams State University, Colorado State University, Fort Lewis College, Metropolitan State University
of Denver, Regis University, University of Alaska Fairbanks, University of Colorado, University
of Denver, University of Northern Colorado, University of Wyoming, Utah State University, and
Western Colorado University.

∞ This paper meets the requirements of the ANSI/NISO Z39.48–1992 (Permanence of Paper).

ISBN: 978-1-64642-116-9 (hardcover)
ISBN: 978-1-64642-311-8 (paperback)
ISBN: 978-1-64642-117-6 (eBook)
https://doi.org/10.7330/9781646421176

Library of Congress Cataloging-in-Publication Data

Names: Paulos, Michael H., editor. | Smith Hansen, Konden, editor.
Title: The Reed Smoot hearings : the investigation of a Mormon senator and the transformation of an
American religion / edited by Michael Harold Paulos and Konden Smith Hansen.
Other titles: The investigation of a Mormon senator and the transformation of an American religion
Description: Logan : Utah State University Press, [2021] | Includes bibliographical references and index.
Identifiers: LCCN 2021001145 (print) | LCCN 2021001146 (ebook) | ISBN 9781646421169 (hardcover)|
ISBN 9781646423118 (paperback) | ISBN 9781646421176 (ebook)
Subjects: LCSH: Smoot, Reed, 1862–1941—Political and social views. | Mormons—Political activ-
ity—Utah—History—20th century. | Mormon Church—United States—History—20th century. |
Mormons—Civil rights—United States—History—20th century. | Religion and politics—United
States—History—20th century. | Legislators—Utah—History—20th century. | Legislative hear-
ings—United States. | Polygamy—United States.
Classification: LCC E664.S68 R44 2021 (print) | LCC E664.S68 (ebook) | DDC 328.73/092—dc23
LC record available at https://lccn.loc.gov/2021001145
LC ebook record available at https://lccn.loc.gov/2021001146

Earlier versions of chapter 1 and 6 were published in The Journal of Mormon History. Chapter 7 is
reprinted with the permission of the Smith-Petit Foundation.

On behalf of our members, authors, and readers, the volume editors thank the Gonzaba Medical Group
for the generous support toward the publication of this book.

Cover Illustration: "While the Watchman Sleeps" by Charles Nelan, 1898. Public domain image from the
Library of Congress, with special thanks to Roslyn P. Waddy.

To Kim, whose efforts have provided the opportunity to pursue
this unexpected avocation in Mormon history

and

To Mary Hansen Smith, who has borne with me the long
and unstable world of academia, and the inevitable life
transformations that it has inspired.

Contents

Preface

PART I: THE NATIONAL PICTURE

Introduction

Preface

Michael Harold Paulos and Konden Smith Hansen

The Reed Smoot Senate hearings have been a rewarding venture for each of us, both personally and professionally. Our collaboration on this book has been a choice experience for friendship and shared interests and one that has indeed left us indebted to many. We would also like to express thanks to the many authors who contributed outstanding essays amidst busy schedules and life transitions. We didn't feel it necessary to be above groveling, and are grateful for each author's contribution. Also deserving our heartfelt appreciation are the mentors, friends, and family members whose encouragement and other assistance contributed substantially to the success of this project. These include Newell Bringhurst, Troy MacDonald, Tom Kimball, Rob Holland, Stephen Q. Wood, Bruce Quick, Harold and Tina Paulos, Gary Bergera, Ron Priddis, Joe Geisner, Harvard S. Heath, Kathleen Flake, Doug Gibson, Lavina Fielding Anderson, Cristine Hutchinson-Jones, Kenneth L. Cannon II, Moses N. Moore, Tracy Fessenden, Linell Cady, James Foard, Daniel Ramirez, Klaus Hansen, Leslie Chilton, Tisa Wenger, Peter Iverson, Matthew Garrett, Colby Townsend, Megan Badger, James Badger, and Richard E. Wentz. Also deserving of praise are our long-suffering and sup-portive spouses (Kim Paulos and Mary Hansen Smith) and families (Addison Paulos, Brandon Paulos, Cardon Paulos, Delaney "Laney" Paulos, Elizabeth "Libby" Paulos, Faith Paulos, Grayson Paulos, Hudson Paulos; Zacharie Smith, Eliza Smith, Edward Smith, Aster Smith, and Norah Smith) who have witnessed over several years our Smoot hearings fascination, which on occasion could be classified as passionate overkill. There are also others who remain unnamed that we owe our gratitude to, from the "blind" reviewers of the various essays, to those who offered helpful critiques or ideas to the various authors as they worked their essays to fruition. Our original vision for this project was to offer fresh perspectives on the Reed Smoot hearings from differing angles, including national and local. It is our sincere hope that this book will add, even if only in a small way, to the existing scholarship on the Reed Smoot hearings and the important role they played in shaping American, religious, political, and Mormon history.

THE REED SMOOT HEARINGS

FIGURE 0.1. Reed Smoot portrait (ca. 1904). Photo courtesy of the Church History Library collection.

Part I

The National Picture

DOI: 10.7330/9781646421176.c000

Introduction

Konden Smith Hansen

Mormon apostle Reed Smoot's provocative 1903 Utah election to the United States Senate sparked an intense debate and reconsideration of the relationship between religion and American politics during the "Progressive Era," a time of heightened cultural, religious, and political transformation. The central question was if America's political establishment would permit a high-ranking official of the Church of Jesus Christ of Latter-day Saints (also referenced as the "Mormon Church," "LDS Church," "Mormonism," or just "the Church"), a small religious group deemed outside the mainstream of American ideals, to hold high elective office. Moreover, the disputed aspects of the so-called Smoot Question, as it was colloquially called at the time, were widely publicized in Protestant churches as well as media outlets when formal Senate hearings commenced in Washington from 1904 to 1906. For many religious residents of the Progressive Era, Smoot's presence in the Senate accelerated the already waning influence of Protestant hegemony within American public institutions. Indeed, the outcome of the hearings in 1907, which resulted in Smoot's favor, not only indicated an expansion of American religious pluralism but also displayed the continued and complex religious nature of America's budding secularized nation-state. Conversely, the flexible and accommodating response to the hearings by the LDS Church indicated a fresh openness from Church leadership to pursue a strategy of rapprochement with the country during a time of increased secularization, which in turn granted the Utah Church access to a wider berth of national acceptance.

This olive branch of inclusion extended to the Church was not to be interpreted as a blanket acceptance of religious differences, but rather it was a straightforward and uncompromising declaration that previous iterations of Mormonism would not be tolerated. Only a more secular expression of Mormonism, the one carefully presented by Smoot and his defenders, was acceptable for a seat at the table of full American citizenship. In other words, acceptance of Reed Smoot's Mormonism into the tapestry of America's expanding religious plurality, depended upon the Church falling in line with the "progressive" Protestant expectations of this newly emergent secular-modern era.

Often, "the secular" is defined diametrically opposed to "the religious," inspiring the false oversimplification that a "secular society" is one without religious influence, which has led to a zero-sum perception that distorts how the religious and the secular are considered, along with the dynamic relationship these forces have with American politics. But, as anthropologist Talal Asad explains, the secular is neither a break from nor an evolutionary expansion beyond the religious but rather is a modern expression of it. Notably, the term "secular," as it has been used in the West, is an idiomatic, mid-nineteenth-century expression that reframes moral progress from "human nature," as established by the Christian doctrine of the Fall, to that of autonomous human agency. And rather than being a sui generis force that explains a cultural phenomenon, the "secular," in this context, refers to a specific historical development that plants itself inside a unique American religious environment. In American Protestant thought, the individual was understood to be depraved and in need of the coercive moral power of the righteous state, thereby defining religious liberty via exclusion and suppression. Although unnamed and even denied, this religious influence in American politics denigrated individual liberty, argued David Sehat in his study on religious freedom, and it both established and imposed a narrow version of Protestant moral order on all Americans. Under this structure, and using the influence of ministers and other professors of religion, state actors (often ministers or former ministers) were enabled to prosecute blasphemy, enforce Sabbath day observance, and at times constrain religious belief.[1]

The end-of-the-century turn toward the secular in America, however, with its new emphasis on human autonomy and individual religious liberty, was likewise rooted in Protestant assumptions, norms, and values. These secularization trends proved crucial to Smoot, since one outcome of these shifts was wider participation in the modern state, regardless of religious belief. William Cavanaugh explained that this so-called secular movement in American politics utilized new terminology that demarcated itself from this earlier ecclesiastical political influence and subordinated this moral establishment to the new secular modern state. Moreover, in Robert Crunden's study of turn-of-the-century progressive reform, he argues that democratic reformers, even after abandoning explicit expressions of faith, retained and were guided by moral principles taken from their earlier religious training. Religious influence did not disappear within this new secular environment but instead became subtler and implicit. Assessing this nuanced development, Cavanaugh argues that there was nothing new or substantial with this fabricated religious-secular binary, but, rather, the semantic revision created a political myth that expanded the moral authority of a new set of American political elites.[2] At its core, the secularization of American politics took shape inside American Protestantism and redefined the theological principle of the human agent as well as the human agent's relationship to the modern nation-state. For Smoot to carve out a place within this new structure, he would have to do so as an autonomous agent within this Protestant moral worldview, rather than construct-ing a schematic specific to Mormonism.

In late nineteenth-century America, the term "religion" referred to Protestant Christianity, representing a denominationally diverse tableau that claimed a col-lective ownership over society and pursued political exclusion on theological grounds. At the same time, the American nation-state, being informed by these secularization trends at the turn of the century, cast political participation in stra-tums that deemphasized Christian partisanship and the influence of clergy while prioritizing autonomous human agency and the privatization of religious expres-sion. Secularity, then, notes Charles Taylor, means that individuals in society can "engage fully in politics without ever encountering God." These shifts vibrated across American society and influenced how intellectual, social, political, and religious leaders approached societal issues, giving priority to the tangible and observable over that of the metaphysical. For Taylor, this transition toward secu-larity was revolutionary, and represented "the first time in history" that "a purely self-sufficient humanism came to be a widely available option"—a schematic whose main goal was that of "human flourishing," with no "allegiance to anything else beyond this flourishing," including religion.[3] As Protestant hegemony and homogeneity over American politics began to recede on account of this wave of secularity, the Smoot hearings similarly questioned Mormonism's commitment to these same human-focused ideals, regardless of how religiously heterodox the Utah-based Church was to the Protestant establishment. And even though Smoot's theological worldview and heterodox religious practices were probed throughout the ordeal, these views and performances were not, in the end, dis-qualifying. What proved most important was Smoot's ability to define himself as an autonomous moral agent, despite his religious affiliation and ecclesiastical position, which placed himself and his religion squarely within the parameters of the new modern-secular age.

In his exploration of the idea of religious freedom in America, David Sehat notes that religious dissenters were the ones most adversely impacted by the inherent coerciveness of the moral religious establishment, and these dissenters in turn extended the strongest opposition to it. While this establishment remained unnamed and therefore largely invisible to accusations of inappropriate religious influence in American politics, the effort to exclude Smoot based on explicit religious grounds proved unworkable in this new era. Yet despite these ineffectual efforts, Smoot's victory in 1907 was by no means assured, as federal protections of unorthodox religious belief or nonbelief had not been fully established, nor had the First Amendment been applied to all levels of government. In this context, the Smoot hearings stand as a case study that highlights the awkward restrictions of religious liberty in America, based on principles of exclusion and coercion, and it opened to public gaze the inconsistencies these principles posed for a new century of secular progress. Although still powerful in 1907, it became clear that this "disciplined moral militia" of partisan Protestants that justified its power by minimizing the religious belonging of other groups had been built, notes Sehat, on "shifting sands."[4] Though this moral militia, so to speak, retained great power, the Smoot hearings also demonstrate a significant questioning of this power on a national stage.

For much of the nineteenth century, the Church of Jesus Christ of Latter-day Saints defined itself as an isolationist and polygamist community that blurred the lines between religion and politics, thereby placing itself outside popular notions of acceptable religion and these new definitions of secularity. Like other nineteenth-century Protestants, Mormons in the Utah basin linked their vision of human autonomy to ecclesiastical influence and the larger Church collective. But facing these new potentials toward belonging in American politics, LDS Church leaders argued before the Senate that it was the individual, not ecclesiastical authority, that reigned sovereign in the Mormon kingdom, which was increasingly being redefined in more denominational terms. Although this framework may have seemed inconsistent with earlier perceptions of an uncritically obedient Mormon collective, President Joseph F. Smith testified in Washington that Mormons were free to disregard Church teachings, even "essential doctrines," and remain in good standing. Smoot himself argued during his testimony that his loyalty as a senator was to the nation and its constitution, over that of the LDS Church and its doctrines. Thomas G. Alexander's formative work, *Mormonism in Transition*, incisively observed the salience of a new outlook for the institutional Church beginning in the 1890s by noting that the Church began to develop a new religious and cultural paradigmatic framework that shifted away from a parochial focus to a more cosmopolitan one, which in turn allowed for both mainstream party politics and improved relations with Americans at large.[5] Expanding upon Alexander's work of Mormonism's transitional period, this volume adds new insights into what the Smoot hearings meant for American politics and its dynamic relationship to religion, including how religious minorities navigated the demands of this new secularity. Beyond this, this volume also looks at these shifts within the institutional Church and how the event affected individuals, including Reed's wife, Allie Smoot, as well as his personal secretary Carl Badger and his wife, Rose Badger. These and other personal accounts provide texture and clarity on this changing relationship of the Latter-day Saints with the American public, as well as what it meant for their own church and faith community. Moreover, essays in this volume flesh out new perspectives on trends within American society and the LDS Church during this tumultuous period, when progressive voices challenged the status quo and abetted a reconsideration of the boundaries and relationship of religion and politics. When the Reed Smoot hearings began, this progressive strain had been percolating across the country for at least a decade and caused many Americans to reconsider the explicit and exclusionary nature of Protestant privilege and the tight grip it had on American politics. At the same time, several chapters in this volume reveal the nation's continued relationship with religion itself, thereby offering a deeper understanding of America's newly emergent secularity at the start of the twentieth century.

Mainstream American perspectives of Mormonism began to shift favorably near the end of the nineteenth century, based in part by the Church's celebrated participation in the 1893 World's Fair in Chicago and the positive publicity surrounding Utah's 1896 achievement of statehood. America's turn toward secularization began to grasp Mormonism only after it promised to abandon polygamy in 1890, ended its more isolationist economic practices, and joined without interference the American two-party political system. Smoot's election in 1903 ignited widespread protests and revealed that many unresolved concerns remained about the LDS Church becoming a legitimate American religion. The precipitating events leading up to the hearings, such as the abandonment of polygamy and Utah statehood, along with the Church's accommodating response to these hearings, highlight that the Church's march toward national acceptance was a piecemeal process rather than an overnight shift and that the national context of secular progress and of the demands of a privatized religious faith was anything but settled.

Despite these continued concerns about the Church, the backdrop of the Progressive Era worked as gravitational pull for both Mormonism and America, motioning the Church toward accommodation through the abandonment of nontraditional religious practices, while simultaneously forcing the country to agitate against and inch away from its own exclusionary instincts. Secularization trends were eroding a specific strain of religious influence within American politics while simultaneously establishing another. This nuanced shift toward the secular within American politics profoundly influenced both the line of questioning at the Senate hearings and the ultimate outcome of the contest, clearing the path for the Church to reset its relationship with the nation generally. Although imperceptible to some of Smoot's contemporaries, this minor victory for Smoot over contemporary Protestant sectarians seeking to exclude religious difference not only opened the door of Mormon inclusion but also created new potential for future inclusion of other minority religious groups who were similarly compliant with the developing secular-progressive expectations of the day. And though more accommodating to religious diversity, these new secular standards were rooted in liberal Protestant assumptions of the individual, together with the expectations of good citizenship and morality, thereby demanding Mormons publicly embrace marital monogamy. The secular state, that as Cavanaugh explains, subordinated a more conservative moral establishment and ecclesiastical authority to itself, likewise subordinated Mormonism and its claims of moral ecclesiastical and revelatory authority.

BACKGROUND ON REED SMOOT AND THE SENATE HEARINGS

Born in Salt Lake City, Reed Smoot was the third of seven children sired by Abraham O. Smoot with his fifth wife, Anne Kirstine Mauritsen (Morrison) Smoot.[6] Reed's birth in 1862 occurred a few months before President Abraham Lincoln signed into law the Morrill Act, the first legislative act by the federal government targeting Mormon plural marriage. Smoot's birth year is surely ironic, given that forty-five years later, this monogamous LDS apostle, born into a polygamous household, was the focal point of the federal government's final effort to end the practice. This generational divide between Reed and his father, Abraham, showcases the dramatic influence the Progressive Era had on Reed's generation of Mormons as well as how startling President Smith's Senate testimony was when he placed Mormonism within this new liberal vision of privatized faith.

Reed's father, Abraham, played a prominent role in early Utah as a businessman, a political leader—where he was mayor of Salt Lake City and Provo for more than twenty years—and an ecclesiastical leader—where he was Stake President for twenty-seven years.[7] Reed followed his father into each of these three areas, while surpassing his success and influence in each sphere. Reed's personal ambition and inner drive were transmitted to him by both his mother and father in what historian Harvard Heath explains as a type of "noblesse oblige." From Reed's early years in Utah, he had a strong Mormon-centric identity that came with a sense of "specialness" and "mission" and which motivated and permeated all his life's endeavors.[8]

Although the two men were similar in many respects, Reed was certainly not a carbon copy of his father. Many of their differences reflect the generation shifts within the Church more generally, while others reflected larger cultural trends in America. Smoot was determined to be his own person, carving his own path that in many ways was the opposite of his father's. Abraham's life reflected an earlier era of Mormonism that included plural marriage, theocracy, and business insularity. Reed's, on the other hand, symbolized a new image, in which monogamy was the divine standard, theocratic political leadership was phased out, and business cooperation with American enterprise accelerated. And while Abraham Smoot owned slaves, Senator-elect Reed Smoot stirred national controversy by inviting African Americans to a banquet in Provo with the Utah Legislature and other State officials, seating them next to "some white people" and assigning two willing "white girls" to serve them as waitresses, when others had refused. Smoot's racially inclusive gesture was contentious, and some of the white guests at the banquet protested by changing tables. In response to criticism, Smoot was unapologetic and defended his actions by pointing to Washington, DC. "If President Roosevelt isn't too good to entertain a colored man at the White House, I don't see why I shouldn't have colored people as my guests." Smoot here was referencing Roosevelt's controversial meal with prominent African American leader and educator Booker T. Washington.[9]

Another significant departure from his father was that Reed became an ardent Republican, when his father had been a stalwart Democrat who preached "the Democratic gospel" at home and in public."[10] Reed's political split from his father, or "metamorphosis" as Harvard Health described it in his study of Smoot, began in 1891 during his ten-month mission to the British Isles,[11] when the LDS Church

FIGURE 0.2. Painting portraits of (a) Abraham O. Smoot (early 1850s) and (b) Reed Smoot (1901). Images courtesy of Kathryn Smoot Egan, great-granddaughter of Reed Smoot.

in England was struggling and the missionary work was at times "intolerable." His experiences with local conditions and interactions with the working class convinced him that economic protectionism via tariffs was the best way to protect American workers back home and to ensure social stability and economic prosperity. Protectionism was a plank of the Republican Party's platform and eventually became Smoot's signature legislative issue as well as his political downfall in Washington. During Smoot's fifth term in the Senate, he coauthored and passed in 1930, largely on partisan lines, a piece of legislation known at the time as the "Smoot-Hawley" Tariff. Ignoring a petition signed by over a thousand economists, this bill was signed by President Herbert Hoover during the early stages of the Great Depression, and the legislation failed to stimulate the American economy or reduce unemployment. In fact, the bill had the opposite result of stoking retaliatory measures by foreign governments, leading to trade isolationism that exacerbated the severity of the overall global economic downturn. Smoot lost his 1932 reelection bid based in part on his involvement with the Smoot-Hawley Tariff.[12]

As a successful businessman in Utah, who began working in his father's businesses at age fifteen while attending Brigham Young Academy, Reed's substantial business acumen was recognized by Church leaders who in 1900 called him into the Mormon hierarchy at age thirty-eight to become a member of the Quorum of the Twelve Apostles.[13] Not known for deep theological or spiritual propensity,[14]

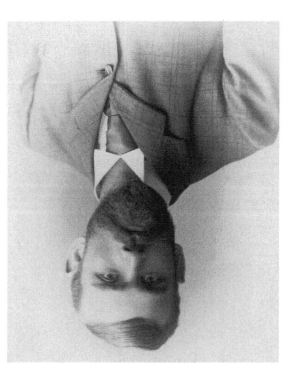

FIGURE 0.3. Portrait of Reed Smoot as a missionary in Liverpool, England 1891. Smoot was a missionary in England for ten months, where he was persuaded of the importance of using trade barriers such as tariffs to protect the working class. Photo courtesy of the Church History Library collection.

Reed contributed financial and administrative expertise at a time when the institutional Church was modernizing and seeking greater economic and structural stability. Smoot was part of Church president Lorenzo Snow's progressive vision for the Church, wherein he believed that all Progressive Era advancements, including those of "science" and "mechanism," were prompted by God's revelatory influence to benefit "all flesh that will receive it."[15] Despite his call into the LDS hierarchy, Smoot was eager to explore a political career and considered a 1900 run for the Senate but was advised against it by President Snow, who said it was not the right time.[16] Snow passed away the next year, in 1901, and the newly called Church president, Joseph F. Smith, who was a fellow Republican, approved of Smoot's desire to run the next year for Utah's open Senate seat.[17]

On January 20, 1903, the Utah State Legislature elected Reed Smoot to the US Senate.[18] This electoral action provoked political, commercial, and religious opponents of the Church to submit two separate, though related, petitions to the federal government protesting Smoot's seating. The first petition, dated January 26, 1903, and signed by nineteen (later eighteen when one of the signers withdrew) Utah non-Mormons—most of whom represented the state's "gentile" (i.e., non-LDS) churches—was known as the Citizens' Protest, and averred that Smoot was unfit to serve on several grounds connected to his ecclesiastical calling in the LDS Church. These signatories contended that the Mormon Church continued to perform plural marriages despite an 1890 Church-adopted manifesto ostensibly banning all such nontraditional marital relations. The second petition, dated February 25, 1903, was issued separately by John Luther Leilich (1854–1905), superintendent of missions of the Utah District for the Methodist Episcopal Church. Leilich, who became known in some LDS circles as "lie like," and who even provoked criticism from the Ministerial Association and other Methodist leaders in Leilich's jurisdiction, had also attached his name to the Citizens' Protest.[19] His separate charges were especially inflammatory, contending that Smoot was a practicing polygamist and that his position as an apostle disqualified him from taking the oath of US senator, since the "object" of the Church was to "subvert" the "aims and ends" of the US government.[20]

Smoot was invited by the Senate Committee on Privileges and Elections to respond to both protests in late November 1903. Smoot's written defense, submitted in early January 1904, was carefully constructed. He nimbly sidestepped the issue of his ecclesiastical position as irrelevant and answered simply that there were only two points that might prohibit him from retaining his seat: first that he was a practicing polygamist and, second, that he was bound by a religious oath that would be incompatible with the oath administered to all incoming senators. Smoot's strategy was clear: any investigation should focus on him and not on the Church, and he was going to do everything in his power to keep Joseph F. Smith and the Church out of the fight.[21] The committee's members, chaired by Michigan

"DURN!"

FIGURE 0.4. "An Interrupted Ramble." This Alan L. Lovey cartoon depicts newly elected Utah senator Reed Smoot being tripped up by the "Utah Citizens Protest" on his 2,000-mile journey to Washington, DC, from Utah. *Salt Lake Herald*, February 10, 1903. Courtesy of the Brigham Young University Family History Center.

Republican senator Julius Caesar Burrows (1837–1915), met on January 16, 1904, to discuss the charges and to hear the two teams of attorneys' oral arguments. Robert W. Tayler and Thomas P. Stevenson represented the Citizens' group. Defending Smoot was non-Mormon, Washington lawyer Augustus S. Worthington and Salt Lake City–based Mormon attorney Waldmar Van Cott. After considerable discussion, it became evident that the case against Smoot, despite his and his lawyers' maneuvering, would be directed more at the LDS Church and would rest on three points: (1) the LDS Church had not entirely abandoned polygamy, (2) LDS authorities continued to practice polygamous cohabitation, and (3) the LDS Church interfered in and influenced to some extent the politics of Utah and of surrounding states.

Formal committee hearings began in early March 1904 and continued intermittently over the next two years until April 13, 1906, when a second round of concluding arguments were completed.[22] Stenographers recorded the testimony of ninety-eight witnesses, some of whom were called to the stand multiple times. The full Smoot hearings testimony, along with numerous other documents included as part of the formal record by both senators and lawyers, was then published and distributed in four volumes totaling 3,432 pages.[23] The committee completed its investigation on June 1, 1906, recommending to the full Senate by a committee vote that Smoot should not be allowed to retain his seat. Eight months later, on February 20, 1907, the full Senate voted 42–28 against this recommendation, and Reed Smoot kept his Senate seat.

There are a few reasons that explain why it took four years for the "Smoot Question" to get resolved. From a political perspective, the US Senate then and today, known popularly as the world's greatest deliberative body, is governed by obtuse rules, parliamentary procedures, inconsistent voting requirements and schedules, frequent recesses, and complex committee structures intended to decelerate major legislative changes and to prevent abrupt decision making. Smoot's case represented such a situation in which the Senate rules along with political personalities inside the committee created a protracted outcome. Since Smoot was constitutionally qualified to serve and was well liked by fellow senators after being sworn in, removing him from office would require a two-thirds super-majority vote. In addition, at the time of the final vote, Republicans dominated the Senate with a 58 to 38 seat advantage. Overcoming this partisan hurdle would require that Smoot's opponents produce incontrovertible evidence of Smoot's or the LDS Church's criminal complicity that would convince fellow Republican senators to vote against one of their own. Over the four years, hearings and votes were scheduled, postponed, closed, and then reopened while Smoot's opposition scoured Utah for a "smoking-gun" that would implicate Smoot. Other delays occurred because some senators preferred to vote on the Smoot question after the 1906 midterm elections.

In a broader sense, the hearings represented a high-stakes negotiation in which a significant stakeholder, this earlier Protestant moral establishment, categorically refused to surrender any ground or control of the status quo, including just one Senate seat. Aligned with modernist Protestant progressives at the head of this newly emergent secularity, Smoot's inclusion symbolized a disruption of the moral religious establishment's stewardship over American society that left many outraged and uneasy. Lashing out, these traditional religious forces kept up the struggle against Smoot and his supporters for as long as they could, but they ultimately failed to persuade this new generation of political elites to exclude a constitutionally qualified apostle of the Church of Jesus Christ of Latter-day Saints.

NOTABLE SCHOLARSHIP ON THE HEARINGS

Kathleen Flake, in her landmark 2004 study published by the University of North Carolina Press, *The Politics of American Religious Identity: The Seating of Senator Reed Smoot, Mormon Apostle*, positions the Smoot hearings as a watershed moment when the country worked out a solution to the "Mormon Problem."[24] Flake focused on the mechanics of how the Church convinced outside critics that it had fundamentally changed while simultaneously assuring believing members inside that nothing material had been revised. Flake addressed the political and religious compromises that took shape during the hearings that allowed Church leaders to drop the salvific sacramental practice of plural marriage in a way that allowed its Protestant critics to accept the Church as politically acceptable within constitutional boundaries. The significance of Flake's study extends beyond Smoot and his personal faith and provides scaffolding for broader questions about religious memory as well as narrative details on how the "political terms" were nego- tiated to allow for "increasingly diverse" religious traditions to be "recognized and accommodated in America for the remainder" of the twentieth century.[25]

The current volume does not attempt significant revisions of Flake's important interpretations of the hearings, though some exist. Instead, our focus is to build on her interpretations by considering unexplored political and religious milieux connected to the event. Some chapters in this book provide new perspectives on how religious and political institutions adapted and shape-shifted in response to larger societal and ecclesiastical trends, while others focus on key historical per- sonalities mostly ignored by the existing scholarship. In addition, this introduc- tion provides insights into secularism during the Progressive Era, unexplored by Flake, which influenced the approach to the hearings while also setting the stage for their existence. The Church's protracted abandonment of plural mar- riage was not an amiable separation, but rather, if expressed metaphorically, it was a messy, drawn-out divorce, in which leading participants compromised both themselves and loved ones in a struggle to protect the stability of the family unit. Not surprisingly, a few loyal followers sustained collateral damage as the institu- tion's revelatory credibility was tarnished. Reed Smoot's personal secretary Carl A. Badger, whose experiences at the hearing are explored in chapter 7 by Gary James Bergera, was one such individual disillusioned by what he witnessed, and his vignette is a crucial addition to the discussion offered by Flake.

Other scholars have ably analyzed various areas of the Smoot hearings but, like Flake, have appraised the impact the hearings had on institutions such as the fed- eral government and the LDS Church; moreover, these scholars have assessed the influence the hearings had on Reed Smoot the apostle-senator or other male elites during the early part of the twentieth century. Milton R. Merrill, in his doctoral thesis, "Reed Smoot: Apostle in Politics" (Columbia University, 1950), published posthumously by the same title forty years later by Utah State University Press, approached the hearings as one chapter in Smoot's thirty-year political biogra- phy. Merrill assessed Smoot's motivations in running for political office, ascribing his motives to an unquenchable ambition, while also analyzing Utah's elections leading up to Smoot's 1903 success. Merrill concludes that the "investigation years changed Smoot very little fundamentally," but rather, it had the effect of solidify-ing his "deeply grooved principles," including such views that "patriotism was a religious principle" and that the "Republican party was the party of intelligence and righteousness." In essence, Smoot's character was validated, not shaped, by the four years of limbo he endured during the hearings.[26] Also in 1990, the same year that Merrill's biography was published, historian Harvard S. Heath completed a dissertation, "Reed Smoot: First Modern Mormon" (Brigham Young University, 1990), in which he treated the hearings as a Bar or Bat Mitzvah moment, as it were, for the LDS Church by contextualizing the hearings as Mormonism's attempt to secure an adult seat within the "American community." Further, Heath posits that if the Church's early nineteenth-century struggles to survive persecution and vio-lence in Missouri and Illinois can be pithily labeled a "quest for refuge," then the institutional challenges precipitated by the Smoot hearings in Washington, DC, can most aptly be described as a "quest for legitimacy."[27]

More recently, Jonathan H. Moyer's unpublished dissertation, "Dancing with the Devil: The Making of the Mormon-Republican Pact" (University of Utah, 2009), contextualizes the Smoot hearings within the LDS Church's turbulent but symmetrical relationship with the Republican Party. Specifically, Moyer traces the radical trajectories "of the Mormon Church and the Republican Party," each of which arose from the "religious and political turmoil of Jacksonian America," and argues that each entity's transformation reflects a similarity and "underlying symbiosis." Moyer frames the Smoot hearings as a "key episode" and "decisive moment" in the relationship and suggests that this intersection can best be under-stood when the Republican Party is viewed as redefining itself away from being a "radical reform vehicle" during the nineteenth century, to a political party in the twentieth century that was the "embodiment conservative stability." And over the same time period, the LDS Church is seen abandoning its radical religious practices such as communalism and plural marriage, to a faith community that embraced conservative ideals. Moyer concludes that each of these two institutions reinvented themselves in response of external conditions and created an "alliance" and "lasting partnership," which in a previous era would have been considered impossible.[28]

One last relevant Smoot hearings publication is Michael Harold Paulos's 2008 one-volume abridgement of the hearings that includes the most salient testimony provided by subpoenaed witnesses. This documentary volume does not develop a synthesized thesis on the importance or place of the hearings in American or Mormon history but includes primary resource annotations that illuminate behind-the-scene events connected to Senator Smoot and specific testimony given at the hearings. The information provided in these footnotes are derived primarily from Reed Smoot and his personal secretary Carl Badger's contempo-raneous correspondence.[29]

These important studies provide insights on the hearings but, as mentioned above, have largely focused on how the hearings impacted American institutions and its elites. This current volume not only adds to the arguments of Kathleen Flake, Milton Merrill, Harvard Heath, and Jonathan Moyer summarized above, but also adds fresh insights and correctives into how the hearings impacted other spheres of American society, religion, and culture. One area illuminated in this book is how the hearings interfaced with the political debate for a constitutional amendment defining marriage between one man and one woman. Another area considered afresh is how the protracted hearings impacted laypersons, women, and other individuals hitherto given sparse attention. This discussion includes an essay by Reed Smoot's great-granddaughter Kathryn Smoot Egan on how the hearings impacted Allie Smoot, Reed's wife, who for most of the hearings oper-ated as a single parent back in Provo, Utah. Each chapter in this volume makes a unique contribution on the hearings, positing new arguments and narrative that broaden the story while at the same time providing new political, religious, famil-ial, and personal images that augment and garnish public understanding of the event and its significance within American religious history. A central storyline that emerges from these essays are the strains felt between an earlier generation of Latter-day Saints who were brought up during a time of ecclesiastical moral influence and explicit expressions of religion in politics, to a new generation of Latter-day Saints who valued individual agency and privatized expressions of faith. Although loosely connected by topic, these chapters, when considered in totality, provide new flashes of illumination, making visible neglected aspects of this con-troversial and intense moment of political and religious transition at the begin-ning of the twentieth century.

AMERICAN HISTORY CONTEXT

Over the course of US history, technological advancements have been lead-ing drivers of cultural, economic, and societal change. These changes are rarely uncontested and often spur protests from those fearful of losing social position, economic stability, and privilege. Anxieties of citizens regarding these larger cul-tural changes frequently find expression in the political discourse and legislative priorities of elected officials. The Smoot hearings were held during a tumultu-ous period when urbanization and technological breakthroughs sparked major changes and displacements in society that evoked passionate responses from cit-izens concerned about the new directions in which the nation was headed. The vociferous opposition by this moral establishment to Smoot's admission to the US Senate was similar to the opposition voiced against immigrants, labor unions, and striking workers and reflected a pattern to these tensions and fears. Furthermore, as David Sehat argues, the American economy matured over the latter half of the nineteenth century, which led to the emergence of large corporations with the attendant rise of concentrated wealth. Up to this point, America's economy had mostly been entrepreneurial and run by individual proprietors. The rise of large corporate firms with multiple shareholders and salaried managers led to the pooling of monies for corporate leadership, who in turn used it to influence American life.[30] Reed Smoot's own rise to power was based on his success in this sector of the economy, together with the Church's own investments in corporate wealth and its own presumption of wealth as an inherent good.

These Progressive Era developments, including the rise of urban industry, expedited the growth of America's cities by creating a magnetic pull for both immigrants and unskilled workers. This trend set off warning bells for Protestant moral reformers, who observed a waning of religious influence in these burgeoning population centers. Social Gospel theologian and general secretary of the Evangelical Alliance Josiah Strong observed in 1893 that the ministering efforts of Protestant churches in America's major cities were "sadly deficient," warning of the need to "awake to their duty" and "opportunity"; or else the "present tendencies will continue until our cities are literally heathenized."[31] In response to this need, moral reform societies were established, and existing institutions found renewed zeal as they sought to counter the spread of irreligion and "heathenism" in America's metropolitan areas.[32] A few prominent social reformist groups—such as the Women's Christian Temperance Union (WCTU), the National Reform Association (NRA), and the National Christian League for the Promotion of Social Purity (NCL)—also targeted Smoot and fused their effort to protect the American home with the fight against the Utah senator. Margaret Dye Ellis, general superintendent of the WCTU, reflected these conflated concerns when she read a resolution on behalf of "millions of women" to President Theodore Roosevelt that insisted, in the name of both "womanhood" and "motherhood," that Smoot be removed from the Senate.[33]

Opposition to Smoot and related efforts to protect the home were a few of the several religious concerns outlined by these national reform societies. Other issues of focus were temperance, blasphemy, marriage and divorce, Sabbath observance, and prayer and the Bible's place in public schools. One influential moral reformer of the day, Thomas P. Stevenson, who cofounded the NRA's influential magazine *Christian Statesman*, and who also presented the NRA's protest against Smoot before the Senate committee in early 1904 by testifying that his purpose in opposing Smoot was to "maintain and promote the Christian features of the American Government."[34] had been a standard-bearer in the fight to establish Sabbath laws across America. Stevenson and his religious allies believed that the American Civil War had been a punishment to the country for not formally accepting God, Jesus Christ, and the Bible as the foremost sources of authority in its founding documents. Seeking to rectify this statutory omission, Christian reformers lobbied Congress unsuccessfully over five decades to amend the Constitution in a way that enshrined Christianity and acknowledged its paramount authority within the country. Blocked in these attempts because of a negative report by a House of Representatives judiciary committee in 1874, moral reformers were forced to consider other ways to find resolution. Kathleen Flake, in explaining this context, pointed out that the Smoot hearings not only required a compromise from the leadership of the LDS Church to completely abandon plural marriage, but also a compromise by the Protestant establishment to adjust its exclusionary vision of an explicitly Christian America.[35]

Many American Protestants shared these concerns about the rise of religious and ethnic diversity in American cities and its threat to white Protestant supremacy but disagreed that an explicit statement of Christian devotion needed to be added to the US Constitution. Church historian Philip Schaff countered the efforts of the NRA by stating that such a push to rewrite the preamble of the Constitution was "impractical" and gave the wrong impression that the founding document was hostile to religion. Although perhaps not in form, Schaff noted that the Constitution was Christian in substance and that only through the principles of Christianity could such a system of justice and humanity ever have emerged.[36] Founder of the NRA, William Strong, an associate justice of the US Supreme Court in the 1870s with a reputation of being "somewhat excessive" in his Presbyterian faith, agreed with the idea that Christian churches should remain separate from the state but that God should not be separate and as such pushed for the addendum.[37] Strong and Schaff shared the idea that Protestantism monopolized principles of morality and liberty, yet their disagreement was in how that religious influence filtered through society and thus related to American law. Fearful of the growing political influence of Mormon polygamists in Utah and Catholic immigrants in the city, it was argued at an NRA convention that the initial step toward societal reform was to "place all Christian laws, institutions and usages in our government on an undeniable legal basis in the fundamental law of the nation." A change like this, Schaff explained, would forbid, under penalty, the public exercise of non-Christian religions. Moreover, this enshrinement of Christianity may not "convert the infidel or save a soul," but it would inject "the Christian feeling of the American people into the law on marriage, the Sabbath, and honesty, until our laws adequately represent our belief." Relatedly, Strong argued in 1875 that though the government could not forbid Mormons from believing in polygamy, it could on moral grounds outlaw the actual practice. Despite the failed addendum, Jon C. Teaford notes that three years later in the *Reynolds v. US* decision, the Supreme Court upheld Strong's logic against Mormonism and officially adopted "orthodox Christian views of marriage as the law of the land."[38]

In *Church and State* (1888), Schaff similarly referenced Mormonism as "altogether abnormal and irreconcilable with the genius of American institutions," and though, as he wrote, the general government could not "attack the religion of the

Mormons, as a religion, . . . it can forbid polygamy as a social institution, inconsistent with our western civilization," an arrangement upheld by both Congress and the Supreme Court. Demonstrating the intrinsic religious nature of social reform, Schaff argued that the "state cannot be divorced from morals, and morals cannot be divorced from religion." Although this relationship between religion and the state was often denied by those who pushed it, this moral establishment over American society depended upon orthodox Protestant moral codes, and as such, "the Mormons must give up this part of their religion, or emigrate." As the morality of America and its predominant religious faith were intertwined, Schaff believed American laws were naturally reflective, and constitutional permission was unnecessary.[39] Revealing their Calvinist roots, Strong and the NRA articulated the need for an explicit guarantee of Christian sovereignty over American society, which would serve as an impetus to enforce orthodox Protestant principles. Following this failure to amend the Constitution, however, William Strong secularized his rhetoric in order to impose these same theological principles on American society, in the same way that he had inveighed against polygamy. In 1880 for example, Strong pushed the idea that the majority of Americans desired "laws for the observance and protection of a weekly rest day for all our people; not because such a day is a Divine institution, but because they believe that such a day properly regarded is of immense importance to our political and social interests."[40] When it came to American law and faith, particularly when more explicit controls were rejected by Congress, Protestants utilized secular techniques to impose religious dogma on the American public. It's not that Schaff and Strong were in disagreement that America was ideally Christian, or even that Mormonism was antagonistic toward that ideal and therefore needed to go; instead, their disagreement with each other was in the necessity to impose such Christian ideals in explicit constitutional terms.

While Schaff criticized the NRA for its impractical efforts to "christianize the Constitution and to nationalize Christianity," he strongly ridiculed the efforts of Free Thinkers and the National Liberal League (NLL) to impose an absolute separation of church and state, or as he put it, "to heathenize the Constitution and to denationalize Christianity."[41] In 1854 Schaff warned against "political atheism," which included "reckless efforts to uproot all that is established" and denies "the divine origin of civil government altogether." For Schaff, Thomas Jefferson's so-called wall of separation was nothing more than "social despotism, or downright mobocracy."[42] Francis Abbot, founder and president of the NLL, decried the NRA's proposals to redefine American law through religious terms as hostile to a free system of democracy and as dangerously theocratic. While many in Abbot's camp agreed with the religious notion that fostering public morality and civility was critical for the success of society, these liberal reformers opposed expanding an explicit role for religion and argued that narrow religious dogma brought

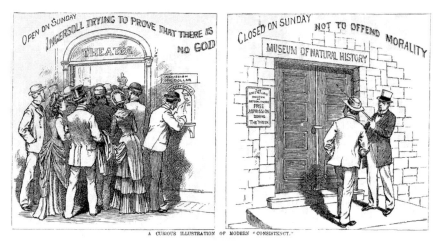

FIGURE 0.5. Playing off the national debate over the consistency of imposing Sabbath regulations, Frank Leslie's *Illustrated* draws out the irony of closing the free admission Museum of Natural History, while Robert Ingersoll draws in paying crowds on the same day, preaching against God. "A Curious Illustration of Modern 'Consistency'" from *Frank Leslie's Illustrated Newspaper*, May 28, 1881. Image courtesy of the Wikimedia Commons.

fear, hate, and persecution. National Liberal League officer and popular lecturer Robert G. Ingersoll, known as "the great agnostic," propounded his position that for a free and liberal society to emerge and endure, it must rest upon facts, science, and quantifiable data, not upon subjective claims of faith and the supernatural. Indeed, Ingersoll's suggestion was to wholly separate religious influence from the state, which would guarantee "the equitable taxation of church property, secularization of the public schools, abrogation of Sabbatarian laws, . . . [and] prohibition of public appropriations for religious purposes." Using these principles as guidelines, liberal reformers responded to the Christian amendment by calling for their own constitutional amendment establishing a "total separation of Church and State," or in other words, a full restriction of government entities to base public policy decisions on partisan religious dogma.[43] While Schaff acknowledged that there were "some good religious people" who supported the platform of the NLL, he argued against their support by contending that any attempt to create an "absolute separation is an impossibility," because it would inimically require the expulsion of the "Christian religion from the national life," which in his view was the entire "basis of the common wealth."[44]

In addition to these polarized proposals for constitutional amendments, new modernist reformers advocated in the 1890s for a more nuanced collaboration of religion and state, one that conflated Protestant Christian morality with the social mechanisms of government. Addressing the delicate linkage between the kingdom of heaven with those with frailties on earth, Congregationalist minister and college professor George D. Herron argued that separating religious and societal obligations was unwarranted and rooted in selfishness, being "the origin of evil." Bearing the name of Christ was not an abstract belief but required personal effort, with those serving others being "made sacred for the social service, and thus fully sacrificed in bearing away the sins of the world." Although later he was forced to resign from his teaching post at the Congregationalist college for his more radical political and socialistic views, while also being defrocked from the ministry and expelled from the church, Herron was adamant that if properly understood, social and economic problems were at heart religious problems.[45] Similarly, philosopher and psychologist John Dewey articulated in his 1897 "pedagogic creed" that institutions that did not directly connect student learning with the raw, contemporaneous societal context were inert and dead. Dewey further propounded that individuals were fundamentally social creatures, and the institutions and educators who continued to define the world in abstract and objective ways that ignored individuals and their place within the world were failing students by presenting information devoid of any meaning or value. From this standpoint, Dewey continued, public education would not replace the moral teachings of the home but, rather, act as its social extension of parental efforts. Teachers were not simply facilitators of objective memorized facts, rubrics, and categorizations; rather, they stood as social servants "set apart for the maintenance of proper social order and the securing of the right social growth" and "in this way the teacher always is the prophet of the true God and the usherer in of the true kingdom of God." Under Dewey's construction, professors and parents, together with ministers of faith, held a sacred responsibility in the creation of democratic citizens and the "formation of the proper social life."[46]

Historian Robert Crunden, in his study on this progressive movement, contextualized the 1890s as a pivotal decade in American creativity, when religious thought permeated questions of social reform. Herron's aforesaid aspirations for the coupling of religion and social reform were inspired by an evangelical ideal that did not advocate for specific government policy but assumed instead, as had Schaff, that Christianity's values would organically move its adherents to seek for and contribute to the regeneration of society. Conversely, Dewey, using secular terminology that reflected rationality and science, looked to institutional governmental structures to play a key role in facilitating a society that guaranteed divine sanction.[47] Translating the essence of these ideas into a practical political solution, President Theodore Roosevelt became a patron saint for progressive reformers seeking a shift toward a more religiously fused secular democracy. Throughout his presidency, Roosevelt threaded a nuanced needle between the approaches of Herron and Dewey and couched his religious vision with secular language. In chapter 1 of this volume, I explain that Roosevelt's embrace of a subtler form of religious stewardship and its emphasis on "merit, not metaphysics," provides context for why Roosevelt supported Smoot and also how Roosevelt's vision proved to be a leading influence during the era. In sum, Roosevelt's support of Smoot gave voice and stability to the shifting sands of America's political landscape along with the undergirding religious vision of social reform during the Progressive Era.

As mentioned previously, attempts to modify the Constitution failed over the latter part of the nineteenth century, leaving the debate on Protestantism's place in American politics unsettled when the Smoot hearings convened and offered a new touchpoint for consideration. Protestant reformers, after failing to unseat Smoot, used the pages of the *Christian Statesman* to reassure readers that the fight was far from over, while also reframing the political loss by reiterating its strategic vision that the US Constitution must be amended to acknowledge the "law of Christ" as the "basis and standard" for all "legislation touching the family." To these partisan religious opponents of the Utah senator, Smoot's success was a mere pyrrhic victory, no different from the Union's defeat at the first battle of Bull Run during the Civil War and that ultimate victory over this "false and abominable religion" was inevitable and would redound to their favor, like the Union eventually prevailed over the Confederacy. And since "no question is settled until it is settled right," the *Statesman* further enjoined, the reformers' efforts to inform and educate "the [American] people" was preparing "the way for the next stage" of the conflict, which would be one step closer to the goal of an aforesaid constitutional amendment.[48]

Gaines Foster, in his study on moral reform during the nineteenth century, identified slavery, prohibition, and polygamy as the three vehicles used by reformers to align American jurisprudence with Christian doctrine.[49] An important voice of the era, Frank Ellinwood, who was founder of the American Society of Comparative Religion, and a Presbyterian missiologist and Princeton Seminary graduate, wrote an essay in 1903 for the progressive Protestant magazine the *Homiletic Review* entitled, "Mormonism, a New Religion of the Nineteenth Century." A critic of the LDS Church, or "monstrous cult" as he described it, Ellinwood argued that the growing secular sentiment that Mormonism should "enjoy freedom of religious opinion," as other religions received under the Constitution, was misguided because the central consideration was not of "theology" or "religious opinion," but rather it was a matter of "ethics" and "conformity to the laws of marriage ... [as] enforced in all other States," which Mormonism, because of its polygamist past, was clearly incapable of compliance.[50] Furthermore, an editor's note in the same issue of the *Review* averred that polygamy stood as "an essential and inseparable feature" of Mormonism and that Ellinwood's essay championed both "the interests of the family and ... [of] fundamental morality." Continuing on this thread, the *Review's* editor encouraged religious leaders to enlist churchgoers to expose the "infamous system" of Mormonism and to prepare for "the coming battle against the beastly immorality incarnated in Reed Smoot and thrust upon the nation in the Senate of the United States."[51] Efforts to exclude Smoot and to revise the Constitution were each unsuccessful, which both placed the Smoot hearings at the heart of the national discussions of religion in the public square and further exposed the moral establishment as discriminatory and religiously fueled, in spite of the cleverly used secular rhetoric. These religious discussions within American politics played an important role in the national debates over social reforms and the meaning of American secularity in the context of progressive impulses at the beginning of the American modern secular era.

CURRENT WORK OVERVIEW

Because of the diversity of approach and content of the essays included in this work, and the reality that the Smoot hearings were both a national American and local Mormon story, this volume is divided into two sections that reflect this demarcation. Part I features essays of national perspectives and themes that address broad questions and current academic concerns. Part II contains essays that take a more intimate approach that assess the impact individuals had on the trajectory of the hearings as well as the impact the hearings had on people locally. This dividing line between the local and national is not absolute and in some cases has been arbitrarily applied; consequently, some spillover content exists.

CHAPTER BREAKDOWN: PART I—THE NATIONAL PICTURE

The first chapter, "The Reed Smoot Hearings and the Theology of Politics: Perceiving an 'American' Identity," written by Konden Smith Hansen, a lecturer in religious studies at the University of Arizona, examines the national picture surrounding the hearings and expands upon the argument made in this introduction, namely, that the changing cultural attitudes within the country are what provided space for Smoot to retain his seat in the Senate, which in turn illuminates the expanding notion of religious pluralism and secularity in American politics during the Progressive Era. While the Smoot hearings were not the overriding impetus impelling religious pluralism, they served as an episode of political theater that previewed these shifting assumptions about what it meant to be an American and the role religion played in assessing that category. By accepting the LDS Church into this national pantheon of acceptable American religions, the nation symbolically turned a corner, so to speak, which reshaped, if only slightly, the boundaries of what it meant to be an American and acceptably religious, and, as this chapter shows, this new national secularity was not devoid of theological and moral significance. The LDS Church, for its part, enthusiastically embraced this new Protestant-fused secularity of political inclusion and acceptance. However, this embrace was not without costs but required historical, doctrinal, and familial modifications, including the painful sacrifices of beloved personalities upheld as "prophets, seers, and revelators." During the hearings, the LDS Church made substantial efforts to show members of the US Senate that Mormonism was a different religion from what it had been and that it was no longer interested in kicking against modernity's pricks. This display of discontinuity mimicked that of more liberal progressive Protestants, such as in the refashioning the Church's public image as apolitical, reframing its kingdom ideals as spiritual, keeping its religious expressions as private, modifying its preferred family structure to marital monogamy, and demonstrating its commercial activities to be clearly outside of ecclesiastical interference. Thus, Smith Hansen concludes, the Smoot hearings played the dual role of transforming Mormonism into a more "acceptable" religion by way of redefining it as "American," while at the same time allowing space for this new secular-Protestant definition of religion and national belonging to be hashed out in a national debate.

As previously noted, Smoot's success relied upon his legal team's ability to convince the Senate as well as the nation that Mormonism had undergone important changes and that Smoot himself stood at the forefront. In the second chapter, "'Justice Is Never Permanently Defeated Anywhere': Reed Smoot's Confirmation Vote in the United States Senate," independent historian Michael Harold Paulos evaluates the Senate's final plenary debate and subsequent confirmation vote. On this final day, Smoot and his supporters articulated his belonging in the Senate through the lens of secularity that insisted upon the irrelevance of his private faith, even as Smoot's opposition targeted his faith as a public threat. But as Smoot's allies argued, such a focus on religion was intolerant and not in harmony with the progressive advancements being made in the country. In arguing for his retention in the Senate, Smoot's fiercest advocates did not defend his religion per se; rather, they dismissed it as both "foolish" and even "grotesque." Within these new political-religious trends in the country, Paulos demonstrates that the discussion of Smoot's place in the Senate constructed a new framework for Mormons that enabled service in high public office. With the opportunity, Smoot embraced this new progressive model of secularity that implicitly disempowered religion, by exclaiming that a "man's religious belief" remained the property of the individual, and expulsion from public office for simply "belonging to any religious denomination" was not an acceptable practice of politics. This victory speech of Smoot's is one iteration of the progressive trends sweeping across America, that is, the idea that religion was a person's private business and that morality based upon principles of humanism, not theology, sat at the heart of civic service. In a similar way that Roosevelt stood as a masculine model for American politics, Smoot offered a privatized faith model of monogamy and evident morality that satisfied the demands of his Protestant colleagues.

An important component of the hearings was the massive, yet mostly neglected by scholarship, role that women's groups played in shaping the national debate. Female religious and benevolent societies united with the National League of Women's Organizations to campaign against Mormonism and Senator Reed Smoot. These nationwide efforts had an important impact on the public perception of Mormonism, which served as a moral backdrop for Congress to act. In chapter 3, "Antipolygamy, the Constitution, and the Smoot Hearings," emeritus Brigham Young University (BYU) professors, the late Byron W. Daynes (political science) and Kathryn M. Daynes (history) demonstrate the influential role these women's organizations had on social reforms promoting marriage. Providing a statistically detailed study of proposed constitutional amendments on marriage, Daynes and Daynes offer analysis on these efforts attempted to establish the moral authority of motherhood and the home on the federal level and how the threat of Mormon polygamy was used at times on these efforts. Indeed, when Smoot arrived in Washington in early 1903, these female opponents were seasoned political activists who had championed for decades the Christian notion of traditional marriage. Between the years 1871 and 1924, these groups helped propose 114 different constitutional amendments concerning marriage and divorce, of which 55 specifically posited the specter of polygamy. Additionally, Daynes and Daynes's analysis demonstrates the larger secular patterns in America outlined in this introduction, that is, the rescinding of support for the activities of Smoot's opponents as well as the increased discomfort with explicit uses of sectarian sentiment at the public square. Moreover, these trends coincided with the Republican Party's focus on muscular expressions of Christian piety, which privileged implicit forms of religious expression and relegated explicit utterances of faith as politically inadvisable. Considering the decades-long efforts of these female groups to enshrine Christian marriage into the American constitutional order, Daynes and Daynes's work demonstrate that these efforts during the hearings were not a watershed, per se, but instead represent the moment when the efforts had reached a peak, and the momentum for such marital reform against polygamy had begun to recede.

When evaluating the historical significance of the hearings in the context of national opposition to the LDS Church, it can be tempting to simplify Smoot's victory as the inflection point at which opposition to the LDS Church ebbed. Flake, in *The Politics of American Religious Identity*, concludes that "the Mormon Problem faded relatively quickly from the nation's consciousness after the 1907 decision to seat Apostle Smoot," and whatever opposition remained looked more and more like publicity stunts intended for religious audiences that framed Mormonism as a useful foil to shape "sectarian identities." Meanwhile, the "rest of American moved on."[52] This volume, however, provides a larger context for the lingering concern over the political integration of the Church of Jesus Christ of Latter-day Saints. Daynes and Daynes's essay reveals that antipolygamy efforts by

Women's groups did not begin with Smoot, nor disappear once Smoot was confirmed, but rather, the women "accelerated their crusade against polygamy with the help of the anti-Mormon articles and lecture tours." Furthermore, in chapter 4, "Do I Hear an Echo? The Continuing Trial of the Mormon Church after Smoot's Retention," Salt Lake City attorney and independent historian Kenneth L. Cannon II, surveys this persistent criticism of Mormonism that continued for more than a decade after Smoot's retention. This opposition to the LDS Church was intense, and it included a wave of muckraking articles, published in national magazines, lambasting the Church between the years 1910 and 1911, as well as the activities of staunch Church critic Frank J. Cannon, editor of the *Salt Lake Tribune* during the hearings, who spent the decade inciting popular sentiment as a prolific author, editor, and highly public lecturer. Using his unique insider perspective of the Church as the son of high-ranking Church official George Q. Cannon, Frank J. Cannon's insights into Mormonism's practices and its relationships with politics were heard or read by over a million curiosity seekers. In several ways outlined by Kenneth L. Cannon II, the specific themes of criticism leveled after Smoot's confirmation make it seem like the hearings settled little, or that the published record of the hearings did not, after all, exonerate Smoot but instead served as a blueprint for future attacks on the Mormon Church.

Kenneth L. Cannon II's conclusions temper Flake's thesis that the country necessarily "moved on." In the years following Smoot's confirmation vote, Kenneth L. Cannon II illustrates instances in which women's groups reassembled over new rumors of plural marriages, provides new examples of rekindled conflicts between Joseph F. Smith and the media, and provides evidence of reignited concerns over treasonous temple oaths and continued hierarchical influence in politics. Amid these controversies, and using the encore help of powerful progressive figures such as Theodore Roosevelt, Smoot and the LDS Church weathered this storm and avoided the threat of a second investigation. It was not until around 1917, ten years after the hearings, when the Church enthusiastically supported America's entrance into World War I, that the public's appetite for Mormon sensationalism began to recede. As a side note concerning the Church's prominent support for the American war effort, newspapers noted the distinction held by Smoot that he was the first senator to offer a prayer on the Senate floor, in which he implored God to "bless and approve" the action of the Senate in declaring war on Germany.[53] Kenneth L. Cannon II argues that LDS patriotism during the war transformed the way Americans viewed Mormons, and this display of wartime patriotism provided Mormons with the inverse benefit of feeling a strong sense of nationalist belonging after decades of alienation. As Mormons fought alongside other Americans, rather than against them, the country was ready to move beyond the intractable "Mormon Question" and accept Mormonism as an American reality.

Part II of this volume looks at the hearings from a more local and biographical perspective. These essays, though narrow in scope, should not be interpreted as culturally or politically insignificant, since they focus on how individual persons, both political and religious, encountered, embraced, and responded to this larger political event.[54] Mormon apostle Reed Smoot's struggle before the US Senate represented more than just his electoral future, or the electoral viability of future Mormons; rather, the hearings served as a touchpoint for Mormons to reorient themselves and claim religious and national belonging in a shifting cultural and religious environment. Also included in this section are personal stories of how individuals influenced the course of the hearings and shaped Mormonism's modern face.

In the chapter 5, retired BYU Communications professor and Smoot great-granddaughter Kathryn Smoot Egan contributes an original essay, "My Darling Allie, Your Reed: Letters 1903–1907," on the family life of Reed and his wife, Alpha (Allie) May Eldredge, during the Senate hearings. Egan's essay tells the story of Reed and Allie Smoot's personal strain in raising a family amid heavy national prejudice, as well as living thousands of miles apart. It was a delicate time for the Smoot family, and Egan crafts an intimate narrative of the couple, where Reed yearns for his family's support and Allie faces the struggles of single parenthood during the prolonged absences. The familial costs incurred from Reed's senatorial ambitions were substantial for Allie and their six children, but Egan demonstrates that they survived the ordeal by privately leaning on each other, which, intentionally or not, publicly modeled a new monogamous paradigm of national citizenship for Mormons in the twentieth century. At the same time, Allie's public monogamous relationship with Reed patterned familiar Protestant Victorian patriarchal mores, demonstrating a new Mormon morality that was acceptable to the Protestant establishment, when polygamy had been deemed a relic of barbarism.

In chapter 6, "Under the Gun at the Smoot Hearings: Joseph F. Smith's Testimony," Michael Harold Paulos analyzes the testimony and events surrounding the Smoot hearing's first and most important witness, President Joseph F. Smith. Smith's testimony not only set the tone for other Church witnesses, but his physical presence in Washington conveyed a new willingness toward change and national engagement. Paulos takes us through what historians such as Carmen Hardy and Kathleen Flake have noted as Smith's evasive and equivocating responses at the hearings, which not only frustrated elites and embarrassed allies in Washington, but also bewildered some believing Mormons back home in Utah. But it was Smith's selective use of candor about his personal polygamous life that proved most troublesome to Smoot's defenders in the Senate. Yet ironically, it was this candid testimony that ultimately bolstered Smoot and steered "the Church towards long-term success." President Smith's admissions of continued illegal cohabitation, considering earlier promises of discontinuance, reinforced prevailing notions of Mormon duplicity. However, Smith's testimony simultaneously established a form of Mormon independence and separation from established institutional practices and teachings, thus painting Smith's continued polygamous lifestyle as that of an individual, rather than the formal policy and action of the institution. Indeed, when questioned if Smoot ever advised him "to desist from polygamous cohabitation," Smith simply responded that Smoot did not know about such arrangements. Distinguishing himself as a free individual agent apart from the institutional Church, Smith pleaded ignorance to the activities of his ecclesiastical subordinates after the 1890 Manifesto, including whether they sired additional children thereafter. Within this schematic of a newly argued privatized form of Mormonism, Paulos shows that both Smith and Smoot used the "shopworn playbook of craftiness and guile" that the "LDS hierarchy" had developed over the preceding decades to defend against the antipolygamy efforts of the federal government. By redefining Mormonism as a more individual privatized faith separate from its institution, Smith's testimony helped secularize and modernize the LDS Church, which thus opened a wider circumference for political participation. Smith's testimony was a "calculated risk," Paulos propounds, but one "that set the stage for Mormonism's acceptance into America's religious pantheon, where it would start the process of assimilation into American society at large."

In chapter 7, "'Some Divine Purpose': Carl A. Badger and the Reed Smoot Hearings," managing director of the Smith-Pettit Foundation Gary James Bergera tells the story of Carl A. Badger, Smoot's twenty-five-year-old personal secretary who was attending Columbian College's law school (later George Washington University) and how the hearings challenged his religious faith. A youthful idealist and a committed member of the Church of Jesus Christ of Latter-day Saints, Badger found the testimony he attended from President Joseph F. Smith and other Church leaders unbearable and fretted at the duplicity he detected in their words before Congress. After several painful committee hearing sessions, Badger began to believe that only external pressure from the federal government would provide the impetus to inspire internal LDS reform. Badger, who represented the youthful generation of Church members oriented toward twentieth-century assumptions of American modernity and religiosity, confided in his letters home to his wife, Rose, that he was struggling to reconcile traditional LDS presumptions of ecclesiastical goodness and wisdom with what he was witnessing in Washington. For instance, Badger was bothered that some Church leaders nonchalantly testified to "have broken the law of God" by continuing polygamous relationships and giving off the impression that God was "a very easy 'Boss.'"

In important ways, Badger's disenchantment with Church leaders mirrored the "doubt and skepticism" felt by a few similarly situated Utah Mormons attending eastern universities between 1896 and 1920. Thomas W. Simpson, in his book *American Universities and the Birth of Modern Mormonism*, presents the story of a few LDS students, who after leaving Utah and entering the university, adopted a "critical attitude" toward the Church, which was based on the ethos of their academic training. These young scholars placed "the intuitions of their fathers on the dissecting table for analysis" and concluded that some "good men," or in other words Church leaders, had "made serious mistakes." Badger's religious trajectory during the hearings followed a similar course, though he is not mentioned in Simpson's book. Ironically, two of the leading champions of this "academic migration" to elite eastern universities—Benjamin Cluff, the principal of Brigham Young Academy, and Joseph Marion Tanner, the Church school superintendent—were forced to resign in the context of the Smoot hearings because of post-manifesto marriages they had entered into. These illegal marriages not only caused problems for Senator Smoot but also had the effect of slowing "the progress of Mormon intellectual history."[55] Simpson's book is silent on the impact testimony given at the Smoot hearings had on this cohort of Mormon students, though it is reasonable to assume they had a similar reaction to that of Badger's or other young non-academically trained Mormons residing in Utah. In response to this fallout from the hearings, Joseph F. Smith undertook damage control measures that restored credibility to the Church's tarnished public image and prophetic mantle. Badger, in these ways, is also representative of this new generation of Mormons, ones who did not feel as strong a connection to the Church's polygamous and collectivist past but who identified "with the respectable moralistic religion of the Protestant establishment." Ultimately, concludes Bergera, Badger's personal struggle reveals the personal crisis faced by individual Mormons who identified with a privatized, moralistic faith yet continued to encounter unsettling contradictions with hierarchical allegiance.

As discussed in this introduction, Smoot's opponents consisted of a diverse alliance of Christian, business, and political constituencies, who joined the coordinated populist campaign against his presence in the US Senate. Senator Fred T. Dubois, a Democrat from Idaho, a former federal official enacting "night raids" against polygamists, and a close ally to Frank J. Cannon, played a leadership role in this campaign against Smoot and the LDS Church. Historian John Brumbaugh, in chapter 8, titled "'A Systematic, Orderly, and Unusually Intelligent Fight': Senator Fred T. Dubois and Reed Smoot" argues that Dubois's actions to organize national protests against Mormonism represent "an interesting case study of Mormon 'Orientalism'" and explains in part the how and why Mormon "otherness" was perpetuated during the early twentieth century. Holding a senior position on the Senate committee investigating Smoot, Dubois shrewdly criticized Smoot in a way that advanced the specter of Mormon otherness that resonated both inside and outside America. Distrustful of Mormon leadership and their claims of reform, Dubois sought unsuccessfully to neutralize the LDS Church's influence in Washington. Just months before Smoot's final confirmation vote, Dubois suffered several political defeats after years of advocacy, including the failure to disenfranchise Mormon voting rights, the failure to pass an antipolygamy constitutional amendment, and the failure to win reelection in Idaho. Dubois's many defeats present a microcosmic illustration of this introduction's thesis, that the Smoot hearings suggest an important expansion of religious pluralism in America, where outmoded ideas of prejudiced elites were replaced by more secular-minded progressive politicians. Part of this "changing of the guard" came from the shifting national mood that favored an increased level of inclusivity and religious toleration.[56] Moreover, the replacement of two LDS apostles, John W. Taylor and Matthias Cowley, who engaged in illegal polygamous marriages and then refused to testify before the Senate committee, is likewise analogous to these larger secular shifts that allowed for a fuller cooperation between the LDS Church and the federal government.

The last item in this volume, "LDS Officials Involved with New Plural Marriages from September 1890 to February 1907," is an appendix by historian D. Michael Quinn. Based on research that began in the 1960s, Quinn's appendix includes a careful chronology of matrimony dates and names, together with relevant pronouncements and comments by ecclesiastical leaders. This list includes 289 polygamous marriages that occurred from September 30, 1890, the day before Church leaders voted "unanimously" to "sustain" the recently published manifesto, through February 21, 1907, the day after the US Senate voted to retain Smoot in the US Senate. On April 5, 1907, Joseph F. Smith, Anthon H. Lund, and John R. Winder of the First Presidency, the Church's highest ranking ecclesiastical body, presented to the Church in General Conference an "Address To the World," which was adopted by the general Church by way of a vote. Among other things, the address declared that the Church had been "true to its pledge respecting the abandonment of the practice of plural marriage" and that any plural marriages after 1890 were merely "sporadic cases" performed by "a few over-zealous individuals who refused to submit even to the action of the Church in such a matter." Quinn's appendix, however, provides extensive documentation of plural marriages engaged in and performed by top Church authorities from 1890 to 1907, including President Smith and his two counselors Lund and Winder. Indeed, by the time Smoot secured his seat in the Senate, twenty-five LDS officials had "knowingly performed post-manifesto polygamy" and, "remarkably," at least thirty-one of those marriages "occurred from the start of testimony until the end of the Smoot Case in February 1907."

Quinn's research provides an important glimpse into the internal complexities and contradictions encountered when a religious institution undergoes a dramatic metamorphosis, which in this case required the stoppage of a sacred marital practice that Apostle John W. Taylor declared was essential to achieving "a fullness of glory." Church leaders had little interest in completely ending the practice with the Woodruff Manifesto in 1890, including future LDS president Lorenzo Snow, who stated privately to fellow apostles in 1896 that the principle of plural marriage was "as true today as it ever was" and "will again be practiced by this people." Reed Smoot himself spoke in 1902 before the Twelve of his hope for its future restoration, while others prophesied that the practice would remain on earth in one form or another, until Christ's return. Those who continued to perform and sanction polygamous unions post-1890 in defiance of national law and Church pronouncements were not rogue actors but highly revered leaders caught between the significance of Smoot's election and the commandment to live a divine practice that threatened it. An overview of Quinn's appendix makes it clear that the Smoot hearings played a critical role in forcing a complete repudiation by the LDS Church of the practice of plural marriage, together with how it was publicly spoken of and understood by a younger generation of Mormons. The distinction and even overlap between authorized and unauthorized violations of Church pronouncements against polygamy that took shape during these hearings represented an important shift within LDS history and the Church's entrance into the Progressive Era, leading to the emergence of schismatic groups known as "Fundamentalist Mormons." This appendix is a preview of a full-length study with detailed footnoting that D. Michael Quinn is preparing about post-manifesto plural marriages.

The scholarship in this volume complements, challenges, and expands upon the existing work on the Reed Smoot hearings. In addition, this volume adds new insights into the role religion and the secular played in the shaping of American political institutions and national policies, the intrinsic religious nature of the secular itself, the intimacies and challenges of religious privatization, the dynamic of federal power on religious reform, and the role individuals played in impacting these institutional and national developments. While additional aspects of this story remains to be told, the present study provides an important case study of religious dynamism as seen through the LDS Church during this period of theological and political crisis. Leaders of the Church made internal adjustments, some of which were the result of public outcry and government coercion, that allowed for the Church to achieve an embrace of religious inclusion in America. In the decades that followed the Smoot case, the Church transformed itself into a twentieth-century beacon of corporate patriotism, patriarchy, and monogamy. Last, this volume adds to the corpus of scholarship on the Smoot hearings new stories of ancillary and tertiary characters who played a role in this transitional moment for the Church of Jesus Christ of Latter-day Saints and America at large.

Reed Smoot's vindication has been viewed by some as Mormonism's "coming of age" moment and the entrance of the Mormon people to the modern world.

However, when placing this victory more broadly in the American story, what results is a clearer picture of how religious accommodation and assimilation eventuated in an emergent modern and coercive nation-state, as well as how the two entities (Mormon Church and US nation-state) were changed simultaneously by the encounter. Mormonism "came of age" because they became what a Protestant nation wanted them to be—that is, in part, monogamous and privatized. In crucial ways, such religious pluralism was not entirely dependent upon the waning influence of America's quasi-religious establishment but was, instead, equally predicated on Mormonism's willingness to abandon the practice of sacred salvific rituals as well as a willingness to remove beloved personalities from the Church's hierarchy as a type of symbolic sacrifice on the altar of American religious pluralism.

This volume does not address all pertinent questions surrounding the importance of the hearings or its social context, and as such additional work remains. However, it is hoped that this volume spurs historians and other scholars of Mormon and American history to ask new questions about this important historical moment in America.

NOTES

1. Talal Asad, *Formations of the Secular: Christianity, Islam, Modernity* (Stanford, CA: Stanford University Press, 2003), 24–26; David Sehat, *The Myth of American Religious Freedom* (New York: Oxford University Press, 2011), 4–7, 58.

2. Robert M. Crunden, *Ministers of Reform: The Progressives' Achievement in American Civilization, 1889–1920* (New York: Basic Books, Inc., 1982), 25, 62–62; William T. Cavanaugh, *The Myth of Religious Violence* (New York: Oxford University Press, 2009), 57–60, 77, 80–81.

3. Charles Taylor, *A Secular Age* (Cambridge: The Belknap Press, 2007), 1, 18.

4. Sehat, *The Myth of American Religious Freedom*, 4, 8–9, 154–159, 183–184.

5. Thomas Alexander, *Mormonism in Transition: A History of the Latter-day Saints, 1890–1930* (Urbana: University of Illinois Press, 1996), 14–15.

6. Loretta D. Nixon and L. Douglas Smoot, *Abraham Owen Smoot: A Testament of His Life* (Provo, UT: Brigham Young University Press, 1994), 315–320.

7. Nixon and Smoot, *Abraham Owen Smoot*, 2, 17–32.

8. Each of Reed's parents played a major role in his development. For the best treatment of Reed Smoot's early life, see Harvard S. Heath, "Reed Smoot: First Modern Mormon" (PhD diss., Brigham Young University, 1990), 12–83.

9. "Reed Smoot Dines Negroes," *New York Times*, February 13, 1903, 1; Jonathan H. Moyer, "Dancing With the Devil: The Making of the Mormon-Republican Pact" (PhD diss., University of Utah, Salt Lake City), 307, 415.

10. Heath, "Reed Smoot," 54–56.

11. Heath, "Reed Smoot," 35, 41–58. After serving for ten months, Smoot was summoned home early by President Wilford Woodruff because his father was in poor health and they needed Reed to handle the family's business affairs.

12. Heath, "Reed Smoot," 51–56. For background on Smoot's protectionist career, see Milton R. Merrill, *Reed Smoot: Apostle in Politics* (Logan: Utah State University Press, 1990), 285–347; Michael Harold Paulos, "'Smoot Smites Smut': Apostle-Senator Reed Smoot's 1930 Campaign

against Obscene Books," *Journal of Mormon History* 40, no. 1 (Winter 2014), 53–96; Matthew Lyman Rasmussen, *Mormonism and the Making of a British Zion* (Salt Lake City: University of Utah Press, 2016), 78–102; Douglas A. Irwin, *Peddling Protectionism: Smoot-Hawley and the Great Depression* (Princeton, NJ: Princeton University Press, 2011) 3, 40–42, 50–53, 65–79, 82–88, 90–92, 145–146, 190–194.

13. Heath, "Reed Smoot," 34–37, 68–74. Many of Smoot's ecclesiastical colleagues at the time, and Reed Smoot himself, were surprised at his call to the Quorum of the Twelve. President George Q. Cannon admonished Smoot at the time that he needed "to change his course in life," to which Smoot replied that he would make it his "first consideration."

14. Smoot's calling to the apostleship was a surprise to some in Utah and is reflected by the apocryphal story of a conversation between the colorful LDS general authority J. Golden Kimball and Reed Smoot soon after his calling: "When Reed Smoot was called as a[n] apostle, J. Golden Kimball came into his office to speak with him. 'Brother Smoot,' he said, 'I just wanted you to know that I really and truly believe that your calling was inspired by God. It must have been a genuine revelation from the Lord because sure as hell nobody else would have ever thought of you.'" Eric A. Eliason, *The J. Golden Kimball Stories* (Urbana: University of Illinois Press, 2007), 71–72.

15. Lorenzo Snow, "Greeting to the World," January 1, 1901, in James R. Clark, ed., *Messages of the First Presidency of the Church of Jesus Christ of Latter-day Saints* (Salt Lake City: Bookcraft, 1965–1975), 3:333–35. For more background on the LDS's embrace of Progressive Era values, especially from LDS Women, see Coleen McDaniel, *Sister Saints: Mormon Women since the End of Polygamy* (New York: Oxford University Press, 2019), 36–37, 40–42.

16. Moyer, "Dancing with the Devil," 272.

17. Heath, "Reed Smoot," 74–78.

18. Thanks to Gary James Bergera for his assistance in writing this background of the Smoot hearings and for this paragraph and the following two paragraphs.

19. See Joseph Fielding Smith, *Life of Joseph F. Smith, Sixth President of the Church of Jesus Christ of Latter-day Saints* (Salt Lake City: Deseret Book Co., 1938), 330; "Attack on Smoot's Accuser," *New York Times*, March 22, 1903, 3; "Ministers Act on Smoot," *New York Times*, March 1, 1903, 2.

20. US Senate, Committee on Privileges and Elections, Proceedings before the Committee on Privileges and Elections of the United States Senate in the Matter of the Protests against the Right of Hon. Reed Smoot, a senator from the State of Utah, to Hold His Seat, 59th Cong., 1 Sess., Senate Report No. 486, 4 vols. (Washington, DC: Government Printing Office, 1904–1907), 1:1–30 (hereafter, Smoot Hearings). Leilich's charge that Smoot was a polygamist was quickly disproved.

21. Reed Smoot to Joseph F. Smith, January 9, 1904, Reed Smoot Papers, L. Tom Perry Special Collections, Harold B. Lee Library, Brigham Young University, Provo, UT (hereafter, Smoot Papers).

22. The following list displays the formal committee meeting schedule at the Smoot hearings:

> March 1, 1904, through March 12, 1904—Testimony
> April 20, 1904, through May 2, 1904—Testimony
> December 12, 1904, through December 20, 1904—Testimony
> January 10, 1905, through January 27, 1905—Testimony and First Round of
>   Concluding Arguments
> February 6, 1906, through February 9, 1906—Testimony
> March 26, 1906 through March 27, 1906—Testimony
> April 12, 1906, through April 13, 1906—Second Round of Concluding Arguments

23. At different times over the two years of formal hearings, the entire testimony of specific witnesses was published by the government printing offices and distributed in tract format to interested readers and politicians unable to attend the testimony in person.

24. The "Mormon Problem" was used throughout the nineteenth century as a catchall phrase and rhetorical reduction to describe the repeated political problems America had with Mormonism during much of the nineteenth century.

25. Kathleen Flake, *The Politics of American Religious Identity: The Seating of Senator Reed Smoot, Mormon Apostle* (Chapel Hill: University of North Carolina Press, 2004), 1–2, 8, 10–11.

26. Milton R. Merrill, *Reed Smoot: Apostle in Politics* (Logan: Utah State University Press, 1990), 16–26, 98; Milton R. Merrill, "Reed Smoot: Apostle in Politics" (PhD diss., Columbia University, 1950).

27. Harvard S. Heath, "Reed Smoot: First Modern Mormon" (PhD diss., Brigham Young University, 1990), 84–197; Harvard S. Heath, "The Reed Smoot Hearings: A Quest for Legitimacy," *Journal of Mormon History* 33, no. 2 (Summer 2007), 1–80.

28. Jonathan H. Moyer, "Dancing with the Devil: The Making of the Mormon-Republican Pact" (PhD diss., University of Utah, Salt Lake City), 1–2, 606–618.

29. Michael Harold Paulos, ed., *The Mormon Church on Trial: Transcripts of the Reed Smoot Hearings* (Salt Lake City: Signature Books, 2008).

30. Sehat, *The Myth of American Religious Freedom*, 183–184.

31. Josiah Strong, *The New Era, or the Coming Kingdom* (New York: Baker and Taylor Company, 1893), 201, 209–211, 253, 255.

32. Gaines Foster, *Moral Reconstruction: Christian Lobbyists and the Federal Legislation of Morality, 1865–1920* (Chapel Hill: University of North Carolina Press, 2002), 222–225.

33. Flake, *The Politics of American Religious Identity*, 60; "Women against Smoot," *New York Times*, June 9, 1906, 4.

34. Proceedings before the Committee on Privileges and Elections of the United States Senate in the Matter of the Protests against the Right of Hon. Reed Smoot, a Senator from the State of Utah, to Hold His Seat (Washington, DC: US Government Printing Office, 1906), 1:70–72.

35. Jon C. Teaford, "Toward a Christian Nation: Religion, Law and Justice Strong," in *Journal of Presbyterian History (1962–1985)* 54, no. 4 (1976): 431; Flake, *The Politics of American Religious Identity*, 10; Foster, *Moral Reconstruction*, 22, 25, 82–83; William R. Hutchison, *Religious Pluralism in America: The Contentious History of a Founding Ideal* (New Haven, CT: Yale University Press, 2003), 78–80; John G. Turner, *The Mormon Jesus: A Biography* (Cambridge, MA: Harvard University Press, 2016), 180–183.

36. Philip Schaff, *Church and State in the United States, or The American Idea of Religious Liberty and its Practical Effects* (New York: Charles Scribner's Sons, 1888), 39–40.

37. Teaford, "Toward a Christian Nation," 426, 430.

38. Teaford, "Toward a Christian Nation," 430, 432; Schaff, *Church and State*, 39.

39. Schaff, *Church and State*, 44, 48.

40. Teaford, "Toward a Christian Nation," 432.

41. Schaff, *Church and State*, 43.

42. Philip Schaff, *America, a Sketch of the Political, Social, and Religious Character of the United States of America, in Two Lectures, Delivered at Berlin with a Report Read before the German Church Diet at Frankfort-on-the-Maine, Sept* (New York: C. Scribner, 1855), xi.

43. Robert Ingersoll, *Some Mistakes of Moses* (Buffalo, NY: Prometheus Books, 1986), 14, 26–28; Philip Hamburger, *Separation of Church and State* (Cambridge, MA: Harvard University Press, 2002), 293–313, 327; *Equal Rights in Religion. Report of the Centennial Congress of Liberals, and Organization of the National Liberal League, at Philadelphia, on the Fourth of July 1876* (Boston: Published by the National Liberal League, 1876), 10, 175; Foster, *Moral Reconstruction*, 2, 22, 29–30, 46; David Sehat, *The Myth of American Religious Freedom* (New York: Oxford University Press, 2011), 176–178; George M. Marsden, *Fundamentalism and American Culture* (New York: Oxford University Press, 2006), 29.

44. Schaff, *Church and State*, 40, 45.

45. Crunden, *Ministers of Reform*, 40–48; James H. Smylie, *The Encyclopedia Americana: International Edition*. vol. 11 (Danbury: Grolier Inc., 1995), 238.

46. Crunden, *Ministers of Reform*, 58–63; John Dewey, "My Pedagogic Creed," *School Journal* 54, no. 3 (January 16, 1897): 77–80.

47. Crunden, *Ministers of Reform*, 40, 48, 62–63.

48. T. P. Stevenson, ed., *The Christian Statesman* 41, no. 5, [National Reform Association] (May 1907): 135; T. P. Stevenson, ed., *The Christian Statesman* 41, no. 6 [National Reform Association] (June 1907): 187–188.

49. Foster, *Moral Reconstruction*, 230–233.

50. Frank F. Ellinwood, "New Religions of the Nineteenth Century: Mormonism." *Homiletic Review* 46, no. 5 (November 1903): 323–329.

51. "Editorial Section." *The Homiletic Review* 46, no. 5 (November 1903): 399–400.

52. Flake, *The Politics of American Religious Identity*, 159–162.

53. Smoot noted in his diary that the newspaper coverage of his prayer was "favorable." Harvard S. Heath, *In the World: The Diaries of Reed Smoot* (Signature Books, Salt Lake City, 1997), 351–353.

54. For an interesting and relevant discussion about human agency that "conditions other people's lives," which represents its own type of "system" or cultural force that is governed by probability rather than causality, see Talal Asad, *Genealogies of Religion: Discipline and Reasons of Power in Christianity and Islam* (Baltimore: Johns Hopkins University Press, 1993), 6–7, 10.

55. Thomas W. Simpson, *American Universities and the Birth of Modern Mormonism, 1867–1940* (Chapel Hill: University of North Carolina Press, 2016), 54–91.

56. Secularity deals with religion in the public space, where older religious models encounter a new "secular age" of expanded ideas and practices of how the nation-state can be conceived and made relevant to the individual, producing a "new age in which the older religion is no more at home." This shift toward the secular does not imply a simple story of religious decline in society, but rather, as Charles Taylor explains, "of a new placement of the sacred or spiritual in relation to individual and social life. This new placement is now the occasion for recompositions of spiritual life in new forms, and for new ways of existing both in and out of relation to God." For a broad discussion of this "secular age," see Taylor, *A Secular Age*, 26, 280–281, 437.

1

The Reed Smoot Hearings and the Theology of Politics

Perceiving an "American" Identity

Konden Smith Hansen

And here let me add, the feelings of pure and unalloyed loyalty to our government which were deep-seated in the hearts of the Mormon people then, are still a part and parcel of our very being now, and indeed could not be otherwise, for the simple reason that as a community, we are an integral part of the nation itself, and the God whom we worship is the God of this nation.
—JOSEPH F. SMITH, 1907[1]

The Reed Smoot hearings of 1904–1906 reveal important insights into shifts within American religious and secular history. Upon winning a seat in the US Senate, Utahn Reed Smoot (1862–1941), an apostle in the Church of Jesus Christ of Latter-day Saints, received significant protestation that his election demonstrated an unforgivable breach of the separation of church and state that threatened the stability of the republic. It is important to note, however, that numerous Protestant ministers from differing denominations, as well as several Christian organizations, many who had long lobbied to unite their religion with the state, felt the most intense threat from Smoot's religion and feared for the soul of the country. The fact that Smoot ultimately retained his seat after an intensive four-year investigation suggests an important shift in the power dynamics of American politics over the late nineteenth and into the early twentieth centuries. As developed in the introduction, this shift is an outward expression of the changing role of religion in American public life, as well as a symbol of the waning role of partisan ecclesiastical influence. In short, the Smoot case demonstrates not only the embrace by the LDS Church of a more secular vision of privatized religion, but also a similar embrace by the US Senate. Observing this movement toward secularity

DOI: 10.7330/9781646421176.c001

and its deep synthesis with liberal Protestantism in American society and politics reveals important connections between an emerging "modern" Mormon identity, and an "American" identity that was then being redefined.

These national transformations toward secularism changed how Americans perceived themselves and others, including their Mormon countryman. Moreover, the LDS Church itself experienced shifts in how its membership perceived themselves as legitimate Americans, and not just as a community on the margins marking time for a separate millennial kingdom to appear. This chapter explores what it meant in the popular mind, at the start of the twentieth century, to be American and how religious outsiders such as Mormons came to identify themselves *within* this changing ideal during the Progressive Era. Often cited roughly as beginning in the 1890s and ending in the 1910s, this "progressive" era looked for new ways to understand societal advance in light of the failures of an earlier Protestant Era. As discussed in the introduction, the Progressive Era was a period of growing religious pluralism and cultural secularization, as well as a time when the powerful Protestant hegemony in American society began to noticeably recede. As previously noted, this recession of traditional religious influence should not be misunderstood as the cessation of religion from American public life, but rather it should be recognized as the time when a new Protestant secularity was initiated that transformed how religion related to the American nation-state. This new relationship as defined by a new breed of liberal Protestant elites can be observed at the senatorial hearings focused on whether Mormon apostle Reed Smoot could retain his seat. Smoot's ultimate victory was in attaining the status of being "American," despite his religious affiliation, a key thrust of this new Protestant American secularity.

THE PROGRESSIVE ERA, 1890S–1910S

The political, economic, and religious remodeling of America during the Progressive Era was unprecedented in American history. Between 1870 and 1900, the United States moved from an agricultural nation of farmers to a world industrial power.[2] Rural isolationism was a thing of the past, noted Congregational minister and social theologian Josiah Strong in 1893, for "steam and electricity are making the whole world a neighborhood and every man a neighbor."[3] Indeed, new technologies revolutionized how Americans lived and traveled, refashioning the literal landscape where citizens lived. Moreover, growing divisions in American thought increased with the rise of secular scientific thought, urbanization, and industrialization, heightening the levels of social and economic anxiety.[4] As noted in the introduction, American Protestants had traditionally perceived the individual as depraved and dependent upon the government to provide a Christian moral framework to ensure social order and a civil society. Providing individuals with too much liberty, it was then understood, would cause the downfall of civilization.

This concern over the continuation of this Christian civilization, notes Tisa Wenger and David Sehat, created a situation in which Protestant churches actively worked against the advancement of religious liberty.[5] The emergence of America's new industrial economy, however, with the attendant growth of religiously diverse cities in the last half of the century, brought social shifts that directly challenged the influence of this earlier moral establishment. Economic developments, such as the rise of corporations and concentrated wealth, with the unseemly underbelly of labor exploitation, were embraced by Protestant elites as God's divine economic-social order. As Congregationalist minister Henry Ward Beecher famously remarked when criticizing the Great Railroad Strike of 1877, "God has intended the great to be great and the little to be little." Workers responded by organizing labor unions and strikes, but when challenging this reputedly divine economic system, these laborers were dismissed as depraved individuals who peddled in dark conspiracies that threatened the moral integrity of the nation.[6] Alarmed by the efforts to dismiss the urban working class and other urban concerns, Josiah Strong sermonized against the drawbacks of technology and industry and lamented that corporations were exploiting the services of unskilled workers, to the detriment of skilled workers who could not find work.[7]

Concurrent with these labor anxieties was the national myth in America about science and social progress, then embraced by liberal Protestants. Traditional Protestantism had long assumed the role of being the foremost cultural arbiter within American society and was naturally unwilling to let go of this privileged position despite the era's liberalizing centrifugal forces. While some progressive Protestants recognized these shifts as an intellectual and a scientific form of modern Protestantism, defensive responses by traditional Protestants reveal their preference to conserve the status quo. Josiah Strong inveighed against this form of Protestant class prejudice, warning that it threatened to transform Protestant Christianity into an exclusive "steepled club," attractive only to an elite "sort of folks" and not welcoming to the working-class citizens then residing in large cities. Strong opposed the ideas of men such as Reverend De Witt Talmage of the Central Presbyterian Church in Brooklyn, who promoted a form of class segregation in churches by arguing that if the "common people" are mixed with the affluent and "uncommon" folks in worship, it would keep "one-half of Christians sick at their stomach" and would "kill the church . . . with bad smells."[8] Prominent ministers, such as Beecher and Talmage, viewed monetary success as evidence of God's favor, and those less fortunate were determined to be deserving of their poverty. For Strong, prosperity theology and Christian elitism such as this were false doctrinal concepts, and he believed an embrace of these ideas would lead to a widespread loss of faith in Protestantism's social relevance. Thus, the transformations of the Progressive Era not only brought social and economic problems to the country, as noted by Strong, but also exposed the limitations of the existing moral establishment to resolve them. Strong, an influential social critic, sounded the alarm, and pushed for a new level of Christian urban activism that embraced scientific advances as a method to address the challenges of the era.

As the Progressive Era evolved, the myth of progress also shifted notions that religious obligation required the mechanisms of the government to force religious perfection across the world in preparation of Christ's millennial reign, to the concept of a private faith that influenced the social-political system through subtle and more implicit ways.[9] To begin the Progressive Era, it is important to note, many Americans did not see as separate their religious beliefs and their everyday industrial lives, which included science, economics, and politics. As an example, ethnographer and theorist of religion Stanley Tambiah argued that Protestant theology and modern science, prior to the Progressive Era, were strong allies. Also, American historian Edward Larson suggests that secular scientific theory at the turn of the century was not antireligious but incorporated theistic elements that conjoined the two. Furthermore, according to many Protestant intellectuals of the day, including Henry Ward Beecher, science played an important part in bringing forth Christ's millennial kingdom in America.[10] Thus, at the beginning of this transitional era, Protestant Christianity was upheld as an important element of scientific and social progress, even as this understanding of progress was shifting away from more explicit theological concerns.[11]

By embracing the link between religion and science, observed George Marsden, these "faithful" intellectuals focused on both theology and geology, classifying the certainties of religion while avoiding speculative hypotheses, and using geology to further establish theology. Josiah Strong, adding his voice, not only argued in 1893 that science represented an extension of the Protestant kingdom, but also considered science an incipient form of revelation. Scientists, Strong averred in his work *The New Era, or Coming Kingdom*, were akin to ancient prophets who declared, "the kingdom of heaven is at hand."[12] Despite these discussions on the intersections of science and religion, many Americans, by the start of the twentieth century, increasingly decoupled the linkages between the two. And over time, methodological shifts in how science and religion were approached in the universities and in the larger society accelerated this bifurcation. Namely, the field of science placed its focus on empirically obtained knowledge, devoid of religious significance, while religious communities emphasized a more private form of faith that claimed less authority over secular knowledge.[13]

At the time Strong wrote of scientists being prophets, the scientific community was exploring hypotheses that threatened traditional understandings of Christianity, at least according to a growing number of alarmed millennialists. Popular theories such as Darwinian evolution brought into question the biblical account of the earth's creation and the divine genesis of humankind. In response, Charles Hodge, professor of systematic theology at Princeton, agreed that Darwinism, as a symbol of atheistic empiricism, threatened to "dethrone God" in the quest for ultimate truth.[14] Other challenges to religion emerged, including German Higher Criticism studies that questioned the authenticity and historicity of Christ's life, death, and resurrection, and the infallibility of the Bible. German moral relativists, such as Friedrich Nietzsche, even questioned the very concept of a moral civilization itself, and refuted Christianity's claims to divine truth and morality.[15] The resistance to these intellectual and scientific challenges highlights the divisions within American Protestantism that occurred around the time the Smoot hearings began. Although independent of these hearings, these fissures within Protestantism, existing within the context of an emergent modern secular nation-state, foisted challenges to the fitness of using explicit expressions of traditional religion in American politics. This shift redefined an earlier public morality against the more "progressive" modality of an implicit faith that emphasized human empiricism and reason.

The liberal impulse that shifted explicit religion toward implicit religion was the modernists' attempt to adapt Christian practice to fit within the scientific era in which the Protestant establishment wielded dwindling influence. In what William Hutchison labeled the "modernist impulse," liberal theologies infiltrated large denominations and by the new century had become accepted aspects of Protestant life. These impulses countered earlier Calvinist dogmas that denigrated individuals and demarcated their dependence on repressive theocratic rule. Further, other liberal theologies, though not fully embraced, suggested that Christ's life, as the incarnation of God, infused the world with divine autonomy, thereby rejecting any moral distinction between religious belief and the physical world. For modernists, God was found in both nature and human nature, and any disunion of the two was artificial truth. These modernists also rejected literal readings of the Bible, deemphasized religious dogma, and instead taught that divinity is within each individual and emphasized the importance of offering good works. During the 1880s, battle lines between modernist and traditionalist voices were drawn within some congregations, and by 1890, notes Hutchison, the modernist's vision had become as strong a movement as any.[16] As modernists questioned long-held conventions, they also provided solutions on how to combat and adapt to the challenges being made against Christianity. These adaptations provided dignity to the individual within an implicit religious faith that prioritized righteous action over dogmatic belief. This growing division within American Protestantism percolated for decades until its formal severance at the time of the Fundamentalist movement during the 1910s.

Throughout the nineteenth century, Protestants upheld a postmillennial worldview of God's kingdom returning, despite the tension created by these later anxieties and social challenges. Many Protestants, however, both evangelical and nonevangelical, began to lose faith in an explicitly religious approach to these deep societal concerns that were expected to be solved prior to Christ's return. Pessimistic about their ability to control an increasingly complicated and troubled society, Christian millennialists began to define themselves apart from American politics, holding the belief that Christ's second advent and millennial reign would occur only after the destruction of the increasingly wicked and hopeless world.[17] The key distinction between these two oversimplifications of American millenarianism, explained Grant Underwood, was in the basic attitude of optimism on the one hand, or pessimism on the other, regarding the ability of religion to positively influence society.[18] Modernist Protestants, for their part, resisted more explicit claims of a literal imminent kingdom of God for one more spiritual and aloof, representing a more modern vision of Christian politics that aligned with these newly secularized visions of American science and politics, and they thus avoided the more problematic millennial Christian concerns. While some progressives, remarked Robert Crunden, advocated for an explicitly religious vision of societal reform, such as the Social Gospel movement, progressivism's true influence came when a more implicit form of Christian social engagement matched the tendencies and assumptions of this new scientific era.[19]

Liberal Protestants gravitated toward "natural" as opposed to theological principles, when considering social and political concerns. Defined by moral actions rather than orthodox beliefs, these natural principles erected a philosophical barrier, as it were, for the moral establishment opposed to Smoot to negotiate around during the Progressive Era. These progressive shifts were so dramatic and far reaching that sociologist Christian Smith broadly described it as a "secular revolution," stating that the secularization of American public life was a "contested revolutionary struggle" rather than "a natural evolutionary progression."[20] Indeed, as the moral establishment lost ground in American public life traditional Protestants grew more pessimistic and premillennial, which in turn allowed moderate Protestants the secular space to redefine American politics based on modern principles and implicit forms of Protestant faith.

Despite losing some ground to secular trends, traditional Protestants were still a force to be reckoned with at the time the Smoot hearings commenced. The country was determined to not apply a theological litmus test on Smoot and was disposed to let individuals in the leadership of the Church of Jesus Christ of Latter-day Saints speak for themselves and defend against the barrage of allegations leveled against the Church. Given this opening, the Church seized the opportunity to cast itself in a less threatening light—a privatized and "progressive" Church that was more "acceptably American."[21] Articulating this shift was Mormon prophet Lorenzo Snow, who on the first day of 1901, trumpeted Mormon "modernity" by celebrating, as had Strong and Beecher before, scientific progress as a type of revelation from God. As the Church moved into the Progressive Era, President Snow downplayed the immediate return of Christ and embraced the social developments of the day and as "prompted by His Spirit which before long will be poured out upon all flesh that will receive it."[22] This pronouncement reflected an enthusiastic embrace of certain progressive trends by the LDS prophet, which was likewise echoed by other LDS leaders such as Emmeline B. Wells, who declared, "The spirit of progress of this age is the work of God."[23] Despite some caveats, the Mormons were expanding their religious vision along the lines of the modernist impulse, not dissimilar to many Protestants, which created a sense of national inclusion and religious privatization that embraced modern-secular-progressive societal trends as part of God's plan.

Church leadership declared the times a "building era" and in a 1906 "Christmas Greeting" suggested that "a healthy, progressive spirit has been manifested in almost every part of Zion." In Zion over these short years, or the growing "inter-mountain metropolis," Latter-day Saints pushed to become better organized internally and better situated to press forward with social advancements that modernized communication, architectural structures, agriculture, transportation, and medical care.[24] Additional modifications were made in education, theology, ecclesiastics, business, politics, medicine, and proselytizing that fit more closely with the progressive sentiments of the era. For instance, in 1894, prospective missionaries who could not read were no longer sent out until they had developed a baseline of literacy; in 1898 those who did not pay tithes were discouraged from Temple attendance; in 1899 a Churchwide budgeting committee was initiated; in 1902 record keeping was strongly reiterated and encouraged, while congregational "floating," also known as "congregation hopping" was roundly condemned and discouraged; in 1903 stake presidents were advised to be more selective when calling stake patriarchs; in 1905 widespread Church nonattendance was strongly rebuked; and in 1908 Church members who did not keep the Church's health code known as the Word of Wisdom had their memberships threatened.[25]

During his last general conference address in 1901, Lorenzo Snow stated, "The Church is now seventy-two years of age," and continued, "We are not expected to do the work of the days of our youth, but to do greater, larger, and more extensive work."[26] Following Snow's death, his successor, Joseph F. Smith, christened Snow's message as the "word of the Lord to us all" and stated that the way forward "is to zealously and arduously labor to successfully accomplish all that is required at our hands."[27] Smoot, in his election to the Senate, and subsequent defense of his seat, thrust the Church into the Progressive Era's spotlight and put on trial the Church's renewed sense of progressive purpose and destiny. Smoot's new modernist trajectory symbolized the trajectories a new generation of Church members felt and anticipated during this time of profound change within the nation. Although some prominent Mormons initially questioned the wisdom of Smoot's run for Senate, LDS president Joseph F. Smith assured himself and other believers that God supported this electoral pursuit.[28]

This new progressive approach brought a sense of national inclusion and belonging for many Latter-day Saints. Indeed, there were some periodic flints of inclusiveness, such as in Chicago during the 1893 World's Fair, when the Mormon Tabernacle Choir was enthusiastically cheered and awarded a prize, or in 1896 when Utah became the forty-fifth state to join the Union. Some news outlets, including the *New York Times*, at times softened its coverage of the LDS Church, including in 1894 when it quoted the statement of non-Mormon Colonel Isaac Trumbo, an organizer and leader of the struggle to achieve statehood for Utah, in which he declared that Utah had much to offer the nation on a secular-progressive level and that Mormons were no longer dangerous religious fanatics but rather "intense Americans" due to their proper moral rectitude.[29] Based partially upon Church promises to abandon plural marriage, but also its ability to better present its members in these new secular-progressive ways, statehood was an important achievement signifying a new level of national acceptance. Of course, ridicule and suspicion of the Church remained, but as explicit expressions of religious faith became less important, in some ways, Americans were more easily able to shift their gaze from Mormonism as a dangerous institutional faith to Mormonism as a people who were much less threatening and more recognizably American. And though America's national identity remained unquestionably Protestant, sidelining these theological standards for that of more progressive ones opened the nation to a wider scope of religious diversity. This new openness within American society, remarked Thomas Alexander, provided better opportunities for the Church to conduct "concerted efforts to explain the Latter-day Saints to the outside world."[30]

VOICES AGAINST, VOICES FOR

These adjustments of emphasis within Mormonism are further illuminated by contextualizing the shifts in the national mood toward religion and the adapted role it played within US politics. Many Americans at the turn of the century, however, harbored doubts as to whether members of the LDS Church were sufficiently American to serve in high public office, an objection that persisted as a major topic of questioning throughout the hearings and beyond. Hannah Schoff, president of the National Congress of Mothers and leader of the National League of Women's Organizations, declared Mormonism in March of 1905 "a menace to every home in America." Mary E. James, in her speech at the same anti-Smoot assembly, declared the Church's origin "one of fraud and duplicity."[31] A month later the National Society of the Daughters of the American Revolution passed a resolution that embodied its view that the Mormon "hierarchy" sought "the overthrow of the government."[32] Marian Bonsall, of Minneapolis, following a two-month visit to Utah in the summer of 1905, declared the state "practically a bit of foreign territory in the midst of our country" and a greater menace than previously thought.[33] Such sentiments against the Church were merely chords in a loud chorus of skeptical voices against Mormonism's national belonging and its ability to remain aloof of American politics.

Reaching a height of antipathy at the time of the Smoot hearings, anti-Mormon rhetoric ran parallel to anti-Catholic rhetoric, which had long percolated within America, exposing popular assumptions about religion and its relationship to power. As historian William Shea explains, "Anti-Catholicism was never purely a religious matter for American Protestants; it was from the outset a political fear as well, for the Catholic Church was never a purely or merely an objectionable *religious* system."[34] Catholicism's threat was portrayed not just that it could not separate itself from state power, but rather that Protestants defined American politics and democracy in such a way that it excluded all expressions of faith but their own. Samuel Finley Breese Morse (1791–1872), the developer of the electric telegraph and Morse Code, made the comparison that "Popery, from its very nature," favored "despotism," whereas Protestantism, "from its very nature," favored "liberty."[35] Historian Nathan O. Hatch demonstrated that the religious revivals of the early nineteenth century democratized aspects of American culture, including the religious and political, thereby establishing an important link between them. As this democratizing influence reshaped popular understandings of both American religion and power, which Protestants claimed a monopoly over, non-Protestants were understood to be, by definition, excluded from both. Regardless of denominational affiliation, Protestant individuals assumed local and national leadership roles that linked American politics with God's earthly work, creating an anxiety for moral reform that played to this trend toward the theologizing of American politics.

Catholicism and Mormonism, with their visible hierarchical structures, were discerned by many Americans to be rival political organization, and thus embodiments of corrupt religion and threats to national stability. Protestantism, by contrast, did not have a visible hierarchical structure and instead relied on an invisible democratic network of Christian individuals and organizations across denominational lines to wield political influence. In this sense, the Protestant "church" was not a single entity with a centralized body of leaders, but instead a collective *movement* of Christ-motivated individuals.[36] And because this religiopolitical movement lacked a visible head—in contrast to Catholics and Mormons with their prophets, priests, bishops, and popes—it was christened appropriately republican and idealistically democratic. Being thus invisible and amorphous, this Protestant influence on American politics, however intense, was not in violation of the rules of religious disestablishment or separation.[37] This brand of American religious disestablishment followed the understanding of separation between church and state that allowed adherents to act collectively as individuals to influence state programs and governance while also simultaneously excluding Catholics and Mormons from exercising the same citizenry privilege. "Separation of Church and State" meant that individual Protestants, not institutional churches, had the legal right to interfere with matters of the state, even if these coercive laws regulated religious practice and religious belief. As a result, Protestants believed themselves entitled to have sole stewardship over American public life, a designation made more serious by these visible hierarchical threats. Ironically, the formation of the Latter Day Saint restorationist movement in 1830 was directly attributable to this revivalist sentiment of religious democratization, but for the Protestant moral establishment of this era its reliance on ecclesiastical authority removed it from this acceptability.

Prior to the emergence of Mormonism, Catholicism in America was the quintessential version of the "other." Over much of the nineteenth century, Protestant Americans cordoned off exclusivist boundaries that isolated minority groups based on intolerance and a narrow definition of religious liberty. Catholic immigrants were welcomed into the United States, explained the eminent New England pastor Lyman Beecher in 1836, but only if they conformed to "American" standards, which for Beecher meant Protestant.[38] Mormonism, with a similar hierarchical structure as Catholicism, provoked familiar fears among Americans that the religion would promote nondemocratic values. Despite the many changes to the way in which people thought about religion and politics in the Progressive Era, hierarchies were still distrusted, even if theological beliefs and membership to such groups were not necessarily deemed disqualifying. The entrance fee to join America's new sense of religious plurality was that groups like the Mormons embrace the national myth of progress, which over the early part of the Progressive Era had become explicitly secular though still reliant upon earlier Protestant moral norms and social privilege. A new rhetorical element of this myth was the growing belief that church and state should be more explicitly separate, with individual religiosity being more of a private matter within the contextual corridors of Protestant norms, regardless of institutional or sectarian belonging. This understanding contributed to the growing view that Smoot's personal religion, as long as it was not explicitly visible, was no longer a qualifying or disqualifying factor. The more Americans perceived Mormonism via Smoot as a privatized faith with acceptable Protestant morals, the more Smoot's religion was, as suggested in the *Washington Post*, "nobody's business but his own."[39]

Trends toward a privatized form of religious pluralism based upon Protestant moral norms did not obviate anti-Smoot and anti-Mormon sentiment within America. To the contrary, opposition to Smoot and his Church persisted through the hearings and well beyond, as the specter of Mormonism and the political influence of its hierarchy continued to provoke strong religious passions. However, given this larger cultural shift toward religious privatization, some prominent voices within Protestant churches began to question the appropriateness of a religious crusade directed against the politician Reed Smoot. As Americans decoupled the assumption that political power was contingent upon religious orthodoxy, they in parallel began questioning the role of ecclesiastical bodies to speak on issues of political significance. For instance, ruling elder from New York and chairman of the Committee on Polity, John I. Platt of the Presbyterian General Assembly, created a stir within the assembly by strongly opposing the assembly's effort to oppose Smoot based upon his religious affiliation. "Hold on gentlemen," Platt insisted, "I have a right to my opinion. I hold this as a political question with which this Assembly has nothing to do."[40] Platt contested that the Presbyterian Assembly's opposition to Smoot was not hurting Mormonism per se but, rather, that efforts frustrated the American principle of separation of church and state. He did receive some support from colleagues, but Platt was in a minority with the assembly, which had opened with a prayer that God would help to expel Smoot from office. Within these actions by the Presbyterian Church, which served as a bright flashpoint for the national debate on the role of religion and politics, Platt's objections were summarily voted down by his peers, but his concerns over the role of religion in American public life continued to percolate in America. Moreover, Platt's views symbolized the increasing groundswell toward privatized religion, as well as the withdrawal of influence for religious institutions to set political standards.

Women's organizations were on the forefront of public and religiously organized efforts against Smoot, with some official protests numbering millions of supporters.[41] Being harnessed by the Protestant moral establishment of the era, women's groups upheld the patriarchal model of female moral supremacy, as well as the legal doctrine of coverture that maintained female invisibility in domestic relations.[42] For these female leaders, Smoot epitomized the perceived threats then being leveled against the American home and family. Yet some prominent female leaders began to see such efforts against Smoot as improper and not befitting of the era's progressive standards. Having mingled with and made friends with Mormon women at the Chicago World's Fair ten years earlier, prominent suffragist leader Susan B. Anthony denounced these female voices against Smoot as religious prejudice and a misguided effort: "The idea of crushing polygamy by action against an individual who does not practice it, instead of a general enforcement of the law, seems to be a small way for our country to be acting."[43]

President Theodore Roosevelt's support of Smoot during the hearings is a salient example of this shift of thinking during the Progressive Era. While accepting the classist implications of social Darwinism, Roosevelt rejected the dismissiveness toward the marginalized and urban poor that pastors Henry Ward Beecher and De Witt Talmage had long encouraged and that Josiah Strong had warned against as being socially and religiously corrosive. Progressivism, which included the

Social Gospel movement,[44] became a religious beacon that men such as Roosevelt engaged to develop solutions for the ills of an increasingly secularized society.[45] Quoting from James 2:18 in the New Testament, Roosevelt demarcated his fledgling creed as "I will show my faith by my works."[46] Merit, not metaphysics, became the main reference point of judgment for Roosevelt and like-minded Protestant progressives involved in national politics. Religious influence on politics was to be indirect and private, and any explicit political exclusion of citizens based on theological lines was suspect. Soon after Smoot's election in early 1903, Roosevelt, in conversing with C. E. Loose, a Smoot political ally and mutual friend, had two questions regarding Smoot: "Is Smoot a polygamist?" and "Are Mormons good Americans?"[47] The term "Good American" was pregnant with meaning, and Loose's subsequent defense of Smoot satisfied the president and led to Roosevelt's later belief that the national outcry against Smoot was nothing more than bigoted ignorance and religious persecution.

Roosevelt's decision to support Smoot generated wide controversy and criticism. As noted above, women's groups and Christian moral reform societies, particularly the Council of Mothers, for which Roosevelt had once served as its advisory committee chairman, decried his support.[48] National newspapers editorialized against the president's support of Smoot, including the *New York Times*, which noted that even Roosevelt's own friends found his actions "extremely unfortunate." Consequently, notes the *Times*, "He is believed to have alienated powerful friendships for the party."[49] None of this backlash dissuaded Roosevelt, for he sought to emulate the "unfaltering resolution" and "unyielding courage" of his hero, the progressive mythical icon Abraham Lincoln, and serve as the champion of the "plain people," rather than advocate for the "demagogue." For progressives at the turn of the century, remarked Robert Crunden, Lincoln's death represented "the present," and the emancipation of slaves signaled the opening of the progressive Christian movement.[50] As "chief" of this "democratic republic," Lincoln was the embodiment of "masculine Christianity," an idea that Roosevelt was introduced to at Boston's Trinity Church while a student at Harvard. Trinity's pastor, Philip Brooks, instructed his congregation while Roosevelt sat in the pews that selfish concern for "one's self" is at the "root of every cowardice."[51] It was under this notion of a newly defined progressive Christian gospel, infused with the conceptions of muscular Christianity rather than the aforesaid prosperity gospel, that undergirded some of Roosevelt's determined support of Smoot. America's popular understanding of religion and its relationship to power was shifting, leading to this conflict over Smoot. Furthermore, despite Smoot's detractors' conflation of Smoot with Mormonism's un-American hierarchical structure, which painted Mormonism as a political entity rather than a religious institution, the president, as had Susan B. Anthony, insisted that Smoot's privileges as a private American citizen were independent of his church, or even hierarchical membership.

FIGURE 1.1. Theodore Roosevelt epitomized the conflation of Christian manliness with American patriotism. In this image, a muscular Roosevelt clenches an American flag while leading a group of oversized Rough Riders into battle against the Spanish in Cuba during the Spanish-American War. Udo J. Keppler, Puck cartoon, July 27, 1898. Caption: "The Rough Riders. They are rough on the Spaniards, whether they ride or walk." Courtesy of the Library of Congress, https://www.loc.gov /item/2012647584/.

Public misrepresentations of Smoot, being bandied about in the media, was something Roosevelt had little tolerance for.[52] Moreover, Roosevelt valued the "strenuous life," which influenced his support of Smoot. Historian Joan Smyth Iversen, in her study of antipolygamy and women's movements, makes the observation that Roosevelt's support of Smoot coincided with a new understanding of sexuality that was indicative of the new secularism of the Progressive Era.[53]

Roosevelt's worldview represented an important national shift in perceptions of male sexuality and manhood, from genteel Victorian manliness, to a sturdier yet composed masculinity—one less focused on theology and more on individual character and merit. Therefore, Roosevelt's initial opposition to Mormonism had more to do with the Church's support of a perverse view of masculine sexuality than it did with Mormonism's breach with mainstream Protestantism and earlier theological definitions of American power.[54]

CRUSADE IN THE HALLS OF CONGRESS

What about the hearings themselves? Did the rhetoric used during the investigation reflect these progressive shifts? The fact that it was mainly Protestant ministers and organizations that spearheaded the outcry against Smoot and his religion, such as the aforementioned Presbyterian Convention that sought to influence Congress to "stamp it [polygamy] out forever," remained relevant.[55] Guided by more conservative concerns, the safety of America was conflated with this demographic redrawing of American belonging that Smoot's inclusion redefined. Chairman of the committee on Privileges and Elections, and Smoot opponent Senator Julius C. Burrows (R-MI), claimed in April 1905 that to allow Smoot to retain his seat would drag "the churches of this land, Jew and Gentile, down to the level of abomination." Women in the gallery enthusiastically applauded his statement.[56] Clearly, a substantial faction of these American politicians and their Protestant supporters considered the placing of Mormonism on the same level as the "churches of this land" to be a grave insult, thus reaffirming the exclusionary posture of the moral establishment and a reminder of the part they played in previous battles against Mormonism and the moral integrity of the nation. The very extremity of these statements cast into clear view what was at stake in the Smoot case for all involved, which was not merely control of the Senate but the country's very salvation and identity as a "Christian nation," as well as its ability to uphold national moral integrity and religious honor. Indeed, the national identity of America as Christian was at stake, and the forces of this moral establishment sounded the bells of alarm by rhetorically framing the contest in patriotic terms that gave protection to Christianity and the concept of a moral civilization as they perceived it.

Although overshadowed by polygamy and hierarchal influence, issues of Mormon theology and its ritual practices were investigated at the hearings, particularly how such beliefs might influence individual believers. Late in the afternoon on March 3, 1904, Robert Tayler, attorney for Smoot's opponents, questioned President Joseph F. Smith about the nature of God in LDS thought and how this belief interacted with the Christian notion of individual free will, a doctrinal component Tayler sought to show missing from Mormonism's hierarchical system.

Smith explained that even though leaders of the LDS Church declare that they have divine authority to speak for God, "there is not, and can not be, any possible restraint held over the members of the Church of Jesus Christ of Latter-Day Saints except that restraint which people themselves voluntarily give." Intrigued by this response, Tayler continued questioning Smith on this subject:

> MR. TAYLER: In your conception of God, then, He is not omnipotent and omniscient?
> MR. SMITH: Oh, yes; I think He is.
> MR. TAYLER: But do you mean to say you, at your pleasure, obey or disobey the commands of Almighty God?
> MR. SMITH: Yes, sir.
> MR. TAYLER: Communicated to you?
> MR. SMITH: I obey or disobey at my will.
> MR. TAYLER: Just as you please?
> MR. SMITH: Just as I please.
> MR. TAYLER: And that is the kind of a God you believe in?
> MR. SMITH: That is exactly the kind of a God I believe in.

In this exchange, Tayler attempted to flesh out Smith's perspective regarding man's role as an autonomous free agent, hoping to obtain an answer that revealed the Church's hierarchical stewardship over individual believers, though sensing a trap Smith was careful to downplay. After this exchange, Senator Joseph B. Foraker (R-OH) reminded Tayler that the doctrine of free will, or, in his words, "free moral religion," was the same doctrine that "every good Methodist believes in."[57] Moreover, Smith's conception of free will, which aligned with the contemporaneous notions of "moral agency" over God's sovereignty, had become a core philosophical issue among early twentieth-century progressives. Thus, according to Smith, Mormonism's top hierarchical authority, members of the Church were "free agents," able to dictate their own life decisions, rather than being mere tools of a higher divine purpose, or in this context, under the control of the Mormon hierarchy. Questioned along similar lines, Smoot made the startling claim for a Mormon apostle that if God had commanded him to break American law, he would ignore God's commands or move out of the country.[58]

Mormonism's hierarchical control over its membership was a central topic at the Smoot hearings and represented the core concern of what Protestants most feared about Smoot's occupancy in the Senate. Smith in his testimony was careful to soft-pedal his position in the Church's hierarchy, indicating that his ecclesiastical office was merely that of seniority in the Twelve and granted to him by way of custom. Smith did not deny the role of revelation to his position but rather minimized its significance as well as the nonbinding nature that his actions held on individual members. When pressed by Chairman Burrows on the matter, Smith stated that he had "never pretended to nor do I profess to have received revelations," except "so far as God has shown to me that so-called Mormonism is God's divine truth; that is all." Senator Bailey, a Democrat from Texas, objected to this line of questioning because it focused narrowly on "religious opinions," which he reasoned were irrelevant to Congress. Furthermore, Bailey explained that unless Smith's religion could be shown to "connect itself in some way with their civil or political affairs," it was of no concern to him whatsoever. Notwithstanding this objection, these sorts of questions continued, as Tayler was determined to show that the Church exercised supreme control over the political affairs of its members, which included control of Smoot's votes in the US Senate. In addition to downplaying his leadership office, Smith also sought to persuade the committee that "members of the Mormon Church are among the freest and most independent people of all the Christian denominations." Smith, in rebutting popular notions that all Church members were nothing more than drones of the hierarchy, contended that Mormons were "not all united on every principle" and that, as autonomous agents with free will, were entitled to their own opinions and views. To illustrate this point, Smith explained that he knew of hundreds of Latter-day Saints who rejected polygamy as a true principle, who "never did believe in it and never did receive it," yet remained in good fellowship with the Church.[59] In essence, Smith was making the case that his church was not dissimilar to other volunteer organizations, where individual members held full discretion, based on individual conscience, whether to follow or not follow leadership counsel and to obey or not obey Church teachings. Moreover, if members believed in revelation or did not, or if members of the hierarchy engaged in politics, or illegally continued to practice polygamy, it was based on their individual prerogative and not at the behest of by the Church. When Brigham H. Roberts was asked by Burrows if his continued polygamous living placed him in defiance of the laws of God and the laws of man, he took personal responsibly by stating, "I suppose I am."[60] These responses by Church witnesses that abandoned earlier attitudes of authority and obedience minimized the unique aspects of Mormonism's prophetic claims and the power the institution held over its members, thereby aligning Mormons with the progressive forces of the era.

As leaders of the LDS Church defined themselves within more progressive themes such as private religion before the Senate committee, they did not aim to contradict God's omniscience in human affairs. Instead, Church leaders acknowledged the limitations of humanity in tapping into that omniscience, whether in the Mormon context of prophetic revelation and leadership, or otherwise. By averring the tenet of free will over obedience to Church leadership, Smith and Smoot refuted the accusation that Mormons were controlled by the Church's hierarchy, thereby placing the LDS Church's theology directly in line with the ideas of other notable Progressive Era figures such as Woodrow Wilson and Theodore

Roosevelt.[61] For Smoot's opponents, religion and politics shared an important relationship where the theology of the former informed the policies and perspectives of the latter. And as can be deduced from the assumptions underlying Tayler's interrogation, Mormonism's hierarchical structure implied supremacy to authoritative voices over ordinary voices in the Church, thus leading to a culture of uncritical obedience. Due to the existence of this hierarchy, Mormonism, in Tayler's construction, was not able to be considered authentically "American."

The next morning, March 4, Senator George F. Hoar (R-MA) continued to question President Smith's conceptions of free will, this time using biblical passages and polygamy as a backdrop. Hoar's use of the Bible created a paradox on whether Mormonism adequately separated religion from politics, setting the stage in which a senator of the United States was using religious literature to explicitly "size up" Smoot's political fitness. Plural marriage was at the heart of this exchange between Smith and the committee, when Hoar quoted 1 Timothy 3:2 from the New Testament, which states that a bishop must be the "husband of one wife," a verse frequently used by Protestant ministers to discredit plural marriage:

> SENATOR HOAR: I understood—and I am not sure I understood you aright—that it [the injunction of polygamy] was permissive, but did you mean to say that or do you mean to say that it is obligatory, so far as a general principle of conduct is concerned, but not mandatory under the circumstances?
>
> Now I will illustrate what I mean by the injunction of our scripture—what we call the New Testament.
>
> MR. SMITH: Which is our scripture also.
>
> SENATOR HOAR: Which is your scripture also?
>
> MR. SMITH: Yes, sir.
>
> SENATOR HOAR: The apostle says that a bishop must be sober and must be the husband of one wife.
>
> MR. SMITH: At least.
>
> SENATOR HOAR: We do not say that. [Laughter] The bishop must be sober and must be the husband of one wife. I suppose that is generally construed to enjoin upon bishops the marriage relation. But I have known several bishops, two in my own State, of great distinction, who were bachelors. . . .

To support the idea that plural marriage was a legitimate biblical practice, Smith posited that the scripture was given "in the midst of polygamous people, and that all of the people believed in the practice of polygamy at that time."[62] However inaccurate Smith's editorial comments were, neither Hoar nor any other member of the committee disputed them, since Hoar's point was to demonstrate Mormonism's unscriptural marital practices, rather than to quibble with the

Church president's scriptural commentary. Indeed, while these exchanges give perspective on how Mormons of this era interpreted Christian scripture, the tenor of the questioning, more important, exposed the deep Protestant influence within American politics that was often denied existing.

Such theological interpretation of "our scripture" continued throughout the hearings as a litmus test to determine Smoot's fitness for the Senate. But some members of the committee, including Senator Albert J. Beveridge (R-IN), found such questions inappropriate to determining Smoot's fitness: "I do not think questions as to what are his conceptions of God, or his private, personal duty, are competent."[63] Later on at the hearings, Tayler shifted his framing of questions to use more secular and progressive themes, such as Mormonism's "manhood," that attempted to expose the LDS Church's patriotic inadequacies as well as its overall incompatibility with American political and social culture.

In building upon this theme of hierarchical control, Tayler put former Mormon apostle Moses Thatcher on the witness stand and presented him as the heroic embodiment of democratic individuality and independence. Thatcher had been removed as an apostle in 1896 when he refused to sign the Church's "Political Manifesto," a document requiring Church officials to obtain permission for a "leave of absence" prior to running for public office.[64] For Thatcher's religiously toned acts of ecclesiastical disobedience, Taylor framed the defrocked apostle, who was a member of the Democrat Party, as a hero of democracy who defied hierarchical control over individual conscience. Judge Calvin Reasoner, the "Gentile" editor of a Utah-based periodical *Men and Women*, and a Republican friend of Thatcher, self-published a pamphlet in 1896 entitled *The Late Manifesto in Politics* that detailed the controversy, which Tayler added to the official Senate record.[65] Reasoner's tract, which contradicted the assertions of Church leaders that Thatcher was removed for his "rebellious spirit," posited the interpretation that Thatcher's actions were the result of his own progressive American values that proved incompatible. Thatcher's heroism was the antithesis of the "unmistakable . . . narrowness, prejudice, and injustice" of the LDS Church hierarchy. "Of all the Mormon high priesthood," the pamphlet continued, "Moses Thatcher is the one that stands for the principles of Jefferson and Lincoln as the American people understand those principles." Thatcher's surrendering of his apostolic position because of this refusal to accept an "emasculated manhood and civil agency," enshrined him, in Reasoner's words, "a humble instrument in His Omnipotent hand."[66]

Tayler's use of Reasoner's pamphlet reinforced the theme that the LDS Church and its domineering hierarchy was out of step with the Progressive Era and opposed "to the true spirit of progress." In addition, "Thatcher's war with the Church," intoned Reasoner's pamphlet, "was not a religious or personal one," but rather it was "a war with the individuality and independent manhood required by the Declaration of Independence." And given the Church's treatment of Thatcher,

"Everyone [in Utah] relinquishes his individuality . . . [and] no longer acts from the dictates of his own will, but from the will of the Church," which, according to Reasoner, was inimical to the basic tenets of the modern American character of freedom and manhood.[67] In summation, Reasoner predicted ruination if Mormon dictation of politics continued: "In the end there will be violence and loss of life; the whole State will be storm-swept," resulting in the "end of Jeffersonian Democracy in Utah."[68]

Although Reasoner couched his arguments in more secular terms, his further clarifications demonstrate the contribution of theology to his formulation. Gender constructions, such as the notion of "manhood," were not merely political demarcations of power, but theological, and stood central to Protestantism's concern over moral order and the preservation of the family and country. Injecting scripture into his understanding of the American metaphor of the separation of church and state, Reasoner contended, "Under the American system there are two distinct spheres for church and state, and they must be kept separate from inception to culmination. In the one sphere, according to the words of Christ, we must 'render unto Caesar the things that are Caesar's.'" While on the other, Reasoner maintained, the "individual souls of men and women created by God in His image and after His likeness" were "endowed in the nature of things with inalienable rights of life, liberty, and happiness," where these God-endowed rights were independent of the government and exist as "an expansion and administration of these primal rights."[69] Not only did this theological metanarrative of American power define the government as a tool of deity, but it also created an exclusionary schematic against those who defied it. Interpretations of church-state separation had long served as a powerful tool to uphold Protestantism's tight grip on religious privilege and moral authority over the state but were being redefined within more progressive notions of individual independence that actually served to open space for non-Protestants such as Thatcher who had demonstrated this independence. Americans at the time of the hearings grappled with this new understanding of separation, together with more radical views that called for the absolute removal of religion from the state, which traditionalists considered "political atheism," demonstrating the complicated contest over Smoot's seat.

Reasoner's pamphlet was an obscure piece of literature for audiences outside of Utah; however, the ideas propounded by it revealed important shifts in how Americans spoke about separation and spoke to the fears of Smoot's emergence onto the national stage. Tayler, by placing Thatcher on the witness stand, sought to reinforce Reasoner's postulation of Mormon-clerical influence with explosive testimony from the deposed apostle. But his stratagem fell short, and fortunately for Smoot, Thatcher argued the entire episode to be little more than an unfortunate misunderstanding.[70] In responding to Smoot's attorney Waldemar Van Cott, Thatcher explained that the manifesto "left all the officers of the church absolutely

WHILE THE WATCHMAN SLEEPS.

—New York Herald.

FIGURE 1.2. With its tail stretching back to "Utah," the reptilian monster "Mormonism" creeps up the steps and enters the US Congress while Uncle Sam, "the Watchman," sleeps. Brigham H. Roberts won his election as the Democratic Representative from Utah to the Fifty-Sixth Congress on November 8, 1898, but after significant protests and debates, his seat was declared vacant by way of a vote on January 23, 1900. Opponents accused Roberts of continuing the illegal practice of polygamy, but more dangerously he was seen to be an extension of Mormon hierarchal control and influence in American politics—a shadow that continued into the Smoot hearings. This cartoon quickly followed Roberts' election and was reprinted in several important newspapers throughout the country, highlighting salient fears Americans had concerning Utah's representatives immediately following statehood. Charles Nelan, Chicago Daily Tribune, cartoon, November 27, 1898. Caption: "While the Watchman Sleeps." Courtesy of the Library of Congress, with special thanks to Roslyn P. Waddy.

free" to exercise their rights as "American citizen[s]," with the main caveat being that the document specifically "applied to the higher authorities of the church," for which he "had no objection." In later testimony, Thatcher further undermined Tayler's contentions as specious by avouching that nothing had "come to my knowledge" which shows that "the church had ever undertaken to dominate the political affairs of Utah."[71]

Tayler also subpoenaed high-ranking Church official Brigham H. Roberts to answer questions on the Political Manifesto. Roberts had been nominated by the

Democratic Party in 1895 to run for the House of Representative in Utah's first
state elections. After he and the Democrats sustained losses, Roberts blamed the
results on Church involvement.[72] With the Political Manifesto developed in the
context of this election, Roberts's initial interpretation of the document was negative and similar to that of Moses Thatcher's, believing it an attempt by the Church's
top leadership to control Utah's emergent political structures. However, unlike
Thatcher, Roberts ultimately signed on to the manifesto after hours of painful
deliberation with Church authorities who, he now claimed before the Senate
committee, had "enlightened" him "in reference to their purposes."[73] Roberts and
Thatcher, though not sharing the apostle-senator's Republican political party and
politics, proved more supportive of Smoot's claim of individual Mormon autonomy that contradicted Tayler's attempt to paint the Church as a political autocracy.

For Smoot's detractors, Mormonism was the problem since the hierarchal
structure breached religious and political norms within a free American society.
Frank J. Cannon, Utah's first senator and son of prominent Church official George
Q. Cannon, utilized his position as editor of the *Salt Lake Tribune* to criticize
Smoot, Joseph F. Smith, and the LDS Church. Cannon's March 1905 excommunication was seen as a demonstration of American patriotism and manhood by
the Mother's Congress who christened him that same month a hero to be "welcomed into the ranks of loyal, law abiding citizens as a brave defender of home
and purity"—an ironic assessment considering his well-known drinking habits
and engagement with prostitutes while a married man. Whatever Cannon's personal failings, the Mother's Congress held the LDS Church as the antithesis of
American individualism and of masculine agency, associating Cannon's "valuable service" and "manly American" citizenship with his public dissent from
Mormonism itself.[74] As was attempted at the hearings with Moses Thatcher and
Brigham H. Roberts, opponents of Smoot upheld the Church as the inverse of
what it meant to be properly religious and acceptably American, thereby clarifying the meaning of both. It can be argued then that the deeper question probed
at the hearings was less about Mormonism and more about what it meant to be
American and the relationship religion continued to play within that privileged
identity. Although it was widely understood that Mormonism itself was un-
American and discursive, the real question was whether individual adherents of
the Church were compatible with American values and thus able to be included in
this larger national vision. Was the Church made up of individuals acting according to their own conscience? Or did the Church determine peoples' conscience
for them? Would Smoot's inclusion in the Senate validate the Mormon hierarchy
and its ecclesiastical interests, or would his inclusion validate the moral agency
of individual Mormons and their constitutional rights? Questions at the hearings of political influence, plural marriage, free will, manliness, and prophetic
leadership revealed the outlines of American power, which demanded a modern

Protestant form of private faith, sexuality, and spiritual independence. Despite its description within the secular rhetoric of separation, liberty, and masculinity, the continuation of Protestant privilege in politics was revealed in national protests, congressional arguments, and submitted testimonial, complicating the question of Smoot's qualifications for high public service and the role religion continued to play in American politics.

It is easy to dismiss such linkages of religion and politics as anything more than generic theopolitical talk, rather than an enforcement of Christian theology in the public realm. The very fact, however, that Smoot's seat was hotly debated for four years, attacked primarily by Protestant ministers, women's Christian organizations, attorneys, and congressmen quoting both the Declaration of Independence and the Bible demonstrates that the Smoot hearings, beyond confirming Smoot's fitness to sit in the Senate, confronted the definition of what it meant to be an American, masculine, and Christian—three themes that were not seen as separate. Smoot and Joseph F. Smith went to great lengths to redefine the Church into these shifting national progressive demands, permanently altering the Church toward more Protestant sensibilities of private faith. Although similarly spoken in coded secular terms and ideals, both Smoot and Smith ultimately perceived their efforts as advancing Christ's kingdom on earth. Notably, as Smoot retained his contested seat in February 1907 despite much religious clamor and uncertainty, it was now clear that religious influence, for Mormons as well as Protestants, had to be implicit in order to be acceptable—representing a new decline in Protestantism's more explicit hold on American society and earlier theological definitions of what it meant to be American.

During the drawn-out debate of Smoot's retention of his seat, national acceptance of Mormonism and the relationship its hierarchy had over its members had been intensely questioned. But with the Church's adamant denial of such hierarchical control, together with the waning of influence of more explicit long-held Protestant theological standards, Smoot was reluctantly and conditionally accepted. Indeed, the very framework of congressional inclusion and action that had presupposed the implementation of God's law as found in the Bible that stood above the Constitution, referred to as the "higher law," was now criticized as unworkable, particularly as it pertained to exclusionary actions such as those waged against Smoot.[75] During the plenary debate preceding the final Smoot vote, Senator Foraker justified his support for Smoot by recognizing the dilemma, even contradiction, between the higher law and the oath of office as established by the US Constitution, together with new sensibilities of the Progressive Era concerning the secularization of American polity and the privatization of religion.

> This higher law we all appreciate. The Senator from North Dakota [Mr. HANS-
> BROUGH] is not the only man who thinks of the higher law; we all think of it; but

the trouble about following the higher law is that every man writes the higher law to suit himself. [Laughter.] What we are here to follow and to be governed by and to observe—and we violate our oaths of office if we do not do it—is the Constitution of the United States in its requirements.[76]

The long national debate surrounding Smoot in some ways crowned a remarkable journey that Americans, which, with the waning of the notion of this vague but profoundly influential "higher law," now applied to Mormons. It is this recession of "higher times," notes Charles Taylor, that marks a society's move toward the secular.[77] This journey from the Protestant hegemony of the nineteenth century to a broader sense of religious inclusion at the beginning of the twentieth brought a new kind of national identity and marked new reference points for American legislation and national belonging. Religious pluralism as it was now being forged transformed what it meant to be an American, together with its redefined privatized faith and spiritualized kingdom of God that reconfigured how religion related to the state and highlighted the rise of a new liberal secular Protestant elite.

Mormons had long insisted upon their patriotism and religious legitimacy, but Smoot's victory and the related progressive transformations of his church marked a new level of national acceptance of these claims. As the Church forged alliances with this new class of liberal Protestant elites, Mormonism had been "discovered," as it were, and like the American continent, the discovery did not so much bring it into existence but instead brought into view the perception of its existence by a people of privilege and power who provided this new inclusion based upon these markers of privilege.[78] Mormonism, at least as perceived on the secular-national level, turned out not to be so bad after all, and, in important ways, its submission to this newly formed secular nation-state became a boon to the new progressive Republican elite. When Reed Smoot walked into the Senate chamber and sat in his accustomed seat after the vote, he symbolically placed Mormonism into a context of acceptable religion and true Americanness, an acceptability that played a role in defining these larger standards of religious inclusion—an inclusion predicated upon a new submissive stance on the part of religion toward the secular state. Indeed, Smoot's occupancy in the Senate and his submission to this more privatized form of Protestant faith revealed a new secularity that defined American politics at the beginning of the twentieth century, one that was not devoid of religion but rather insisted on a more implicit form. At last, these dramatic national transformations established that Mormons were viable participants in this newly forged political system and that more explicit theological sentimentalities and traditional forms of religious influence were no longer able to forbid it.

NOTES

1. Joseph F. Smith, letter to Reed Smoot, February 23, 1907, in James R. Clark, ed., *Messages of the First Presidency of the Church of Jesus Christ of Latter-day Saints* (Salt Lake City: Bookcraft, 1965–1975), 4:141.

2. David Goldfield, Carl Abbott, Virginia DeJohn Anderson, Jo Ann E. Argersinger, and Peter H. Argersinger, *The American Journey: A History of the United States*, 2 vols. (Upper Saddle River, NJ: Prentice-Hall, 1998), 2:594.

3. Josiah Strong, *The New Era or the Coming Kingdom* (New York: Baker and Taylor, 1893), 344–345.

4. The new sense of optimism was astounding. Henry Adams wrote in 1900: "It is a new century, and what we used to call electricity is its God . . . The period from 1870–1900 is closed . . . The period from 1900–1930 is in full swing, and, gee-whacky! How it is going! It will break its damned neck long before it gets through, if it tries to keep up the speed." Qtd. in Paul F. Boller, *American Thought in Transition: The Impact of Evolutionary Naturalism, 1865–1900* (Boston: University of Massachusetts, 1969), 227.

5. Tisa Wenger, *Religious Freedom: The Contested History of an American Ideal* (Chapel Hill: University of North Carolina Press, 2017), 3, 234–239; David Sehat, *The Myth of American Religious Freedom* (New York: Oxford University Press, 2011), 50.

6. Sehat, *The Myth of American Religious Freedom*, 184.

7. Strong, *The New Era*, 143.

8. Strong, *The New Era*, 253, 255, 201, 209–211; qtd. in Boller, *American Thought in Transition*, 118–119.

9. George Marsden, *Fundamentalism and American Culture*, 2nd ed. (New York: Oxford University Press, 2006), 50–55; Ferenc M. Szasz, *The Divided Mind of Protestant America*, 1880–1930 (Tuscaloosa: University of Alabama Press, 1982), 72–75. Szasz offers an important overview of the Bible Conferences that started in 1876 and that popularized a form of premillennialism that would continue to define itself against the growing tides of both modernity and liberal-progressive Christianity. Adherents of this reactionary movement against modernity and liberalism in the 1910s self-titled themselves the "Fundamentalists."

10. Nineteenth-century Protestants in America allied themselves with the American philosophy of Francis Bacon, who had established that careful observation and classification of the facts presented the avenue toward scientific truth. This approach was connected to the popular notion of "common sense realism," which asserted that things were just as they appeared to be to the common person. As Marsden, *Fundamentalism and American Culture*, 7, 14–15, notes, far from excluding religion, as the next century would do, scientists could focus on theology as well as science, needing only to classify the certainties of science and avoid speculative hypotheses. "The Bible, of course, revealed the moral law; but the faculty of common sense, which agreed with Scripture, was a universal standard. According to Common Sense philosophy, one can intuitively know the first principles of morality as certainly as one can apprehend other essential aspects of reality." See also 24, 50, for more on Beecher and the larger theological connection between science and this earlier Protestant vision of America, which was to be a literal historical kingdom of God, taking place "in this world," not otherworldly, but "here and now." Ernest Lee Tuveson, *Redeemer Nation: The Idea of America's Millennial Role* (1968; repr., University of Chicago Press, 1980), 29–30, had earlier argued that redemption of society had its appointed progression and that natural laws could not be ignored. See also a copy of Beecher's sermon "Evolution and the Church." Henry Ward Beecher, *Evolution and Religion* (Boston: The Pilgrim Press, 1885), 127–143.

11. Stanley Tambiah, *Magic, Science, Religion, and the Scope of Rationality* (1900; rpt., Cambridge: Cambridge University Press, 2004), 17; J. Edward Larson, *Summer for the Gods: The*

Scopes Trial and America's Continuing Debate over Science and Religion (New York: Basic Books, 2006), 23.

12. Strong, *The New Era*, 11, 12, 22, 30.

13. Marsden, *Fundamentalism and American Culture*, 48–51, shows that as the popularity of premillennialism rose near the end of the century, postmillenarianism did not disappear but rather transferred hope for the kingdom from this world to the heavens. Although the Social Gospel demonstrates a continued interest in a type of here-and-now amelioration, postmillennialism became secularized in the sense that it dropped many earlier supernatural expectations, becoming more figurative and less literal. For early controversies surrounding Darwinism and religion, see Bert J. Loewenberg, "The Controversy over Evolution in New England 1859–1873," *New England Quarterly* 8, no. 2 (June 1935): 232–257.

14. Boller, *American Thought in Transition*, 22.

15. German philosopher Friedrich Nietzsche, following his intellectual forerunners Karl Marx and Ludwig Feuerbach, tore apart traditional notions of good and evil in 1887. He questioned the very value of values, noting that morals are all manufactured to oppress lower classes, priests being the worst offenders, and classifying "all religions" as being "at bottom systems of cruelty." Nietzsche, *The Birth of Tragedy and The Genealogy of Morals*, trans. Francis Golffing (1872, 1887; rpt., New York: Doubleday, 1956) 167, 192.

16. William R. Hutchison, *The Modernist Impulse in American Protestantism* (Durham, NC: Duke University Press, 1992), 2–9, 106–113.

17. Marsden, *Fundamentalism and American Culture*, 49.

18. Brigham Young University scholar of religion Grant Underwood, *The Millenarian World of Early Mormonism* (Urbana: University of Illinois, 1993), 3–5, 8, 41, 74, recognized that the "simplistic differentiations about whether Christ will come before (pre-) or after (post-) the millennium are hardly sufficient to distinguish these two schools of thought." The eschatology of Mormonism, for example, "is thoroughly premillennial," despite its postmillennial Protestant evangelical drive, its social sense of responsibility, and its heavy political aspirations. As a general rule, premillennialists are literalists, while postmillennialists were more allegorists. Mormonism, however, represented a mix of figurative, literal, and allusive tendencies in their biblical interpretations. Therefore, the major differences between the two camps can be seen as differences of scriptural interpretation on such key points as what the kingdom will look like, humanity's role (or nonrole) in bringing forth this kingdom, the need for evangelism, and notably the relation of the state in this coming messianic millennial kingdom.

19. Robert M. Crunden, *Ministers of Reform: The Progressives' Achievement in American Civilization, 1889–1920* (New York: Basic Books, Inc., 1982), 40.

20. Christian Smith, ed., *The Secular Revolution: Power, Interests, and Conflict in the Secularization of American Public Life* (Berkeley: University of California Press, 2003), 1.

21. Thomas Alexander, *Mormonism in Transition: A History of the Latter-Day Saints, 1890–1930* (Urbana: University of Illinois Press, 1996), 126.

22. Lorenzo Snow, "Greeting to the World," January 1, 1901, in Clark, *Messages of the First Presidency*, 3:335.

23. Alexander, *Mormonism in Transition*, 96.

24. First Presidency, letter to Francis M. Lyman, August 21, 1903, in Clark, *Messages of the First Presidency*, 4:64–65; First Presidency "Christmas Greeting" December 17, 1904, and December 15, 1906, in Clark, *Messages of the First Presidency*, 4:92–98, 128–132.

25. These developments are identified in various First Presidency statements during the period. Clark, *Messages of the First Presidency*, 3:265, 266, 288, 315; 4:12, 35, 58, 64, 100, 130, 182–185.

26. Lorenzo Snow's "last address" from *Conference Reports*, October 1901, in Clark, *Messages of the First Presidency*, 4:11.

27. Brigham H. Roberts, *A Comprehensive History of the Church of Jesus Christ of Latter-day Saints, Century I*, 6 vols. (Provo, UT: Brigham Young University Press, 1965), 6: 389–390.

28. "If I have ever had the inspiration of the spirit of the Lord given to me forcefully and clearly it has been on this one point concerning Reed Smoot, and that is, instead of his being retired, he should be continued in the United States Senate." Joseph F. Smith, qtd. in Alexander, *Mormonism in Transition*, 30. Milton Merrill, *Reed Smoot: Apostle in Politics* (Logan: Utah State University Press, 1990), 29, notes that President Smith was the only one who could have persuaded Smoot to retire, but never did, despite the opposition by many LDS who felt that now was no time for the Church to engage the nation in another struggle with public opinion.

29. "Sees a Bright Outlook for Utah," *New York Times*, July 23, 1894, 5.

30. Alexander, *Mormonism in Transition*, 257.

31. Joan Smyth Iversen, *The Antipolygamy Controversy in U.S. Women's Movements, 1880–1925: A Debate on the American Home* (New York: Garland Publishing, 1997), 217; "Mormonism Scored," *Washington Post*, March 15, 1905, 2.

32. "Congress at an End," *Washington Post*, April 23, 1905, 2.

33. "Mormons a Menace," *Washington Post*, July 11, 1905, 7.

34. William M. Shea, *The Lion and the Lamb: Evangelicals and Catholics in America* (New York: Oxford University Press, 2004), 56; emphasis his.

35. Qtd. in Shea, *The Lion and the Lamb*, 60.

36. Nathan O. Hatch, *The Democratization of American Christianity* (New Haven, CT.: Yale University Press, 1989), 3–16.

37. Law professor Philip Hamburger outlines this religious dynamic within American politics but also how Protestants conflated the individual with the institution by ignoring "the possible distinction between Catholic images affixed to the wall of a schoolroom and the cross and clothing of an individual Catholic teacher." Hamburger, *Separation of Church and State* (Cambridge, MA.: Harvard University Press, 2002), 284, 379–380.

38. Qtd. in Shea, *The Lion and the Lamb*, 60, 64.

39. "The Storm Will Soon Die Out," *Washington Post*, January 19, 1903, 6.

40. "Presbyterian Union in Sight," *New York Times*, May 29, 1904, 7.

41. "Want Smoot Unseated," *Washington Post*, October 28, 1905, 4; "Signed by 1,000,000 Women." *Washington Post*, November 26, 1905, 8; "Smoot Keeps His Seat," *Washington Post*, February 24, 1907, 4.

42. Sehat, *The Myth of American Religious Freedom*, 98–104, 154–155.

43. "Miss Anthony for Smoot," *New York Times*, January 27, 1903, 1; see also Iversen, *The Antipolygamy Controversy*, 219.

44. The "social gospel" represented a more aggressive social awareness of this religious obligation to the poor. In this mentality, righteous action, not dogmatic belief, lay at the heart of "true religion." Consequently, as historian William Hutchison explained, "Social gospel activity meant exposure to minorities and their problems. Quite often, it involved exposure to their religious forms and religious experience." Of interest, this emphasis on progressive Christian social engagement on the part of Roosevelt helps explain his softer and more affirming stance toward Smoot. For more on these social movements of the early twentieth century, see William R. Hutchison, *Religious Pluralism in America: The Contentious History of a Founding Ideal* (New Haven, CT: Yale University Press, 2003), 85–88, 101–106, 175, 177.

45. Clifford Putney, *Muscular Christianity: Manhood and Sports in Protestant America, 1800–1920* (Cambridge, MA.: Harvard University Press, 2001), 40.

46. George E. Mowry, *The Era of Theodore Roosevelt, 1900–1912* (New York: Harper and Brothers, 1958), 48.

47. Merrill, *Reed Smoot*, 28.

48. Kathleen Flake, *The Politics of American Religious Identity: The Seating of Senator Reed Smoot, Mormon Apostle* (Chapel Hill: University of North Carolina Press, 2004), 12–13, 146, 162. See also Merrill, *Reed Smoot*, 92; "Riis Misled President, Says a Senator's Wife," *New York Times*, December 19, 1906, 10.

49. "Smoot Is Assured of Victory To-day," *New York Times*, February 20, 1907, 5.

50. H. W. Brands, *The Selected Letters of Theodore Roosevelt* (New York: Cooper Square Press, 2001), 375; Crunden, *Ministers of Reform*, 4–5.

51. Kathleen Dalton, *Theodore Roosevelt: A Strenuous Life* (New York: Alfred A. Knopf, 2002), 62–63.

52. H. W. Brands, *T. R.: The Last Romantic* (New York: Basic Books, 1997), 519. In November of 1904, Roosevelt announced an embargo on news from all federal departments in Washington after the Boston Herald published "deliberate falsification" and "malicious inventions" about his own family.

53. Iversen, *The Antipolygamy Controversy*, 224–227.

54. Gail Bederman, *Manliness and Civilization: A Cultural History of Gender and Race in the United States, 1880–1917* (Chicago: University of Chicago Press, 1995), 190.

55. "The Mote and the Beam," *Los Angeles Times*, May 27, 1903, 6.

56. "Congress at an End," *Washington Post*, April 23, 1905, 2.

57. US Senate, Committee on Privileges and Elections, Proceedings before the Committee on Privileges and Elections of the United States Senate in the Matter of the Protests against the Right of Hon. Reed Smoot, a Senator from the State of Utah, to Hold His Seat, 59th Cong., 1st Sess., Senate Report No. 486, 4 vols. (Washington, DC: Government Printing Office, 1904–1907), 1:161 (hereafter, Smoot Hearings).

58. Jonathan H. Moyer, "Dancing with the Devil: The Making of the Mormon-Republican Pact" (PhD diss., University of Utah, Salt Lake City, 2009), 494; Michael Harold Paulos, ed., *The Mormon Church on Trial: Transcripts of the Reed Smoot Hearings* (Salt Lake City: Signature Books, 2008), 558.

59. Smoot Hearings, 1: 92–93, 98–99, 156.

60. Smoot Hearings, 1: 718–719.

61. For a detailed social and political analysis of moral agency as understood at this time, see Mowry, *The Era of Theodore Roosevelt*, 50.

62. Smoot Hearings, 1:209–210.

63. Smoot Hearings, 1:161.

64. "Controls Utah Politics," *Hartford Courant*, April 23, 1904, 9; Davis Bitton, *George Q. Cannon: A Biography* (Salt Lake City: Deseret Book, 1999), 353–355, 412–413; Smoot Hearings, 1:1023–1024; Kenneth W. Godfrey, "Moses Thatcher in the Dock: His Trials, The Aftermath, and His Last Days," *Journal of Mormon History* (Spring 1998): 67–73. For more in Thatcher's episode with the Church and the Political Manifesto, see Thomas G. Alexander, "'To Maintain Harmony': Adjusting to External and internal Stress, 1890–1930," *Dialogue: A Journal of Mormon Thought* 15, no. 4 (Winter, 1982), 48–49; Edward Leo Lyman, "The Alienation of an Apostle from His Quorum: The Moses Thatcher Case," *Dialogue: A Journal of Mormon Thought* 18 (Summer 1985): 67–91; Roberts, *Comprehensive History*, 6: 330–336. Letters between Moses Thatcher and Lorenzo Snow were reprinted in the Smoot Hearings, 1:1025–35.

65. Calvin Reasoner, "The Late Manifesto in Politics: Practical Working of 'Counsel' in Relation to Civil and Religious Liberty in Utah," as reproduced in the Smoot Hearings, 1:947–1037.

66. Smoot Hearings, 1: 967, 1035–1037.

67. Smoot Hearings, 1:987, 1007–1008; For more on masculinity and its relevance to this era see Bederman, *Manliness and Civilization*, 44. See also literary historian Ann Douglass, *The Feminization of American Culture* (New York: Doubleday, 1977), 327, on the new masculinization of American culture in reaction to growing concerns of an overly effeminate one. Revivalist Billy Sunday embodies this cultural shift in his depiction of Jesus as "the greatest scrapper that ever lived."

68. Smoot Hearings, 1:968–971.

69. Smoot Hearings, 1:1017.

70. Despite this testimony by Thatcher, the Political Manifesto of 1896 continued to be a topic in the Smoot hearings. This document's existence was for many a prime example of political influence by the Church, since it inferred that no one in the Church could run for office unless they had permission, or "counsel" from Church authorities. "Smoot's Moot Question Up," *Los Angeles Times*, December 12, 1906, 12.

71. Smoot Hearings, 1:1038–50.

72. Gustive O. Larson, *The "Americanization" of Utah for Statehood* (San Marino, CA: Huntington Library, 1971), 297.

73. Smoot Hearings, 1:727–728.

74. "Mothers Denounce Smoot," *New York Times*, March 18, 1905, 1. See also Jeffrey Nichols, *Prostitution, Polygamy, and Power: Salt Lake City 1847–1918* (Urbana: University of Illinois Press, 2002), 65, 138.

75. This pre–Progressive Era view of the "higher law" was articulated before Congress by Senator William H. Seward (R-NY) more than fifty years earlier. As he explained before Congress: "The Constitution regulates our stewardship; the Constitution devotes the domain to union, to justice, to defense, to welfare, and to liberty. But there is a higher law than the Constitution, which regulates our authority over the domain, and devotes it to the same noble purposes." Qtd. in Frederick W. Seward, *William H. Seward: An Autobiography from 1801 to 1834. With a Memoir of his Life, and Selections from his Letters, 1831–1846* (1877; rpt., New York: Derby and Miller, 1891), 126.

76. Congressional Record: Containing the Proceedings and Debates of the 59th Congress, 2nd Session, Volume 41, Part 4 (Washington, DC: Government Printing Office, 1907), 3414.

77. Charles Taylor, *A Secular Age* (Cambridge: Belknap Press, 2007), 719.

78. This framework comes from Richard E. Wentz, *The Culture of Religious Pluralism* (Boulder, CO.: Westview Press, 1998), 21: "'Discovery' also incorporates the expectations and memories of those who meet, those who discover each other. It would have been impossible for Columbus to have discovered anything except what he was enabled to perceive on the basis of the imagined order and meaning of the world of which he was a part . . . One can never discover raw empirical reality; one discovers perceptions of reality." In the fight over public opinion regarding Smoot, together with the state's role concerning religion, the nation was in discovery of itself, as much as it was of Reed Smoot's religion.

2

"Justice Is Never Permanently Defeated Anywhere"

Reed Smoot's Confirmation Vote in the United States Senate

Michael Harold Paulos

On Wednesday morning February 20, 1907, two chaplains, residing thousands of miles apart, offered contrasting prayers to begin the legislative activities of the day. The first prayer, given at 11 AM. Washington, DC, time,[1] was uttered by Unitarian Minister Edward E. Hale, then serving as chaplain to the United States Senate. A dignified man with a distinctive look, Hale was known to give "unconventional, familiar and impressive" prayers while serving Congress.[2] When once asked, "Do you pray for the Senators, Dr. Hale?" the bearded chaplain replied, "No, I look at the Senators and pray for the country."[3] Hale's idealism indicated both seriousness of character and a deep skepticism of politicians.[4] On the docket this day was Senate resolution 142, "That REED SMOOT is not entitled to a seat as a Senator of the United States from the State of Utah";[5] it was juxtaposed against the constitutional imperative of Article V, "that no State, without its Consent, shall be deprived of its equal Suffrage in the Senate." Smoot had been serving for forty-eight months as both a US Senator and an LDS apostle, the second-highest governing body of the Church of Jesus Christ of Latter-day Saints. Within five hours of Hale's prayer, Smoot's political future was decided by a roll call vote of his senatorial colleagues.

Concurrent with Chaplin Hale's prayer was a prayer spoken in Salt Lake City by Elder David Hess, a former LDS bishop then serving as a Chaplain to the Utah State legislature.[6] This "petition to the Throne of Grace" did not focus on the country at large, rather the parochial interests of Utah and Mormonism. Hess

DOI: 10.7330/9781646421176.c002

supplicated the "Hand of Providence" to actively influence "the senate of the United States at Washington, to the end that the members of that body may stand by the constitution of the fathers and that they may not abridge the rights of a sovereign state of this union." With direct concern over Smoot's confirmation vote, Hess beseeched protection for Utah by praying, "that those who have sought to bring this great state into contempt may be brought to confusion" and that by so doing, America "may continue to be a land of freedom as declared by the mouths of thy holy prophets."[7] The backdrop for these prayers was a country in transition, where cultural changes across society kindled anxieties for many Americans. Senators were faced with not only the narrow question if Smoot, a high-ranking Mormon official, could enter the Senate, but more saliently, if a person's religion disqualified them for public service. Competing definitions of morality were at play, the result of which would determine the priority given to one's theology or one's inherent worth in relation to the state.

A few year earlier, in January of 1903, Smoot had been elected by the Utah State legislature despite the earnest warnings of two Non-Mormon state officials,[8] State senator George N. Lawrence and Utah State representative William E. White, who "fervently" plead "with the (Utah) legislature . . . not to elect Apostle Reed Smoot" and cautioned "against a union of church and state" that "would bring upon Utah the censure of the nation and humiliation before all."[9] As predicted by these two men, Smoot's election ignited a national maelstrom that placed Smoot, the state of Utah, and the LDS Church in the national spotlight.[10] Moreover, the two dissimilar prayers offered in 1907 symbolized some of the divisions and disparate ideas colliding within the country. This question was, explained by Republican senator John C. Spooner of Wisconsin, a "very grave concern," and one that "created very great and almost universal interest in the country;" one that engendered "a very great deal of prejudice . . . one way and another." Partisan fervor was apparent to start the debate when Senators bickered for fifteen minutes over the "arrangement of time" between those who desired "to briefly explain the vote which they intend to cast on this matter."[11] Smoot's detractors, including "veteran campaigners against Mormonism" Republican chairman Julius Caesar Burrows of Michigan and Democratic senator Fred T. Dubois of Idaho,[12] reserved to themselves the majority of the five hours as an indiscreet way to filibuster expressions of support for Smoot.[13] Despite these political machinations, Democratic senator Augustus O. Bacon of Georgia spoke proudly of the work being performed by the Senate that day, lauding it "as the most valuable and the most important branch of the constitutional framework of our Government" and the "only branch of the Government which is clothed

"WILL HE RISE AGAIN?"

FIGURE 2.1. "Will He Rise Again?" Cartoonist Alan L. Lovey presents the prickly obstacles Senator Reed Smoot faced in Washington, DC, as he sought to protect his duly elected Senate seat there. *Salt Lake Herald*, December 15, 1903. Courtesy of the Brigham Young University Family History Center.

with legislative, executive, and judicial functions."[14] On this day, Smoot faced the Senate's judicial versatility, or as one Senator self-importantly inferred, the "highest court this world has ever known."

Smoot's political status attracted a wide berth of national publicity and back-lash. Women's coalitions spearheaded efforts to deluge "the Senate with memo-rials, petitions, [and] personal applications" demanding that "Senators should see things in certain lights and act accordingly."[15] One such demand was made by Maria Weed in a letter to *Outlook Magazine*, imploring that the "legislative, restrictionary power" of the federal government be used to enact an antipolygamy constitutional amendment that "compel[s] a recognition of the Governmental authority and jurisdiction [by the Mormon Church], heretofore utterly and successfully ignored."[16] Numerous other women, fearing for the sanctity of the

FIGURE 2.2. "On The Toboggan: 'One! Two! Thr—!'" "Anti-Smoot Petitions" sent by women from across the country flooded senators in Washington demanding that Smoot be removed from office. *Chicago Chronicle* as reprinted in *Salt Lake Tribune*, June 11, 1906. Courtesy of the Brigham Young University Family History Center.

American home, effectively used "the petition . . . as if it were the ballot" to declare "war on the Mormon Senator," believing that "had [they] not kept up a steady fire of petitions his right to his seat would not have been seriously questioned" nor would there have been an "investigation."[17] Other female petitioners raised concern over Smoot's divided loyalties, believing his allegiance to the Church superseded his loyalty to the country. Smoot was stung by this onslaught and explained to his spiritual file leader, Joseph F. Smith back in Utah, that most of these petitions were sent "from the Eastern states."[18]

Petitions, "signed by thousands of women," were also sent from constituents to senators in Western States, including Republican senator Perkins of California. Following parliamentary procedure, Senators dutifully presented them for recognition during session hours. On one occasion in early 1906, Senator Perkins "took the occasion" of presenting petitions to frame Smoot's situation as a question of secularism and religious freedom: "Religious views should not be considered in passing upon the qualifications of a Senator and that his honesty and the attributes that command confidence and respect should be considered above all else."[19] Defending Smoot was an unpopular position to take in the Golden State, and once reports reached home of Perkins's support, religious leaders living there "denounce[d] the stand [Perkins] has taken."[20] Halfway through his third six-year term, Perkins did not face immediate electoral peril; however, Perkins must have worried about the long-term political implications his support would bring. Ultimately, the California senator did not incur lasting deleterious political effects, nor did he alienate his state's legislature, who eventually reelected him to a fourth term.[21]

Protestant leaders across America mobilized to oppose Smoot, making it clear they viewed religious inclusion as a national threat. This mobilization included religious leaders on the local level who spearheaded community demonstrations against Smoot while at the same time rhetorically denouncing Mormonism at weekly Sunday services. Nationally, prominent magazines, such as the influential *Christian Observer*, published strident stories outlining the supposed danger, as it were, faced by the country if Smoot and his Mormon faith were let into the Senate. The following excerpt, appearing in the *Observer*, reflects the views of these protestant leaders in 1906:

> The Mormon Church is one of the bitterest enemies to evangelical religion, and the deadliest foe to Republican institutions in this country . . . The United States Senate is now called on to give a national indorsement to Mormonism, by recognizing as one of its members and as a law-maker for the United States, an official of the Mormon Church, who holds that there is no lawful or authorized Government on this continent but the Government of the Mormon priesthood. The triumph of this claim would threaten the existence of every evangelical Church in this country, would make the Bible a forbidden book, and relegate the United States to the condition of priest-ridden Europe in the dark ages. The political aspect of this question no less than the religious aspect of it, therefore, threatens every Church in the Land.[22]

Soon after Smoot's triumph, the *Observer* became more vociferous with specious arguments predicting the Mormon hierarchy would move "stealthily and steadily" to enact a "political overthrow of the Constitution," which would lead to "the domination of the Mormon Church over the land." These religious opponents of Smoot, then determined not to surrender, viewed his election as a direct attack upon Christianity, which they viewed to be a foundational pillar of the country.[23] Allowing Smoot to remain in the Senate would unleash a Trojan Horse of false religion, as it were, that would apocalyptically erode true Christianity and lead to spiritual turpitude within the country's borders.

National vituperation of this caliber drained the patience of many Utahns, including Governor John C. Cutler, who restively could not "sit idly by and allow my state and its people to be maligned and vilified . . . by disappointed politicians, ambitious plutocrats, or recreant sons of the soil." Taking his indignation to the pages of the *Chicago Daily Tribune*, Cutler provided a political case for Smoot's retention and an update to readers on the status of Americanization of Utah. His approach was two-tiered, to first concede the reality that "a few cases of plural marriage have occurred since the adoption of the manifesto" but, second, to contextualize this admission by reminding readers Smoot was not sent to Washington by the institutional Mormon Church, nor, by implication, the handful of post-manifesto marrying perpetrators, but by the Republican Party of Utah. The sitting governor also extolled the merits of Utah's immigration successes, stating Utah "is absorbing and Americanizing its large immigration [population] in a perfectly satisfactory way . . . notwithstanding the fact that our immigrants come from nearly all parts of the world, the great industrial, and educational, and social advantages existing here are thoroughly effectual in fusing these heterogeneous elements into a homogenous citizenship."[24] In other words, the governor was allaying national fears that Utah was brainwashing new immigrants into a balkanized ideology of Mormon theocracy.

Wide interest in Smoot's case was also "evident in the thronged condition of the [Senate] galleries," where a "great majority of visitors" watching the plenary debate were women, "many of whom managed to invade the reserved precincts of the men's galleries." These enthusiastic spectators left a mark on the afternoon by turning it into a campaign rally or athletic event, "vigorously applauding Senators who were speaking against [Smoot]" and providing "hearty handclapping" upon the completion of Chairman Burrows's concluding speech. These occasional interruptions elicited the ire of the Senate's vice president, who was caught off guard by the spectacle of a throng of women jeering at a beleaguered US senator, and threatened "dire punishment if there was any more applause" coming from the gallery.[25]

Nine senators, three supporting and six opposing, took turns articulating their positions on the Smoot case. Republican senator Shelby M. Cullom of Illinois, who favored Smoot's retention but did not vote on this Wednesday, provided a written retrospective on the solemn occasion and subject: "Every Senator was obliged, of necessity, to assume the position of a judge upon the bench—a judge from whose verdict there could be no appeal."[26] This statement was particularly pungent for Smoot, knowing that he had no judicial recourse if the votes went against him. Prior to the vote, national newspapers reported the results of a "careful" poll of senators showing Smoot was safe,[27] but this did not allay the fears of the apostle-senator. Smoot did not feel at ease from the prospect of becoming a martyr of religious liberty until the last vote was cast.

FIGURE 2.3. "After a Weary Wait." Smoot's case dragged on for many years in the US Senate, and the Senate barber, as it were, was ready to give Smoot's hoary status his full attention. *Salt Lake Herald*, February 2, 1907. Courtesy of the Brigham Young University Family History Center.

For "three years," Cullom continued, the Senate Committee on Privileges and Elections labored arduously, "probing every charge and taking voluminous testimony." The committee contemplated its contents within the context of "the demands of public opinion and the demands of the Constitution" as well as "the rights of the people and the rights of Reed Smoot." A skeptic of the negative sentiment billowing against Smoot, Cullom believed the public at large had been "supplied" with "voluminous fiction" and "prejudiced" information that led to a warped view of the truth and skewed conclusions.[28]

During his forty years in Congress, Cullom had been a "violent believer in the power of the federal government to do anything in the name of justice."[29] This vehemence included two instances in which he unsuccessfully introduced "proscriptive legislation against" Mormonism.[30] This legislation not only stripped away the freedoms of practicing polygamists but also echoed "the debates on Reconstruction measures," when "southern states" were forced to re-qualify "for readmission to the Union."[31] Cullom was proud of his past opposition to Mormonism, boasting that the first anti-Mormon bill passing the House bearing his name was his "signal honor." And even though this bill was "buried in the Senate," it served as the "frame and substance" for future, successful anti-Mormon legislation enacted into law. As any seasoned politician would, Cullom implicitly took credit for the reforms of Mormonism, crowing that "the ethics of Mormonism had really and radically changed," to where the Church is no longer a "threat or a menace to the United States."[32] When Smoot arrived in Washington, the Illinois senator was "friendly" and supportive and offered his assistance to the end of the hearings.[33]

Other Senate colleagues were swayed to Smoot after seeing the "many good qualities" he exhibited. By the time of the vote, Smoot was viewed by a majority of rank-and-file Republicans as an "earnest, honest, conscientious" man, whose "home life is without a known blemish."[34] Leaders of the GOP, including the chairman of the Military Affairs Committee Redfield Proctor of Vermont and Senate leader Boeis Penrose of Pennsylvania, provided helpful advice on legal and political aspects of the hearings.[35] Penrose's support of Smoot was immortalized by his apocryphal but iconic phrase "As for me, I would rather have seated beside me in this chamber a polygamist who doesn't polyg than a monogamist who doesn't monog."[36] Proctor, for his part, was also involved in a moment of levity that demonstrates Smoot's personal appeal. When an "earnest delegation" of women stormed the Capitol to demand that the Vermont senator vote to expel "Mr. Smoot from the Senate," he glibly responded by summoning for Smoot, who soon appeared. Always a gentleman, Smoot "bowed and smiled pleasantly" before them, "wait[ing] for someone to say something." Flummoxed by the turn of events, one of the crusading women awkwardly spoke up: "We were telling Senator Proctor . . . about our memorial temple we are building," to which Smoot replied, while pulling out a twenty-dollar bill, "[sounds] like a worthy object. I trust you will allow me to contribute something."[37] Smoot's good-natured friendliness in the face of intense opposition disarmed some opponents, including a few initially skeptical senators.

Seconds into the first speech of the plenary debate, Senator Dubois fired an opening salvo by reiterating a potent political case against the Mormon Church. "Our contention," declared the senator, "is that the Mormon Church as an organization is so un-American, so lawbreaking, and law defying that he, on account of his position in it, is not fit to represent, he does not possess the qualifications to represent, the people of the United States in this Chamber."[38] Iterations of this reasoning of guilt by association were repeated by subsequent senators at the debate. Most adversarial senators would have preferred to argue that Smoot was unqualified to serve based on strict constitutional merits, rather than on this indirect argument. But this was not possible since he was older than "the age of 30 years," had "been nine years a citizen of the United States," and was "an inhabitant" of the State of Utah at the time of his election.[39]

Other senators mitigated the importance of these requirements by applying novel constitutional interpretations vis-à-vis Smoot. For example, Republican senator Henry C. Hansbrough of North Dakota, who broke ranks with his party to vote against Smoot, downplayed these "legal aspects," suggesting they were "of secondary importance," because "the Mormon Church [today] is on trial for high crimes and misdemeanors," the seriousness of which requires we look "beyond the mere application of written law." In other words, the "higher law" must be invoked and the "unwritten law" embraced to justifiably render a "long-delayed verdict" against the Mormon Church.[40] The senator left undefined exactly what constituted the "unwritten law" and its appropriate application, though he was using this notion as an explicit argument to justify his public policy and religious worldviews. Similar arguments had been used in previous decades to justify the fight against the so-called twin relics of barbarism, that of slavery and polygamy.[41] Hansbrough creatively repackaged the argument for a new context, appropriating it to Smoot as a stratagem to moralize the issue for Christians. Hansbrough's departure from his party's line was an attempt to improve his reelection chances, but unfortunately for Hansbrough, he was not victorious in a "direct senatorial primary," in part because he alienated Scandinavian voters in his state who learned Smoot's mother was a Norwegian immigrant.[42]

Chairman Burrows, during his plenary remarks, tackled Smoot's fitness from a different angle, explaining that the framers of the Constitution never intended that these requirements serve as the "be all and end all" for senatorial qualification per se and then argued a federal-government-centric position. Using consecutive quotations from Thomas Jefferson and Pomeroy's Constitutional Law textbook that ostensibly appeared harmonious, the Wolverine State's senator postulated his thesis that the Constitution merely placed "a limitation upon the power of the States" in elections by "restricting the choice to a certain class of citizens." Congress, under this interpretation, was the final arbiter relating to the "qualifications of the Senator or Representative when elected from this eligible list." Otherwise, Burrows warned, men such as Joseph F. Smith "would be entitled to admission to this body if elected by the legislature of Utah, and his five wives and forty-three children could witness from the galleries of the Senate his triumphal entry, unquestioned and unopposed, into the membership of this august assembly."[43] By juxtaposing Smoot to President Smith, a very unpopular polygamous man in America, Burrows linked the apostle-senator with the political deadweight of Mormon polygamy and menacing patriarchy. Furthermore, Smoot's opponents, including Burrows, saw no material difference between Smoot's situation and that of B. H. Roberts, a polygamist Church leader blocked, because of his polygamous marital status, from entering the US House of Representatives after being elected in 1898.[44]

Despite making some good points that extenuating circumstances could exist whereby Congress could rightfully expel an elected representative, Burrows undercut his credibility by misusing quotes that served his political ends. For example, he strip-quoted Thomas Jefferson to give the impression that this founding father advocated for Congress and the federal government to be the final judge of elections returns, when in actual fact Jefferson's full quotation argued for the opposite conclusion. That is, states and the people residing therein, rather than the central government, hold the power to define the qualifications of congressional representatives as they see fit.[45] This was not the first time Burrows wrested a quote: earlier in the afternoon Beveridge had rebuffed the committee chairman senator for misquoting Smoot to gain a tactical edge. But this criticism was quickly qualified with senatorial polite speak, and Beveridge exonerated Burrows, averring that "[Burrows] is incapable of doing any human being an injustice knowingly," and the "clipping was prepared for him" by those "who are interested in the cause" and motivated to manipulate the outcome.[46]

Differing with Burrows's constitutional interpretations were the opinion editors at the *New York Times*, who, several months previously, sided with Jefferson's actual sentiments and wondered "how any man trained in the American principles of civil liberty could take the side that a State is not entitled to choose its own representatives," and condemned those who used "sentimental considerations . . . to outweigh the legal and rational considerations." Furthermore, the *Times* editors continued, "The Senate knew," when Utah was admitted as a state, that the Beehive State's constituents would "return a Mormon Senator," and therefore, reneging on democratic principles was not a viable option for the country.[47] Moreover, for these *Times* editors, America had rejected multiple statehood attempts pushed by LDS leadership spanning over a forty-year period; the country had had ample time to enter this Utah relationship with eyes wide open.

These senators' specious arguments against Smoot's fitness were intended to countervail several anticipated assertions for Smoot, namely, that he did not "practice polygamy," that there was no "evidence that he has personally and individually encouraged the practice of polygamy," and that he should not "be condemned because of the acts of his associates."[48] Opponents also cited legal precedent to illustrate examples in which courts sanctioned guilt by association, including the following snippet published in the Majority Report of the Committee on Privileges and Elections:

> It is an elementary principle of law that where two or more persons are associated together in an act, an organization, an enterprise, or a course of conduct, which is in its character or purpose unlawful, the act of any one of those who are thus associated is the act of all, and the act of any number of the associates is the act of each one of the others.[49]

Dubois's hostility for Smoot reflected a jaded perspective developed over a twenty-year period extending back to the 1880s, when he was a "violent persecutor of Mormons" while serving as a US Marshall in Idaho.[50] But the Idahoan's relationship with the Church was not always adversarial. About a decade earlier, in the mid-1890s, LDS apostle Abraham Cannon wrote that then Republican Senator Dubois was "a very good friend [to the Church], and helped very much to make Utah a State."[51] But this stint of rapprochement with Mormonism was merely a blip on the radar as intervening events in Idaho politics turned the tides back to opposition, with the last straw being Apostle Smoot's 1903 election. An irresistible provocation for Dubois, who believed the Church had not kept its word since Utah had become a state, the senator renewed his virulent anti-Mormon crusade and spearheaded the national fight against the LDS Church because he felt "it is the only right thing to do under the circumstances."[52] By advocating that Mormonism was a legitimate threat to democracy, Dubois sacrificed his political career in waging a no-holds-bar fight on Smoot.[53] With senate elections held in Idaho a month prior to the plenary debate, Dubois suffered an ignominious electoral defeat at the hands of the Idaho State legislature, thus, making him a lame duck at the time of this speech.[54]

Despite periodic criticism from Senate colleagues that his persecution of a religious minority group was "playing to the galleries," Dubois remained undeterred.[55] In a Senate floor speech given on December 13, 1906, a month prior to his election defeat, Dubois berated President Theodore Roosevelt for his support of Smoot. As background for this criticism, the Senator quoted snippets from previous presidential annual messages, known today as the State of the Union, of seven former commander-and-chiefs (including Presidents Buchanan, Grant, Hayes, Garfield, Arthur, Cleveland, and Harrison) showing their deep suspicion of "the menace of Mormonism."[56] His purpose for reading these quotations was "to mark the contrast between [former US Presidents] and the present occupant of the White House," who he felt was blinded by political expediency and willfully ignorant of the imminent peril faced by the country:

> Mormonism is more insidious, more dangerous, and a greater menace to our Government and civilization to-day than it was at any particular period when these messages were addressed to Congress. Yet President Roosevelt does not deem the subject worthy of mention in a message filled with suggestions. A majority of a great committee of the Senate, after patient and exhaustive research, have reported that Reed Smoot is not entitled to his seat as a Senator. It was not a partisan report. It should not be a partisan subject. No President heretofore has made it a matter of partisan politics. President Roosevelt has.[57]

Dubois's foregoing assertion that Roosevelt did not "deem the subject" of Mormonism "worthy of mention in ... [an annual] message filled with suggestions" strained credibility. Only ten days earlier, at Roosevelt's sixth annual message, which Dubois likely attended and was certainly aware of, the president posited his belief, without explicitly mentioning Mormonism or the state of Utah, that a "constitutional amendment" should be passed relegating the "whole question of marriage and divorce . . . to the authority of the National Congress." This would confer, Roosevelt continued, to "Congress the power at once to deal radically and efficiently with polygamy" because it "is neither safe nor proper to leave the question of polygamy to be dealt with by the several States. Power to deal with it should be conferred on the National Government."[58] Interestingly, Roosevelt's foregoing endorsement of a constitutional amendment represented a change in position for the Rough Rider, who five years prior had assured Mormon leaders that "he would do anything he could for us and that the proposed Constitutional amendment should not go through."[59] The president's maneuvering on the marriage issue was his way to triangulate his support for Smoot and his seat in Congress, while at the same time defending traditional marriage and circumscribing his opposition to marital practices then associated with the Mormon Church.

As for Dubois's statement that Smoot's seat should not be a partisan issue, the apostle-senator and his acolytes agreed in substance but from the opposite perspective. Weeks after the vote, Smoot expressed disappointment that he had not received a "unanimous" vote. In his opinion, "there was no reason for a single vote being cast against me, not a single reason."[60] Dubois's criticism of the president for partisanship revealed his frustration with the White House's last-ditch efforts to whip up votes. Over four years, Roosevelt had shrewdly created political ambiguity on his position regarding Smoot's future. Behind the scenes, he provided support to Smoot through private meetings and indiscreet lobbying. Publicly, the president maintained neutrality by avoiding any declarations of support, instead being content to allow the matter to play out in committee.[61] However, days before the final roll-call vote, Roosevelt allowed his staff to leak to the press his pro-Smoot position; thereafter, front-page stories reporting his Smoot support appeared in newspapers, including in the *New York Times*, which "add[ed] zest to the closing hours of the fight against the Apostle-Senator," giving him a final nudge toward redemption.[62]

Also criticizing President Roosevelt for his "alleged friend[ship]" with Smoot was Dubois's wife, Edna Dubois. Well schooled in the art of bare-knuckle politics, Edna Dubois supplemented her husband's efforts by using politically charged rhetoric against Roosevelt and the LDS Church. Speaking to a public gathering held at a Methodist Church a few days after her husband's foregoing December speech, Edna explained that Roosevelt's support of Smoot was based on misinformation relayed to the president by an advisor, which caused him to become impervious to any contradictory information about Smoot or the Beehive State being offered by the "women of the land." Punctuating these allegations, Edna Dubois unloaded,

FIGURE 2.4. "Located and Cinched at Last." President Theodore Roosevelt's support of Reed Smoot, which was criticized by Senator Fred Dubois of Idaho along with his wife, Edna Dubois, was a key factor in the Utah's senator's retaining his seat. *Salt Lake Herald*, February 21, 1907. Courtesy of the Brigham Young University Family History Center.

"Mormonism . . . is a greater blot than was slavery. The men and women of this country must fight it with the same courage and willingness that William Lloyd Garrison and the New England reformers displayed in the cause of freedom. Mormon children in Utah spit upon the American flag." In essence, Edna Dubois was labeling the Mormon Church "a treasonable organization," not worthy of being accepted into the American family.[63]

Dubois likewise did not pull punches when leveling criticism. Moving his sights away from the president, he lambasted the "misstatements," "misrepresentations," and "subterfuges" made by his colleagues in the Senate who had recently spoken for Smoot. Dubois, an expert on the testimony, having attended more than 80 percent of the hearings, offered little senatorial courtesy to his colleagues, whom he snidely described as "learned lawyers" that skewed the facts. And to prove this point, the senator dispensed specific examples. When multiple senators insisted that a former LDS bishop served penitentiary time for engaging in "polygamous living," Dubois refuted the assertion by using the bishop's own testimony showing he had committed adultery, not polygamy, and concluded, "No Mormon has ever prosecuted any other Mormon for living in the polygamous relation."[64] When Republican Senator Dillingham of Vermont stated that no evidence had been presented implicating Apostle John W. Taylor in taking new wives after the 1890 Manifesto, Dubois reminded that Apostle Taylor conceded guilt by fleeing the country and "hiding" from the "Senate committee." Additionally, Dubois quoted from reputable testimony showing that two of Taylor's five wives were not of marital age when the manifesto was released, explaining they were approximately ten years old.[65] Dubois was correct on both points; Taylor had married wives after the manifesto as well as evaded a federal subpoena by fleeing north to Alberta, Canada, where he claimed Canadian citizenship, and disclaimed any allegiance to the US government.[66]

Fred Dubois also responded to previous statements of his Senate colleagues. Future secretary of state Philander K. Knox, then serving as senator from Pennsylvania, asserted in a floor speech that he did "not see how the sanctity of the American home is at stake in this issue" because Smoot has "from his youth up set his face and lifted up his voice against polygamy."[67] To this, Dubois rebutted by summarizing Smoot's pedigree: "Senator Smoot is the son of a polygamist. His father had four wives, and he was raised in this polygamous atmosphere with polygamous half brothers and sisters. When he reached the age of manhood he married a polygamous child, his wife being the daughter of the fourth wife of her father." Given this upbringing, Dubois challenged every senator "to point to any single utterance in public or any single act of Reed Smoot" in which Smoot "attempted in the slightest degree to suppress polygamy or to put his seal of condemnation on polygamous living." Without an immediate response to his challenge, Dubois continued, "There is no record of it anywhere. All his life, all his acts, all his teachings are to the contrary."[68]

Smoot "listened attentively" and "sat unmoved" as Dubois and other senators "alternately defended and condemned" his fitness to serve.[69] The entirety of the hearings had been an emotionally taxing time for the Utahan, and his health had suffered. Only a few hours remained before deliverance, but Dubois had more arrows left in his quiver. Expressing contempt for those senators preparing to vote for Smoot, Dubois chafed, "[only] ten Senators in this body . . . would vote to retain Reed Smoot in his seat if they had carefully read the testimony."[70] Smoot had attended nearly every minute of committee testimony, but today he was not allowed to cast a vote.[71] And among those senators voting, most did not consume the entirety of the thirty-four hundred pages of testimony. Each senator, however, was aware of hotly contested aspects of the proceedings, given the duration of the hearings and its ubiquity in the news.

Following Dubois's floor speech was one for Smoot by Republican Albert J. Beveridge of Indiana, a well-informed Senator who had carefully studied the full testimony while a member of the committee. Known for his "eloquent speeches,"[72] the forty-four-year-old second-term senator was "young, handsome, magnetic," spoke with a "ringing voice, and a manner that compels admiration even from his foes."[73] This senator from Indiana was recently described as "the most important progressive in the US Senate during the first decade of the twentieth century" and perhaps the "chief senatorial ally" of President Roosevelt on a variety of political issues, including the Smoot affair.[74] A champion of reformers and conservationists, and a believer that the arc of history bends toward justice and progress, the Hoosier senator was skeptical of the tactics used at the investigation, believing the "whole matter has developed into a fight by Fred Dubois ... against the Mormon Church."[75] When formal testimony began, Beveridge pleased LDS leaders in Washington by being a rigorous but friendly questioner. Thirty years after this debate, when Smoot was no longer serving in national politics, he publicly surmised at an LDS General Conference that Beveridge's friendliness to the Church revealed his genuine interest in its divinity and furthermore was intrigued how Church "members were willing to sacrifice so much of their time and their substance" to further the work. Certainly it is true that Senator Beveridge was impressed by some aspects of Mormonism, but a potential convert he was not, since Smoot's memory did not recall that the senator from Pennsylvania described Mormonism as "incomprehensible, grotesque, and absurd" at this plenary debate.[76]

A devout Christian with spiritual curiously, Beveridge had ideas about the world that can be easily discerned within the pages of his book, *The Young Man and the World*, published just months before the plenary debate. Containing a collection of previously published essays, Beveridge's book was intended to be a road map for success to young male readers, guiding them toward religious and professional fulfillment. Still in print today, copies of this popular work were available in Europe in 1906, when exiled apostle Heber J. Grant was serving as LDS mission president. Three years prior in 1903, Grant had fled to Europe from Utah in haste after making the incriminating "admission" before students at the University of Utah that he proudly had "two wives" and if the "laws of the United States would permit I would make it three."[77] Intended as a tongue-and-cheek remark, which elicited laughter in the student audience, Grant's comments spread quickly in the early twentieth-century media environment, eliciting national headlines and hurting Smoot's precarious political situation. Utah law enforcement officers immediately issued a warrant for Grant's arrest on the charge of polygamous cohabitation but were not able to detain the apostle before he skipped town.[78]

Grant, who succeeded Joseph F. Smith in 1917 as the seventh president of the Church, purchased a copy and read *The Young Man and the World* while serving in Europe. Inspired by the book's ideas, Grant frequently shared quotations from it with Mormon audiences, explaining its words "have greater meaning" to LDS audiences.[79] Also contained within *The Young Man and the World* was a framework that illuminates, in part, why Beveridge willingly supported Smoot. In the chapter entitled "The Young Man and the Pulpit," Beveridge argued against the view that "minister[s] of the Gospel" should not "mix [it] up in politics" or use "pulpits to express views on our civic and National life." Instead, the senator from Indiana recommended that men of the cloth should look to Jesus, who "took a considerable part in public affairs," even scourging "money-changers from the Temple." Beveridge's apparent advocacy for ecclesiastical activism was tempered by his cautionary caveat that ministers limit the number of causes they undertake, "For there is always the danger that if he takes part in many political agitations he will become so monotonous that all his power for good will be dissipated."[80] Ironically, some of Smoot's colleagues in the Quorum of Twelve believed that Smoot had fallen prey to the situation Beveridge warned of and were displeased by the microscope being placed on the Church. They blamed Smoot for being the cause of much "unpleasantness and trouble."[81] Others in leadership positions were disappointed by the apostle-senator's lack of knowledge of doctrinal matters within LDS theology, presumably compared to his prodigious knowledge of public policy.[82]

Beveridge began his floor speech by framing himself to be a "democrat to the bone," who believed in the common axiom of the times, *Vox Populi, Vox Dei*, or "the voice of the people is the voice of God." But in regards to Smoot and his personal life, the country had been misinformed; Smoot was a victim of a smear campaign, propagated by "misguided millions" who were trying to "ruin the reputation" of a man "whose life has been stainless."[83] Adding color to this depiction, the youthful senator compared Smoot to Alfred Dreyfus, a Jewish captain in the French Army who, in the year 1894, was arrested, falsely convicted of treason, and thrown into prison at Devil's Island. In the decade following his imprisonment, one historian surmised that Dreyfus became "one of the best-known men in Europe, if not the world."[84] Another recent author characterized the "Dreyfus Affair" as a "miscarriage of justice" that polarized France and remains controversial to this day.[85] Dreyfus was fresh on Beveridge's mind, since only months early the Frenchman had been exonerated and released. By placing Dreyfus and Smoot in juxtaposition, Beveridge assured those inside the Senate gallery that "Justice is never permanently defeated anywhere." Beveridge then expanded:

Dreyfus was charged with treason; and this man [Smoot] is charged with treason—and worse . . . he is charged with infamy, as well as treason, before the American people; before the bar of public opinion he has been tried on the charge of the vilest of offenses. And because the American people have been made to believe this infamy, they have petitioned this court for judgment against the guiltless. This fact is important, for who can say what has been the influence on the members of this court that clamor which has assailed us, a clamor as erroneous as that which sent the loyal French Jew to Devils Island?[86]

Dousing the comparison with hyperbole while ignoring Dreyfus's half-decade imprisonment, Beveridge submitted that the senator-apostle's plight was more severe than Dreyfus's because in addition to being charged for treason, Smoot had suffered through "three long years" of infamy, where the "average man and woman has been told that Reed Smoot is a criminal guilty of a disgusting and filthy crime—a crime abhorrent to our race and destructive of our civilization. The country has been told that this man is a polygamist."[87] Indeed, legitimate similarities existed between these two men, but to elevate Smoot's suffering above Dreyfus's represented unwarranted political grandiosity. Moreover, the topic of Dreyfus's plight has been far more important historiographically and geopolitically as it inspired Austrian journalist Theodore Herzl's influential tract on political Zionism called *The Jewish State* (1896), as well as the publication of hundreds of books on the topic of Dreyfus.[88] Smoot's situation, on the other hand, has only generated a handful of monographs and other scholarly attention, nor has it spawned a serious political movement outside of motivating other American Mormons to seek high political office.

In addition to Beveridge, two other GOP Senators, Joseph B. Foraker of Ohio and Jonathan P. Dolliver of Iowa, spoke eloquently on the apostle's behalf. Each of these men used similar rhetorical approaches, lauding Smoot's personal life on one hand, while criticizing Mormonism on the other. Foraker praised Smoot as "so good a man" that he "sometimes" doubts that he is real. "He seems to have no vices," Dolliver explained, and listed off the habits of drinking, chewing, swearing, and smoking, all vices Mormons are taught to avoid. This praise was paired with the Iowa senator's mention of the many "misdeeds" committed by the Church during the years it practiced polygamy.[89] Dolliver complemented Smoot for obtaining "a position of leadership in the church . . . without turning aside from the path of virtue or by precept or example defiling the purity of his own home" but made clear that he harbored "deep prejudices against the Utah branch of the Mormon Church" and did "not like its history nor the record which it has made in the past."[90] Dolliver purposefully demarcated Smoot's Utah Mormonism from the off-shoot branch of Mormonism headquartered in his home state of Iowa, then known as the Reorganized Church of Jesus Christ of Latter Day Saints (RLDS Church), for political purposes. Although similar in many core beliefs, these churches held irreconcilable perspectives on the historicity and provenance of the practice of polygamy. These differences were stark enough that the president of the RLDS Church, Joseph Smith III, the eldest son of Mormonism's founder Joseph Smith Jr. and cousin of Joseph F. Smith, strategically joined the national fight to unseat Smoot and mitigate the influence of Utah Mormonism.[91]

Dolliver's speech for Smoot was an exercise in political courage or foolhardiness, given the prevalence of RLDS constituents in his state. Eight months earlier he had voted for Smoot's ouster as a member of the committee,[92] but at that time, as the Hawkeye Senator rehearsed, he was a recent appointee to the committee who "acquiesced with the majority of the committee" because he did not have time to carefully examine "the voluminous record" and was under the "general impression that Senator Smoot was guilty" of the crime of polygamy.[93] As with any politician forced to explain a change of position to a disappointed constituency, Dolliver carefully crafted his words for the RLDS audience back home. Tiptoeing gingerly, Dolliver dismissed Smoot's Mormonism, explaining that it "is a feeble and struggling affair" outside of Utah, while at the same time praising the "immediate descendants of Joseph Smith" living in his state as an "industrious, law-abiding, God-fearing" people, who "for half a century [have been] an influence for good throughout the entire community." Iowa Mormons, Dolliver propounded, have a "creed [that] differs from the theology of Utah Mormonism" in two important ways: first by its opposition to "the crime of polygamy" and second by "the absence of all secret rituals." Even though Dolliver found Smoot's Mormonism a "strange faith," this time around he opted to vote for the Utah senator under the rationalization that he preferred to err "on the side of justice and fair dealing," rather than risk branding an innocent man a "malefactor."[94] As for the political repercussions of Dolliver's support, he incurred none, since he shrewdly withheld public knowledge of his support for Smoot until after reelection in January of 1907. Passing away three years later, Dolliver's did not thereafter have another election.[95]

Beveridge also used this template of commending Smoot personally while denigrating the institution of Mormonism, averring Smoot had lived a "blameless life" prior to arriving in Washington and since being sworn in had been a paragon of loyalty and fealty. But when speaking of Mormonism, Beveridge denigrated the faith with words such as "grotesque" and "absurd."[96] For Beveridge, the most pertinent question of the day had nothing to do with the doctrinal deviances of Mormonism vis-à-vis Protestantism, nor the improprieties of Smoot's ecclesiastical colleagues. What concerned the senator about the resolution was the threat it posed to the "corner stones of this Republic," namely, "religious tolerance" and "religious liberty." This opposition to Smoot, continued the Hoosier, was not any different than the "Know Nothing movement of the [eighteen] fifties" or the "A.P.A. [American Protective Association] movement of a few years ago." Each rooted in anti-Catholic nativism, these two uprisings were viewed by the political class of 1907 as a "black-eye" to American pluralism.[97] Arguments made against Smoot's Mormonism were actually recycled attacks used by the thought leaders within the Know-Nothings and APA movements. For instance, Know Nothings feared that Catholic assertiveness, not dissimilar to Mormon assertiveness, would have a subversive influence upon both American Protestantism and democracy and, if allowed to take root, would result in the banishment of the bible.[98] By the same token, the APA sought to limit the "ecclesiastical power" of the Catholic Church, similar to the Mormon Church, "which claims higher sovereignty" than the United States and "is irreconcilable with American citizenship."[99]

Senators speaking against the resolution in favor of Smoot were also cognizant of the hefty cost taxpayers bore in funding the hearings. Beveridge complained the investigation had "taken place at the cost of" $26,000 of the "people's money," which was spent "to ruin this man."[100] The financial burden to Smoot personally was also substantial. According to reports, he paid an out-of-pocket amount of $30,000, larger than that of the US government, but was reimbursed half of the total shortly after his vindication, when Senator Sutherland offered an amendment to the deficiency bill coming out of the appropriations committee.[101]

Weeks after Beveridge's "stirring speech," the Church-owned *Deseret Evening News* reprinted in its entirety the ninety-minute stem-winder. With a staff reporter inside the Senate chamber, the *News* favorably compared Beveridge's oratory to that from the "lips of a Burke, or a Patrick Henry" and further avouched that even though the "great majority of the audience was not in sympathy with the speaker's views, they paid him the rare compliment of several times interrupting" with applause. *Deseret News* readers of the speech were left to imagine the intensity of the elocution and drama of the event, where "arch foe" Burrows sat "directly in front of" Beveridge, watching his delivery as sweat "poured down his face," wilting his "shirt collar . . . into shapelessness."[102]

If Beveridge held adversarial contempt for the Republican chairman, as implied by the foregoing quote from the Church's newspaper, his speech revealed no such animus. The Senate hearings had been an enormous undertaking, described by one astute analyst as "the most thorough and exhaustive instigation of Mormon affairs ever made," with inquiries made into its "history . . . organization, creed, practices, business affairs, and even the lives of its prominent members."[103] For these efforts, which included testimony from ninety-eight witnesses and two rounds of closing arguments by four attorneys, Beveridge complimented: "[Chairmen Burrows] has labored through his mighty task . . . perform[ing] his enormous duties with industry, fidelity, courage, and uniform courtesy to his associates."[104] Other observers, including University of Illinois associate professor of political science James Wilford Garner, were less enthused by the proceedings. Writing in *The North American Review*, the professor considered the hearings a waste of time and resources, opining, "The present investigation has brought nothing to light that has not already been well known." Smoot, notorious for his miserly tendencies and belt-tightening instincts, certainly agreed with these sentiments. However, compared with other governmental misappropriations and largesse's of the day, the Smoot hearings would not have registered at the top of the pork-barrel list.

For Garner, the hearings identified just one "serious consideration" to remove Smoot: the claim that his membership in a polygamous hierarchy rendered him "unfit, morally, to occupy a seat in the National legislature." Not persuaded by this allegation, Garner denominated it "mental thralldom" and not "convincing to a judicial mind." Moreover, Smoot was duly sworn in and possessed "all the requisite constitutional qualifications"; thus, his seat could only be deprived by the statutorily mandated two-thirds majority delineated in Section 5 of Article 1 of the Constitution. Not applicable to Smoot's case, Garner continued, were instances when a "bare majority" of senators voted to remove members who had "become insane, idiotic or violent, or . . . afflicted with a dangerous contagious disease." Nor were the abnormal actions of past Congresses who prevented elected representatives from taking their seat on account of being deemed legally unqualified to service. This included when "self-confessed criminal" B. H. Roberts was prevented from taking his seat because of his plural wives, or earlier when elected representatives during the Civil War were blocked from entering Congress for disloyalty to the Union.[105] The question of Smoot's fitness to serve in the Senate was based upon morality, rather than his belief in a particular religious institution per se. Under this schema, it was polygamy, a criminal act of individual agency based on supreme court jurisprudence, rather than Mormonism per se, that disqualified Smoot.

Burrows, in his concluding remarks, was not persuaded by this two-thirds majority line of reasoning offered by Garner and others but recognized he was fighting a losing battle, since even sympathetic Senators to his cause believed a two-thirds majority was required to oust Smoot.[106] He disclaimed any "desire to discuss that question [of the two-thirds majority]" or "the contention that Mr. Smoot" is a polygamist, though he could not refrain from expressing dismay that his "friend from Iowa [Mr. Dolliver]" was conned into the impression that Smoot was a polygamist, since from "the beginning to the end of the investigation not one solitary word was submitted to the committee on that point [that Smoot is a polygamist]." Furthermore, the Chairman rejected the notion that his committee was waging a "war against a religious faith" and took offense at the assertion that if Smoot is denied his seat, "then the presiding authorities of every church of whatever faith, Jew or Gentile, Catholic or Protestant, may be denied a seat in this national council chamber."[107]

Frustrated by these allegations, Burrows forcefully distilled his perspective: "It is not a war on a church, but it is a protest against the admission into the Senate of the representative of an organization confessedly criminal. Churches of this country . . . guard and protect the purity of the home as the altar of their faith, and I protest against this effort to drag the Christian churches of the land down to the low level of this abomination."[108] These colorful highlights from Burrows's speech belie its overall stodginess, which according to one newspaper was as "dry as tinder, replete with constitutional arguments and . . . precedents without number."

FIGURE 2.5. "A Pointed Argument." Republican Chairman Julius Caesar Burrows of Michigan used many creative tactics to make life uncomfortable for Reed Smoot during Smoot's first few years in the US Senate. In this illustration, cartoonist Charles L. Bartholomew depicts a coy Senator Burrows sportfully watching Smoot's reaction to being pricked by a sharp Salt Lake temple trap set by Burrows on the contested Utah Senate seat. The *Minneapolis Journal*, December 11, 1906.

Burrows was filling time with this speech to filibuster Smoot's allies from speaking in his favor, and only rabid "anti-Smoot [Senators] all the way through" remained in the chamber, and even they passed the time by "chatting" on other topics. Overflow gallery crowds also lost interest in the Michigander's speech, resorting to quiet conversations and hushed "whispering." Aware of these discourteous onlookers, the senator from Kalamazoo periodically interrupted his remarks to either quiet the crowd or to apologize for its prosaic content.[109]

Adding to Burrows's perspective on the abominable aspects of the Mormon Church was Democratic senator from Nevada, Francis G. Newlands, who proffered a postscript on Mormonism's control of "temporal matters" in Utah, as well as its "thoroughly accomplished" union "of church and state." Newlands, the only western Senator, along with Dubois, voting against Smoot, worried his vote would unfavorably redound to his political demise. The "Mormon Church is a strong political factor in a portion of Nevada, and the man who antagonizes that church takes his political life in his hands."[110] Newlands overstated the political peril he faced and was reelected twice thereafter.

After five hours of plenary discussion, the vice-president rapped his gavel to end debate. Members of the House of Representatives as well as "employees of the Senate" poured into "the standing room on the floor of the Senate" to get a closer view of the final vote.[111] Smoot, not interested in watching the actual vote, repaired alone to the Republican Party's cloakroom, where he "nervously [walked] up and down" while also receiving as near to real-time updates from a Senate page he "had stationed" just outside the cloakroom door.[112] Three roll-call votes commenced on the resolution, "*That REED SMOOT is not entitled to a seat as a Senator of the United States from the State of Utah.*" The first two votes were on proposed amendments to this resolution, and the third vote on the full resolution. The final vote on the full resolution was 42–28 in Smoot's favor. Republican Senators, trailed by GOP House members, rushed the cloak room to "heartily" congratulate the apostle-senator with handshakes and expressions of "admiration" for his comportment during the "trying ordeal."[113] Smoot opponents, including a disappointed Chairman Burrows, did not congratulate Smoot at this spontaneous reception, nor at any time after the debate.[114]

Mixed reactions to the Senate vote spread across the country, reflecting the polarization engendered by the topic, while also resembling the differing priorities of those who gave prayers to begin the day. Christian ministers vented indignation, while LDS leaders in Utah expressed jubilation. Dr. T. C. Iliff of Nebraska struck a shrill tone by his condemnation of the US Senate for perpetuating "the Mormon monstrosity" in enacting the "greatest shame of the decade and the greatest insult ever offered the American people" by seating Apostle Reed Smoot.[115] Reverend S. E. Wishard in California followed suit, deriding Mormonism as a system that "begins with lust and is founded upon lust" and teaches that "Jesus was married to both Mary and Martha, and other women, and that He lived to see His own children." Feeling angst by Smoot's victory, Wishard continued his attack: "The greatest source of revenue in the Mormon church is the baptising of the living relatives, who stand sponsor for relatives who have died, outside the church. They exact a heavy fee for this service, and it is going steadily on every day at four centers in Utah."[116]

Conversely, celebratory responses in Utah likewise exuded dramatic flair. Writing in the opinion section of the Church's *Deseret Evening News*, Apostle Charles Penrose extolled the vote as a vindication to Smoot, the LDS Church, and

Christianity.[117] Smoot's victory represented "a literal fulfillment" of the spurious White Horse prophecy, which articulates that "Latter-day Saints" would one day "take up" the mission of defending both "the government of the United States" and the "Constitution of this Republic" from "anarchistic assaults." "Smoot and his friends," Penrose expanded, deserved thanks "for the courage and integrity with which they took up the defense of that divinely inspired magna charta." A task they undertook, "not because of any personal ambition, but because of the firm belief that the world needs this country, this free government, for the further advancement of the cause of humanity toward the Millennial condition."[118] Speaking off-the-cuff at a Church meeting house dedication, President Joseph F. Smith added his perspective on the subject. Smoot's "victory in Senate was a fulfillment of God's Will," and a missionary opportunity where "the American people" and "high officials of the government" learned of the "true doctrines of Mormonism," and now "have a true conception of the faith of the Mormon Church."[119] For Church leaders, Smoot's grueling political victory in Washington had the salutary effect of advancing Church interests, and it represented a providential pot of gold for the transitioning faith.

Smoot's tone was more measured and less parochial. He interpreted the success as a victory for American religious liberty rather than a vindication per se of Mormonism's "true doctrines." Celebratory receptions were held up and down the Wasatch Front upon his return home to Utah. At one event held in his hometown of Provo, Smoot lamented that "the hardest accusation which he had to face was when he was called disloyal to his country and to his flag."[120] At another event, Smoot's expressed nostalgic emotion:

> I pray that this will be the last great battle for the upholding of our Constitution guaranteeing religious liberty to all citizens. I hope it will never occur again in the senate or house of representatives [sic] of the United States, where a man's religious belief is brought in question; or wherein the senate or house is asked to expel him for belonging to any religious denomination; and I believe it will not. And if I have been an instrument in any way, shape or form, as it was settled by our forefathers, all that I have suffered, all I have passed through, or all that it has cost me, I would willingly undertake again for the same great cause. I know I am right, because I never felt more humble in all my life. I know, my friends, that the result is as it should be, for it appeals to and makes me feel in my soul the same as I always do when I have done something to advance humanity, or assist a brother or sister anywhere upon this earth.[121]

For Senator Smoot, political justice was achieved, fulfilling Beveridge's progressive prediction and perspective that justice is "never permanently defeated anywhere"—not permanently for Smoot personally, not permanently for the evolving Church he represented. Although the fight seemed interminable, fraught

—Berryman in the Washington *Star.*

FIGURE 2.6. "Smoot's Victory." Senator Reed Smoot believed his retention in the US Senate was victory for religious liberty in America. Cartoonist Clifford K. Berryman portrays Smoot's win as less than secure, with the Utah senator clinging to his seat tightly as his opposition lie in wait behind him. *Washington Star* as reprinted in the *Literary Digest*, March 2, 1907. Courtesy of the L. Tom Perry Special Collections, Brigham Young University.

with uncertainly and ambiguity, the overwhelming vote in Smoot's favor provided him with the freedom to serve the American people an additional twenty-five years. Smoot may have been hyperbolic in his excitement, but he was not entirely off base by suggesting that his victory played a part in the larger national shift toward secularization and its related principle of religious pluralism. Smoot, like many progressives within the Republican Party, defined religious liberty as religious belonging, where citizens enjoyed the freedom to not have their religious beliefs questioned at the public square, even if these religious beliefs were outside the mainstream. The process and outcome of Smoot's case helped to articulate this new understanding of religious liberty and offered a new framework for modern Mormonism and political progressives to operate within. Historian Kathleen Flake, in her important study of the Smoot hearings, persuasively argued that Smoot's victory served two important purposes. First, it provided a one-hundred-year solution "to the Mormon problem," an agreement that has held firm until recently with Mitt Romney's multiple runs for the US presidency, where once again Mormonism was a subject of political derisiveness.[122] And second, Flake continues, the compromise "articulated the terms for extending religious liberty to an increasing non-Protestant and non-Christian citizenry."[123] Smoot saw his victory on the same terms, that it was a success for both religious liberty and the country's fealty to the Constitution, enabling a positive step forward vis-à-vis secular reform, where one's religion was not the primary determinant of national belonging or the most important qualifier for political leadership.

With over a century of hindsight since Smoot's vindication, the two morning prayers, spoken by Chaplain Hale in Washington and Chaplain Hess in Utah, each supplicating deity for national and provincial ends, have been effectively answered to the benefit of Mormonism, Utah, and America at large. Mormonism as an institution has become an integral part of American society and culture, with members prominent in the fields of business, academia, media, and government. Over time the country has integrated many different religious or nonreligious groups into the working fabric of daily life and politics, however limited this inclusion remains. Latter-day Saints today make contributions to America that bear the earmarks of Smoot's approach to citizenship, rather than the insular, collectivist course pursued by the senator's nineteenth-century ecclesiastical contemporaries who determinedly amassed, over several decades, a substantial record of civil disobedience by openly flouting national antipolygamy laws.[124] Indeed, historian Harvard Heath's pithy assertion that Reed Smoot was "the first modern Mormon" is truer in modern America than the apostle-senator could have imagined.[125]

NOTES

1. US Congressional Record, 59th Cong., 2nd Sess., 1906 [sic; the Congressional fiscal year was March to February/March], vol. 41, p. 3398 (hereafter, Congressional Record).

2. "Edward Everett Hale (1822–1909)," in *Heralds of A Liberal Faith*, edited by Samuel Atkins Elliot (Boston: The Beacon Press, 1952), 4: 150–51, 154. This vignette also explains, "No one who ever saw Edward Everett Hale could possibly forget him. No one who knew him could fail to be impressed by his personality. Physically he was a big man. He was built on generous lines and his head was Homeric. He was large, too, in his grasp of things. In all his outlooks he enjoyed a wide horizon. It was written of him that, 'Probably no man in America aroused and stimulated so many minds as Hale, and his personal popularity was unbounded.'"

3. I have not located any contemporaneous sources for this famous, oft-repeated quote attributed to Hale. However, Hale's foregoing quote has appeared in many books over the years,

including the following: Suzy Platt, ed., *Respectfully Quoted: A Dictionary of Quotations* (New York: Barnes and Noble Books, 1993), 60; Brook Thomas, *Civic Myths: A Law-and-Literature Approach to Citizenship* (Chapel Hill: University of North Carolina Press, 2007), 264.

4. At the 1893 World's Parliament of Religions, Hale gave a speech entitled "Spiritual Forces in Human Progress," where he outlined his twentieth-century vision for America. This included "peace among all nations of the world," "Universal education . . . for everyone," healthcare equally available to all citizens, and all people voluntarily living pure lives of chastity, devoid of drunkenness. For a reprint of his speech, see Rev. John Henry Barrows, ed., *The World's Parliament of Religions* (Chicago: Parliament Publishing Company, 1893), 1:523–526. Approximately eight years earlier, in the late 1880s, Hale was affiliated with the National Anti-Polygamy League that campaigned against polygamist B. H. Roberts when he was elected to Congress. Hale's Unitarian Church joined the sectarian opposition to Roberts's seating by protesting "to Congress that seating a Mormon would be 'prejudicial to the best interests of the country.'" Jonathan H. Moyer, "Dancing with the Devil: The Making of the Mormon-Republican Pact" (PhD diss., University of Utah, Salt Lake City, 2009), 197, 215.

5. Congressional Record, 3404.

6. "Preliminaries in the Forenoon," *Salt Lake Herald*, August 26, 1904, 3. In 1904, "Bishop" David Hess served as the chaplain to the Republican State Convention and "delivered a prayer in which he petitioned the Almighty to be with the Republican Party in the campaign." Hess was a bishop of a congregation located in Davis County, UT.

7. "Elder Hess' Prayer," *Salt Lake Herald*, February 21, 1907, 2. According to this report, Hess did not write out this prayer for publication, but a "transcript of his prayer was submitted to Chaplain Hess, who said it was substantially correct. He said that was the way he felt about the Smoot case and that he had consulted no one about the matter before making his prayer." Two days after this conspicuous prayer, the editor of the Mormon-owned *Salt Lake Herald* opined, "The more we think of that prayer the less we like it. It seems to us that Hess was praying more to the galleries than to his God . . . if Hess had gone into his closet and prayed his prayer in secret . . . there could have been no complaint about it . . . But no man, be he a preacher or layman, has the right to stand up and, under the pretense of addressing the Almighty, make a political harangue for the delectation of an aggregation of politicians . . . Chaplain Hess may possibly believe that his prayer saved Smoot . . . We do not believe that the prayer by Hess had any effect whatever." See "A Gallery Prayer," *Salt Lake Herald*, February 23, 1907, 1.

8. Near the conclusion of the Smoot hearings, when Mormon antagonist Charles M. Owen was called to testify a second time, Chairman Julius Caesar Burrows entered into the Congressional Record information on each elected member of Utah State Legislature's religion back to 1896 when Utah became a state. Mormons were marked with an "M" and Gentiles (non-Mormons) were marked with a "G." Both George N. Lawrence and William E. White were demarcated with a "G." See Proceedings before the Committee on Privileges and Elections of the United States Senate in the Matter of the Protests against the Right of Hon. Reed Smoot, a Senator from the State of Utah, to Hold His Seat (Washington, DC: US Government Printing Office, 1906), 4:143 (hereafter, Smoot Hearings).

9. "Smoot Chosen Senator by Majority of Thirty," *Salt Lake Herald*, January 21, 1903, 1. White also "declared in effect that the election of an apostle meant the choice of the prophet, seer and revelator of the church of Jesus Christ of Latter-day Saints." In response to White's statement, Rep. James B. Wilson of Wasatch County "declared he welcomed any storm which might arise from the election of Smoot. 'Let it come,' he declared. He bade defiance to the opposition."

10. For background and context on the Reed Smoot hearings, see Milton R. Merrill, *Reed Smoot: Apostle in Politics* (Logan: Utah State University Press, 1990), 11–104; Kathleen Flake, *The Politics of American Religious Identity: The Seating of Senator Reed Smoot, Mormon Apostle* (Chapel Hill: University of North Carolina Press, 2004); Jonathan H. Moyer, "Dancing with the

Devil: The Making of the Mormon-Republican Pact" (PhD diss., University of Utah, Salt Lake City, 2009); Harvard S. Heath, "The Reed Smoot Hearings: A Quest for Legitimacy," *Journal of Mormon History* 33, no. 2 (Summer 2007): 1–80; Michael Harold Paulos, "Senator George Sutherland: Reed Smoot's Defender," *Journal of Mormon History* 33, no. 2 (Summer 2007): 81–118; Michael Harold Paulos, "'Horribly Caricatured and Made Hideous in Cartoons': Political Cartooning and the Reed Smoot Hearings," in *Mormons and American Popular Culture*, vol. 2 (Praeger Publishers, 2012). For an abridgement of the Smoot hearings with annotations, see Michael Harold Paulos, ed., *The Mormon Church on Trial: Transcripts of the Reed Smoot Hearings* (Salt Lake City: Signature Books, 2008).

    11. Congressional Record, 3404; "Sen. Smoot Retains His Seat and is Given a Big Ovation" *Ogden Standard*, February 20, 1907, 1.

    12. Moyer, "Dancing with the Devil," 354.

    13. Congressional Record, 3404–3405; "Sen. Smoot Retains His Seat and Is Given a Big Ovation," *Ogden Herald*, February 30, 1907, 1. Senator Dubois initially said he only needed thirty minutes but quickly retracted to a full hour. Chairman Burrows insisted he needed a full ninety minutes to conclude the debate. Dubois and Burrow's requests were interesting given that just two months prior both men had spoken on the Smoot topic on the Senate floor for more than three hours each. See Paulos, "Senator George Sutherland," 89–90. For reports on the two speeches, see "Burrows Argues for Expulsion of Smoot," *Hartford Courant*, December 12, 1906, 15; "Dubois Roast the President," *Los Angeles Times*, December 14, 1906, 14; "Dubois Attacks President," *New York Times*, December 14, 1906, 7. Senator Spooner was likely a causality of this time gimmick by Burrows and Dubois. During the preliminary dickering over time allocation, Spooner included himself within the "number of Senators . . . who desire to briefly explain the vote which they intend to cast on this matter." But over the five-hour debate, Spooner did not take the floor to explain his vote in favor of Smoot. Congressional Record, 3404; "Senator Smoot is Vindicated; Retains Seat By Large Margin," *Inter-Mountain Republican*, February 21, 1907, 1.

    14. Congressional Record, 3417.

    15. Cullom, "The Reed Smoot Decision," *North American Review*, March 15, 1907, 572. In early June 1906, when the Senate committee voted on Smoot, the National League of Women's Organizations adopted a resolution decrying that Smoot "sits in the Senate as an apostle of polygamy and the representative of a treasonable organization, and therefore should no longer remain a member of its body." Later delegates from this organization met with President Roosevelt and presented him with an anti-Smoot resolution. "Women against Smoot," *New York Times*, June 9, 1906, 4. For more on the historical context surrounding the protest, see Joan Smyth Iversen, *The Antipolygamy Controversy in U.S. Women's Movements, 1880–1928* (New York: Garland Publishing, Inc. 1997), 213–238; Moyer, "Dancing with the Devil," 227–349. Media sources and politicians at the debate averred that millions of women protested Smoot's seating. For example, Chairman Burrows asserted during his speech that "four million women in this country . . . ask that Mr. Smoot may be excluded from the Senate." See Congressional Record, 3421. Additionally, the anti-Smoot *Salt Lake Tribune* reported that "Ten Million American Women" were waging a battle for the purity of the Nation's homes. "'Big Stick' Saves Smoot from Deserved Exclusion," *Salt Lake Tribune*, February 21, 1907.

    16. "Letters to The Outlook," *Outlook*, February 3, 1906, 280.

    17. "Woman's Influence," *Chicago Daily Tribune*, June 3, 1906, B4. In the introduction of a 1905 reprint of the confessions of John Doyle Lee, participant and only legally prosecuted Mormon associated with the Mountain Meadows Massacre, journalist Alfred Henry Lewis explained that the "womanhood of the nation . . . compelled the present Senate investigation," which has "uncovered Mormonism in many of its evil details, . . . pious charlatanism and religious crime." According to Lewis, the Smoot hearings were merely an "incident" battle in war to defend womanhood, not "wholly won with Smoot's eviction from his Senate seat," but when "all of Mormonism and what it

stands for is destroyed." John Doyle Lee and Alfred Henry Lewis, *The Mormon Menace* (New York: Home Protection Publishing Co., 1905), vii–xxii.

18. Reed Smoot to Joseph F. Smith, November 14, 1903, Reed Smoot Papers, L. Tom Perry Special Collections, Harold B. Lee Library, Brigham Young University, Provo, UT (hereafter, Smoot Papers). Throughout the hearings, letters flooded into Washington. At one point, Smoot explained to President Smith in Utah that "Senator Beveridge is receiving from one to two thousand letters a day, and the other Senators are being deluged with requests to vote to unseat me." Reed Smoot to Joseph F. Smith, March 23, 1904, Smoot Papers. However, these letters to Beveridge do not appear to have been sent by people in his home state of Indiana. In his floor speech, Senator Beveridge suggested that "out of Indiana's nearly 3,000,000 people but few have written me on this subject, although my correspondence with my constituents is enormous. I am prouder of that evidence of faith and trust in me of Indiana's people than I am of the place in this body which they have given me, I am proud that they know that not all the letters that could be written in a hundred years nor all the petitions that could be gathered by any propaganda, . . . would swerve me if I knew the writers of those letters and the signers of those petitions to be misinformed." Congressional Record, 3409. Additionally, Mormon historian Harvard Heath explained, "The states with the greatest numbers of petitions against Smoot seemed to follow the Saints' route west from New York to Utah, especially Colorado and Idaho." See Heath, "The Reed Smoot Hearings," 13–14. Heath's dissertation graphically displays this dynamic, showing a map of the Saints' route west, with the number of petitions for each state. See Harvard S. Heath, "Reed Smoot: First Modern Mormon" (PhD diss., Brigham Young University, Provo, UT, 1990), 98–99. Last, Jonathan Moyer posits his complementary insight that "the states most pronounced in their anti-Smoot petitions also displayed some of the nation's most intense religiosity." Moyer, "Dancing with the Devil," 329–330.

19. "Smoot Petitions Presented," *New York Times*, February 20, 1906, 2.

20. Reed Smoot to Joseph F. Smith, March 6, 1906, Smoot Papers. Smoot enumerated the backlash in a letter home to President Smith, "I feel sorry for Senator Perkins, of California, for since he made a speech in submitting the petition against me, the Churches of his State have been passing resolutions against him, and some preachers have written him insulting and threatening letters. They have charged him with upholding bigamy and polygamy, . . . The Senator . . . has not weakened a particle; and he told me the other day, that if he had the thing to do over . . . he would do just as he had done. . . . Senator Warren, of Wyoming, is receiving his share of abuse for endorsing the remarks made by Mr. Perkins."

21. "Senatorial Elections," *Outlook*, January 23, 1909, 129.

22. "Mormonism a Menace," *Christian Observer*, August 29, 1906, 3.

23. The *Observer* continued, "Optimistic and ease-loving gentlemen may cry, peace, peace. But there is no peace when such a hydra-headed monster of treason and immortality begins to creep in the highest council of our nation. Rome had no such reason for her stern watchword: 'Delenda est Carhtoago,' as our land has for the eradication of this cancerous growth on our American civilization." See "The Mormon Triumph," *Christian Observer*, March 13, 1907, 2. This essay relied upon the following Orson Pratt quote from his essay entitled "The Kingdom of God" to exhibit Mormon treachery: "The only legal government that can exist in any part of the universe. All other governments are illegal and unauthorized." For a convenient reprint of Pratt's foregoing essay originally published in 1848 in Liverpool, England, see David J. Whittaker, ed., *The Essential Orson Pratt* (Salt Lake City: Signature Books, 1991), 48–60. "Delenda est Carhtoago" is Latin for "Carthage must be destroyed."

24. "Utah Defamed Only to Serve Ends of 'Sore' Politicians, Governor Says," *Chicago Daily Tribune*, February 11, 1907, 8.

25. "Senate Refuses to Oust Smoot," *New York Times*, February 21, 1907, 5. The threats of punishment "so cowed the galleries that the announcement of the vote was heard without any

demonstration whatever, although scores of women were just aching to hiss" at senators for voting in favor of Smoot.

26. Shelby M. Cullom, "The Reed Smoot Decision," *North American Review*, March 15, 1907, 575.

27. "Smoot Is Sure of His Seat: Poll of Senate Discloses Fact That Enough Cannot Be Obtained to Oust Him," *Chicago Daily Tribune*, February 19, 1907, 6. Also see "Smoot Is Assured of Victory To-day," *New York Times*, February 20, 1907, 5. Back in Utah, the official organ of the Republican Party in the State of Utah, the *Inter-mountain Republican*, also reported that Smoot was "Certain to Retain Seat." See "Short Address by Reed Smoot Clinches Seat in Upper House," *Inter-mountain Republican*, February 20, 1907, 1.

28. Cullom, "The Reed Smoot Decision," 572. Smoot found that most people had misinformation related to Mormonism, including one of non-Mormon attorneys (Mr. Worthington) hired to represent his case. Confiding to the First Presidency six weeks before the hearing began, Smoot explained, "We . . . have embraced every opportunity that has been offered . . . of posting [Worthington] as to the real condition of affairs and the true inwardness of the case. We found that [Worthington] had imbibed many anti-Mormon notions and therefore it took more time to get him to understand things aright, but he seems to have a fair conception of the subject and a desire to do all he can to insure [*sic*] a success." Reed Smoot to Presidents Joseph F. Smith, John R. Winder, and Anthon H. Lund, January 16, 1904, Smoot Papers.

29. Howard R. Lamar, "Political Patterns in New Mexico and Utah Territories 1850–1900," *Utah Historical Quarterly* 28, no. 4 (October 1960): 385.

30. Moyer, "Dancing with the Devil" 332.

31. Gustive O. Larson, *The "Americanization" of Utah for Statehood* (San Marino, CA: Huntington Library, 1971), 65–67; Edwin Brown Firmage and Richard Collin Mangrum, *Zion in the Courts: A Legal History of the Church of Jesus Christ of Latter-day Saints, 1930–1900* (Urbana: University of Illinois Press, 1988), 41, 47; Edward Leo Lyman, *Political Deliverance* (Urbana: University of Illinois Press, 1986), 126–133.

32. Shelby M. Cullom, "The Meaning of Mormonism," *Independent*, April 26, 1906, 979–982.

33. Late in 1903, Smoot was pleasantly surprised with the following experience: "Senator Cullom came to me and said, 'The presenting of these petitions has not worried you, has it?' I remarked to him, 'Not in the least.' He said, 'I do not think they ought to, for they come from a lot of old women and Sunday-school children.'" Reed Smoot to Joseph F. Smith, November 14, 1903, Smoot Papers.

34. Cullom, "The Reed Smoot Decision," 575. After the first round of closing arguments in early 1905, Smoot had a conversation in the Senate cloakroom with Republican senator McComas of Maryland. After complaining about several aspects of the Mormon Church, McComas "remarked . . . that it was a lucky thing for the church that I was sent here as Senator for I was liked by both Democrats and Republicans and for that reason he did not expect I would be unseated." Reed Smoot to Joseph F. Smith, February 10, 1905, Smoot Papers.

35. For instances in which Smoot sought out Proctor's advice, see Reed Smoot to Joseph F. Smith, December 16, 1903, Smoot Papers; Reed Smoot to Joseph F. Smith, January 4, 1904, Smoot Papers; Reed Smoot to Joseph F. Smith, February 10, 1905, Smoot Papers. Despite Smoot's frequent mention of Proctor's support, the senator from Vermont's unpublished biography is completely silent about any aspect of his behind-the-scenes role during the Smoot hearings. See Chester W. Bowie, "Redfield Proctor: A Biography" (PhD diss., University of Wisconsin, Madison, 1980), 413–492. In an interesting voting twist, Proctor cast only the first of three roll-call votes impacting Smoot on February 20. For unknown reasons, he did not vote on the final resolution that determined Smoot's future and was the only senator to follow this abstention pattern. Congressional Record, 3429–3430.

36. Paul B. Beers, *Pennsylvania Politics Today and Yesterday* (University Park: Pennsylvania State University Press, 1980), 51. Multiple versions of Penrose's colorful phrase have appeared in

print, which was "supposedly said in the Senate where a protest had arisen against seating Reed Smoot . . . [but] not verified in newspapers or accounts of that time." Moreover, a similar phrase, "with variation in the wording" has been attributed to "President Theodore Roosevelt, while he was campaigning in 1902." See Suzy Platt, ed., *Respectfully Quoted: A Dictionary of Quotations* (Barnes and Noble, Inc, 1993), 222; *Reader's Digest*, June 1958, 142. It's unlikely that Roosevelt used the phrase, since he was opposed in 1902 to Smoot coming to the Senate. Also, *Salt Lake Tribune* historian O. N. Malmquist printed this with the caveat, "This delightful sidelight on the Smoot controversy was a frequently told story at the *Tribune* when the author first joined the staff. He could not trace it to any printed source." See O. M. Malmquist, *The First 100 Years: A History of The Salt Lake Tribune 1871–1971* (Salt Lake City: Utah State Historical Society, 1971), 229, 435. Last, on an interesting sidebar, Elder Dallin H. Oaks of the Quorum of Twelve Apostles gave an interview in 2006 as Mitt Romney prepared for his first presidential run; Oaks brought up the Smoot hearings, remarking, "At a critical point a powerful senator said he would vote for Smoot . . . He said: 'In the United States I would rather have a polygamist who doesn't polyg than a monogamist who doesn't monog.'" "Is America ready for a Mormon president? Governor Must Fight Old suspicions on Road to the White House," *Daily Telegraph*, February 12, 2006, 16.

37. "The Sterner Sex," *The American Lawyer* 14 (July 1906): 323. At the General Conference held in April 1907 just days after the vote, Smoot shared the following message about his meetings with "hundreds of leading women of the country," who after speaking with him for "ten or fifteen minutes" about the Church's "beliefs and aims," would say, "Why, Senator Smoot, I signed the petition asking your expulsion from the United States Senate, because I believed the stories published and told against you and the Mormon Church." Conference Report (Salt Lake City: Church of Jesus Christ of Latter-day Saints, April 1907), 29–30.

38. Congressional Record, 3405. The *Salt Lake Tribune* reported that Dubois gave his thirty-minute "impromptu" speech. See "'Big Stick' Saves Smoot from Deserved Exclusion," *Salt Lake Tribune*, February 21, 1907.

39. Article 1, Section 3. All see Congressional Record.

40. Congressional Record, 3414. Republican senator Joseph B. Foraker of Ohio was skeptical of Hansbrough's "higher law" argumentation, stating, "I have understood from the beginning that not the Mormon Church, not Joseph F. Smith, not anybody but only Reed Smoot, was on trial, and that we had in the trial of Reed Smoot to bear in mind not what the Senator from North Dakota said he thought it our duty to be governed by, namely, a higher law, but the Constitution of the United States . . . His duty is at all times governed by his oath of office, which requires him to support and uphold the Constitution of the United States. There is nothing in his oath of office about a higher law . . . There is a great moral question involved and I would think I was violating all the morals of this case if I were to vote in this matter contrary to the requirements of my oath of office . . . This higher law we all appreciate. The Senator from North Dakota is not the only man who thinks of the higher law; we all think of it; but the trouble about following the higher law is that every man writes the higher law to suit himself. [Laughter.] What we are here to follow and to be governed by and to observe—and we violate our oaths of office if we do not do it—is the Constitution of the United States in its requirements."

41. See Sarah Barringer Gordon, *The Mormon Question: Polygamy and Constitutional Conflict in Nineteenth-Century Utah* (Chapel Hill: University of North Carolina Press, 2002), 78–80, 139.

42. Flake, *The Politics of American Religious Identity*, 161–62; "Another Senatorial Victim," *Chicago Daily Tribune*, September 11, 1908, 8.

43. Congressional Record, 3419. In a letter to Joseph F. Smith prior to the start of the Senate hearings, Smoot addressed ways in which he could show his independence from the Church hierarchy. One way was his disinclination to hypothetically attest that he would not vote for Joseph F. Smith to be "Governor of the State" but that "any act in voting to honor you as President of the Church was solely a religious affair." Reed Smoot to Joseph F. Smith, January 9, 1904, Smoot

Papers. In response to this Smoot comment, the LDS First Presidency advised, "You suggest that you might say that you could not vote for [Joseph F. Smith] for a secular office. We do not think you will gain anything by this, as the senators, knowing the strong regard the leaders of the Church have for one another, would hardly believe it." First Presidency to Reed Smoot, January 20, 1904, Smoot Papers.

44. For more on Roberts's case, see Moyer, "Dancing with the Devil," 183–241; Davis Bitton, *The Ritualization of Mormon History and Other Essays* (Urbana: University of Illinois Press, 1994), 150–170. On a parenthetical note, B. H. Roberts, a staunch Democrat, opposed Smoot's continuing to serve as both an apostle and a senator and was frustrated by some of the tactics Smoot's campaign used. Roberts believed these efforts blurred the lines between church and state and obligated Mormon Democrats to vote for Smoot "in order to strengthen" him, and by implication the Church, "with the leaders of the Republican Party at Washington." Responding to this ploy, Roberts stated the following at a Democratic Party gathering: "If the issue in this campaign is to be the vindication of Reed Smoot, then let me say to you that no Democrat owes Reed Smoot any allegiance. I honor Mr. Smoot in his ecclesiastical position, but if his claim to a seat in the United States Senate possesses intrinsic merit he should retain it by reason of that intrinsic merit. If it does not he should be put out. The fact that he has, or claims to have, the power to dominate the political destinies of this State should not be a factor in consideration . . . The Church to which I belong decrees individual political independence to every man in the Church. The distinguished leader of the Church recognizes that fact. I honor him as my leader in spiritual things. Under God any man who pretends to say that that leader favors other [than] separation of Church and State I brand as a liar. No priesthood has the right to dominate the political acts of men in this great free Republic of the West. Stand by your colors as Democrats. Let us have no suggestion of fusion. Peace can only come to Utah through the success of the [Democratic] Party." See "Roberts Denounces Smoot," *New York Times*, August 25, 1906, 4; "Roberts and the Machine," *Salt Lake Herald*, August 25, 1906, 4; Joseph Geisner, "Very Careless in His Utterances," *Sunstone* (December 2011): 15–16.

45. "Thomas Jefferson to Joseph C. Cabell," January 31, 1814, in Philip B. Kurland and Ralph Lerner, eds., *The Founders' Constitution*, University of Chicago and Liberty Fund, http://press-pubs .uchicago.edu/founders/documents/a1_2_2s9.html (accessed 11 February 2021). This Jefferson letter contained his musings on the notion of federalism, and the appropriateness of states, rather than Congress, in adding qualifications to members of Congress over and above what is defined within the Constitution. Jefferson was conflicted by the topic and over time had taken multiple positions on the subject. Ultimately, Jefferson argued that the power of the federal government would encroach upon the Tenth Amendment, which gave power to states on these matters.

46. Congressional Record, 3410. Over five consecutive pages in the Congressional Record, Burrows excerpted numerous quotations from Smoot hearings testimony. This includes one section where he silently omitted the following italicized testimony without attribution, which would have provided a more sympathetic view of Angus M. Cannon's testimony:

> THE CHAIRMAN: Since that time you have cohabited with these wives?
> MR. CANNON: It has been my practice, if I can not live the law as the Lord gives me, I come as near to it as my mortal frailty will enable me to do.
> THE CHAIRMAN: Then, in cohabiting with these wives since the manifesto, you have violated the law of God, have you not?
> MR. CANNON: I know I can not live without violating His laws.
> THE CHAIRMAN: Answer that question whether you have violated, that particular law we are talking about.
> MR. CANNON: I presume I did.

See Smoot Hearings 1:780–86; Congressional Record, 3423.

47. "Senator Smoot's Case," *New York Times*, June 5, 1906, 8. In a subsequent editorial, the *Times* argued that Congress was fully aware of Utah's religious demographics when it was admitted into the Union and could "have taken the ground that Utah should not be admitted to Statehood until the Mormons were statistically shown to be outnumbered, and were sure to be outvoted by the Gentiles." "The Case of Utah," *New York Times*, June 12, 1906, 8.

48. Smoot Hearings, 3:483–84.

49. Smoot Hearings, 3:484–85.

50. Beverly Alice Berry, "Methods of Support Used in the Senate Debate on the Seating of Reed Smoot: A Content Analysis" (MA thesis, Brigham Young University, Provo, UT, 1968), 50–52.

51. Leo Lyman, ed., *Candid Insights of a Mormon Apostle: The Diaries of Abraham H. Cannon 1899–1895* (Salt Lake City: Signature Books, 2010), 758. Also see Moyer, "Dancing with the Devil," 139–140.

52. Leo W. Graff Jr., *The Senatorial Career of Fred T. Dubois of Idaho, 1890–1907* (New York: Garland Publishing, 1988), 369. Dubois was upset with the recent "crushing defeat" of his Democratic Party, which he blamed on the influence of the Mormon Church in Idaho, and he vindictively used the Smoot hearings to get payback.

53. Graff, *The Senatorial Career*, 502–504. In a letter dated November 17, 1903, from Dubois to Reverend John L. Leilich, a virulent Mormon opponent who incorrectly alleged that Smoot was a polygamist, Dubois explained, "I myself have burned all the bridges behind me, and will fight this context out to the end, regardless who suffers. I know, to begin with, that it ends my political career." A few months later, Dubois suggested, "I expect the bitter opposition of the Mormon leaders, and . . . while they will destroy me politically, I can be a strong factor in destroying . . . the curse of polygamy." Dubois's biographer critically summarized Dubois's political demise, saying his "sincere devotion to principle" as a "true believer," even when the "sweep of events" had made polygamy a dead issue, "had become twisted fanaticism." Heath explains that Dubois's efforts against Smoot gave his state such a "political black-eye" that it "enraged some Democrats" to work "against him" and "ensure his defeat." See Heath, "The Reed Smoot Hearings," 71–72.

54. See "Election of Borah," *Salt Lake Herald*, January 16, 1907, 2; "Some Senators Selected," *Salt Lake Herald*, January 17, 1907, 1. Dubois was defeated in Idaho "by a vote of fifty-three to eighteen."

55. Moyer, "Dancing with the Devil," 398.

56. "Dubois Attacks President," *New York Times*, December 14, 1906, 7. Dubois quoted from President Buchanan's First Annual Message, President Grant's Third and Seventh Annual Messages, President Hayes's Third and Fourth Annual Messages, President Garfield's Inaugural Message, President Arthur's First, Third, and Fourth Annual Messages, President Cleveland's First and Fourth Annual Messages, and President Harrison's Second and Third Annual Messages. See Congressional Record, 333–335.

57. Congressional Record, 335. During his plenary remarks, Dubois expanded, "For the first time the Mormon question has been made a political one. The President of the United States is an open friend of the Senator from Utah. You all know it. The country knows it. The President wants him seated. You Republicans join with the President in wanting the Mormon vote. You have got it. They are with you; you have every one of them, my friends on the Republican side of the Chamber. But it has cost you the moral support of the Christian women and men of the United States. I hardly think you can afford to pay the price for this temporary political advantage." Congressional Record, 3408. Also see Flake, *The Politics of American Religious Identity*, 146.

58. Theodore Roosevelt's Sixth Annual Message, December 3, 1906. Text can be found online at John Woolley and Gerhard, eds., the American Presidency Project, http://www.presidency.ucsb.edu/ws/index.php?pid=29547#axzz1lqt50mXl (accessed 11 February 2021). A year prior to Dubois's 1906 speech, Smoot reported to Church leaders in Salt Lake that when he met with Roosevelt at his office, Dubois "called" on the President, and Smoot was "pleased to note

they were not very cordial." Smoot then editorialized, "I don't believe the President has much respect for him." Reed Smoot to Joseph F. Smith, December 12, 1905, Smoot Papers. Also, Burrows quoted these passages from Roosevelt's annual message during in his plenary speech as a way to rebut the argument made numerous times by Smoot supporters that polygamy is dying out: "The President of the United States, who never moves by indirection or strikes an aimless blow, is evidently not in accord with the opinion that polygamy is dying out." Congressional Record, 3426.

59. Jean Bickmore White, ed., *Church, State, and Politics: The Diaries of John Henry Smith* (Salt Lake City: Signature Books, Inc, 1990), 505. Also see Moyer, "Dancing with the Devil," 281.

60. "Satisfied With His Vindication," *Salt Lake Herald*, March 8, 1907, 10.

61. Milton R. Merrill, "Theodore Roosevelt and Reed Smoot," *Western Political Quarterly* 4 (September 1951): 440–453; Moyer, "Dancing with the Devil," 404–475. Notably, Roosevelt was opposed to the election of an apostle to the Senate and spoke out publicly against Smoot. See Moyer, "Dancing with the Devil," 293–296. In addition, the adversarial Utah newspaper, the *Salt Lake Tribune*, edited by the Frank J. Cannon, began to mock the emerging alliance between Smoot and Roosevelt, by referring to Smoot as the "Little Stick," playing off the president's iconic "Big Stick" symbolism. See "Smoot's Little Stick," *Salt Lake Tribune*, March 2, 1907; "That National Tithe," *Salt Lake Tribune*, March 3, 1907.

62. Roosevelt's endorsement of Smoot was revealed in a personal letter to Senator Knox, who had recently given a Senate speech on the legal and constitutional framework as to why Smoot should remain in the Senate. "Knox Defends Smoot's Seat," *Los Angeles Times*, February 15, 1907, 14; "Knox Defends Reed Smoot," *Chicago Daily Tribune*, February 15, 1907, 7; "Smoot Is Assured of Victory To-day," *New York Times*, February 20, 1907, 5; "Smoot Defends the Church and Himself," *Salt Lake Herald*, February 20, 1907, 1; "President Praised Knox," *New York Times*, February 19, 1907, 1. In his 2009 University of Utah dissertation, historian Jonathan H. Moyer asserts that Roosevelt's support of Smoot during the Senate hearings was a tactic within a larger strategy that he and other "canny" GOP leaders used to broaden the party's appeal to geographic, religious, and ethnic groups previously considered outcasts. See Moyer, "Dancing with the Devil," 405. Buttressing Moyer's thesis was an op-ed published in 1907 by the Ogden Standard: "[GOP] party leaders could not forget that if they parted with the Mormon apostle, Utah would doubtless be lost to the Republican party for years to come. There is now nothing to prevent it from voting the straight Republican ticket for a generation or more." "Eastern Opinion" *Ogden Standard*, March 2, 1907, 4.

63. "RIIS Misled President, Says a Senator's Wife," *New York Times*, December 19, 1906, 10. On the day of the final Smoot vote, Edna Dubois was invited by her husband to sit in the "Senators reserved gallery." Also sitting in this reserved section were "Rev. Dr. W. N. Paden, pastor of the First Presbyterian church of Salt Lake; Mrs. Margaret D. Yeelds of the National W.C.T.U., Mrs. Frederick Schoff and the representatives of the Women's organizations." "'Big Stick' Saves Smoot from Deserved Exclusion," *Salt Lake Tribune*, February 21, 1907.

64. Congressional Record, 3406–3407; Smoot Hearings, 1:501–505. Despite the bishop's actual testimony to the contrary, Senators Hopkins, Beveridge, and Sutherland each contended that Bishop Harmer was married to Ellen Anderson after the manifesto. Harmer had married two women prior to the manifesto but had fathered two children out of wedlock with Anderson. At the time of this testimony, Harmer was not financially supporting either Anderson or the children, even though they lived on the same square of land as Ida, one of his first two wives.

65. Congressional Record, 3409. Dubois was referring to the testimony of L. E. Abbott, a resident of Farmington, Utah, where Taylor's two post-manifesto wives resided. Abbott conjectured that half-sisters Rhoda Welling (born November 19, 1880) and Eliza Roxie Welling (born July 18, 1880) were "22 to 24 years of age, although I am not absolutely sure." Smoot Hearings, 1:1052. According to the LDS Church's www.FamilySearch.com (as of 11 February 2021), Abbott was cor-

rect: these half-sisters were age twenty-three at the time of Abbott's testimony, and Taylor married both on August 29, 1901.

66. John W. Taylor to Joseph F. Smith, March 16, 1904, Smoot Papers; Joseph F. Smith to Reed Smoot, March 20, 1904, Smoot Papers; Francis M. Lyman to George Teasdale, July 9, 1904, Smoot Papers. For more on the Taylor imbroglio, see Heath, "The Reed Smoot Hearings," 30–37, 44, 48–50, 56–59, 68–70. In April 1906, Taylor and fellow apostle Matthias F. Cowley's submitted their resignations to the Quorum of Twelve Apostles, which was accepted but not made public. Smoot was allowed to mention the resignations, but Burrows and Dubois were skeptical that it was "only a ruse to take the heat off Smoot." Permission was "promptly" granted to Smoot to show the letters only to "trusted friends." Heath, "The Reed Smoot Hearings," 68–71. Burrows and Dubois remained spurious, and used the pages of the Majority Report to express dismay: "The dropping of Taylor and Cowley from the quorum of the twelve apostles was so evidently done for popular effect that the act merits no consideration whatever, except as an admission by the first presidency and twelve apostles that Apostles Taylor and Cowley have each taken one or more plural wives since the manifesto." Smoot Hearing, 3:477. Last, during his remarks at the Smoot debate, Dubois stretched the truth by claiming, "They resigned as apostles one week before the vote was taken on the Smoot case in the committee." Congressional Record, 3408.

67. Congressional Record, 2939. This was a common political defense made by Smoot advocates. In the minority report written in support of the Utah senator, five senators including Knox wrote the following, "[Smoot] has been noted from early manhood for his opposition to plural marriages, and probably did as much as any other member of the Mormon Church to bring about the prohibition of further plural marriages." Smoot Hearings, 4:500. Also, when Senator Hopkins spoke in favor of Smoot on January 11, 1907, he remarked similar sentiments: "[Smoot] stands for the sacred things in the church and against polygamy and all the kindred vices connected with that loathsome practice. In his position as a member of the church, and as an apostle and preacher of the doctrines of the church, he has done more to stamp out this foul blot upon the civilization of Utah and the other Territories where polygamy has been practiced [more] than any thousand men outside of the church . . . The whole life of Senator Smoot is a protest against polygamy. Every act that he has engaged in, either in the church or outside of it, is a condemnation of it." Congressional Record, 938, 945. Last, Senator Beveridge made a similar defense in his floor speech, asserting, "Reed Smoot has been the leader of the younger, wiser, and more modern element of the church that opposes this [i.e., polygamy] insult to marriage." Congressional Record, 3409.

68. Congressional Record, 3409.

69. "Smoot Is Victor in 4 Year Fight," *Chicago Daily Tribune*, February 21, 1907, 6; "Senator Smoot Keeps His Seat," *Hartford Courant*, February 21, 1907, 13.

70. Congressional Record, 3408. "Senate Refuses to Oust Smoot," *New York Times*, February 21, 1907, 5.

71. "Senator Smoot Keeps His Seat," *Hartford Courant*, February 21, 1907, 13.

72. Moyer, "Dancing with the Devil," 343.

73. "Beveridge's Stirring Speech for Smoot," *Deseret Evening News*, March 9, 1907, 13.

74. Jonah Goldberg, *Liberal Fascism: The Secret History of the American Left, from Mussolini to the Politics of Meaning* (New York, Doubleday, 2007), 91.

75. Albert Beveridge to Charles E. Coffin, March 24, 1904 as qtd. in Moyer, "Dancing with the Devil," 398. Beveridge ascribed political motives to Chairman Burrows, saying he was "up for re-election" and is "playing to the galleries." On another occasion, Beveridge called Burrows "a damn liar." Carl Badger, Journal, March 22, 1904, in Rodney J. Badger ed., *Liahona and Iron Rod: A Biography of Carl A. Badger and Rosalia Jenkins Badger* (Bountiful, UT: Family History Publishers, 1985), 256–257.

76. Smoot made this statement thirty-three years later at General Conference. Conference Report (Salt Lake City: Church of Jesus Christ of Latter-day Saints, April 1937), 106 (hereafter,

Conference Report). Also, Carl Badger noted in his diary some of the off-the-record dynamics at the Smoot hearings with the following anecdote: "Someone asked Senator Hoar why he asked the questions of the witnesses. 'To keep Beveridge from joining the Mormon Church,' he answered." Carl Badger, Journal, March 15, 1904, in J. Badger, *Liahona and Iron Rod*, 212. Congressional Record, 3409, 3412.

77. Grant famously joked to a group of "spellbound" students, "Yes, I have two wives, and the only reason I haven't got another is because the Government won't let me. (More laughter and applause). That is, if she would consent." Ironically, Grant's quip was a minor sidebar in a lecture in which he talked about patriotism and loyalty to country and school in the context of fundraising for the University of Utah and his recent mission to Japan. Additionally, he counseled students to never give up and buttressed this advice with a personal story from 1893 when he encountered severe financial difficulties. See "Heber J. Grant Is to Be Arrested," *Ogden Standard*, November 11, 1903, 8; "Salt Lake News," *Ogden Standard*, November 5, 1903, 8; "Apostle Grant Gives Up $1,150," *Salt Lake Herald*, November 5, 1903, 5.

78. "Mormon Apostle Eludes Officers," *Ogden Standard*, November 11, 1903, 6; "Heber J. Grant Is Out of Sight," *Ogden Standard*, November 12, 1903, 4; Reed Smoot to Joseph F. Smith, January 8, 1904, Smoot Papers. Still under warrant for arrest, Grant returned from Europe to Utah to be with his family in December 1906. "Grant Will Be Here to Answer," *Deseret Evening News*, December 28, 1906, 2; White, *Church, State, and Politics: The Diaries of John Henry Smith*, 577. After a short stint in Utah, Grant was reported to have traveled back East for business purposes. Also, his diary reveals he was in Juárez, Mexico, in late January 1907. By March 1907, all charges against him had been dismissed. See "Heber J. Grant Case Dismissed," *Deseret Evening News*, March 4, 1907, 3; Privately Published, *The Diaries of Heber J. Grant, 1880–1945*, abridged (Salt Lake City: Utah, 2010), 285.

79. At this speech given at Mutual Improvement Association (M. I. A.) conference, Grant explained that he had read Beveridge's book while in England: it "did me a great deal of good, and put a good many ideas into my head," and Beveridge "is capable of saying many things that I think are inspiring to the youth of Zion." See "Temperance—Inspirations To Progress," *Improvement Era*, 1908, vol. 11, August 1908, No. 10. Grant also retold the story with quotations at the 1919, 1922, and 1927 General Conferences. See Conference Report (April 1919), 27–28; Conference Report (October 1922), 9; Conference Report (April 1927), 9. Other Church leaders speaking in the General Conference quoted Beveridge's book or quoted President Grant quoting Beveridge, including Rudger Clawson in 1934 Conference Report (April 1934), 51; Reed Smoot in 1937 Conference Report (April 1937), 104–106; LeGrand Richards in 1946 and 1955 Conference Report (April 1946), 48, and Conference Report (April 1955), 123; and Marion G. Romney in 1948 Conference Report (April 1948), 77. President Hugh B. Brown, one of Grant's missionaries in Europe, mentioned in his memoirs that as a young man he "carefully [read] the works of Albert J. Beveridge." See Edwin B. Firmage, ed., *An Abundant Life: The Memoirs of Hugh B. Brown* (Salt Lake City: Signature Books, 1999), 64.

80. Albert J. Beveridge, *The Young Man and the World* (New York: D. Appleton and Company, 1906), 246–277.

81. Reed Smoot to Joseph F. Smith, February 5, 1904, Smoot Papers.

82. James E. Talmage Journal, January 20, 1905, James E. Talmage Collection, L. Tom Perry Special Collections, Harold B. Lee Library, Brigham Young University, Provo, UT. Future LDS apostle and scripture scholar James E. Talmage was summoned to Washington to provide expert testimony on Church doctrine. He was also in the committee room when Smoot was called as a witness. He thought, "Bro. Smoot did his case much good by his own testimony" but was underwhelmed by his grasp of doctrinal concepts.

83. Congressional Record, 3408–3409.

84. Louis Begley, *Why the Dreyfus Affair Matters* (New Haven, CT: Yale University Press, 2010), xi–xiv, 2. Of interest, in Begley's preface to his book written in January 2009, he favorably compares

the current detainees housed in the US military prison Guantanamo Bay to Dreyfus, conjecturing that "some . . . detainees may be as innocent as Dreyfus some surely are not." B. H. Roberts was similarly tabbed "the Dreyfus of American" in 1900 when he was blocked from taking his seat. See Theodore W. Curtis, "Roberts: The Dreyfus of America," *Arena* 23 (February 1900) 120–131; David Brudnoy, "Of Sinners and Saints: Theodore Schroeder, Brigham Roberts, and Reed Smoot," *Journal of Church and State* 14 (Spring 1972), 269; Jonathan H. Moyer, "Dancing with the Devil," 204.

85. Piers Paul Read, *The Dreyfus Affair: The Scandal That Tore France in Two* (New York: Bloomsbury Press, 2012), 1–4.

86. Congressional Record, 3408.

87. Congressional Record, 3409. Beveridge partially based this conclusion on his personal experience: "Since last session I have personally spoken to not less than 300 men and women all over the country on this subject. Every one of them thought the Utah Senator a polygamist, and was therefore against him. And nearly all of them when told the truth frankly changed their attitude." The charge of treason was related to the alleged oaths Smoot had taken in the temple, which were "inconsistent with his oath as Senator; because he owes a higher allegiance to his church than to his country." Congressional Record, 3411.

88. Theodore Herzl, *A Jewish State: An Attempt at a Modern Solution to the Jewish State* (New York: Federation of American Zionists, 1917).

89. Congressional Record, 3415.

90. Congressional Record, 3417.

91. For scholarship on the history between the LDS and RLDS churches, see Valeen Tippetts Avery, *From Mission to Madness* (Urbana: University of Illinois Press, 1998); Linda King Newell, "Cousins in Conflict: Joseph Smith III and Joseph F. Smith," *John Whitmer Historical Association Journal* 9 (1989), 3–16; Roger D. Launius, *Joseph Smith III: Pragmatic Prophet* (Urbana: University of Illinois Press, 1988).

92. The adverse committee vote for Smoot was held on June 1, 1906. After voting was completed, Smoot confidently telegrammed home to President Smith, "Do not allow Committee on Privileges and Elections report worry you. I am satisfied I will be successful." In reply, Smith reassuringly replied, "The old saying, better late than never, is applicable in this case, for the press dispatch reporting the action of the committee yesterday was very disappointing indeed, and we concluded that Senator Dolliver had changed front and gone over to your opponents. However we had already commended to get over the first feelings of disappointment caused by the report, and began to feel this morning that a victory won on the floor of the Senate would be very much preferable, in view of the notoriety your case has aroused through the nation, to one achieved in the committee room; and this feeling is now strengthened by the receipt of your telegram expressing yourself satisfied that you will yet be successful. We look for nothing short of success." Joseph F. Smith to Reed Smoot, June 2, 1906, Smoot Papers.

93. Congressional Record, 3417.

94. Congressional Record, 3418. Two Republican Senators, Dolliver and Chauncey M. Depew of New York, voted against Smoot in committee but switched their votes on the final vote. Had "these two men . . . voted in the committee as they on the floor today the question would have never come to the Senate for settlement." "Senate Refuses to Oust Smoot" *New York Times*, February 21, 1907, 5.

95. *The Salt Lake Tribune* editorialized against Dolliver's change of position, writing that only after his reelection was Dolliver comfortable to "gratify the wishes of the White House." See "Dolliver's Motives," *Salt Lake Tribune*, February 23, 1907.

96. Congressional Record, 3409, 3412. Beveridge's pejorative terms here contradict Smoot's assessment that Beveridge was spiritually curious about Mormonism. Twelve years later, in 1920, Smoot told the following story at October Conference, "Yesterday I asked Hon. Albert J. Beveridge . . . to attend the afternoon session of our conference. . . . He asked when the 'Mormon'

people began to build this magnificent structure. I told him the erection of the building was begun in the year 1853, long before there was a railroad in this country, and at a time when the people had very little of this world's goods. I called his attention to the fact that the building of the temple was an evidence of the faithfulness and loyalty of the people to the work established by God in this dispensation ... Said he, 'What do they use the temple for?' I told him of the sacred ordinances of baptism for the dead; I told him of the eternal marriage covenant, and that our people believed in both, and the vicarious work that was preached by the apostles of old was attended to in our temples. He said, 'What do you mean by baptism for the dead?' Said I, 'Senator Beveridge, we mean this, that we are carrying out the same instructions in regard to this wonderful principle as taught in the days of the Savior and his ancient apostles.' ... And he said, 'That is wonderful. Are there any other churches in all the world today that preach and practice it?' 'No.' 'Well, tell me the operation.' I said, 'Suppose my great-grandfather had lived at a time (which he did) before the gospel, as revealed in this dispensation, had ever been preached, or a testimony of an elder of the Church had ever been heard; some relative can be baptized for him.'" See Conference Report (Salt Lake City: Church of Jesus Christ of Latter-day Saints, October 1937), 135.

97. Congressional Record, 3412. For background on these nativistic movements, see Humphrey Joseph Desmond, *The Know-Nothing Party* (Washington, DC: New Century Press, 1905); Humphrey Joseph Desmond, *The A.P.A. Movement* (Washington, DC: New Century Press, 1912); Tyler Anbinder, *Nativism and Slavery: The Northern Know Nothings and the Politics of the 1850s* (New York: Oxford University Press, 1992); Sean Wilentz, *The Rise of American Democracy* (New York: W. W. Norton and Company, 2005), 677–688. Senator Dolliver of Iowa spoke in support of Smoot though acquitted "the opponents of Senator Smoot of any purpose to violate the traditions of religious liberty"; "but," he said, "I could not be one of those who are willing to bring upon him and his little family the humiliation and contempt which would necessarily follow his expulsion from the Senate of the United States without taking the risk which I dare not assume, of laying upon a fellow-man a part, at least, of these burdens which, in other lands and in other ages, have been found too grievous to be borne." Congressional Record, 3418.

98. Anbinder, *Nativism and Slavery*, 112–117. Scholar David Brion Davis has argued that during the nineteenth century, nativist writers used similar rhetorical tactics to expose and attack Mormonism, Masonry, and Catholicism. Davis explained that nativists constructed sensational images of "an American conspiracy" that was "almost indistinguishable" for all three groups. See David Brion Davis, "Some Themes of Counter-subversion: An Analysis of Anti-Masonic, Anti-Catholic, and Anti-Mormon Literature," *Mississippi Valley Historical Review* 47, no. 2 (September 1960), 206–207. Beveridge also noted this rhetorical dynamic used by nativists against other religious groups, saying, "I have on my desk the books that recite formal complaints upon which it was sought to inflame the people, and you could lay them side by side with this particular charge made here now [against Smoot] and not tell the difference." Congressional Record, 3412.

99. Desmond, *A.P.A. Movement*, 39.

100. Congressional Record, 3409–3410. The *Deseret Evening News* inaccurately reported the total expenditure to the government for travel, stenographers, and printing between $50,000 and $75,000. "After Four Years' Delay," *Deseret Evening News*, February 20, 1907, 1; "Senator Smoot to Be Reimbursed for Expenses," *Deseret Evening News*, March 2, 1907, 1.

101. "Smoot Has His Expenses," *Salt Lake Herald*, March 3, 1907, 10; "Wanted to Dip into Treasury," *Deseret Evening News*, March 8, 1907, 5. A similar amendment to reimburse Smoot's opponents for their attorney fees was proposed and rejected. Senator Dubois led this effort as one of his last acts in Congress, explaining that "these expenses had been borne by several ministerial associations, and by women's clubs and associations." Additionally, according to a *Salt Lake Herald* report, many people believed that the Church, rather than Smoot, had spent a "great

deal of church money . . . on the Smoot cause." See "Smoot's Victor Pleases," *Salt Lake Herald*, February 23, 1907, 5.

102. "Beveridge's Stirring Speech For Smoot," *Deseret Evening News*, March 9, 1907, 13. Of interest, Beveridge violated his own guidance contained in his book *The Young Man and the World* to preachers that they limit their sermons to "thirty minutes," though twenty "minutes is long enough." This advice was given because "this is America and everybody is in a hurry." However, Beveridge gave himself an out by saying his counsel applied to "all great orators except" politicians, "who necessarily must cover all the 'issues.' The political speaker is sorry enough that this is true—but there is no help for it; 'the questions of the day' must all be answered. But you, Mr. Preacher, need not be so encyclopedic; and you ought to be illuminating and uplifting on one subject in half an hour—and no longer. That light is brightest which is condensed." Beveridge, *The Young Man and the World*, 272–274.

103. James Wilford Garner, "The Case of Senator Smoot and the Mormon Church," *North American Review* 184, no. 606 (January 4, 1907): 46–58.

104. Congressional Record, 3410.

105. James Wilford Garner, "The Case of Senator Smoot and the Mormon Church," *North American Review* 184, no. 606 (January 4, 1907): 56–58.

106. Congressional Record, 3429–30. Eight senators voted for the "two-thirds" requirement but voted against Smoot keeping his seat.

107. Congressional Record, 3421.

108. Congressional Record, 3427.

109. "Senator Burrows Lost Hard Fight" *Salt Lake Tribune*, February 25, 1907.

110. Congressional Record, 3428.

111. "Senator Smoot Keeps His Seat," *Hartford Courant*, February 21, 1907, 13.

112. "Smoot Is 'Sustained' after Long Struggle," *Salt Lake Herald*, February 21, 1907, 1; Carl Badger to Rose Badger, February 31, 1904, in Rodney J. Badger, *Liahona and Iron Rod*, 369.

113. "Smoot Is Victor in 4 Year Fight," *Chicago Daily Tribune*, February 21, 1907, 6.

114. "Burrows Has Not Congratulated Smoot," *Salt Lake Tribune*, March 3, 1907.

115. "Seating of Smoot Is Shame of the Nation," *Salt Lake Tribune*, March 20, 1907. Iliff was speaking at a Methodist mission convention and was peeved that "the greatest part of that shame rests on the four Senators, Dolliver, Beveridge, Foraker, and Dillingham who, though members of the Methodist church, gave their votes in support of the Mormon apostle."

116. "Tells of the Mormons," *Los Angeles Times*, February 26, 1907, II-7.

117. "The Meaning of the Vote," *Deseret Evening News*, February 21, 1907, 4.

118. "A Prophecy Fulfilled," *Deseret Evening News*, February 23, 1907, 4. Historian Craig Foster has recently argued against the authenticity of the so-called White Horse prophecy. This prophecy, purportedly spoken by Church founder Joseph Smith, avers that the day would come "when the destiny of the nation will hang by a single thread. At this critical juncture, this people will step forth and save it from the threatened destruction." See Craig L. Foster, *A Different God? Mitt Romney, the Religious Right and the Mormon Question* (Salt Lake City: Greg Kofford Books, 2008), 49–60.

119. "Joseph F. Smith Talks of Smoot," *Salt Lake Herald*, April 1, 1907, 10.

120. "Reception to Senator Smoot," *Ogden Standard*, March 14, 1907, 2.

121. "Senator's Speech to His Townsman," *Deseret News*, March 9, 1907, 5.

122. For a sage analysis of public perception surrounding Mitt Romney's presidential runs in 2008 and 2012, see J. B. Haws, *The Mormon Image in the American Mind: Fifty Years of Public Perception* (New York: Oxford University Press, 2013), 207–281.

123. Kathleen Flake, "Mr. Smoot Goes to Washington: The Politics of American Religious Identity, 1900–1920" (PhD diss., University of Chicago, 2000), 227. For information on the similarities between Romney and Smoot and the fraying of the Mormon Question agreement, see Brooke

Adams, "Mormon Apostle Paved the Way for LDS Candidates" *Salt Lake Tribune*, December 8, 1907, C1, C3; Michael Harold Paulos, "Meet the Original Mitt Romney," Realclearpolitics.com, March 15, 2012, http://www.realclearreligion.org/articles/2012/03/15/meet_the_original_mitt _romney_106447.html (accessed 11 February 2021); Michael Harold Paulos, review of Craig L. Foster, *A Different God?* and Newell G. Bringhurst and Craig L. Foster, "The Mormon Quest for the Presidency," *Journal of Mormon History* 36, no. 1 (Winter 2010): 243–258.

124. J. David Pulsipher, "Prepared to Abide the Penalty: Latter-day Saints and Civil Disobedience," *Journal of Mormon History* 39, no. 3 (Summer 2013): 131–162.

125. Heath, "Reed Smoot: First Modern Mormon."

3

Antipolygamy, the Constitution, and the Smoot Hearings

Byron W. Daynes and Kathryn M. Daynes

Although the Smoot hearings did not greatly affect the patterns of proposed constitutional amendments against polygamy, the numbers and timing of these amendments do reflect, in a general way, national antipolygamy attitudes. Several trends prepared the ground for the proposed amendments and the increasingly harsh legislation against polygamy. In the wake of the Civil War, women, denied the vote, turned to political action through a variety of organizations. Many of these were rooted in various Protestant home missionary societies. The most prominent was the nondenominational Women's Christian Temperance Union (WCTU). Organized in 1873, the WCTU not only promoted temperance but also social purity, which meant protection of the ideal Christian home in which the mother was the moral authority. To women in these organizations, polygamy was the antithesis of the social purity they sought to impose through political action.

Important to incorporating these organizations into the antipolygamy movement was the Salt Lake Ladies' Anti-Polygamy Society. Former Mormon and non-Mormon women were galvanized by the tale of Carrie Owens, a Mormon convert who promised to marry John Horne Miles. When she learned he was also betrothed to two other women, she hesitated but reluctantly married Miles on condition that she be the first wife. Learning that another woman was considered the first wife, she left the marriage, finding sympathy with non-Mormon women who found polygamy abhorrent. The Carrie Owens affair prompted the women of Salt Lake to organize in 1878. They changed the name of their organization in

DOI: 10.7330/9781646421176.c003

1880 to the Woman's National Anti-Polygamy Society to reflect its growth, with chapters around the country.[1]

Proliferation of these women's groups was augmented by various religious groups also concerned with the social purity of the nation. Deep concerns had surfaced regarding marriage and divorce in the postbellum period. The marriage question involved not only polygamy but also free love, fertility, contraception, the status of women, and divorce. In the wake of the American Revolution, judicial decisions had weakened public regulation of marriage and expanded the legal freedom to marry. But in the second half of the nineteenth century, the divorce rate was rising—albeit at levels much lower than at present—and was higher in the United States than in Europe, creating concern about challenges to traditional lifelong marriage. In addition to proposed constitutional amendments giving the federal government more control over marriage and divorce were eleven proposed amendments before 1924 devoted solely to providing Congress the power to establish laws regarding divorce.[2] The increasing numbers of divorces and Mormons openly flouting the long-held value of monogamy prompted a retreat from earlier marital freedom at the state level.[3] Such concerns meshed with Republican moral reform, of which antislavery had been only part. Polygamy was the unfinished business of "those twin relics of barbarism—Polygamy, and Slavery" mentioned in the 1856 Republican Party platform.[4]

Heightened concern about marriage and divorce in America prompted the proposal of 114 constitutional amendments from 1871 to 1924. The first amendment ever proposed regarding marriage was in 1871; it prohibited interracial marriages. The fifty-five antipolygamy amendments were proposed between 1879 and 1924. Most of the other 114 proposed amendments increased Congress's power to pass legislation regarding marriage or divorce or both. All of these proposed amendments increasing Congress's jurisdiction over marriage in the states would have necessarily included power to make laws regarding polygamy, even when polygamy was not specifically mentioned.[5]

Among the fifty-five proposed amendments concerned solely with polygamy, some simply prohibited polygamy altogether, others gave Congress power to make laws regarding polygamy, while others limited polygamists' rights. A few, however, went beyond that. In 1899 Congressman Joseph Baltzell Showalter (R-PA) proposed an amendment incorporating the language that polygamy "shall be treated as a crime against the peace and dignity of this Republic." The next year he again proposed amendments prohibiting polygamy but which now included the reason that it was "condemned by the law of Christ governing the marriage relation."[6] In arguing for his proposed amendment to prohibit polygamy, Senator Joseph Dolph (R-OR) contended: "The true theory of marriage is that it is not only a contract between the man and the woman, but is also a contract between them and the state, by which they undertake to perform the duties growing out of the marital

FIGURE 3.1. "Smoot—'Well. I Guess It's Me to the Woods Now.'" Cartoonist Alan L. Lovey captures here the indignation that many American women felt toward Reed Smoot's election and his presence in the US Senate. *Salt Lake Herald*, March 3, 1904. Photo courtesy of the Church History Library collection.

relation to the state, and upon this theory the contract can only be lawfully entered into or annulled with the consent of the state."[7] These explicit statements reflect both the religious and political cultural values of most Americans at that time.

Some policy makers saw polygamy as an "abomination in a Christian country" that had to be destroyed for the sake of the reputation of the standards and ideals of the nation.[8] Others saw Mormon polygamy as a source of "national embarrassment" and a "political threat to the integrity of the United States."[9] The preamble to House Joint Resolution 50, introduced by Congressman William Rosecrans (D-CA) in 1883, described polygamy as being a "barbaric practice," needing to be banned so it would not cause injury to our "liberties, interests, and good name of the whole people."[10] Still others saw plural marriage as "anti-American" and incompatible with "our civilization." Francis Lieber, an advisor to President Lincoln, argued that "monogamic marriage . . . is one of the preexisting conditions of our existence as civilized white men."[11] Others were concerned that the idea of polygamy might spread to other territories and other states. Senator Dolph suggested in 1888 that the

Mormon Church has been allowed until recently to violate the laws of the land, to defy the power of the Government with impunity, so that polygamy has grown to alarming proportions, is firmly established in the Territory of Utah, and has sent its roots into the surrounding Territories to poison the social life of other inchoate States and to threaten them with the ultimate domination of the political power in its interests.[12]

Nevertheless, Mormons claimed that the First Amendment protected their plural marriages. That claim was undercut by the *Reynolds* decision announced in January 1879. The Supreme Court concluded: "Laws are made for the government of actions, and while they cannot interfere with mere religious belief and opinions, they may with practices."[13] With heightened concern about marriage and reform organizations in place, the *Reynolds* decision signaled the beginning of concerted and increasingly harsh laws to stamp out polygamy. In his message to Congress in December 1879, President Hayes urged that means be found to both prevent and punish polygamy in Utah, a territory with sufficient population to be admitted as a state. Nine days later, on December 10, the first antipolygamy constitutional amendment was proposed, declaring that "polygamy shall not exist within the limits of the United States" and giving Congress power to enforce this. It was proposed by none other than Julius Caesar Burrows, then a congressman from Michigan but a quarter of a century later chair of the Senate Committee on Privileges and Elections that held hearings on Reed Smoot.[14]

Michigan was active in opposing polygamy. The Michigan legislature had passed resolutions favoring the abolition of polygamy as a condition for admitting Utah as a state, which Burrows then submitted to the House five days after he proposed the first antipolygamy constitutional amendment in 1879. The same day, Burrows's colleague from Michigan, Edwin Willits (R-MI), proposed two bills in the House dealing with polygamy. Not until January 12 the following year was the first petition from the Women's Anti-Polygamy Society of Utah presented to the House. Tellingly, it asked, not that polygamy be abolished but rather that LDS Church leader George Q. Cannon be expelled from the House for violating the laws on polygamy, one indication of the centrality of political power in antipolygamy movements in Utah.[15]

Congress greatly strengthened the 1862 Morrill Anti-Bigamy Act in the 1882 Edmunds Act by providing for the punishment of unlawful cohabitation, not only polygamy; revoking polygamists' right to vote or hold political office; and making those who believed in polygamy ineligible for jury duty in polygamy cases. The judicial crusade was effective in sending hundreds to prison and others into hiding in Utah and other territories. It did not, however, change the Church's policy on plural marriage. The Edmunds-Tucker Act, passed in 1887, thus sought to punish the Church itself, not only its polygamous adherents. Among its provisions, this act annulled the incorporation of the Church of Jesus Christ of Latter-day Saints and provided the process for escheating its property above the value of $50,000. Moreover, the act changed family law in the territories, mandating that a record of all marriages be filed in the appropriate court. Such a provision could only apply to the territories, where Congress had jurisdiction, because states had always regulated marriage and divorce within their own boundaries.

Congress had been flooded with petitions against polygamy in the wake of the *Reynolds* decision, and public opinion was aroused again in 1882. Two antipolygamy amendments were proposed that year, one before the Edmunds Act was introduced and the other as that act made its way through Congress. Both prohibited polygamy as well as voting or office holding by any polygamist. But with prosecutions under the Edmunds Act, signed on March 22, 1882, off to a slow start, two additional amendments were proposed in December 1883. By 1886, with the Edmunds Act effective in putting many polygamists behind bars but not in eliminating polygamy, a number of bills and four antipolygamy amendments were proposed. That year marked the first amendment introduced in the Senate, proposed by Shelby Cullom (R-IL), who had sponsored a bill in 1870 in the House giving the federal government exclusive control over prosecution of polygamy cases.

Another of the amendments in 1886 was proposed by the House Judiciary Committee after considering two amendments referred to the committee. Accepting *Reynolds* as a justification for prohibiting polygamy, the committee offered additional rationale. First, Franklin S. Richards had testified before the committee that some Mormons believed entering plural marriage was mandatory to attain exaltation while others did not.[16] The committee report interpreted this testimony to mean that plural marriage was "not commanded, but was allowed by God." If it was not commanded, stated the report, then its prohibition would not invade anyone's conscience. Second, there could not be one law permitting Mormons to practice polygamy and one prohibiting others from doing so because that "would create the supremacy of this one system of religion over the civil authority of the Government," in effect establishing a religion. Third, polygamy is "an offense against the order and best interest of society," a wrong to women but more especially to children born in "partial bastardy" who had not given consent to their "unhappy birth" into a polygamous family. The committee justified amending the Constitution by indicating that territories should be prepared for statehood but could not enter the Union with an "Asiatic type" marriage; hence, polygamy must be prohibited in the United States.[17] The proposed amendment was superseded by the proposed changes to the Edmunds bill that the same Judiciary Committee, chaired by John Randolph Tucker (D-VA), reported three weeks after its report on the antipolygamy amendment. Nevertheless, the hearings and report on the proposed amendment provided context for the Tucker bill, some of whose provisions were incorporated into the punitive Edmunds-Tucker Act of 1887.[18]

Passage of the Edmunds-Tucker Act claimed attention during the spring of 1887. Nevertheless, in September the report of the Utah Commission, established to enforce the Edmunds Act, recommended that a constitutional amendment be passed,[19] and in December, when Congress began its new session, two amendments were proposed—including another by Senator Cullom—and four more followed in January 1888. One of these was proposed by William Springer (D-IL), chair of the House Committee on Territories, on January 9, the day before the delegate from Utah introduced a bill seeking admission of Utah as a state. Springer explained to Mormons that one objection to Utah statehood was the concern that the clause prohibiting polygamy in the proposed Utah constitution would not be enforced, hence his proposed constitutional amendment giving Congress the power to act if a state did not.[20]

Although David B. Culbertson (D-TX), chair of the House Judiciary Committee, initially gave the Springer amendment his approval, the Judiciary Committee took up the issue and in February proposed its own amendment. For the second time the committee proposed an amendment defining polygamy: "Polygamy shall consist in a marriage relation, by contract or in fact, existing at the same time between one person of either sex and more than one person of the other sex." The amendment reflected the ideas of Joel Bishop, one of the foremost legal writers of the day, that marriage was more than a contract; it was a civil status. This definition did not mesh with the distinction made by Mormons and others between the ceremony—viewed as polygamy—and the subsequent cohabitation. The Judiciary Committee's substitute amendment omitted mention of "polygamous association or cohabitation," language included in the Springer and the previous Judiciary Committee amendments and was thus thought to meet Mormon objections. It did not. The committee's proposed amendment did not come up for a vote in the House.[21] Nor did the two constitutional amendments proposed in December 1889 fare better.

By 1890 action shifted to the Supreme Court. In *Davis v. Beason* the Court upheld the oath Idaho required of voters to attest they did not belong to any group advocating polygamy, thus disfranchising Mormons. Also that year in *Late Corporation v. United States* the Court upheld the Edmunds-Tucker Act's provisions for dissolving the corporation of the Church and escheating its property.[22] Congress echoed these decisions with a number of proposed bills clarifying and expanding these decisions. Among these was the Cullom-Struble bill essentially excluding Mormons in general from the political process. After much prayer, President Wilford Woodruff issued a manifesto in 1890 saying he advised members of the Church to refrain from contracting plural marriages. This declaration signaled a change in the political trajectory, and not until 1892, after bills had been submitted to Congress giving Utah Home Rule (Democratic proposal) or statehood (Republican proposal) was another antipolygamy constitutional amendment introduced.[23] It too languished.

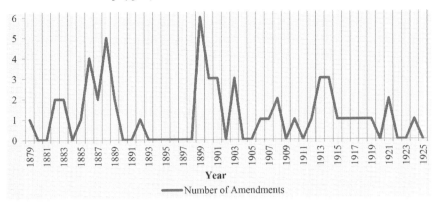

FIGURE 3.2. Number of Amendments per year, 1879–1924. *Source*: Edward Stein, "Past and Present Proposed Amendments to the United States Constitution Regarding Marriage," *Washington University Law Quarterly* 82, no. 3 (Fall 2004): 666–682.

Antipolygamy activism was quiescent as Utah was admitted as a state in 1896 but burst into flame after Utah elected polygamist Brigham H. Roberts to Congress on November 8, 1898. In the lame duck session immediately following, petitions began to pour into the House against Roberts, mainly from religious and women's groups. Fewer than three months after Roberts' election and before he presented himself to take the oath of office, the first constitutional antipolygamy amendment in seven years was proposed in the House. Hearings held the same month titled the amendment "A joint resolution proposing amendments to the constitution disqualifying polygamists for election as Senators and Representatives in Congress, and prohibiting polygamy and polygamous association or cohabitation between the sexes."[24] While other proposed amendments had included provisions barring polygamists from any governmental office, this was the first to specify the offices of representative and senator. In December 1899, at the beginning of the session in which Roberts was to be seated, seven antipolygamy amendments were introduced within two months, the largest number of such amendments in so short a time. Not surprisingly, all these proposed amendments, plus another proposed shortly after the vote in the House to exclude Roberts, prohibited any polygamist from holding any office in the government.[25]

Exclusion of Roberts from his seat in the House was insufficient to dampen antipolygamy flames. Three more constitutional amendments were proposed in 1901, and the House Judiciary Committee held hearings in 1900 and 1903 on two of the amendments introduced in the wake of Roberts's election. The witnesses in these hearings, leaders in religious and women's organizations, conveyed an almost paranoid fear of growth of the LDS Church. Rev. William R. Campbell, clerk of the Presbytery of Utah, compared the number of Mormons in the United States in 1890 with a 1900 figure rounded to the next higher 100,000, yielding a doubling of the Church's membership in a decade, something the Latter-day Saints could only have hoped would have happened. Tunis L. Hamlin, president of the Presbyterian Society of Washington City, claimed that the Mormons gathered "great numbers" of converts—based on comments made by her two maids—while Margaret Dye Ellis, superintendent of a department of the Woman's Christian Temperance Union, claimed that "many sections" of Montana were being colonized by Mormon converts from eastern states. Because Mormonism planned "the union of the church and the state," witnesses asserted that the Church's growth posed a danger to the republic. They also averred that the Mormons were not living up to their promises and that polygamy was expanding. Members of the Judiciary Committee were skeptical of assertions and unsupported evidence presented by the various witnesses, but questions were planted in fertile soil about whether Mormon polygamy and Church control of politics continued. The congressmen wanted reliable facts, either from a congressional commission or from some trustworthy source.[26] The hearings on these proposed amendments, the last of which was conducted less than a year before Smoot's election, kept alive doubts about whether Mormons had kept the implied bargain about polygamy that had led to Utah statehood.

When newly elected Reed Smoot arrived in Washington in early 1903, Congress was already demanding answers to the Mormon question. On January 5, 1903, before the Utah legislature elected Smoot as senator but when his selection seemed certain, another antipolygamy amendment was introduced into the House. Immediately following his election, two additional amendments, one in the House and one in the Senate, were proposed disallowing any polygamist to hold office.[27] But those opposing the seating of Reed Smoot had a major problem to resolve. They found few violations against Smoot himself that would strip him of his seat—he was not a polygamist, and his behavior and background were fully in compliance with constitutional requirements and the standards of the Senate. There was nothing, in other words, to disqualify him from Senate service.

Protestant churches throughout the country, however, were particularly critical of Senator Smoot continuing in office. On May 21, 1903, the Northern Baptist Home Mission Society unanimously voted to call for Smoot's unseating, and then several days later the 115th General Assembly of the Presbyterian Church asked its member churches to go on record against polygamy and the Mormon Church.[28] Aroused by the Roberts case, women's groups continued their antipolygamy struggle by opposing Smoot. The Interdenominational Council, WCTU, Christian League for Social Purity, National Congress of Mothers, and the Daughters of the American Revolution organized the National League of Women's Organizations in 1904 to coordinate their efforts to stir up opposition to the Utah senator. They claimed 1.5 million women in their crusade and spurred their adherents to send a spate of petitions to Congress.[29] In many small towns around the nation, Protestant churches passed resolutions condemning the Mormon faith and polygamy and calling for Smoot's expulsion.[30]

Opposition to Smoot resonated with many members of Congress. At the forefront was the chairman of the committee investigating Smoot, Senator Julius Caesar Burrows (R-MI), a long-term critic of the Church who had proposed the first constitutional amendment against polygamy.

On February 20, 1907, the Senate voted on the resolution of the Committee on Privileges and Elections stating, "That REED SMOOT is not entitled to a seat as a Senator of the United States from the State of Utah." In the plenary debate prior to the vote, which is covered in detail in chapter 2, the question had arisen about whether excluding a senator, which the committee's resolution proposed, should require a two-thirds majority, given that the Constitution requires such a super majority for expulsion from the Senate (Article I, Section 5). Senator Albert Hopkins (R-IL) (who proposed an antipolygamy constitutional amendment early the following year) proposed that the resolution be amended to require a two-thirds majority for passage. The amendment to the resolution passed easily, with 69 percent of those voting and 58 percent of all senators favoring the amendment.[31] The procedural amendment virtually assured that Smoot would retain his seat: the vote on his retention needed only twenty-four of the senators voting that day or thirty-one of all senators to vote against the committee's resolution. With the GOP in control of 64 percent of Senate seats in the Fifty-Ninth Congress, some amount of party cohesion among Republicans could handily defeat the unseating of one of its members.

Senator Edward Carmack (D-TN), one of the 46 percent of Democrats who voted in favor of the necessity of a two-thirds majority to unseat Smoot, then submitted a substitute resolution that Smoot be expelled from the Senate. The substitute failed: the vote was 27 yeas and 43 nays, with 20 not voting. The Senate then considered the original resolution, stating that Smoot was not entitled to his Senate seat amended to require a two-thirds majority for passage. The only senator to change his vote from the previous resolution about expulsion was Senator Henry du Pont (R-DE), who opposed expulsion but voted in favor of the resolution that Smoot was not entitled to his seat.[32]

The final vote on the resolution to unseat Smoot failed 28 to 42, with nine Senate Republicans voting against retaining his seat. Not only did the vote not reach the necessary two-thirds, but only 40 percent voted in favor of the resolution. While the vote was not strictly by party, 81 percent of Republicans voting supported Smoot, and 86 percent of the Democrats who voted favored the resolution that Smoot was not entitled to his Senate seat. No senator from the Deep South, all of whom were Democrats, voted in support of Smoot. On the other hand, longtime opponent of Mormonism Republican Shelby Cullom paired instead of voting, but his colleague announced that if he had been present he would have been in favor of seating Smoot.[33] By pairing, Cullom was spared from voting against the majority of his party but did not cast a vote that counted for Smoot to retain his seat.

To a remarkable degree, the final vote on Smoot demonstrated a large amount of party loyalty, as shown by the party unity scores. The higher the party unity score, the more often the senator had voted with the majority of his party. The nineteen Democrats voting in support of the resolution to unseat Smoot merited an average party unity score of 92.13, while the three Democrats who voted with the majority had a lower score of 74.16. Similarly, the thirty-nine Republican senators voting against the resolution were more likely to vote with their party, having an average party unity score of 89.84, than those Republicans voting to unseat Smoot, whose average party unity score was only 72.93.[34] Elmer Burkett (R-NE) was the only Republican voting with the majority of Republicans whose party unity score (69.86) was lower than the average score of those Republicans opposing Smoot. He counterbalanced his vote in support of Smoot by proposing an antipolygamy constitutional amendment at the end of the year. Equally ambivalent was Jonathan Dolliver (R-IA), the Republican senator voting in support of Smoot with the next lowest party unity score (75.39). He had signed the committee report opposing Smoot but then gave a speech in his behalf on the Senate floor and voted against the committee resolution.[35]

Party unity among Republicans was decisive in Smoot's retention of his Senate seat. To be sure, the LDS Church had had to prove its loyalty to the nation by accepting the resignations of two apostles responsible for encouraging post-manifesto polygamy and by Mormon participation in the Spanish-American War and giving aid during domestic crises.[36] All fifteen of the senators previously expelled from the Senate had been disloyal: one for treason and support of an anti-Spanish conspiracy and fourteen for support of the Confederate rebellion. This history of reasons for expulsion highlights some initial beliefs about the threat Mormonism posed to the nation, but the hearings had shown no taint of disloyalty attached to Smoot and mitigated concerns about his church. Moreover, during the time the hearings were dispelling concerns among party leaders about Smoot, he racked up a party unity score of 96.67.[37] A loyal Republican himself, he retained his seat through the support of other loyal Republicans.

The relationship between the Smoot hearings and the fifty-five proposed constitutional amendments is tenuous, however. For example, the hearings had little to do with the number of amendments introduced since the majority was introduced prior to the hearings. As is made plain in tables 3.1 and 3.2, prior to the hearings—beginning in 1879 through 1902, thirty-two antipolygamy amendments were proposed to the Congress. During the period from Smoot's election in 1903 to the vote on the Senate floor—January 1903 through February 1907—four amendments were proposed concerning polygamy; another nineteen marriage

TABLE 3.1. Proposed amendments introduced in the Senate

Amendment	Year	Senator	State	Population*	State Voting History†
S.J. Res. 68	1886	Sen. Cullom (R)	Illinois	3,077,871	14 dem, 9 rep, 3 others
S.J. Res. 2	1887	Sen. Dolph (R)	Oregon	317,704	5 dem, 3 rep
S.J. Res. 3	1887	Sen. Cullom (R)	Illinois	3,826,352	14 dem, 9 rep, 3 others
S.J. Res. 5	1889	Sen. Dolph (R)	Oregon	317,704	5 dem, 3 rep
S.J. Res. 164	*1903*	Sen. Hansbrough (R)	North Dakota	319,146	3 rep
S.J. Res. 56	*1906*	Sen. Platt (R)	New York	9,113,614	13 rep, 10 dem, 25 others
S.J. Res. 13	1907	Sen. Burkett (R)	Nebraska	1,192,214	13 rep, 2 others
S.J. Res. 19	1908	Sen. Hansbrough (R)	North Dakota	577,056	3 rep
S.J. Res. 46	1908	Sen. Hopkins (R)	Illinois	5,638,591	14 dem, 10 rep, 3 others
S.J. Res. 91	1913	Sen. Weeks (R)	Massachusetts	3,366,416	9 rep, 1 dem, 30 others
S.J. Res. 96	1914	Sen. Weeks (R)	Massachusetts	3,366,416	9 rep, 1 dem, 30 others
S.B. 3000	1916	Sen. Thomas (D)	Colorado	939,629	9 rep, 5 dem
S.J. Res. 147	1918	Sen. Myers (D)	Montana	548,889	6 rep, 5 dem

Note: Italicized dates indicate amendments proposed from the month of Smoot's election until the final vote confirming his seat.

* According to the most recent census previous to proposed amendment.

† Voting history is determined by how many senators from each party were voted into office from the year the state was created to the year the amendment was proposed.

amendments concerning polygamy were proposed after the Senate vote on Smoot's seat in 1907.

Nor did the Smoot hearings bear much relationship to which party the representative or senator who proposed those amendments belonged. While Reed Smoot was a Republican, this mattered little in terms of those who proposed amendments opposing polygamy, as tables 3.1 and 3.2 indicate. Indeed, Republicans, still living in the shadow of the 1856 party platform condemning "those twin relics of barbarism—Polygamy, and Slavery," proposed 78.2 percent of the fifty-five antipolygamy constitutional amendments, with Democrats proposing only 18.2 percent and the House Judiciary Committee proposing two (3.6 percent). Thirty individual senators and representatives proposed amendments from 1879 to 1924, 70 percent of whom were Republican.

Before Smoot was elected in January 1903, two Republican senators proposed four amendments, and during the Smoot ordeal from his election to the final Senate vote in February 1907, two Republican senators each proposed an antipolygamy amendment. Neither before nor during the Smoot affair did any Democratic senator propose such an amendment. Only after Smoot's seat was confirmed did two Democratic senators offer amendments against polygamy, but twice as many Republican senators proposed such amendments in the aftermath of the Smoot hearings (see table 3.3). The two Democratic senators came from the western states of Colorado and Montana. Among Republican senators, two were from Illinois, and one each was from Oregon, North Dakota, Nebraska, New

TABLE 3.2. Proposed amendments introduced in the House

Amendment	Year	Representative	State	District #	Population*	Year Created	Voting History†
H.J. Res. 54	1879	Rep. Burrows (R)	Michigan	4	1,636,937	1853	6 rep, 2 dem
H.J. Res. 87	1882	Rep. Thomas (R)	Illinois	18	3,077,871	1873	2 rep, 1 dem
H.J. Res. 166	1882	Rep. Cox (D)	North Carolina	4	1,399,750	1790	2 rep, 6 dem, 23 others
H.J. Res. 12	1883	Rep. Thomas (R)	Illinois	20	3,077,871	1883	1 rep
H.J. Res. 50	1883	Rep. Rosecrans (D)	California	1	864,694	1865	4 rep, 3 dem
H.J. Res. 16	1885	Rep. Thomas (R)	Illinois	20	3,077,871	1883	1 rep
H.J. Res. 140	1886	Del. Voorhees (D-WA)	Washington Territory	At Large	357,232	1854	6 rep, 6 dem
H.J. Res. 143	1886	Rep. Van Eaton (D)	Mississippi	6	1,289,600	1873	2 rep, 2 dem
H.J. Res. 176	1886	Committee on Judiciary					
H.J. Res. 45	1888	Rep. E. B. Taylor (R)	Ohio	19	3,672,316	1833	4 rep, 2 dem, 7 others
H.J. Res. 49	1888	Rep. Springer (D)	Illinois	13	3,826,352	1863	5 rep, 5 dem
H.J. Res. 64	1888	Rep. Stewart (R)	Vermont	1	332,422	1791	6 rep, 14 others
H.J. Res. 67	1888	Del. Voorhees (D-WA)	Washington Territory	At Large	357,232	1854	6 rep, 6 dem
H.J. Res. 116	1888	Committee on Judiciary					
H.J. Res. 23	1889	Rep. E. B. Taylor (R)	Ohio	19	3,672,316	1833	4 rep, 2 dem, 7 others
H.J. Res. 77	1892	Rep. Bushnell (D)	Wisconsin	3	1,693,330	1849	5 dem, 7 rep
H.J. Res. 354	1899	Rep. Capron (R)	Rhode Island	2	428,556	1843	10 rep, 5 dem, 4 others
H.J. Res. 1	1899	Rep. Capron (R)	Rhode Island	2	428,556	1843	10 rep, 5 dem, 4 others
H.J. Res. 10	1899	Rep Bromwell (R)	Ohio	2	3,672,316	1813	8 rep, 7 dem, 10 others
H.J. Res. 45	1899	Rep. Grout (R)	Vermont	2	343,641	1791	6 rep, 0 dem, 15 others
H.J. Res. 69	1899	Rep. Showalter (R)	Pennsylvania	25	6,302,115	1833	9 rep, 3 dem, 3 others
H.J. Res. 93	1899	Rep. Shafroth (R)	Colorado	1	539,700	1893	1 rep, 1 other
H.J. Res. 112	1900	Rep. Gibson (R)	Tennessee	2	2,020,616	1813	5 rep, 2 dem, 17 others
H.J. Res. 137	1900	Rep. Showalter (R)	Pennsylvania	25	6,302,115	1833	9 rep, 3 dem, 3 others

continued on next page

TABLE 3.2—*continued*

Amendment	Year	Representative	State	District #	Population*	Year Created	Voting History†
H.J. Res. 203	1900	Rep. Showalter (R)	Pennsylvania	25	6,302,115	1833	9 rep, 3 dem, 3 others
H.J. Res. 40	1901	Rep. Showalter (R)	Pennsylvania	25	6,302,115	1833	9 rep, 3 dem, 3 others
H.J. Res. 55	1901	Rep. Capron (R)	Rhode Island	2	428,556	1843	10 rep, 5 dem, 4 others
H.J. Res. 68	1901	Rep. Gibson (R)	Tennessee	2	2,020,616	1813	5 rep, 2 dem, 17 others
H.J. Res. 240	*1903*	Rep. Parker (R)	New Jersey	6	1,883,669	1873	6 rep, 3 dem
H.J. Res. 258	*1903*	Rep. Jenkins (R)	Wisconsin	10	2,069,042	1893	2 rep
H.J. Res. 170	1910	Rep. Madden (R)	Illinois	1	5,638,591	1818	12 rep, 6 dem, 2 others
H.J. Res. 277	1912	Rep. Sweet (D)	Michigan	5	2,810,173	1863	10 rep, 7 dem
H.J. Res. 91	1913	Rep. Gillett (R)	Massachusetts	2	3,366,416	1789	6 rep, 1 dem, 25 others
H.J. Res. 144	1913	Rep. Gillett (R)	Massachusetts	2	3,366,416	1789	6 rep, 1 dem, 25 others
H.J. Res. 200	1914	Rep. Gillett (R)	Massachusetts	2	3,366,416	1789	6 rep, 1 dem, 25 others
H.J. Res. 201	1914	Rep. Gillett (R)	Massachusetts	2	3,366,416	1789	6 rep, 1 dem, 25 others
H.J. Res. 9	1915	Rep. Gillett (R)	Massachusetts	2	3,852,356	1789	6 rep, 1 dem, 25 others
H.J. Res. 216	1917	Rep. Gillett (R)	Massachusetts	2	3,852,356	1789	6 rep, 1 dem, 25 others
H.J. Res. 74	1919	Rep. Gillett (R)	Massachusetts	2	3,852,356	1789	6 rep, 1 dem, 25 others
H.J. Res. 131	1921	Rep. Gillett (R)	Massachusetts	2	3,852,356	1789	6 rep, 1 dem, 25 others
H.J. Res. 137	1921	Rep. Gillett (R)	Massachusetts	2	3,852,356	1789	6 rep, 1 dem, 25 others
H.J. Res. 114	1924	Rep. Gillett (R)	Massachusetts	2	3,852,356	1789	6 rep, 1 dem, 25 others

Note: Italicized dates indicate amendments proposed from the month of Smoot's election until the final vote confirming his seat.

* According to the most recent census previous to proposed amendment.

† Voting history is determined by how many representatives from each party were voted into office from the year the state was created to the year the amendment was proposed.

York, and Massachusetts. No senator representing a southern or border state proposed an antipolygamy amendment.

In the House, Democrats were slightly more active in proposing amendments about polygamy, composing a third of representatives who offered such amendments, in comparison to slightly fewer than a quarter of senators. Before Smoot's election, 10 Republicans in the House proposed 19 amendments, while 6 Democrats proposed 7. Thereafter House Republicans were considerably more active. While Smoot's seat was in jeopardy, two Republicans each proposed an amendment; no Democrat did. After the Senate vote on Smoot's seat, one Democrat proposed an amendment, while two Republicans proposed eleven amendments—ten proposed by Frederick Huntington Gillett (R-MA). Three representatives from southern states proposed antipolygamy amendments prior to the Smoot hearings, two Democrats—from North Carolina and Mississippi—and a Republican from Tennessee, while none did so during or after the hearings.

Reform tendencies in the Republican Party were strong after the Civil War but declined as other issues came to the fore. Native-born Protestants in northern states, many of whom were Republican, supported using government power to control a variety of moral issues, such as temperance, gambling, prostitution, and, of course, polygamy. Reform movements had not been strong in the South, even before the Civil War, and the reforms instituted by Reconstruction state governments only hardened attitudes after white Southerners took control of state politics through the Democratic Party by 1877. Northern urban Democrats, with their large immigrant base, also eschewed the moral reforms supported by the native born. Neither party countenanced polygamy, but Republicans, with its reform wing, were more aggressive in using federal power to effect social change, whereas Democrats favored local control. The relative number of amendments proposed by members of each party reflects these divergent views.

The size of the state whose representatives or senators introduced antipolygamy amendments was not altered by the hearings (see table 3.4). The states that Democratic House members represented included North Carolina, Mississippi, California, Washington Territory, and the midwestern states of Illinois, Wisconsin, and Michigan. Illinois, Ohio, and Vermont each had two Republican representatives who proposed amendments, while one Republican representative each from Rhode Island, Massachusetts, New Jersey, Pennsylvania, Michigan, Wisconsin, Colorado, and Tennessee did so. There was, however, an overall difference between the House and the Senate in the size of the state congressmen proposing amendments represented. In general, House members offering antipolygamy amendments came from larger, more populous states than did senators proposing amendments against polygamy. The lack of definitive patterns, however, suggests personal predilections of congressmen, active antipolygamy organizations in their constituencies, or both.

TABLE 3.3. Introduction of amendments by senators and representatives according to party (number of individuals in parentheses)

SENATE	Republican	Democratic
Before 1903	4 (2)	0
Jan. 1903–Feb. 1907	2 (2)	0
After Feb 1907	5 (4)	2 (2)

HOUSE	Republican	Democratic
Before 1903	19 (10)	7 (6)
Jan. 1903–Feb. 1907	2 (2)*	0
After Feb. 1907	11 (2)	1

* One of these two amendments was submitted on January 5, fifteen, 15 days before Smoot was elected on January 20, 1903. It was counted with the other amendments during the Smoot ordeal because it was widely assumed after the November elections that Smoot would be elected by the Utah legislature, a valid assumption when he received almost twice as many votes as needed for election. "Possible Future President of the Mormon Church Will Be the Next United States Senator from Utah," Hearst's *Chicago American*, 23 November 1902; "Smoot Chosen Senator by a Majority of Thirty," *Salt Lake Herald-Republican*, 21 January 1903.

In terms of the intensity of the amendment against polygamy, we used a five-point scale to measure this, as tables 3.5 and 3.6 make clear. The "intensity scale" measures how constrained the proposed amendment would have been to a polygamist. The score is based on a series of five questions assessing these constraints: (1) Would the proposed amendment prohibit polygamy? (2) Would the proposed amendment punish a polygamist and/or his family? (3) Does the proposed amendment indicate a particular punishment for the polygamist? (4) Does the proposed amendment include cohabitation as well as polygamy in its language? (5) Does the proposed amendment include a definition of marriage and/or polygamy? As these are applied to every proposed amendment, the amendment is assigned one point for each question answered "yes." Scores varied from 1 to 5, with an amendment receiving a score of "5" being the "most constraining," while an amendment receiving a score of "1" considered the "least constraining."

The average intensity for the proposed amendments prior to Smoot's election was 3.00, while the average score for those amendments after Smoot's seat was confirmed in February 1907 was 1.84.[38] The results of these two tables reveal that the hearings diminished the intensity of feeling—or fear—regarding polygamy. Although Smoot was not a polygamist, the long and extensive hearings essentially precluded any polygamist from holding high government office in the foreseeable future.

The Smoot hearings thus had some, but limited, impact on the patterns of proposed constitutional amendments against polygamy, but they did bring about

TABLE 3.4. Population of the states from which senators and representatives introduced antipolygamy amendments

Large States	Population*	Small States	Population
Senate			
New York	9 million	Colorado	939,000
Illinois	3 million	Montana	500,000
Massachusetts	3 million	North Dakota	300,000–577,000
		Nebraska	350,000
		Oregon	300,000
House			
Pennsylvania	6 million	California	846,000
Illinois	3 million	Colorado	539,000
Massachusetts	3 million	Rhode Island	400,000
Ohio	3 million	Washington Territory	350,000
Tennessee	2 million	Vermont	300,000
Michigan	1–2 million		
Wisconsin	1–2 million		
Mississippi	1 million		
New Jersey	1 million		
North Carolina	1 million		

* Population in this table is approximate population at the time the amendments were proposed.

some renewed apprehensions regarding polygamy. After all, critics had had a high-ranking member of the LDS Church—a church that had introduced polygamy to the American polity—who wanted to sit in the US Senate representing a state that had been known for its polygamous activities. Two amendments were proposed in the immediate wake of Smoot's election, both mandating that a polygamist could not "hold, occupy, or enjoy any office of honor or profit under the United States."[39] Nevertheless, this language was less explicit than that proposed when polygamist B. H. Roberts was elected to the House of Representatives but was excluded from the House by an overwhelming majority vote.[40] Then two amendments were proposed in 1899 stating: "No person shall be Senator or Representative in Congress, or elector, or President, or Vice-President, or hold any other office of honor or emolument, whether civil or military, under the United States or under any State or Territory thereof, or be permitted to vote at any election for any of said officers in either State or Territory who shall be found guilty of polygamy or polygamous cohabitation."[41] Still, amendments proposed in the wake of the elections of Roberts and Smoot evinced concern over lawbreaking polygamists holding any government office, whether elected or appointed.

TABLE 3.5. Breakdown of amendments by intensity score

Score	Before 1903	1903 and After
5	3	0
4	14	0
3	2	4
2	6	14
1	7	5

Source: Table created by authors.

Note: For the criteria of how the intensity score was created, see page 119 in the text.

TABLE 3.6. Antipolygamist amendments by data and intensity

Amendment	Date*	Score
H.J. Res. 54	1879	1
H.J. Res. 87[†]	1882	5
H.J. Res. 166[†]	1882	3
H.J. Res. 12[†]	1883	5
H.J. Res. 50	1883	1
H.J. Res. 16[†]	1885	5
H.J. Res. 140	1886	1
H.J. Res. 143	1886	1
H.J. Res. 176	1886	4
S.J. Res. 68	1886	2
S.J. Res. 2	1887	1
S.J. Res. 3	1887	2
H.J. Res. 45	1888	4
H.J. Res. 49	1888	4
H.J. Res. 64	1888	4
H.J. Res. 67	1888	1
H.J. Res. 116	1888	2
S.J. Res. 5	1889	1
H.J. Res. 23	1889	4
H.J. Res. 77	1892	2
H.J. Res. 354**	1899	4
H.J. Res. 1[†]	1899	4
H.J. Res. 10[†]	1899	3
H.J. Res. 45[†]	1899	4
H.J. Res. 69[†]	1899	4

continued on next page

TABLE 3.6—*continued*

Amendment	Date*	Score
H.J. Res. 93†	1899	4
H.J. Res. 112†	1900	2
H.J. Res. 137†	1900	4
H.J. Res. 203†	1900	4
H.J. Res. 40†	1901	4
H.J. Res. 55	1901	4
H.J. Res. 68†	1901	2
H.J. Res. 240	**1903**	1
H.J. Res. 258†	**1903**	3
S.J. Res. 164†	**1903**	3
S.J. Res. 56	**1906**	3
S.J. Res. 13	**1907**	1
S.J. Res. 19	**1908**	3
S.J. Res. 46	**1908**	2
H.J. Res. 170	**1910**	2
H.J. Res. 277	**1912**	1
H.J. Res. 91	**1913**	2
H.J. Res. 144	**1913**	1
S.J. Res. 91	**1913**	1
S.J. Res. 96	**1914**	2
H.J. Res. 200	**1914**	2
H.J. Res. 201	**1914**	2
H.J. Res. 9	**1915**	2
S.B. 3000	**1916**	2
H.J. Res. 216	**1917**	2
S.J. Res. 147	**1918**	2
H.J. Res. 74	**1919**	2
H.J. Res. 131	**1921**	2
H.J. Res. 137	**1921**	2
H.J. Res. 114	**1924**	2

Source: Edward Stein, "Past and Present Proposed Amendments to the United States Constitution Regarding Marriage," *Washington University Law Quarterly* 82, no. 3 (Fall 2004): 666–682.

* Dates in bold indicated amendments proposed after November 1902, when Smoot's election was assured.

† Amendments that include a punishment that does not allow a polygamist to serve in a government office.

** Proposed title of the amendment prohibited polygamists from serving as a representative or senator, but text of amendment does not include this specific prohibition.

Smoot himself indicated his opposition to any additional amendments being proposed:

> I have taken the position that I am opposed to any more constitutional amend-
> ments, and as a citizen of Utah, I am particularly opposed to an amendment that
> is directed against my people and my state. I have suggested that the best way
> to reach this question is to pass a national marriage law, and I have assured the
> Senators that I will support any measure, no matter how strict or what penalties
> it imposes, [with] provisions for the punishment of fornication, adultery, incest,
> unlawful cohabitation, and kindred offences. I hardly think that we need worry
> much about this constitutional amendment proposition.[42]

He was right, of course: no antipolygamy amendments reached the floor of either chamber.

Furthermore, the position a politician took on Smoot bore little relationship to his stand on antipolygamy amendments. Theodore Roosevelt's annual message to Congress in 1906 called for a constitutional amendment to regulate marriage and divorce and give Congress the power to "deal . . . with polygamy."[43] Such a stance allowed Roosevelt to both support Smoot and oppose polygamy. Similarly, Senators Burkett (R-NE) and Hopkins (R-IL) voted to retain Smoot in the Senate but offered antipolygamy amendments within a year after that vote. Senator Platt (R-NY) introduced an amendment a month before the committee's decision on Smoot, but in the vote on the Senate floor he chose to pair, though his colleague announced that had Platt been present he would have voted to retain Smoot. On the other hand, Senator Hansbrough (R-ND) proposed antipolygamy amendments at the beginning and end of the Smoot ordeal, in 1903 and 1908, and voted against Smoot. Offering an amendment could thus be consistent with one's vote on Smoot or provide a means to support him while expressing opposition to polygamy.

Having been brought into action by the Roberts case, religious and women's groups did not fade away quickly after Smoot's Senate seat was confirmed. In the fifteen years between 1910 and 1924, sixteen antipolygamy amendments were proposed. Three-quarters of these were from the Massachusetts delegation: two by Senator John W. Weeks and ten by Representative Frederick H. Gillett. Beginning with an article by Senator Julius C. Burrows—undaunted by defeat—published three months after the vote allowing Smoot to retain his seat, national magazines published a spate of articles over the next few years highly critical of Mormons. Women's groups, continuing their activities after 1907, accelerated their crusade against polygamy with the help of the anti-Mormon articles and lecture tours. The National Reform Association claimed they held more than fifty meetings averaging 1,000 people each and organized a petition campaign that yielded over 20,000 resolutions sent to Congress to support Gillett's proposed antipolygamy amendments in 1914. This was the peak of the antipolygamy campaign in the post–Smoot hearings period. In chapter 4 of this book, Kenneth L. Cannon II chronicles the trajectory of opposition to the LDS Church by national groups after Smoot's confirmation. Nevertheless, the Protestant National Reform Association, Rev. William Campbell, and others continued to advocate passage of a constitutional amendment from 1915 to 1924, and Gillett continued to propose amendments that were sent to committee and never heard of again. The emphasis of women's groups eventually moved to prohibition and woman suffrage, and in 1925, when Gillett moved from the speakership of the House to the Senate, where Smoot was chair of the powerful Senate Finance Committee, he ceased his fruitless effort to pass an antipolygamy amendment.[44]

None of these proposed amendments about marriage was adopted. From 1879 to 1924, the dates of the first and last proposed amendments regarding polygamy, over 1,500 constitutional amendments on various issues were proposed, and only four—the Sixteenth, Seventeenth, Eighteenth, and Nineteenth—were eventually adopted. The bar for passage is indeed a high one. Any congressman or senator may introduce a joint resolution proposing an amendment. It is assigned a number and referred to a committee, where it usually dies. At times public hearings are held, after which a vote of committee members is taken. The resolution may be reported with or without changes, or it may be tabled, its usual fate. If it is reported to the full chamber, it is still likely to be tabled. All fifty-five proposed amendments dealing with polygamy were tabled at some stage: none made it to the full chamber for a vote. Had any made it to the full chamber, it would have taken a two-thirds vote in favor in order to proceed to the other chamber, where it would again need a two-thirds favorable vote. The proposed amendment would then be submitted to the states, two-thirds of which would need to ratify it for the proposal to become a part of the constitution. In the end, none of the fifty-five amendments had been treated seriously enough to ever come to a vote on the floors of either chamber of Congress.[45]

One might ask why an amendment was sought to rid the country of polygamy given that the Congress was so active in passing legislation against plural marriage and the Supreme Court handed down such strong antipolygamy decisions. Opponents to polygamy listed a number of reasons. Fanny Carpenter, of the New York State Federation of Women's Clubs, for one, supported H.J. Res. 40, when it was introduced in the Fifty-Seventh Congress (1902) because she felt it was the only way to finally rid the nation of this threat. As she indicated, "We realize that an amendment to the Constitution of the United States is a serious thing. It is difficult, and it is well that it should be difficult, to add an amendment to the important fifteen which already exist, but this proposed anti-polygamy amendment concerns a matter of such vital importance that it seems to demand this very grave action."[46] H.J. Res. 176, Forty-Ninth Congress (May 24, 1886), posited another reason for passing an amendment prohibiting polygamy. The House

Judiciary Committee stated: "The evils of the Mormon system are deeper than can be cured by ordinary legislation. To punish the offender may be accomplished by law, but to extirpate the system, to eradicate it from this Union of free and civilized Commonwealths, will require a change in the Constitution."[47]

The most important reason to support an amendment was that power over marriage and divorce remained in the states. Congress had power to pass laws for territories, but it was also its duty, stated the House Judiciary Committee in 1886, "to fit the community in the Territory in its formative process to become a State, and then to admit it into the Union."[48] To fit Utah to become a state, polygamy had to be prohibited permanently, which an amendment would accomplish. After Utah became a state in 1896, Congress had no power over marriage in Utah. Its options were to pass a constitutional amendment prohibiting polygamy—or to do what it did by using the election of Smoot to exert enormous pressure so the LDS Church itself would suppress polygamy.

Constitutional amendments giving the federal government power to prohibit polygamy throughout the United States, proposed both before and after Utah achieved statehood, provide one measure of the fluctuating intensity of antipolygamy attitudes. In the end, punitive laws and their vigorous enforcement sufficiently suppressed polygamy to permit Utah to become a state and precluded the necessity of an amendment. When it became clear polygamy was still practiced, however much diminished, the Senate withheld something Mormons wanted—the permanent seating of Senator Smoot—until they made additional concessions on polygamy. But the agitation for an antipolygamy constitutional amendment did channel into political action the passions and outrage of their supporters, and the representatives and senators who had introduced amendments sent a message to the Congress and the polity in general that they represented constituent antagonism toward plural marriage. Reformers had recently fought a war on the conviction that the nation could not remain divided, half slave and half free. Opponents of polygamy doubted, to paraphrase Lincoln, that the government could endure, permanently, half polygamous and half monogamous—or even 1 percent polygamous and 99 percent monogamous. An antipolygamy constitutional amendment for its millions of supporters was not merely a means to suppress polygamy; for them it would have enshrined monogamy in America's fundamental document as a principle and a practice foundational to American civilization.

NOTES

1. An excellent study of women in the antipolygamy movement is Joan Smyth Iversen, *The Antipolygamy Controversy in U.S. Women's Movements, 1880–1925* (New York: Garland Publishing, Inc., 1997). Also see Barbara Haywood, "Utah's Anti-Polygamy Society, 1878–1884" (MA thesis, Brigham Young University, Provo, UT, 1980).

2. Roderick Phillips, *Putting Asunder: A History of Divorce in Western Society* (Cambridge: Cambridge University Press, 1988), 458–473; Nancy F. Cott, *Public Vows: A History of Marriage and the Nation* (Cambridge, MA: Harvard University Press, 2000), 105–107; Edward Stein, "Past and Present Proposed Amendments to the United States Constitution Regarding Marriage," *Washington University Law Quarterly* 82, no. 3 (Fall 2004): 672–682.

3. Michael Grossberg, *Governing the Hearth: Law and the Family in Nineteenth-Century America* (Chapel Hill: University of North Carolina Press, 1985), 64–126.

4. Donald Bruce Johnson, *National Party Platforms* (Urbana: University of Illinois Press, 1978), 1:27.

5. Stein, "Past and Present Proposed Amendments to the United States Constitution Regarding Marriage," 666–685; Richard B. Bernstein with Jerome Agel, *Amending America: If We Love the Constitution So Much, Why Do We Keep Trying to Change It?* (New York: Times Books, Random House, 1993), 195–196.

6. H.J. Res. 69, 56th Cong. (1889); H.J. Res. 137, 56th Cong. (1900); H.J. Res. 203, 56th Cong. (1900).

7. 19 Congressional Record, 165 (1888).

8. Morrill Anti-Bigamy Act, ch. 126, 12 Stat. 501 (1862).

9. Julie Ewing, "Public Vows: A History of Marriage and the Nation," *Journal of Law and Family Studies* 199, no. 4 (2002): 203.

10. See H.R. Res. 50, 49th Cong. (1883).

11. Francis Lieber, "The Mormons: Shall Utah Be Admitted into the Union?" *Putnam's Monthly* 5, no. 27 (1855): 234–236.

12. 19 Congressional Record, 166 (1888).

13. *Reynolds v. United States*, US 98:166 (1879).

14. *Journal of the House of Representatives of the United States*, being the second session of the Forty-Sixth Congress; begun and held at the City of Washington, December 1, 1879, in the one hundred and fourth year of the independence of the United States, Serial Set Vol. No. 1901, 11–12, 76.

15. *Journal of the House of Representatives of the United States*, 2nd sess. 96–97. The resolutions passed by the Michigan legislature had been presented to the House in the preceding Congress as well. *Journal of the House of Representatives of the United States*, being the first session of the Forty-Sixth Congress; begun and held at the City of Washington, March 18, 1879, in the one hundred and third year of the independence of the United States, Serial Set Vol. No. 1874, 24, 28, 191.

16. House Judiciary Committee, Proposed Additional Legislation for Utah Territory, Hearings, April 15, 26, 30–May 1, 3–5, 1886.

17. House Judiciary Committee, Polygamy, Hearing on H.R.J. Res. 176, May 24, 1886, 49th Cong., First Sess., Serial Set Vol. No. 2442, Sess. Vol. No. 8, 3, 7–10.

18. Edward Leo Lyman, *Political Deliverance: The Mormon Quest for Utah Statehood* (Urbana: University of Illinois Press), 34–35, 42–46.

19. Report of the secretary of the interior, being part of the message and documents communicated to the two Houses of Congress at the beginning of the first session of the Fiftieth Cong., Vol. II, Serial Set Vol. No. 2542, Sess., Vol. No. 11, H.Exec.Doc. 1 pt. 5, v. 2, p. 1341.

20. Lyman, *Political Deliverance*, 57–59.

21. Stein, "Past and Present Proposed Amendments to the United States Constitution Regarding Marriage," 667, 670; Grossberg, *Governing the Hearth*, 22–23; Lyman, *Political Deliverance*, 59–62. During the debate on the Senate floor about Smoot retaining his seat, Senator William Dillingham (R-VT) similarly made the distinction between polygamy meaning new plural marriages and polygamous cohabitation as those married before 1890 continuing to live together. 41 Congressional Record, 3271 (1907).

22. Sarah Barringer Gordon, *The Mormon Question: Polygamy and Constitutional Conflict in Nineteenth Century America* (Chapel Hill: University of North Carolina Press, 2002), 209–220, 224–228.

23. Lyman, *Political Deliverance*, 192–192.

24. House Committee on the Election of the President, Vice-President, and Members of Congress, Amendments to the Constitution prohibiting polygamy, etc. February 27, 1899, 55th Cong., 3rd Sess., H.Rpt. 2307, Serial Set Vol. No. 3841, Sess. Vol. No. 2, 6.

25. Stein, "Past and Present Proposed Amendments to the United States Constitution Regarding Marriage," 671–73; Davis Bitton, "The Exclusion of B. H. Roberts," in *The Ritualization of Mormon History and Other Essays*, ed. Davis Bitton (Urbana: University of Illinois Press, 1994), 150–170.

26. House Committee on the Judiciary, Proposed Amendment to the Constitution Prohibiting Polygamy, Hearings, February 20, 1900, 39; House Committee on the Judiciary, Polygamy, Hearings, February 25, 1902, 1–17 (quotations on 16 and 17). For Rev. William H. Campbell's efforts to secure an antipolygamy constitutional amendment, see R. Douglas Brackenridge, "'About the Worst Man in Utah': William R. Campbell and the Crusade against Brigham H. Roberts, 1898–1900," *Journal of Mormon History* 39, no. 1 (Winter 2013): 148–152.

27. H.R.J. Res. 258, 57th Cong., 2d Sess. (January 31, 1903); and S.J. Res. 164, 57th Cong., 2d Sess. (February 5, 1903).

28. Paul M. Holsinger, "For God and the American Home: The Attempt to Unseat Senator Reed Smoot," *Pacific Northwest Quarterly* 60, no. 3 (July 1969): 154–160.

29. Iversen, *Antipolygamy Controversy in U.S. Women's Movements*, 217.

30. Holsinger, "For God and the American Home," 154–160.

31. 41 Congressional Record, 3428–3430 (1907); Anne M. Butler, *United States Senate, Election, Expulsion, and Censure Cases from 1793 to 1990* (Washington, DC: US Government Printing Office, 1995).

32. 41 Congressional Record, 3428–3430 (1907).

33. 41 Congressional Record, 3429–3430 (1907). Pairing is an informal voluntary agreement between House members or senators within each chamber. It can take place on any roll-call vote in the individual chambers. When a member expects to be absent for a vote, he or she may pair with another absent member who would have voted opposite from the absent member and agrees not to vote. A "live pair" is an agreement of one member who is in the chamber with one member outside the chamber. The member in the chamber votes "present" and announces how the pair of them would have voted had they not been in the pair. Pairs are not tabulated in the vote total but are recorded separately at the end of the recorded vote tally in the Congressional Record expressing the positions or attitudes the member had on the issue. On the issues that require a two-thirds vote, a pair in the Senate or House consists of two members in the affirmative to one in the negative. Pairing allows the members to indicate to constituents how they would have voted had they not been in a pair. If the member would have supported the bill had he/she not been in a pair, the member can tell supporters of the bill he/she would have voted for the bill had he/she not been in the pair. To opponents of the bill, the member can provide assurance that at least the member did not vote for the bill because of the pair.

34. The party unity score is calculated on those votes where at least 50 percent of Democrats vote against at least 50 percent of Republicans. The score is determined by dividing the number of such votes in which a particular senator sided with the majority of his party by the number of such votes the senator participated in. For example, Smoot participated in 60 votes where a majority of Republicans opposed a majority of Democrats, and of those, he voted with his party 58 times, resulting in a party unity score of 96.667. All party unity scores are found at or calculated from the data at Elaine Swift, Study No. 3371, Database of Congressional Historical Statistics, 1789–1989, Department of Political Science, University of Georgia, Voteview.com. From its high in the wake of the Civil War, party polarization declined from about the beginning of the twentieth century to World War II but was still relatively high in 1907. Jeff Lewis, "Polarization in Congress," https://voteview.com/articles/party_polarization (accessed January 2, 2021).

35. Kathleen Flake, *The Politics of American Religious Identity: The Seating of Senator Reed Smoot, Mormon Apostle* (Chapel Hill: University of North Carolina, 2004), 161; Elaine Swift, Study No. 3371, Database of Congressional Historical Statistics, 1789–1989. No individual Republican senator who voted against Smoot had as high a party unity score as the average party unity score of all those Republicans who voted for him to retain his seat.

36. Flake, *The Politics of American Religious Identity*, 144–155.

37. US Senate, Art and History, "Expulsion and Censure"; Elaine Swift, Study No. 3371, Database of Congressional Historical Statistics, 1789–1989.

38. Surprisingly, the intensity score rises only to 1.96 if the amendments proposed from 1903 through 1906 are added to those proposed after Smoot's seat was confirmed.

39. Stein, "Past and Present Proposed Amendments to the United States Constitution Regarding Marriage," 675–676.

40. Bitton, "The Exclusion of B. H. Roberts," 167.

41. Stein, "Past and Present Proposed Amendments to the United States Constitution Regarding Marriage," 672–673.

42. Reed Smoot to Joseph F. Smith, April 9, 1904, Joseph F. Smith Letterbooks, LDS Archives.

43. Theodore Roosevelt, Annual Message, December 4, 1906, *Journal of the House of Representatives of the United States*, being the second session of the Fifty-Ninth Congress, Serial Set Vol. No. 5059, 22.

44. Thomas G. Alexander, *Mormonism in Transition: A History of the Latter-day Saints, 1890–1930*, 3rd ed. (Salt Lake City: Greg Kofford Books, 2012), 70–71; Iversen, *Antipolygamy Controversy in U.S. Women's Movements*, 239–255.

45. Stein, "Past and Present Proposed Amendments to the United States Constitution Regarding Marriage," 633.

46. Polygamy: Hearing on H.R.J. Res. 40 Before the House Comm. on the Judiciary, 57th Cong. 7 (1902) (statement from Fanny Carpenter, New York Federal of Women's Clubs).

47. House Judiciary Committee, Polygamy, Hearing on H.R.J. Res. 176, May 24, 1886, 3.

48. House Judiciary Committee, Polygamy, Hearing on H.R.J. Res. 176, May 24, 1886, 3.

4

Do I Hear an Echo?

The Continuing Trial of the Mormon Church after Smoot's Retention

Kenneth L. Cannon II

On February 20, 1907, the US Senate voted convincingly that Reed Smoot was entitled to his seat in that august body.[1] Although Smoot had been the named subject of the investigation by the Senate's Committee on Privileges and Elections, it was really the Church of Jesus Christ of Latter-day Saints, of which Smoot was an apostle, that had been on trial for the preceding three years.[2] The allegations against the Mormon Church and, almost incidentally, Senator Smoot, centered mostly on the continued practice by Mormons of polygamy and their purported disloyalty to the American government, but also included charges of political control by the Church both in Utah and the western United States. Smoot was permitted to retain his seat, due in substantial part to his own integrity and the trust he had built up with his GOP colleagues (then in the majority) during his short tenure in the Senate. His church, on the other hand, was not exonerated by the investigation.[3] After a brief recess in the attacks on the Church following the Senate's decision, the trial of the Mormon Church resumed as critics renewed allegations against the Church in national magazines, on the lecture circuit, and through the political process. Church leaders were forced to combat the sometimes-unfair charges.[4] Only when Americans became obsessed with World War I did this trial of the LDS Church come to an end.

For some reason, perhaps because of the shock of this setback, only a limited number of high-profile attacks on Smoot and the Church appeared in the few years immediately following the 1907 vote. Certainly, anti-Mormon (or at least

DOI: 10.7330/9781646421176.c004

FIGURE 4.1. Frank and Mattie Cannon portrait, 1893. Photo courtesy of Kenneth L. Cannon II.

antipolygamy) activities did not cease entirely, but there was a clear slowdown in attacks during this period. Individuals and institutions that had taken up the fight to have Reed Smoot expelled from the Senate were left discouraged and disorganized. Mercurial Frank J. Cannon was the second-oldest son of longtime LDS First Presidency member, George Q. Cannon, and had been an advisor to senior Church leaders and one of Utah's first two Senators, but had become a virulent enemy of the Church. He had played a critical, behind-the-scenes role in the Senate's investigation of Smoot but eventually left Utah after two traumatic events in his life: the Senate's vote to retain Smoot and the unexpected death of his wife, Mattie, in early 1908.[5] Feeling defeated, Cannon retreated from attacking the Church for several years after Smoot's retention. Even the *Salt Lake Tribune*, which over the years had rarely resisted opportunities to attack the Church, left off its crusade for a time, due in part to Cannon's departure as editor. Although Cannon's close friend and former Idaho senator Fred T. Dubois continued to publish his anti-Mormon *Idaho Scimitar* for a few months, that newspaper soon failed and even Dubois became relatively silent about the Mormons for a while.[6]

By 1909, however, it became clear that the "trial of the Mormon Church" had not ended; it had just receded for a time. In that year, news reports once again accused the Church of the same activities that had prompted the Smoot investigation in the first place. Then, beginning in the last half of 1910, in an unusual convergence of activity, anti-Mormon sentiment surged, with renewed allegations of Mormon "perfidy," including polygamy, political control with a concomitant expansion of political ambitions, and the formation of Church alliances with national financial trusts and "interests" that progressive America found troubling. As a result, national magazines, with combined subscriptions numbering in the millions, weighed in. Books, sometimes serialized first in prominent magazines before publication in book form, reached many more. These publications reenergized women's groups and jump-started a new national campaign against polygamy. Inciting popular sentiment against Mormon polygamy, anti-Mormon agitators took to the Chautauqua and Lyceum lecture circuits to speak on the evils of Mormonism to hundreds of thousands of rapt listeners.

One of the principal allegations against LDS leaders made at the Smoot hearings was that they had secretly encouraged and authorized new polygamous marriages and continued cohabitation between polygamous spouses.[7] In late 1909, the *Salt Lake Tribune* began to reenergize opposition to the LDS Church when it published a list of Mormon men, many of whom were either Mormon leaders or members of leaders' families, who had reportedly entered polygamy after 1890. Over the next year and a half, the *Tribune* carried at least 119 articles accusing the Mormon Church, its leaders, and its members of continuing the illegal solemnization of polygamous marriages.[8] Other long-term opponents of the Church, such as the Women's Christian Temperance Union (WCTU) and the National Reform Association (NRA), stepped up their crusade. New groups such as the Women's Home and Foreign Missionary Society of the Evangelical Lutheran Church (WHFRS) also joined in.[9]

Many Utahns, if not most (be they Mormon or "Gentile"), understood and even expected that polygamous couples who married before 1890, the year polygamy officially ended, would continue to cohabit and those young enough might continue to have children together. Many outside Utah likely shared this pragmatic view of continued relations between couples long married. But allegations of new polygamous marriages were far more troubling. Reports of a few such marriages presented to the US Senate's Committee on Privileges and Elections during the Smoot hearings had been worrisome enough; now the *Tribune*'s reports of hundreds of new plural marriages were cause for alarm.

As the *Salt Lake Tribune* published stories of widespread polygamous marriages and asserted that the LDS Church had done little to curb polygamous activities, an important introduction was made in Colorado during the early spring of 1910. Harvey J. O'Higgins—a prominent New York muckraker, Broadway playwright, detective story writer, and novelist—met Frank J. Cannon through a mutual friend, Judge Ben B. Lindsey, in Denver. As O'Higgins and Cannon talked, the New Yorker quickly realized that Cannon's tale would be his next muckraking work.[10]

O'Higgins later described Cannon as extremely dignified and composed, but with a deathly pallor, reminiscent of someone suffering privately of an incurable disease. O'Higgins blamed Cannon's suffering on the Mormon Church and its president, Joseph F. Smith, who, according to O'Higgins, had ruined him financially, excommunicated him, ostracized him, slandered him, and pushed him out of Utah politics. Fascinated by Cannon's "almost unique human" story, he quickly "persuaded" the editor of *Everybody's Magazine*, a popular Progressive monthly, to underwrite a series of articles detailing Cannon's experiences with the Mormon Church and with Reed Smoot.[11] Word soon spread that Cannon and O'Higgins were preparing articles on the misdoings of the Mormons, and editors of other Progressive magazines scrambled to assign some of their best authors to write competing articles about the Mormons, confident that many Americans were eager to read more reports of Mormon wrongdoing.[12] *McClure's* soon sent its best writer, Burton J. Hendrick, who later won three Pulitzer Prizes for history and biography, to Utah to do in-depth research. Hendrick interviewed many prominent Mormon leaders, including First Presidency counselors, John Henry Smith and Anthon H. Lund, and left Lund "worried" by his extensive knowledge and questions.[13] *Pearson's Magazine* even beat *Everybody's* to the newsstand by several months, carrying three successive articles on the influence the Mormon Church had on American politics, on continued polygamy, and on the close alliance between the Church and Wall Street.[14]

What followed over the following year was a maelstrom of journalistic attacks on the Mormon Church published by four separate Progressive magazines. As the articles appeared, the periodicals varied in their level of vitriol directed at the Church and its leaders, with the highly-respected *McClure's* on one end of the spectrum, taking care to limit its coverage to allegations that Burton Hendrick believed were fully supported, to the thoroughly sensationalized *Cosmopolitan* on the other end, which sometimes made outrageously unsupported charges in the infamous (though clever) "Viper on the Hearth" articles written by the extremely popular writer Alfred Henry Lewis.

All of the magazine series assumed that the Church had to some extent, in Frank J. Cannon's words, engaged in "one of the most direful conspiracies of treachery in the history of the United States."[15] All agreed that the Church had misled the country by secretly continuing the practice of polygamy while asserting that the practice had ended in 1890. All but the careful *McClure's* articles also sought to prove that Mormon leaders were attaining a distressingly high level of political influence and control, at least in Utah and surrounding states (and thereby in the United States), at the same time asserting that they had become extremely wealthy through close association with and participation in the monopolies and trusts of the day.

At the center of the Church's ambitions and perfidy was "the Prophet," Joseph F. Smith, "an old man with five wives and forty-three children," who was an influential millionaire in the Mountain West, a political friend of William Howard Taft, and a power broker on Wall Street. To Richard Barry, writing for *Pearson's*, President Smith was not an impressive man, and Barry criticized his intelligence, oratory, political abilities, and business acumen. The other journals came largely to the same conclusion, with the *Cosmopolitan* painting Smith as a fearsome "viper on the hearth." What made Smith so powerful and influential was his ecclesiastical position that led his people to believe he was in direct communication with God. In light of this, believing Latter-day Saints were prepared to follow his counsel in all matters.[16]

In the first article from the four magazines to address "new polygamy," Richard Barry noted how during what he called the "recrudescence period," even women of intelligence and "superior character," such as Dr. Martha Hughes Cannon, had participated openly in the duplicity. As he eloquently put it, "the lizard of polygamy now basks in the sun of statehood, not at all ashamed and very little afraid."[17] Barry's first *Pearson's* article—which had addressed the Church's alleged political control over a close-knit large group of religiously united people utterly obedient to their ecclesiastical leaders, argued that LDS leaders wielded enough power in the West to control the Senate elections in Utah, Idaho, and Wyoming, and alleged that the Church was well on its way to exercise this same influence in Arizona, New Mexico, Nevada, Colorado, Montana, Oregon, and Washington—attracted little notice from Church leaders.[18] The charges seemed grossly exaggerated.

On the other hand, Barry's accusations of new polygamous marriages secretly ordered by the prophet and his colleagues, which appeared in the October 1910 issue of *Pearson's* (and arrived on newsstands in late September), and other supporting articles by such writers as Frank Cannon and Burton Hendrick, which LDS leaders expected to arrive shortly, caused substantial consternation among the Church's general authorities. The timing of the publications coincided with several difficult cases of local Church leaders involved in new polygamous marriages and worried Mormon leaders.[19] Some apostles, especially Reed Smoot and Francis M. Lyman, lobbied President Smith to subject these local leaders to immediate Church discipline, or at least to have them formally released from their Church responsibilities. Smith was slow to act, however, likely due to his own involvement in "new polygamy" between 1896 and 1904 and his unshakeable belief in plural marriage as a religious principle.[20] Smoot, on the other hand, was particularly sensitive to these allegations of post-manifesto polygamous marriages because evidence of these marriages had nearly cost him his Senate seat.[21] For concerned Church leaders, the renewal of a broad discussion of new polygamy in popular national magazines would elevate this continuing trial of the LDS Church to a new level.

Quickly moving into damage control, the LDS Church responded to these allegations (and anticipated further allegations) of new polygamy. In October 1910, the Church's Council of the Twelve discussed the question regularly in their meetings.[22] Also around this time, the First Presidency issued a clarifying letter to stake presidencies making "known . . . that no one has been authorized to solemnize plural marriages, and that he who advises, counsels or entices any person to contract a plural marriage renders himself liable to excommunication, as well as those who solemnize such marriages, or those who enter into such unlawful relations."[23] Then on Saturday, October 8, sandwiched between two days of General Conference, the First Presidency called a "special priesthood session" in which President Smith and his counselor Anthon H. Lund, referred this letter to stake presidencies and forcefully reiterated that "no one was authorized to celebrate plural marriages."[24]

In late October 1910, the *Salt Lake Herald-Republican*, which had been a Democratic "organ" before having been acquired by Reed Smoot's "federal bunch" in August 1909, asserted that "*Tribune* management" and former Idaho senator Fred T. Dubois, "disappointed, malicious, and vengeful," had visited New York and "arranged with the editors of *McClure's, Pearson's*, and *Everybody's* for the campaign of defamation of Utah which is now in full swing."[25]

Soon thereafter, attacks on the Mormon Church continued with the appearance of the third *Pearson's* article (on the alleged financial practices and control of the Church) and then the first *Everybody's* Cannon-O'Higgins articles under the explosive title of "Under the Prophet in Utah: The National Menace of a Political Priestcraft."[26] In the opening article, Cannon made clear that though he loved his virtuous Mormon brothers and sisters, their leaders had violated the "treaty convention in which the contracting parties were the American Republic and the 'Kingdom of God on Earth,'" and their horrific acts needed to be exposed.[27] The *Everybody's* series, which went through nine installments from December 1910 through August 1911,[28] was an intriguing personal narrative from one of Utah's most talented native sons that helped boost the magazine's circulation from 500,000 to 600,000. It also helped launch Cannon's long-running and remunerative anti-Mormon lecture career on the Chautauqua and Lyceum circuits.[29] Cannon had followed the Smoot investigation closely, and, in fact, helped guide senators in their prosecution of the investigation of Smoot. His firsthand account of the hearings and, more important, the substance of Mormon practices being investigated in the hearings, supplied details found nowhere else. In his articles, books, and lectures, Cannon made the same charges against the Church and its leaders that had been before the Senate committee, but his allegations came from his personal insider experience and knowledge rather than from the transcripts of the hearings.[30]

After the *Pearson's* series had concluded and the *Everybody's* articles on Mormonism had begun to appear, Burton Hendricks' carefully researched and objectively written articles about the Mormons were published by *McClure's Magazine* during January and February of 1911.[31] The *McClure's* essays generally shied away from allegations of political and financial wrongdoing by the Church, focusing instead on continuing polygamy and delving deeply into Mormon theology in an attempt to understand why the Church's leaders seemed so intent upon maintaining the practice in secret, even when public and governmental pressure had brought so much difficulty to the Church and its members.[32] Hendrick concluded that polygamy was at the heart of Mormon theology and that Church leaders would do almost anything to protect and continue the practice. "One of the problems with which the American people will soon have to deal is the revival of polygamy in Utah . . . Mormonism without polygamy largely ceases to be Mormonism. Its whole theological system, from its conception of the Godhead down, is pervaded with sensualism. The Mormon god is not only a just and a vengeful god, but he is a lustful god."[33] Much of Hendrick's second article was devoted to identifying general and local Mormon leaders implicated in polygamy, including seven members of the Church's Quorum of Twelve Apostles, whose photographs were featured prominently in the article. Hendricks wrote that polygamous wives were hidden from public view in "polygamous cities of refuge," including the Forest Dale suburb of Salt Lake City and Mormon colonies in Mexico, Canada, and Hawaii. It was one thing to have the openly antagonistic *Salt Lake Tribune* identify Mormon men who had made new polygamous marriages; it was quite another to have the highly regarded *McClure's Magazine* do the same thing, in more objective terms. Hendrick referred to the Church as a "great secret society" in which "all members . . . are oath-bound, under the most frightful penalties." The manifesto was simply a "trick" to facilitate the Union's admission of Utah.[34] Although Hendrick said little about alleged political and financial wrongdoing by the Church, he did include a short discussion of the Mormon political control in the Intermountain West.[35] Given the relatively objective tone of Hendrick's articles, along with the conscientious accuracy and biting sting of his talented pen, Church leaders were no doubt relieved to realize that the articles narrowly focused on new polygamy rather than including discussion of the additional themes of political control and financial malfeasance.

Reed Smoot was no doubt unhappy when he realized that one final series of articles about the Mormons was being prepared by William Randolph Hearst's *Cosmopolitan Magazine*, whose colorfully written but poorly researched "Viper on the Hearth" articles were consistent with the magazine's reputation of publishing some of the worst yellow journalism of the time.[36] The three *Cosmopolitan* articles were the least objective of the four magazine series. Alfred Henry Lewis was perhaps the most famous political writer of the era and a close personal friend of Theodore Roosevelt and no doubt followed the Smoot proceedings closely from 1904 to 1907. Smoot took immediate notice of the *Cosmopolitan* articles, dryly noting in his diary that "the Cosmopolitan Magazine in its March issue has the first of a series of Anti-Mormon articles by Lewis."[37] These articles can best be described as outrageous. Each of the essays used written and drawn imagery suggesting that Joseph F. Smith was the viper, and other illustrations presented snakes poised on a hearth, snakes surrounding photographs of Mormon leaders, and snakes superimposed on Mormon documents. One image displayed Reed Smoot holding one end of a viper with the other end coiled around the neck of Fred T. Dubois.

Perhaps because he had spent far less time in Utah researching his articles, Lewis relied heavily on the Smoot hearings. Not counting three "dodgers" (senators who had deliberately avoided voting at all on Smoot) and Smoot, who was not permitted to vote for himself, Lewis asserted, all but two senators from western states took their cue from the all-powerful head of the Mormon Church and voted to retain Smoot. Lewis also warned that the political power of the Church was growing and raised the concern that "the Mormon Church might in any campaign be easily strong enough to make or mar a White House." He also portrayed the wealth of the Church as staggering, alleging that the Church's real estate holdings were larger than France, Spain, and Portugal combined; that money it had on deposit "overtowers the Steel Trust or Standard Oil"; and that its annual tithing revenues were between $15 and $20 million.[38] Overarching all was the practice of polygamy, a practice that contributed to the Church being a

> religion of gloom, of bitterness, of fear, of iron hand to punish the recalcitrant. It demands slavish submission on the part of every man. It insists on abjection, self-effacement, a surrender of individuality on the part of every woman. The man is to work and obey; the woman is to submit and bear children. Each is to be for the church, hoping nothing, fearing nothing, knowing nothing beyond the will of the church.[39]

The first two *Cosmopolitan* articles had appeared by the start of LDS General Conference in early April 1911. Hendrick's *McClure's* series had just concluded. Cannon and O'Higgins's April installment of "Under the Prophet in Utah," hit newsstands in late March with cover art showing a white-haired Mormon prophet sitting in a formal wooden chair over the headline "Utah's Treason."[40]

As the "magazine crusade" articles appeared, several high-profile Mormons searched for ways to defend the Church. New York–based Mormon muckraker Isaac Russell, feeling inspired by a "Guiding Hand," enlisted Theodore Roosevelt to write in support of the Mormon Church and in opposition to the critical magazine articles.[41] Senator Reed Smoot, feeling under siege and worried that the US Senate might prompt a second investigation with a less happy outcome also took steps to respond to the articles.[42] As a resident of Washington, DC, Smoot watched closely the effects these articles were having on national perceptions of Mormonism. On a trip back to Salt Lake, he wrote in his diary,

> Held a long meeting with the Presidency and presented my view on the present situation on the new polygamy cases and the sentiment of the leading men of the country. The immediate cause of the renewal of the discussion of this subject is the many magazine articles on the Mormon question charging a return to the practice of polygamy by the church members. I again insisted that the only way the church can clear its self is to handle every new case of polygamy and remove [polygamists] from any position in the church. The church [and] church authorities cannot or will not be believed as to their sincerity in abolishing polygamy if men violating the rule and promise that it should cease are sustained as officers of the church such as Bishops and Presidents of stakes, etc. They seem to think that the fact that the church has not approved or sanctioned the marriages [means] it cannot be held responsible for them—many of them were authorized by President [George Q.] Cannon.[43]

Two days later, Smoot urged the First Presidency to prepare a strong response to the articles, which Smoot would then "try and have the Associated Press carry in full."[44] Around the same time, Smoot learned that Frank J. Cannon was soon to begin lecturing nationally on the Chautauqua and Lyceum circuits. With this news, Smoot urged Church leaders to authorize him to ask the non-Mormon editor of the *Salt Lake Herald-Republican*, LeRoy Armstrong, to prepare an article "for publication in some of the leading magazines on the life of F. J. Cannon" that would "discredit" Cannon by letting the American people "know about his true life and character." Additionally, Smoot asked Church leaders to

> call the question of new polygamy cases up for consideration. Began to tell them of the danger to the church of holding men entering into polygamy since the manifesto in office and stated it was my opinion that we should drop them from all positions where people are asked to vote for them. If we do not do so we cannot convince Pres. Roosevelt or the American people that we are honest or sincere.[45]

At this same meeting, Smoot spoke of Roosevelt's letter to Isaac Russell that would soon be published in *Collier's Weekly*, one of the most popular American weekly magazines. Ironically, Smoot, who wanted in the worst way to "answer" the charges against the Mormons appearing in the national magazines, was concerned about Russell publishing Roosevelt's letter in a popular periodical. The reason was simple: Smoot had read Colonel Roosevelt's letter to Russell and was troubled by the following statement:

If the accusations made against the "Mormons" are false . . . there is no need of
my saying anything. But let me most earnestly insist on the vital need, if there
is the slightest truth in any of these accusations, of the "Mormon" people themselves acting with prompt thoroughness in the matter . . . The people of the United
States will not tolerate polygamy; and if it were found that, with the sanction and
approval or connivance of the "Mormon" Church people, polygamous marriages
are now being entered into among "Mormons," . . . then the United States Government would unquestionably itself in the end take control of the whole question of
polygamy, and there could be but one outcome to the struggle. In such event, the
"Mormon" Church would be doomed, and if there be any "Mormons" who advocate in any shape or way disobedience to, or canceling of, or the evading of, the
manifesto forbidding all further polygamous marriages, that "Mormon" is doing
his best to secure the destruction of the Church.[46]

Smoot did not like the boldness of Roosevelt's warning and doubted "the wisdom of it [having Russell publish the letter in *Collier's*] for we know there have
been new cases [of polygamy]."[47] While Smoot stewed over the matter, he repeated
his admonition to the First Presidency that something needed to be done, due to
the fact that the magazine articles were having a negative impact for the Church
in the minds of national leaders. Smoot believed the First Presidency needed to
"answer" the national "Anti-Mormon articles" with drastic disciplinary actions,
and Russell's article was not the correct course. President Smith's ambivalent reply
caused Smoot disappointment, particularly in light of Roosevelt's warning. Smoot
was perplexed: "[President Smith] does not understand the feeling of the people.
The country will not accept excuses," and if a new investigation were launched
against me, the "testimony given in my case before the Senate Committee [from
1904 to 1906]" would justifiably place the Church "in a bad position," since it had
taken "no action against the persons taking polygamist wives before 1904."[48]

Eventually, Smoot convinced President Smith that a formal statement was necessary, and for his part, Smith assured Smoot that an answer to the "magazine
articles" would be made at General Conference.[49] Smith requested that Smoot line
up eastern media to cover the event, and Smoot in turn contacted Melville Stone,
manager of the Associated Press in New York, to request coverage of the event.
Stone could not promise a full reprint of the statement but indicated he would try
to print a synopsis of the First Presidency statement.[50]

On April 9, 1911, at the Sunday afternoon session of General Conference,
the First Presidency's statement was read publicly by Heber J. Grant, no doubt
because at the time he was both a monogamist (two of his three wives having
passed away) and a well-known Democrat. According to the prepared release, the
Church preferred to maintain its silence, but, the statement explained, "[since]
there are so many requests for replies, or at least explanations," that "perhaps it is

proper that something should be officially stated for the good of the reading public." Indeed, a response was required, continued the statement, as the "mingled nonsense and venom" of the Smoot hearings is now being "poured forth from month and month . . . in present view and in popular form."[51]

Addressing specific allegations made in the magazine articles against the Church, the First Presidency admitted that "some persons" in the Church had incorrectly believed that plural marriage could continue outside the United States, such as in Mexico. However, Church president Lorenzo Snow had previously made clear in a 1900 statement that "the Church has positively abandoned the practice of polygamy, or the solemnization of plural marriages in this and every other state, and that no member or officer thereof has any authority whatever to perform a plural marriage or enter into such a relation." Those offenders "proven by sufficient evidence" to have violated this rule have been "disciplined or excommunicated" by Church tribunals.[52]

Not stopping at charges of illegal polygamy, the statement countered allegations of a "compact" between the Church and the federal government "not to dominate" political matters in Utah. This was a favorite allegation of Frank J. Cannon, in part because he believed that he had negotiated these terms with the federal government on behalf of the Church.[53] Church leaders affirmatively stated that Mormons were patriotic Americans who had courageously served the government of the United States for decades. Finally, the statement addressed assertions of financial impropriety by categorically denying that the Church president had control over tithing revenues or used them for his personal gain and profit.[54]

The Russell-Roosevelt publication appeared in *Collier's Weekly* just a few days after the statement was read by Grant at conference. Isaac Russell's "explanatory note" was the only nationally published defense of the Mormons against the magazine articles. Roosevelt's accompanying letter, though relatively limited in its defense of the Mormons, represented support for the Church from a man of extraordinary influence.[55] Heber J. Grant proudly stated, in a meeting with other senior Church leaders, that "he thought the effect of the Roosevelt article was as though one of the ancient Roman Emperors had written an epistle defending the early Christians, on the ground that Roosevelt is the most powerful figure in the whole world."[56] Caesar had spoken out on behalf of the Mormons, and that was enough. To take full advantage of the positive publicity offered by the article, the Church ordered 6,000 extra copies of the *Collier's* issue to send to government officials in the United States but more particularly to leaders in Great Britain.[57]

Joseph F. Smith also had a last word in the Church's defense against the magazine crusade. Isaac Russell arranged for publication in *Collier's Weekly* of a long letter from the Church president. In the communication, the prophet once again denied the various allegations made against the Church by the muckraking magazine articles.[58] This almost-unprecedented publication in a periodical of national circulation of a letter by a sitting LDS Church president represents an important attempt by Church authorities to control the Church's public image, being an important reminder of Mormonism's still tenuous and uncertain place within American society at the time.

Unfortunately for Smoot, he was not successful in persuading any national press services to publish a story on the Church's defense of itself in the face of the anti-Mormon magazine articles. Locally, however, Smoot enjoyed the satisfaction of undercutting Cannon's credibility by inducing the *Salt Lake Herald-Republican* to publish within its pages ad hominem attacks on Cannon's character. Cannon was vulnerable in his personal life, and the newspaper exploited this. In a harsh editorial entitled "The Unspeakable Frank J. Cannon," the *Herald-Republican* called him "the expatriate, who left Utah for Utah's good." Then, assailing Cannon for what they considered hypocrisy, the newspaper leveled charges that while living in the state, Cannon not only spent much of his time in "lowest resorts" with prostitutes but also fathered illegitimate "children" walking the streets of Salt Lake City. And he did all of this, the editorial continued, while writing self-righteous editorials for the *Tribune* on the "purity of the home and the protection of womanly modesty and virtue." Not leaving any room for interpretation, the *Herald-Republican* scathingly concluded:

> Frank J. Cannon has betrayed every trust that was ever reposed in him, religious, political or commercial, and nothing has been too low for him to stoop to if it gave him funds with which to seek the sort of perversion that most appeals to his debased and corrupted nature. He is a libertine of the worst character, a drug fiend, and a drunkard . . . Cannon probably is the vilest man that ever lived in Utah. Unscrupulous, dishonest, a libertine, with all the decency that God may have given him blotted out by his manner of living.[59]

Smoot was correct to target Frank J. Cannon. Through his "Under the Prophet in Utah" articles, Cannon was attracting national attention, including that of Harry P. Harrison, general manager of the Redpath Lyceum Bureau's Chicago office and one of the most powerful men in the "traveling" or "tent" or "circuit" Chautauqua, a flourishing enterprise during the second decade of the twentieth century.[60] In October 1910, even before the first "Under the Prophet in Utah" article appeared, Harrison made clear to Cannon that he wanted him to sign on with the Redpath Bureau: "We want to be placed in touch and have the first call on your services as a lecturer in case you are able to take up lecture work."[61] By accepting, Cannon ensured that he would have a high-profile platform to counter attempts by Smith and Smoot to improve the public's view of Mormonism.

By early 1911, the Redpath Bureau was preparing a lecture tour for Cannon, who wanted to start immediately, because, as he told Harrison, the window of opportunity to capture the public's sentiments was brief "in this versatile and mobile civilization of ours. And I merely want to clinch the attention of the people while that attention is ready to be clinched."[62] Soon, Cannon took a leave of absence from his job as managing editor of the *Rocky Mountain News* in Denver to embark on speaking assignments in November 1911. He named his lecture "The Modern Mormon Kingdom" as a way to mock the LDS Church's claim that it represented God's kingdom on earth.[63]

A quarto-sized promotion brochure, sent to Chautauqua lecture course committees throughout middle America, extolled the ex-Senator Cannon's speaking abilities as well as the subject of his lectures. This document identified Cannon as the best person to describe what Mormon leaders and their Church were up to, since the ex-senator had been, after all, a "Mormon Ambassador to Washington in 1888 and 1890" and a son of the "first counselor of the Mormon Church." In a now-anachronistic use of the term, the brochure noted that Frank was "racially a Mormon."[64]

Cannon began barnstorming the United States, speaking at Chautauqua gatherings in the summer months and at similar Lyceum lectures during cooler months. In four and a half months, from November to March 1912, Frank gave Lyceum lectures in 103 cities located in twenty-two states. The ensuing summer, he lectured at Chautauqua gatherings in forty-six different cities in nine midwestern states over two and a half months from June to September.[65] Over the next six years, Frank J. Cannon kept up this frenetic pace, giving hundreds of lectures a year under the auspices of the Redpath Bureau and later for the National Reform Association (NRA). Interestingly, presentations attacking a religion were unusual for Chautauqua. As Harry P. Harrison himself put it, there were only two

> subjects that I know of [that] were barred by common consent among Chautauqua managers. No lecturer dared to advocate violent overthrow of the government nor attack the Christian religion. Looking back on it now, the persistent and exceedingly popular campaign by ex-Senator Frank J. Cannon of Utah against the Mormon church, through half the life of the tent circuits, may have come close to sidestepping that second taboo, but managers did not recognize it at that time, perhaps because of the raging polygamy issue.[66]

Cannon's initial speeches were reinforced by the publication of his "Under the Prophet in Utah" articles in book form in December 1911, which received a favorable book review by the *New York Times*.[67] Later speeches were buttressed by the publication in 1913 of his *Brigham Young and His Mormon Empire*, which contained a chapter on how Joseph F. Smith, with supporters such as Reed Smoot, broke with the policies of former Church presidents John Taylor and Wilford Woodruff that focused on the "devotional" side of the religion and instead returned to Brigham Young's "material kingdom." Continuing on a theme of politicians befriending and courting the Mormon vote (in spite of the Church's violations of law), Cannon charged that "visiting presidents of the United States give to him [Joseph F. Smith] as much deference as they receive."[68] Cannon's publications and lectures had the effect of reinvigorating national reform movements against the Church and its alleged insidious practices.

Cannon worked closely with such antipolygamy groups as the WCTU, the Interdenominational Council of Women for Christian and Patriotic Service, and the National Reform Association. By the winter of 1914, Cannon had become the chief spokesman for the latter organization's "anti-polygamy crusade."[69] With Cannon's guidance, Miss C. E. Mason, president of the Interdenominational Council, prepared resolutions that proposed, among other matters, that Congress and the US president move to adopt a federal constitutional amendment against polygamy and polygamous cohabitation. Additionally, the resolution adjured Congress to refuse admittance by "ambassadors of the Mormon Kingdom," such as Reed Smoot, to become senators or representatives.[70]

In his "Modern Mormon Kingdom" lectures, Frank Cannon carefully chose topics that would best resonate with Progressive America, and subsequently he drew heavily upon several arguments and evidence presented at the Smoot hearings.[71] Some of these were also arguments and evidence Cannon had helped develop in leading the charge against Smoot both as a behind-the-scenes instigator of the Senate's investigation and as a newspaper editor.[72] As one of the great orators of his day, Cannon often began his speeches with the bald demand: "What are you going to do about it anyway?"[73] This question both startled and caught the attention of listeners. Drawing on his rhetorical skills, Frank would then make serious allegations about the Mormon Church and its leaders, particularly Joseph F. Smith. Among his chief complaints was that the Mormon Church had made a compact with the US government that ended the federal antipolygamy crusade. In turn, the Church agreed to abandon polygamy and even to require its members to cease cohabiting with polygamous spouses. Based on this understanding, the federal government made Utah a state in 1896, returned escheated property taken under the Edmunds-Tucker Act, and legitimized thousands of children born to polygamous marriages. According to Cannon, the Church had violated this agreement in a number of ways.[74]

One way the Mormon Church had violated the compact, averred Cannon, was by continuing to encourage the practice of polygamy. New plural marriages were performed after the 1890 manifesto, and pre-1890 polygamists were encouraged to maintain financial support of polygamous wives (which he acknowledged was appropriate) but also to continue cohabitating with them. To appeal to his audiences' prurient interests, Cannon would sometimes include a description of a plural marriage sealing ceremony performed in LDS temples.[75] Cannon believed that continued cohabitation violated the aforesaid compact with the nation, and from his perspective, Joseph F. Smith set an example that encouraged all Mormons to persevere in living "the Principle." Smith's continued cohabitation with his five wives, all of whom bore him children after the manifesto, as admitted at the Smoot hearings, served as proof positive of the Church's failure to keep its promises to the government.[76]

Cannon also alleged that the "Prophet of the Church rule[d] with an absolute political power" over Utah and much of the West. Moreover, Cannon argued that Smith had subversively dictated the successful election of Reed Smoot to the Senate. Smith had personally chosen Smoot for the US Senate, and even though honest and fair public servants had properly opposed him on the basis of his "disloyalty," with more than 1 million Americans signing "a memorial to the Senate . . . demanding that this hierarch of the Mormon Kingdom be not allowed to sit in the Senate," the Senate, nevertheless, tragically permitted him to retain his seat.[77] With Smoot safely permitted to retain his Senate seat, President Smith then influenced the election of other "Representatives and Senators" from Utah and surrounding states. These officials, whom Cannon labeled Smith's "ambassadors," then appointed those whom the Church President designated to become local "Federal officials."[78] Feeding the fire of fears he created in his listeners' minds, Cannon persuasively argued that because of the cohesive nature of Church membership, this political power was greatly disproportionate to the relatively small number of Mormons residing in western states. And due to this much larger geographic influence, the Mormon Church was even more politically powerful and frightening than it had been under Utah's People's Party in earlier times. Cannon also claimed that Church leaders were even intent on having sufficient numbers of Mormons in both national parties to tip the balance in close elections. He even suggested that there were sufficient numbers of Mormons in eleven western states that Church leaders could manipulate to sway presidential elections and, in fact, had made the difference in the election of Woodrow Wilson in 1916. As a result, Mormon leaders were in position to extract whatever favors, promises, or support they desired from federal politicians.[79]

Cannon further charged that temple-endowed Mormons were required to take an oath to avenge the blood of the slain founding prophet, Joseph Smith, and his brother Hyrum Smith. In making this case, Cannon quoted testimony from the Smoot hearings about the oath and Cannon stoked the fears of his audiences with the larger claim that Mormon leaders contemplated "supersed[ing] all civil government" with their "Kingdom of God" on earth.

Cannon also criticized the way Joseph F. Smith controlled, without accountability, the Church's "unlimited wealth." Beyond this, Cannon brought attention to the Church's unfair facilitation of wealth by its alliance with Wall Street bankers and trust interests, together with the maintenance of Smith's "absolute" autocracy with "sycophantic defenders" who stood ready to follow the Smith's every command.[80] In drawing attention to these fears, Cannon sometimes bandied numbers so outlandish as to be unbelievable to anyone objectively considering his charges, such as that Joseph F. Smith had $300 million in capital at his disposal and spent upwards of $1 million per year "to chloroform the intelligence of this country," that is, to spread Mormon propaganda and political influence.[81]

Finally, in many speeches, Cannon characterized as a travesty of justice the United States Senate's retention of Apostle-Senator Reed Smoot after the prolonged legitimacy fight. Claiming inaccurately that the Senate and Smoot's accusers "never charged him with polygamy," Cannon alleged that these groups accused Smoot of something far worse, disloyalty to the United States of America. For Cannon, this charge was proven but was hindered by the expenditure by "the Mormon Church [of] several millions of dollars to deceive the people in the United States."[82]

All told, Frank J. Cannon spoke to more than a million people attending these gatherings between 1911 and 1918. His writings were read voraciously by millions more. Giving more than 200 lectures a year, he encouraged listeners to support resolutions calling for the United States to exclude practicing Mormons from holding political office, to require an accounting of "trust funds" held by the LDS Church, to exclude Mormon pamphlets and other religious writings from being transmitted through the US Post Office, and to promulgate and ratify a constitutional amendment prohibiting polygamy. To Cannon, Smoot's first victory in retaining his seat in the Senate did not represent an end to suspicions about the Mormon Church. Rather, it represented an alarm that should raise national concern over Mormonism because LDS leaders had exercised growing power and influence to permit Smoot to retain his seat in the Senate.

As Cannon prosecuted the Mormon Church, he enlisted the help of others in his crusade. Cannon and other agitators tried hard to keep the Mormon Church and its alleged continuing un-American practices of polygamy, political control, and unholy alliances with predatory financial interests in the nation's spotlight. Sometimes they succeeded, but they ultimately failed. The LDS Church survived its continued trial. Neither Reed Smoot nor any other Mormon politician was questioned about whether he deserved to serve in public office because of his religious affiliation. Congress never sent a proposed constitutional amendment prohibiting polygamy to the states for ratification. Many thoughtful Americans did not see a need for such an amendment when the law prohibiting polygamy was already clear. The proposed constitutional amendment was a red herring in the anti-Mormon campaign, and Joseph F. Smith, as early as April 1911, expressed his support for such an amendment with certain conditions.[83] Instead, Reed Smoot continued to gain respect as a prominent member of the Senate. At the same time, national attention was drawn to the "Great War" in Europe and the importance of Mormon polygamy paled in comparison to the extraordinary carnage taking place in Europe, particularly after the United States entered the war in 1917. Contrary to what Cannon had been arguing in his lectures, remaining polygamous Mormons were aging and young Church members were not entering "the Principle." Mormon Democrats were elected to Congress, belying charges of political control by Church leaders. Like other Americans, Latter-day Saints supported the country's war efforts and fought in Europe. Progressive suspicions of "big business" eased. Eventually, even Frank J. Cannon found new pursuits, becoming president of a promising new mining company in late 1917.[84] It had taken a decade beyond the 1907 Senate vote on Reed Smoot, but by 1918 the trial of the Mormon Church during the Progressive Era had largely come to an end.

NOTES

1. The final vote was 27 in favor of expelling Smoot and 43 against expelling him, with 20 not voting. Of the 27 voting to expel, 18 were Democrats and 9 were Republicans. Of the 43 voting against expulsion, 40 were Republicans, with only 3 Democrats voting to permit Smoot to retain his seat. Congressional Record, 59th Cong., 2nd Sess., February 20, 1907, pt. 4: 3429–3430 (hereafter, Smoot Investigation Final Vote). Fortunately for Smoot, Republicans held a large majority in the US Senate in February 1907.

2. An excellent and accessible annotated version of the Smoot hearings is Michael Harold Paulos, ed., *The Mormon Church on Trial: Transcripts of the Reed Smoot Hearings* (Salt Lake City: Signature Books, 2008). Senator Julius C. Burrows, chairman of the Senate Committee investigating Smoot, famously told Senator Smoot, "You are not on trial. It is the Mormon Church that we intend to investigate, and we are going to see that these men obey the law." Reed Smoot and Franklin S. Richards, letter to President Joseph F. Smith, January 18, 1904, Reed Smoot Papers (hereafter Reed Smoot Papers); L. Tom Perry Special Collections, Harold B. Lee Library, Brigham Young University, Provo, UT (hereafter, Perry Special Collections). Not all senators agreed. For example, Senator Joseph Foraker, Republican from Ohio, forcefully stated, "I have understood from the beginning that not the Mormon Church, not Joseph F. Smith, not anybody but only Reed Smoot, was on trial . . ." Smoot Investigation Final Vote, 4:3414.

3. Smoot Investigation Final Vote, 4:3408–3428 (comments of six Republican and Democratic Senators who admired Senator Smoot but felt that his church did not command the same respect).

4. Senators Dubois and Burrows asserted, with substantial truth, however, that Church leaders continued to countenance polygamous cohabitation; that Church leaders continued to exercise or at least attempt to exercise political control over members; that no man had advanced to high Church office without giving "implicit obedience to his leaders," who were mostly lawbreaking polygamists; that no active Mormon had ever prosecuted another member of the Church for polygamy; and that those Mormons who had received temple ordinances had taken some form of oath to avenge the blood of the prophets on the nation. Smoot Investigation Final Vote: 4, 3406–3408, 3422.

5. Frank Cannon knew the Senate well, having served first as Utah's territorial delegate to Congress and then as one of Utah's first senators in the late 1890s. Cannon was bitter about not being reelected to the Senate and not receiving Church support for business and political initiatives after his father's death, and he enthusiastically accepted appointment as editor of the *Salt Lake Tribune* in late 1904. Kenneth L. Cannon II, "Wives and Other Women: Love, Sex, and Marriage in the Lives of John Q. Cannon, Frank J. Cannon, and Abraham H. Cannon," *Dialogue: A Journal of Mormon Thought* 43 (Winter 2010): 91–95; Kenneth L. Cannon II, "'The Modern Mormon Kingdom': Frank J. Cannon's National Campaign against Mormonism," *Journal of Mormon Thought* 37 (Autumn 2011): 62–65. Martha Brown Cannon died unexpectedly at the age of fifty

in March 1908. "Death Claims Mrs. F. J. Cannon," *Deseret Evening News*, March 2, 1908. Mattie had continued to be involved in the LDS Church during her husband's anti-Mormon activities, serving on the General Board of the Church's Relief Society Auxiliary. Report of the Semi-Annual Conference of the Church of Jesus Christ of Latter-day Saints, October 6, 1899 (Salt Lake City: Church of Jesus Christ of Latter-day Saints, semi-annual), 66 (hereafter, Conference Report); Conference Report (October 6, 1905), 24.

6. Leo W. Graff Jr., "Fred T. Dubois—Biographical Sketch," accessed December 2020, http:// libpublic2.eol.isu.edu/old/special/mc004b.htm.

7. US Senate, Committee of Privileges and Elections, Proceedings before the Committee on Privileges and Elections of the United States Senate in the Matter of the Protests against the Right of Hon. Reed Smoot, a Senator from the State of Utah, to Hold His Seat, 4 vols., 59th Cong., 1st Sess., S. Rept. No. 486 (Washington, DC: Government Printing Office, 1904–1906) (hereafter, Smoot Hearings), 1:109–112, 1:130–137 (Joseph F. Smith); 1:430 (Francis M. Lyman); 1:408–414 (Charles H. Merrill); 1:501–502 (Lorin Harmer); 1:515–516 (Thomas H. Merrill); 1:709–712 (B. H. Roberts); 1:780–786 (Angus M. Cannon); 2:42–45 (George Reynolds).

8. B. Carmon Hardy, *Solemn Covenant: The Mormon Polygamous Passage* (Urbana.: University of Illinois Press, 1992), 288. Frank Cannon later reported that the *Tribune* had spent $60,000 obtaining evidence of new polygamous marriages and had "freely tendered the evidence to the prosecuting officers," but, because of the power of "the Prophet" and the political climate of Utah and neighboring states, not a single new polygamist (referred to as "felons" by Cannon) had been brought to justice. Address given by Frank J. Cannon at the Baptist Church in Independence, Missouri, February 25, 1915, typescript, 19 (hereafter Frank Cannon 1915 Address), Archives of the Church History Department, Church of Jesus Christ of Latter-day Saints, Salt Lake City (hereafter, LDS Church History Library).

9. The WCTU had taken an active part in opposing Reed Smoot. Joan Smyth Iversen, *The Anti-Polygamy Controversy in U.S. Women's Movements, 1880–1925: A Debate of the American Home* (New York: Garland Publishing, Inc., 1997), 216–219. The NRA's women's auxiliary was called the "National Order of Anti-Polygamy Crusaders." *Christian Statesman* 48 (June 1914): 282. The mainstream WHFRS used as its study course in the summer of 1913 Bruce Kinney's *Mormonism: The Islam of America* (New York: Fleming H. Revell Co., 1912); "Mormonism as a Religion," *Lutheran Women's Work* 6 (June 1913): 273–276; "Mormonism as a Life," *Lutheran Women's Work* 6 (July 1913): 320–322; and "Mormonism as an Organization and What Is Being Done to Meet It," *Lutheran Women's Work* 6 (August 1913): 426–427. The same issues of the magazine carried extensive articles about the Church and the futility of missionary work among the Mormons.

10. Harvey J. O'Higgins, "Address to the Drama Society of New York on 'Polygamy' (Inside Story of the Play)," [1915], Perry Special Collections. Lindsey and O'Higgins had collaborated on "The Beast and the Jungle," a harsh indictment of corrupt Colorado politics, which first appeared in 1909 as a series in *Everybody's Magazine*, then was published as a book. Ben L. Lindsey and Harvey J. O'Higgins, *The Beast* (New York: Doubleday, Page and Co., 1910). "Muckraker" is an ill-defined term used to describe reform-minded investigative journalists who wrote for Progressive magazines in the first fifteen years of the twentieth century. The fifteen-cent magazines, made possible by newly inexpensive paper, enjoyed immense popularity. The term was applied by Theodore Roosevelt, who compared sensationalized journalists to the "man . . . with the Muckrake in his hand," from John Bunyan's *Pilgrim's Progress*. John Bunyan, *The Pilgrim's Progress, Oxford World's Classics ed.* (Oxford: Oxford University Press, 1998), 164.

11. O'Higgins, "Address on 'Polygamy,'" Perry Special Collections. *Everybody's* would go to substantial lengths to promote articles it wanted to publish. For example, it spent $50,000 in marketing Lindsey's "The Beast and the Jungle" series in 1909. Frank Luther Mott, *Sketches of 21 Magazines, 1905–1930*, vol. 5 of A History of American Magazines (Cambridge, MA: Harvard University Press, 1968), 83.

12. For a detailed discussion of articles about the Mormons in national magazines during this time period, see Kenneth L. Cannon II, "'And Now It Is the Mormons:' The Magazine Crusade against the Mormon Church, 1910–1911," *Dialogue: A Journal of Mormon Thought* 46 (Spring 2013): 1–63. Editors knew that many Americans were outraged that Smoot had been permitted to retain his Senate seat after the shocking exposures reported in the Smoot hearings.

13. John P. Hatch, ed., *Danish Apostle: The Diaries of Anthon H. Lund, 1890–1921* (Salt Lake City: Signature Books, 2006), 440, entry of September 27, 1910.

14. Richard Barry, "The Political Menace of the Mormon Church," *Pearson's Magazine* 24 (September 1910): 319–330; Richard Barry, "The Mormon Evasion of Anti-polygamy Laws," *Pearson's Magazine* 24 (October 1910): 443–451; Richard Barry, "The Mormon Method in Business," *Pearson's Magazine* 24 (November 1910): 571–78. New York–based Mormon journalist and muckraker Isaac Russell understood from his contacts at Progressive magazines (for several of which he wrote editorials and articles), that *Pearson's Magazine* had learned that Cannon and O'Higgins were preparing a series of articles for publication in *Everybody's Magazine* and decided to "scoop" *Everybody's* with its own series. Kenneth L. Cannon II, "Isaac Russell, Mormon Muckraker and Secret Defender of the Church," *Journal of Mormon History* 39 (Fall 2013):14–98.

15. Frank J. Cannon and Harvey J. O'Higgins, "Under the Prophet in Utah," *Everybody's Magazine* 23 (December 1910): 725.

16. Richard Barry, "The Political Menace of the Mormon Church," *Pearson's Magazine* 24 (September 1910): 319–320.

17. Barry, "The Mormon Evasion of the Anti-polygamy Laws," 446, 447–450.

18. Barry, "The Political Menace of the Mormon Church," 320, 324, 327, 330. Barry also retold the story earlier circulated by the *Salt Lake Tribune* that Theodore Roosevelt and the LDS Church had made a "corrupt bargain" by which Roosevelt agreed to support the retention of Reed Smoot in exchange for the Mormon vote. In the third Pearson's article, Barry described the business schemes in which Mormon leaders and their Church invested: banks, mines, salt companies, farm equipment manufacturers, railroads, electric utilities, newspapers. Barry, "The Mormon Method of Doing Business," 572–577.

19. In July 1909, Francis M. Lyman, who previously had testified at the Smoot hearings, was appointed as the chair of a committee charged with investigating and dealing with instances of new polygamous marriages. Thomas G. Alexander, *Mormonism in Transition: A History of the Latter-day Saints, 1890–1930* (Urbana: University of Illinois Press, 1986), 66–68. The so-called Lyman Committee originally consisted of Francis M. Lyman, Heber J. Grant, and John Henry Smith.

20. D. Michael Quinn, "LDS Church Authority and New Plural Marriages, 1890–1904," *Dialogue: A Journal of Mormon Thought* 18 (Spring 1985): 82–103.

21. Reed Smoot, Diary, September 8, 27, October 5, 13, November 15, 1910, March 16, 31, 1911, Reed Smoot Papers. An accessible edition of the Smoot diaries is Harvard S. Heath, ed., *In the World, The Diaries of Reed Smoot* (Salt Lake City: Signature Books, 1997), 63–64, 69, 71–72, 74, 78–79, 95–96, 98.

22. Reed Smoot, Diary, October 1, 1910, Reed Smoot Papers; Heath, *In the World*, 70–71.

23. Joseph F. Smith, Anthon H. Lund, John Henry Smith, letter to Stake Presidents and Counselors, October 5, 1910, copy in the Isaac Russell Papers. A more accessible version is included in James R. Clark, comp., *Messages of the First Presidency*, 4 vols. (Salt Lake City: Bookcraft, 1965–1975), 4:218.

24. Clark, *Messages of the First Presidency*, 4:218; Hatch, *Danish Apostle*, 440–441, entry of October 8, 1910; Reed Smoot, Diary, October 8, 1910, Reed Smoot Papers; Heath, *In the World*, 73.

25. "Democratic-Tribune Deal," *Salt Lake Herald-Republican*, October 27, 1910, 1. The *Herald-Republican* accused *Tribune* management and former senator Dubois of going to New York City earlier in the summer to arrange the crusade against the Mormons by the three identified

magazines. The editorial noted that "it is useless for [Kearns and Dubois] to deny [that they had made arrangements with the national magazines to publish articles on the Mormons], because they were seen in the office of the editor of *McClure's* by a former Salt Lake man, who was told the story of their mission by the editor of *McClure's* himself." Dubois had led the fight against Smoot in the US Senate. Leo W. Graff Jr., *The Senatorial Career of Fred T. Dubois of Idaho, 1890–1907* (New York: Garland Publishing, 1988), 456–492.

26. "And Now It Is the Mormons," *New York Times Review of Books*, November 19, 1910, BR 1.

27. Cannon and O'Higgins, "Under the Prophet in Utah," *Everybody's Magazine* 23 (December 1910): 725.

28. Cannon and O'Higgins, "Under the Prophet in Utah," 722–737, 99–104 (advertising section); 24 (January 1911): 29–35; 24 (February 1911): 189–205; 24 (March 1911): 383–399; 24 (April 1911): 513–528; 24 (May 1911): 652–664; 24 (June 1911): 825–835; "The New Polygamy," 25 (July 1911): 94–107; "The Prophet and Big Business," 25 (August 1911): 209–222. Most of what appeared in the magazine articles was included in the far-better-known book form of the work, *Under the Prophet in Utah: The National Menace of a Political Priestcraft* (Boston: C. M. Clark Publishing, 1911).

29. Cannon, "Frank J. Cannon's National Campaign against Mormonism," 73–78; Frank Luther Mott, *Sketches of 21 Magazines, 1905–1930*, vol. 5 of *A History of American Magazines* (Cambridge, MA: Harvard University Press, 1968), 81–83.

30. Cannon and O'Higgins, "Under the Prophet in Utah," *Everybody's* 24 (May 1911): 656–657, 659–664; 24 (June 1911): 825–835.

31. Burton J. Hendrick, "The Revival of Mormon Polygamy," *McClure's Magazine* 36 (January 1911): 245–62; "The Mormon Revival of Polygamy," *McClure's Magazine* 36 (February 1911): 449–464. There was a broad range of muckraking, from "accurate and penetrating reportage," that appeared in the quintessential muckraking magazine, *McClure's*, to the "irresponsible sensationalism" of *Cosmopolitan Magazine*. Louis Filler, *Appointment at Armageddon: Muckraking and Progressivism in the American Tradition* (Westport, CT: Greenwood Press, 1976), 248.

32. In later correspondence with Mormon journalist Isaac Russell, Hendrick indicated that most of the research materials he used for his articles had come from the transcripts of the Smoot hearings. Burton J. Hendrick, letter to Isaac Russell, May 23, 1911, Isaac Russell Papers. Hendrick did include a short description of the Church's political power and financial wealth that left few government officials who dared attack the Church for fear of losing the Mormon vote. Hendrick, "The Mormon Revival of Polygamy," *McClure's* (January 1911): 252–261.

33. Hendrick, "The Mormon Revival of Polygamy," 245.

34. Hendrick, "The Mormon Revival of Polygamy," 451–458, 461.

35. It was no surprise that *McClure's* was the most temperate in its description of Mormon practices. *McClure's* was the most respected muckraking magazine and was widely known for its quality of writing and research. The magazine became almost synonymous with high-quality muckraking journalism based on the care and quality of its articles. Harold S. Wilson, *McClure's Magazine and the Muckrakers* (Princeton, NJ: Princeton University Press, 1970); Filler, *Appointment at Armageddon*, 248, 251.

36. Alfred Henry Lewis, "Viper on the Hearth," *Cosmopolitan Magazine* 50 (March 1911): 439–450; "Trail of the Viper," *Cosmopolitan Magazine* 50 (April 1911): 693–703; "Viper's Trail of Gold," *Cosmopolitan Magazine* 50 (May 1911): 823–831. Contemporaries, even B. H. Roberts, uniformly referred to the periodical as "the" *Cosmopolitan*. See Brigham H. Roberts, *A Comprehensive History of the Church of Jesus Christ of Latter-day Saints, Century I*, 6 vols. (Provo, UT: Brigham Young University Press, 1965), 6:414.

37. Smoot, Diary, February 17, 1911, Reed Smoot Papers; Heath, *In the World*, 92.

38. Lewis, "Viper on the Hearth," *Cosmopolitan* 50 (March 1911): 446–447; "The Viper's Trail of Gold," *Cosmopolitan* 50 (May 1911): 825–826.

39. Lewis, "The Trail of the Viper," *Cosmopolitan* 50 (April 1911): 700. As Mormon historian B. H. Roberts saw it, "So personal and bitter were these Cosmopolitan articles and so viciously illustrated, that the writer defeated his own ends, or they brought the author and the publishers more censure than praise." Roberts, *A Comprehensive History of the Church*, 6:414. Even Frank J. Cannon found the "Viper on the Hearth" articles to be sensationalized. Frank J. Cannon, letter to Harry P. Harrison, February 10, 1911, Redpath Chautauqua Collection, Special Collections Department, University of Iowa Libraries, Iowa City, Iowa (hereafter Redpath Chautauqua Collection).

40. Ironically, in a remarkable gaffe, the white-haired patriarch illustrated on the cover of the April issue of *Everybody's* was not Joseph F. Smith but his cousin Joseph Smith III, leader of what was then known as the Reorganized Church of Jesus Christ of Latter-day Saints.

41. Cannon, "Isaac Russell, Mormon Muckraker," 46; Isaac Russell, letter to Joseph F. Smith, February 11, 1913, Scott G. Kenney Papers (hereafter Kenney Papers), Special Collections, J. Willard Marriott Library, University of Utah, Salt Lake City, Utah.

42. Cannon, "Magazine Crusade," 22–25, 29–30; Reed Smoot, Diary, March 16, March 31, April 2, April 7, April 8, 1911, Reed Smoot Papers; Heath, *In the World*, 95–96, 98, 99.

43. Reed Smoot, Diary, March 14, 1911, Reed Smoot Papers; Heath, *In the World*, 94–95. In fact, George Q. Cannon played a central role in the renewal of polygamy after 1890.

44. Reed Smoot, Diary, March 16, 1911, Reed Smoot Papers; Heath, *In the World*, 95–96.

45. Reed Smoot, Diary, March 16, 1911, Reed Smoot Papers; Heath, *In the World*, 95–96. The *Herald-Republican* later noted that Cannon's articles in *Everybody's* "are the worst of the lot, and are especially damaging." "Thomas Kearns and Frank J. Cannon," *Salt Lake Herald-Republican*, April 23, 1911, 4.

46. Theodore Roosevelt and Isaac Russell, "Mr. Roosevelt to the Mormons: A Letter with an Explanatory Note by Isaac Russell," *Collier's Weekly* 47 (April 15, 1911): 28. Women's historian Joan Smyth Iversen suggests that Roosevelt's "warning" to the Mormons in the letter published in *Collier's* was connected to his "run for the presidency in 1912, which required the support of reform women." Iversen, *Anti-polygamy Controversy in U.S. Women's Movements, 1880–1925*, 227. This seems unlikely because April 1911 was long before he formally decided to run for president in the 1912 election and he appears to have had genuine concerns about new polygamous marriages, if not about continued marital relations between long-married polygamous couples. I. K. Russell, "Theodore Roosevelt—Staunch Friend of Utah, Incident Is Recalled wherein He Dealt a Staggering Blow to the Defamers of a Maligned People," *Deseret News*, December 20, 1919, Christmas News section, 12.

47. Reed Smoot, Diary, March 16, 1911, Reed Smoot Papers; Heath, *In the World*, 95–96. Isaac Russell later told B. H. Roberts that he understood that "Smoot I believe didn't like the idea of publishing the T. R. letter—feared he'd turn on us: he won't if we're square. I want him to if we're not." Isaac Russell, letter to B. H. Roberts, May 6, 1911, Kenney Papers.

48. Reed Smoot, Diary, March 31, April 2, 1911, Reed Smoot Papers; Heath, *In the World*, 98, 99.

49. Reed Smoot, Diary, April 2, 7, and 8, 1911, Reed Smoot Papers; Heath, *In the World*, 99.

50. Reed Smoot Diary, April 7 and 8, 1911, Reed Smoot Papers; Heath, *In the World*, 99.

51. "Slanders Are Refuted by the First Presidency, Misrepresented from the First," *Deseret News*, April 10, 1911, 3. The statement was reprinted in the June issue of the *Improvement Era* with the memorable title "Magazine Slanders Confuted by the First Presidency of the Church," *Improvement Era* 14 (June 1911): 717–724.

52. "Magazine Slanders." The 1900 statement carefully limited the proscription on polygamous marriages to "states," leaving open the possibility that polygamous marriages might be performed outside the United States, whereas the 1911 statement made clear that marriages outside the United States were also inappropriate. Some of the "persons" who apparently thought such marriages could be solemnized outside of the United States in countries such as in Mexico were George

Q. Cannon and Joseph F. Smith, Lorenzo Snow's two counselors in the First Presidency in 1900. D. Michael Quinn, "LDS Church Authority and New Plural Marriages, 1890–1904," *Dialogue: A Journal of Mormon Thought* 18 (Spring 1985): 61–62, 75–80, 83, 89, 92–93.

53. Cannon, "The Modern Mormon Kingdom," 83–84; Cannon and O'Higgins, *Under the Prophet in Utah*, 395–398.

54. "Slanders Are Refuted," *Deseret News*, April 10, 1911, 3.

55. Isaac Russell, "Mr. Roosevelt to the Mormons, A Letter with an Explanatory Note," *Collier's Weekly* 57 (April 15, 1911): 28, 36. This article was reprinted in the same issue of the *Improvement Era* that carried the reprint of the First Presidency's April 1911 statement. "Mr. Roosevelt to the 'Mormons,'" *Improvement Era* 14 (June 1911): 712–718. Roosevelt basically limited his statements to general support for the Mormons and to responding to arguments that he had made a "corrupt bargain" with the Mormons in the 1904 election by conceding to certain demands of Church leaders in exchange for the Mormon vote. Russell, "Mr. Roosevelt to the Mormons."

56. Charles S. Burton, letter to Isaac Russell, April 29, 1911, Isaac Russell Papers. The letter was marked "strictly confidential."

57. Joseph F. Smith, letter to Isaac Russell, April 25, 1911, Isaac Russell Papers.

58. Joseph F. Smith, "The Mormons To-Day," *Collier's Weekly*, August 12, 1911, 26–27, 29; Joseph F. Smith, letter to Isaac Russell, June 15, 1911, Joseph F. Smith Letterpress Copybooks, Richard E. Turley, ed., *Selected Collections of the Archives of the Church of Jesus Christ of Latter-day Saints*, 2 vols., DVD (Provo, UT: BYU Press, 2002), 1:30.

59. "The Unspeakable Frank J. Cannon," *Salt Lake Herald-Republican*, April 21, 1911, 4. Cannon had at least one illegitimate child and may have had others. Kenneth L. Cannon II, "Wives and Other Women," 84–85.

60. Harry P. Harrison and Carl Detzer, *Culture under Canvas: The Story of Tent Chautauqua* (New York: Hastings House, 1958), xvi–xviii. This form of Chautauqua gathering was variously called "traveling," "circuit," "tent," or "tent circuit" to distinguish it from the similar programs presented in Chautauqua, New York. Circuit Chautauqua brought political figures, actors, entertainers, scientists, musicians, writers, and explorers to cities and towns across America, pitching a circuslike tent in each venue for five or six days in what amounted to the beginnings of adult education in the United States. Circuit Chautauquas were managed by such organizations as the Redpath Bureau.

61. Harry P. Harrison, letter to Frank J. Cannon, October 11, 1910, Redpath Chautauqua Collection.

62. Frank J. Cannon, letter to Harry P. Harrison, February 10, 1911, Redpath Chautauqua Collection.

63. Redpath Chautauqua brochure on Frank J. Cannon, Redpath Chautauqua Collection; Frank Cannon 1915 Address, February 25, 1915, 14, 20, 24, 26–27. The transcript of the speech given by Cannon in February 1915 is the only extant complete copy of an address he gave during this period that I have located. Cannon gave the address to a group sponsored by the NRA and so might be slightly different from the "Modern Mormon Kingdom" lectures he gave before Chautauqua and Lyceum audiences.

64. Redpath Chautauqua brochure on Frank J. Cannon, Redpath Chautauqua Collection.

65. C.M.C. Atkinson of C. M. Clark Publishing, letter to Harry P. Harrison, August 26, 1911; C.M.C. Atkinson, letter to Redpath Slayton Bureau, September 20, 1911; C. M. Clark Publishing, letter to Harry P. Harrison, November 10, 1911; L. B. Crotty, letter to C.M.C. Atkinson, November 13, 1911—all in Redpath Chautauqua Collection. This correspondence does not include a week in January 1912, when the schedule indicated that Cannon would be "booked with our N.Y. office." C. M. Clark Publishing, letter to Harry P. Harrison, November 10, 1911, Redpath Chautauqua Collection.

66. Harrison and Detzer, *Culture under Canvas*, 131.

67. "Utah in Her Chains," *New York Times Review of Books*, December 17, 1911, 1.

68. Frank J. Cannon and George Knapp, *Brigham Young and His Mormon Empire* (New York: Fleming H. Revell, 1913), 386–391.

69. "A Christian Crusade," *Christian Statesman* 48 (February 1914): 88; "Crusade against the Polygamy and Disloyalty of the Mormon Kingdom by the National Reform Association" (Pittsburgh: National Reform Association, [1913]); Frank Cannon 1915 Address, 13.

70. Resolutions, Interdenominational Council of Women for Christian and Patriotic Service, February 1, 1912, Redpath Chautauqua Collection.

71. Andrew Rieser, *The Chautauqua Moment: Protestants, Progressives, and the Culture of Modern Liberalism* (New York: Columbia University Press, 2003), 240–284, describes the close association of 1910s Chautauqua with the Progressive movement.

72. Paulos, "Opposing the 'High Ecclesiasts at Washington,'" *Journal of Mormon History* 37 (Fall 2011): 16, 19, 29–30, 31, 35–36, 40–41.

73. "The Modern Mormon Kingdom," [Sewickley, Penn.] *Herald*, November 16, 1912, in Uncle Dale's Old Mormon Articles, Pennsylvania, 1900–1999, www.sidneyrigdon.com/dbroadhu/PA/penn1900.htm #111612 (accessed 12 February 2021). Even enemies of Cannon grudgingly recognized his considerable talents. J. T. Goodwin, a Utah Gentile and son of sometime *Tribune* editor C. C. Goodwin, once called Cannon "the most brilliant distorter of facts this country has produced in several generations." J. T. Goodwin, *Goodwin's Weekly*, March 4, 1911, as qtd. in Melvin J. Ballard, "Open Letter to Dr. Coyle and the World's Christian Citizenship Conference, June [15], 1913," Official Report, Second World's Christian Citizenship Conference, Portland, Oregon, June 29–July 6, 1913 (Pittsburgh: National Reform Association, 1913), 200. Goodwin, like many non-Mormons in Utah, did not hold a high opinion of Frank Cannon.

74. Frank Cannon 1915 Address, 10–12, 24; Cannon and O'Higgins, *Under the Prophet in Utah*, 395–398; "Would Sue Mormons under Sherman Act," *New York Times*, January 11, 1912, 4; "Ex-Sen. Cannon Bitterly Assails Mormon Church," [Trenton, New Jersey] *Gazette*, April 20, 1914, in Journal History of the Church of Jesus Christ of Latter-day Saints (chronological scrapbook of typed entries and newspaper clippings, 1830–present), April 20, 1914, 4 (hereafter Journal History), LDS Church History Library; "Former Senator Comes to Utah to Attack Utah Faith," *Detroit Journal*, March 17, 1917, *Journal History*, March 17, 1917, 6; "The Topmost Heights of Absurdity Reached by Anti-'Mormon' Campaign," *Deseret News*, April 22, 1916, 3:9.

75. Frank Cannon 1915 Address, 18.

76. Frank Cannon 1915 Address, 14; Cannon and O'Higgins, *Under the Prophet in Utah*, 337–359, 397; "The Modern Mormon Kingdom," [Sewickley, Penn.] *Herald*, November 16, 1912; "Crusade against Mormonism Begun," [Wheeling, WV] *Intelligencer*, April 17, 1914, *Journal History*, April 17, 1914, 4; "Ex-Sen. Cannon Bitterly Assails Mormon Church," [Trenton, NJ] *Gazette*, April 20, 1914.

77. "Ex-Sen. Cannon Bitterly Assails Mormon Church," 26.

78. Cannon and O'Higgins, *Under the Prophet in Utah*, 397–401; "The Modern Mormon Kingdom," [Sewickley, Penn.] *Herald*, November 16, 1912; "Crusade against Mormonism," [Wheeling, WV] *Intelligencer*, April 17, 1914; Frank Cannon 1915 Address, February 25, 1915, 24.

79. "Cannon Flays Mormon Faith," *Detroit Free Press*, March 19, 1917, 3. The 1916 presidential election between Woodrow Wilson and former Supreme Court justice Charles Evans Hughes was very close, and some newspapers reported that Hughes had won. John Milton Cooper, *Woodrow Wilson: A Biography* (New York: Alfred A. Knopf, 2009), 355–360. Although every Western state other than Oregon voted to elect Wilson (putting Wilson over the top) (https://uselectionatlas.org/RESULTS [accessed December 2020]), it was not because Joseph F. Smith had ordered Mormons to vote Democratic that year. Smith was a partisan Republican who had played a central role in the election of Reed Smoot. Quinn, "LDS Church Authority and New Plural Marriages," *Dialogue* 18 (Spring 1985): 96.

80. Cannon and O'Higgins, *Under the Prophet in Utah*, 360–377; Cannon and Knapp, *Brigham Young and His Mormon Empire*, 388; "The Modern Mormon Kingdom," [Sewickley, Penn.] *Herald*,

November 16, 1912; "Ex-Sen. Cannon Bitterly Assails Mormon Church," [Trenton, NJ] *Gazette*, April 20, 1914.

81. Frank Cannon 1915 Address, 22.

82. Frank Cannon 1915 Address, 26.

83. Report of the Annual Conference of the Church of Jesus Christ of Latter-day Saints, April 6, 1911 (Salt Lake City: Church of Jesus Christ of Latter-day Saints, 1911), 8–9. Smith wanted the federal government to regulate marriage and divorce generally and also wanted polygamists married before 1890 and "those who took wives under the authority of the presiding authorities of the Church" to be able to continue to support and, presumably, cohabit with their wives. Report of the Annual Conference of the Church of Jesus Christ of Latter-day Saints. President Smith's cleverly concealed second exception of those polygamists who should be permitted to continue to live with their wives included many men who married plural wives long after the 1890 Manifesto. Different constitutional amendments were proposed between 1908 and 1913. Some would have prohibited only polygamy broadly; others would have banned polygamous cohabitation as well. Edward Stein, "Past and Present Proposed Amendments to the United States Constitution Regarding Marriage," *Washington University Law Review* 82 (2004): 676–677. Smith's professed public support for such an amendment was conditioned on it not making polygamous cohabitation a crime. As Smith had acknowledged in the Smoot hearings and as all of the anti-Mormon agitators had pointed out, Smith himself was living with all of his five wives.

84. "Frank J. Cannon to Be Wyoming Magnate," *Salt Lake Herald-Republican*, June 11, 1917, 10.

Part II

The Local Picture

5

My Darling Allie, Your Reed

Letters 1903–1907

Kathryn Smoot Egan

Loneliness and ambition wove the baseline for my great-grandfather Reed Smoot during his Senate controversy beginning in 1903 and dragging into 1907. His wife, Alpha May Eldredge (Allie), remained in Provo, Utah, caring for their six children for most of the investigation. Reed preferred she not be exposed to the tribulations imposed on him personally and on Mormonism generally, by the "Washington crowd" as he called them. This chapter will bring to light the role Allie played in support of my great-grandfather by contextualizing six letters written to her by the senator during the course of these hearings. In telling her story, I hope to also spotlight the stories of the other women in Reed's life who provided the foundation, comfort, and security required for him to ride out the storm.

I found these six letters written to Allie in my grandmother's attic when I was an honors student at the University of Utah. My grandmother Anita Parkinson Smoot (we called her "Guam") was Reed Smoot's daughter-in-law, married to my grandfather Harlow Eldredge Smoot ("Brownie")[1] who died when I was fourteen. Harlow is the son of Reed Smoot, interviewed in September of 1949 by Milton R. Merrill for his important book *Reed Smoot Apostle in Politics*.[2]

Reed died in 1941, a year before I was born. I know he adored my grandmother Guam; he could count on her cooking. In 1919 Harlow and Anita moved into the house Reed and Allie had built in Provo in 1892—a mansion at the time.[3] Allie considered the house her home—Reed's was in Washington. When Allie and/or Reed came back to Utah after 1919—which Reed did seldom and

DOI: 10.7330/9781646421176.c005

briefly—the front bedroom was theirs. Reed would arrive for dinner bringing friends from Washington, DC, or members of the LDS Church's hierarchy, while Guam would provide the requisite feast. She could cook anything: fish, venison, pheasant—whatever the hunters brought home—or something from nothing when the larder was running low.

My major at Utah was journalism; my honors thesis, "The Role of the Newspaper in the Reed Smoot Investigation: 1903–1907," was submitted to the Department of Journalism in March 1964.[4] I used primary documents discovered in boxes I found in Guam's attic, including Reed's February 20, 1907, tally of Senate votes (42–28) that allowed him to keep his seat and the handwritten letters to Allie. These items I kept as personal treasures. Fortunately, this was prior to my Uncle Sam Smoot's plunder of Anita's attic for all things belonging to Reed Smoot in order to memorialize him by creating a Reed Smoot room that included a wall of portraits currently located at Brigham Young University's Harold B. Lee Library, in Provo, Utah. Sam also wrote a personal history from his experience and perspective growing up in the Provo house. The original compilation of his notes and other materials, entitled "Goodnight Mrs. Smoot," is located within the *Smoot Papers* at the L. Tom Perry Special Collections at Brigham Young University. He also gave copies to the families of his siblings.[5]

For most of the hearings, Reed lived alone in Washington. This physical separation was immensely difficult, and Allie's letters to him were godsends of support and comfort. For the circumspect apostle-senator, writing home to Allie was his way of staying close at hand, sharing his experiences with subtle stoicism and anguish.

The first letter to Allie is postmarked February 27, 1903. A few days prior, Reed had traveled by train to Washington, accompanied by Utah State Republican Party chairman and a lifelong political ally, James H. Anderson. They had heard rumors that a special session in the Senate relating to Smoot's election might be held following the regular session on the Panama treaty. Arriving on February 21, the rumor proved the case, when, after the Panama treaty consideration, Utah's non-Mormon ("gentile") senator Thomas Kearns presented Smoot's credentials on the Senate floor. Michigan senator Julius Caesar Burrows, chairman of the Committee on Privileges and Elections, then introduced a Citizen's Protest against Smoot's seating.[6] During this whirlwind of events, Reed wrote the following letter to Allie. (The six letters abridged in this chapter retain Smoot's original grammar, spelling, and colloquialisms.)

> Darling Allie—Since writing You last I have been almost crowded to death with work. Tuesday evening I attended the Presidents reception at the White House.[7] It was a musicale and the music was grand. Allie I dont beleive [*sic*] I ever will like society and enjoy the gush and hypocrisy of modern gatherings. I dont beleive [*sic*]

FIGURE 5.1. Painting portrait of Alpha "Allie" May Smoot (ca. 1910). Photo courtesy of Kathryn Smoot Egan, great-granddaughter of Reed Smoot.

you will ever feel at home in Washington Society. I believe I saw only two ladies with high neck dresses on and they were from Minnesota and were here on a visit. The balance present did not only have low neck dresses but low body dresses. I will enclose you a programme of musicale. Also tell you more about it when I get home. I am well satisfied with the conditions here and have no doubt of the final outcome. Today Rev [John L.] Leilich presented a charge to [the] Senate through the chairman of Privileges and Elections Senator Burrows of Michigan charging me with polygamy,[8] having married since Statehood but he states it is considered injudicious to give the name of woman or place where marriage was solemnized. It is done to stop my being sworn in, in case of an extra session of Congress and inflame the public mind so they will get up petitions as in the case of [B. H.] Roberts.[9] It looks today like we will have an extra session and I hope and pray that we do for I think it will settle the question very quick. I notice while taking a bath that I am getting skinny as a crow. I am so tired of Hotel food. It almost makes me sick. I cannot complain of the treatment accorded me so far by the Senators or by Washington news papers. I guess I am the best advertised man in the United States and perhaps in the world at present. I hope it will do our people some good. I have not received one word from you as yet. If I was not so crowded I would be awful homesick. Oh give me my Provo home and family for it is the best place on earth. Write and let me know how the children are and kiss them all and tell them to be sure and pray for Papa. . . . many many kisses from Your Reed.[10]

A rational pragmatist, Reed walked a diplomatic line staked at one end by faith and at the other by convictions of how world conditions might be improved through smart legislation. The focus on Smoot being a polygamist was misguided and absurd. Reed was not a polygamist, though both he and Allie had been raised in polygamist families. Reed was the son of Abraham Owen (A. O.) Smoot and Anne Kirstine Mauritsen, A. O.'s fifth wife.[11]

Anne was an extraordinary influence in Reed's life. At age nineteen, she departed Onsu, Norway, over the brutal protests of her parents, with her brother Nelse and his family to join Church members in Salt Lake City, Utah.[12] She was a promising child, the oldest daughter, unusually bright, a weaver, and betrothed to "an exemplary young man" who was the love of her life.[13] Dissatisfied with the Lutheran Church and concerned with the salvation of her soul, she investigated Mormonism with Nelse and found the missionaries' arguments persuasive, though they did not mention plural marriage.[14] After joining the "Mormon Church," Anne arrived in the Salt Lake Valley on September 7, 1855, weakened by the long trip which included a five weeks' crossing the Atlantic Ocean, three months of winter encampment at Mormon Grove in Kansas, and several tedious months crossing the plains with ox teams. Once in Salt Lake, Nelse determined to leave the valley and the Church, and the two siblings parted ways.[15] Left alone, Anne secured a position as a housemaid with Mormon apostle Orson Pratt's family but became too ill to perform the required tasks. She was cared for until deemed "well" but not healthy enough to adequately finish the work required of a maid. Instead she summoned her expertise as a weaver and applied for a position with a family living in Pond Town (later Sugar House). Bishop A. O. Smoot's first and second wives, Margaret (Ma) and Emily, were living in a "rustic cabin" when they hired her for a weeklong trial period and found her work more than satisfactory. Becoming an integral part of the family, Ma Smoot suggested she marry A. O., "as kind and good as any man," and she did. He was forty-one; she was twenty-three. Reed, namesake of A. O.'s brother, was her firstborn son. In 1932, Reed said of his mother, "I relied upon her for guidance, comfort, and sympathetic understanding. In manhood I have been sustained by the faith and the fortitude that she helped to build into my character."[16]

Allie was the beloved, cultured daughter of Horace S. Eldredge and Chloe Antoinette Redfield—the youngest, most beautiful wife of Horace's five[17]—the one with whom he chose to live after the passage of the punitive antipolygamy Edmunds Act of 1882.[18] In his aforementioned family history, Uncle Sam writes "Dad spoke of a tunnel between the house and barn that served General Eldredge when it was found necessary to make a fast exit if the law closed in." Horace was a "merchant prince" in early Mormon history, being both a farmer and frontiersman. He joined the Church when he was twenty and went west with Brigham Young's company in 1846–1847.[19]

Horace was called "General" for his position in the Mormon Militia in Illinois, otherwise known as the Nauvoo Legion. In partnership with Brigham Young, he helped procure and freight merchandise from the "States" to Salt Lake City; was elected marshal of the Provisional State of Deseret (which became Utah Territory); and organized the Bank of Deseret. With a few business partners, including A. O., Horace also organized a firm that became Zion Cooperative Mercantile Institution (ZCMI). He married Chloe Antoinette when she was fifteen; he was thirty-five, producing ten children, including my great-grandmother, Allie, who was the second child and the oldest girl.[20]

Chloe, born on August 10, 1842, was seven years old when her family trekked west in the company led by Aaron Johnson. Family stories tell us that for lack of space in the wagon she had to leave her favorite doll behind, but carried the painted porcelain head across the plains. When the family arrived in Salt Lake, her mother made a new body and dressed the doll elegantly, which Chloe remained attached to for many years. The doll has survived through six generations, encased in glass, and wearing a wedding ring (probably Chloe's) around her arm.

Chloe and her brood lived in a beautiful house. One family photo shows two shaggy ponies standing in the street fronting the house and harnessed to a carriage filled with children. Horace died in 1888, but Chloe maintained the house for thirty years thereafter, holding family and social parties for as long as she was able. Alive until 1920, she was a living reminder of Smoot's polygamous roots during the Senate investigation.

Horace and A. O. Smoot shared entrepreneurial interests as well as high Church positions. A. O. captained the second company of Saints to Utah in 1847, served seven missions for the Church, and, like Horace, went east to secure equipment and supplies. He was Salt Lake's second mayor and founded the sugar factory in Sugar House. Additionally, A. O. became a stake president, founded the Provo Woolen Mill, and, while mayor of Provo, picked up young Reed from Anne's "comfortable home"[21] to accompany him on rounds to his various enterprises. Even at a young age, Reed's father recognized his son's business interest and strong work ethic.[22]

As two scions of Mormon wealth and solid pioneer heritage, Reed and Allie, met when children and married in 1884 at ages twenty-two and twenty-one respectively. Eighteen years later, Reed was a US senator. After sending Reed off at the train station, Allie penned this letter a week later:

My Dear Reed. One week since you left home and we have all been waiting so akesh
[anxious] to hear from you but have only news paper talk. We all felt sorry to hear
[of] your delay, but hope every thing will be all right and as the old saying [goes]
a "poor beginning makes a good ending." I did not have a very pleasant trip home
that night. It was . . . two o'clock [in the] morning when I got in the house. When I
thought of one of the best of husbands gone farther and farther from me I was just a
little blue . . . [I] felt better Wednesday and got the invitations out for the tea party. It
was a grate success . . . The children are all well, and are all trying to be good. I have
got a long much better than I was [afraid] I would. Harold [age 16] trys to be good
but at times is [just] hard to get him to do [just] the right thing. Brownie [age 12]
is been a very good boy, and Chloe [age 15] is a great comfort to me . . . Anne [age
10] is not been well enough to send back to school but I hope she can start Tuesday.
Dear little Zella [age 3] does miss you so much. She says she does wish Papa dear
would get through . . . and come home. Ernest [age 1] walks all over the house, and
gets into all sorts of [mischief]. . . . There is a great deal of sickness all over town. . . .
I am very ankish [anxious] to hear all about things from your own self, . . . I am jest
so shure you will be seated as ever and that the fight will not be so hard when they
all meet and see you.[23]

Early on in the hearings, Allie's support for her absent husband was purposefully
optimistic. She was certain the senators who encountered Reed would see him as
she saw him—a good and valiant man. She supported his political aspirations and
saw herself as his soulmate—as he did her. She longed for him by her side but did
not want to hold him back from what he saw as his destiny—to contribute his
talents to the Church, the Republican Party, and the US economy. Even so, longing
for Reed caused Allie grief, which likely contributed to her frequent illnesses. At
the time Allie penned the aforementioned letter, she believed she would soon join
him in Washington permanently because of a swift investigation and confirmation.
This, however, was not to be and she was consigned to be a single parent for the
majority of the next four years. Allie did have some household help in the person of
Miss Cook, but the six children were a never-ending duty, complicated by absentee
Reed's demands that she enforce his rules with the children. Furthermore, Reed
did not write Allie as often as she wrote him, nor did he write Allie as often as he
wrote LDS Church president Joseph F. Smith or the others helping his cause. Often,
she had to learn of his activities and whereabouts from local newspapers.

For the duration of the separation, Allie worried about Reed's health and eating
habits. She also made it a point to quickly respond to his letters, as can be seen in
this letter sent in early March of 1903:

My Own Dear Reed. . . . [Your letters] both came together last Tuesday and I
should have written before but I took a very bad cold and it settled in my lungs
and I was obliged to lay in bed one day and the next I had to attend my common

work, and as I wrote you last time [Miss] Cook and myself are alone and as you know we are kept pretty busy. I am glad to tell you I am feeling much better . . . and hope to be myself in a few days. I am [sorry] you are getting so thin. We will have to do something for our health. I have never been as tired since Zella came as I am now. . . . Little Zella talks of you most days all day long and those are the days I am very lonesome and to day has been one of those days. . . . Reed if you could look in at us we have the house cleaning all done and I do hope you will like my taste in the things I have chosen and the changes I have made. The house looks beautiful and all the children were so disappointed when we thought how long it would be before you were home. I [told] them all how much better it was for you to have the longer session, and that I felt like God had answered our prayers . . . Harold and Chloe have gone to the Academy for a Basket Ball game between the L.D.S. [and] B.Y.U. . . . I am so glad to let you know [how] good Harold is and he is doing so much better in school. . . . I did not get my letter off yesterday [so I will finish yesterday's letter]. I am sorry to have to tell you my cold is very bad, my lungs have been so sore I can not go out the door. But with care I will be all right in a few days. Reed do not worry about us. Harold letter from you came after I had written. I'm sorry Hotel food does not agree with you better, but you may get used to it . . . Ernest grows every day. He is about all I can lift. . . . God bless and keep you is ever the prayer of us all. Kiss and love Allie[24]

Reed returned home to his family when the Senate recessed in the spring and over the summer of 1903, though he stayed in close contact via mail and telegram with his recently hired private secretary, Carl Ashby Badger, a first-year law student back in Washington. Also away from his family, Carl wrote volumes of letters for the senator and to his wife, Rose. See Gary James Bergera's essay in chapter 7 for more on Carl Badger's experience as Smoot's secretary.

Reed was in Provo in May when an assembly of crusading women's groups—including the International Council of Women for Christian and Patriotic Service, the Women's Christian Temperance Union, and the National Mothers' Congress—met in Los Angeles to pass a resolution calling for the unseating of Reed Smoot. Allie was not spared the vitriol of these activists. My grandfather, Harlow, age twelve at the time, told us stories of letters sent to Allie by members of these groups; they crushed her spirit.

When October arrived, Smoot began preparing for his return to Washington. Writing to Badger, Smoot requested he arrange "a room [for] this coming session of congress." Smoot wanted a room with two beds, since he expected "[Waldemar] Van Cott [Smoot's non-Mormon attorney from Salt Lake City] to be with me most of the time."[25] During these preparations, the *New York Herald* published a full-page article on "the horrors of polygamy," featuring a photograph of Reed standing apart from Allie and the six children next to the fence of their mansion in Provo (see figure 5.3). Alongside the family photo is an image of the Salt Lake Temple. Although Reed Smoot's name was not mentioned in the paper, the story was an "attempt to whip up the emotions of the readers and to associate Smoot with the practice [of polygamy]." Because of the media groundswell against Smoot, the Committee on Privileges and Elections moved to closely examine the protests, and asked Smoot to submit a written defense to the allegations.[26]

Smoot, with the help of hired attorneys for the upcoming hearings, worked "strenuously" to craft a persuasive rebuttal, and soon he finished the formalized reply. His ten-page document addressed each specific charge, which exonerated him from the two most damaging charges: first, the claim that he was a polygamist and, second, "that he is bound by some oath or obligation which is inconsistent with the oath required by the Constitution, which was administered to him before he took his seat as a Senator."[27] Allie explains that she learned of her husband's "answer in the [Utah] news . . . and from what I . . . hear [it] is well received [here in Provo]. I hope it will be as well taken in Salt Lake."[28] Allie's mention of Salt Lake anticipated her husband's concern that some colleagues in the LDS hierarchy would disapprove of the document's boldness disavowing polygamy. Nine days later, Allie wrote to Reed after a trip to Salt Lake: "Your answer of course caused lots of talk but from what I can learn I think was generally well received. I have not seen any one that could tell me anything only jest as I have read in the papers." Sensing this information was not enough to salve Reed's curiosity on the topic, Allie buoyed her husband with candor, "But Reed it is a hard matter in public life to please, and as I have so often thought since you started, one does not need any feeling at all, be honest with one self and do the best one can is all there is to do."[29] However difficult these national investigations were for the Smoot family, Allie now extended a more pragmatic level of comfort given her husband's tenuous future.

By early December, Allie traveled with her rheumatism-stricken mother to New York to visit a medicinal spa for her ailments, followed by a quick stop in Washington to see Reed.[30] Over Christmas break, Reed traveled home to be with his family. Allie savored this time with Reed but was torn emotionally and over-whelmed by the weight of responsibilities she carried. Sometimes, she felt "so lonesome" she could "hardly stand it," with the weeks apart seeming like months. At other times, while thinking over Reed's case, Allie would "get so mad . . . [that she] had to get up to do something to change [her] thoughts." Despite the frustration, Allie provided Reed unqualified support, stating amorously, "words cannot express my appreciation for your love, my love for you grows every day and my consistent prayer is for your success in all things and that our lives may continue to be example[s] for others."[31] Despite the troubles of health and distance, Allie continued her optimism, however challenged, in her husband's success.

Allie's positive nature met the brutal realities of Washington politics and American prejudice. "The tack of the enemy," Carl Badger wrote to his wife, Rose

FIGURE 5.2. Sitting portrait of Alpha "Allie" May Smoot (ca. 1908). Image courtesy of the Church History Library collection and L. Tom Perry Special Collections, Brigham Young University.

mid-January 1904, "into the subject of [post-manifesto] polygamy is a dangerous one . . . that will arouse [public] sentiment [against Smoot]." Smoot's adversaries' strategy was to "hold the Senator responsible [for the new polygamous marriages]," and if successful according to Badger, "out [of the Senate] he will go."[32] Badger's frankness about Smoot's propspects underscored the uncertaintly surrounding the senator one year post election, and at this moment of uncertainty Reed penned the following detailed letter (letter 2) on Tuesday, January 19, 1904, explaining the insider dynamics of the case as well as the shifting tactics of his opponents:

I wanted to write to you on Sunday but I simply could not find the time. I did not get to bed until after midnight and just as I was going to bed I remembered I had

FIGURE 5.3. Sitting portrait of Reed Smoot (ca. 1903). Image courtesy of the Church History Library collection and L. Tom Perry Special Collections, Brigham Young University.

accepted an invitation for dinner . . . Imagine how I felt as I had sent no excuse but had forgotten all about it . . . The reason for this neglect and not writing you was because I worked all day and evening with my attorneys preparing another answer. Last Saturday at the opening hearing of my case before the Committee on Privileges and Elections the opposition presented a new set of [charges] claiming they were the ones they were going to rely on and not the old ones. No one appeared for poor old Lying [John L.] Leilich and R[obert] W. Tayler of Ohio representing the 19 citizens [and he] said they did not intend to defend the charge [of Smoot being a polygamist] and had no intentions of trying to prove them. [Charles Mostyn] Owen was present and is the leader of the opposition. I was compelled to have my answer ready Monday and so [I] had to work Sunday. Yesterday Monday we worked all day and I filed answer at 5 o'clock. Frank Cannon arrived here last night called on me this morning. I received him very coolly and he did not remain in office very long. I dont think he is here for my good purposes.[33] I was so sorry to learn of Ma's continued sickness; I am afraid she will never completely recover from her awful attack of rheumatism.[34] I do wish she was more comfortable. I always notice when ever Ma worries she is always worse. She is not only worrying over her own affairs but about almost every child she has. Allie there is no joy in the world like a contented heart and happy home. Let us always try to have both . . . You don't know how good it makes me feel when your letters come and they state all the children are well and doing nicely. God bless them all and make of them all little men and women.[35] I was going to write to George Brimhall and ask him to take an interest in Harold [age seventeen] and help him out at school but I am much more pleased to learn he has done so without my having to write.[36] Please call on Bro Brimhall and sincerely thank him for me. I do so want Harold to get through school for I want him to help me.[37] . . . Allie I would like the best kind to have you here with me but I do feel it is best for you not to come—will explain why later. Tell Zella [age 4] I received her letter and I enclose you one in answer. I am writing you this during session hours. Next Saturday the Committee meets again to continue hearing of case. God bless you all. Remember me to all Provo friends. Love and kisses to you and children. Your loving Reed.[38]

Irony is the subtext of Reed's letters. He took the attacks on himself as good advertising yet feared for Allie's emotional health if she were to join him in Washington. Rather than bringing her to Washington to weather the storm with him, Reed expected she be his proxy in Utah by shouldering all family responsibilities as well as maintaining their social relationships. Allie, on the other hand, worried about her husband's health, "often wish[ing]" she could be with him to make "it a little pleasant when" he returned from a hard day of work.[39]

In addition to his legislative and political activities, Reed was required to manage his commercial interests back home. His father-in-law had appointed him executor of the Eldredge estate, and thus responsible for the care of his widow, Chloe. Reed often had to make decisions on behalf of Allie's brothers and relied on her to assist. As a woman of her time and station, Allie did not concern herself much with financial issues. The family had always been financially secure, which allowed her space to enjoy shopping, attend parties, and make social calls. Reed's current situation put all this in question; he was short on cash from attorney's fees and low on patience to deal with the Eldredge brothers' finances. His frustration is evident in his letter dated January 23, 1904 (letter 3), in which he asked Allie to assist him with a loan requested by Horace and Ern.[40]

Your telegram stating ["]Horace [Allie's brother, age thirty-five] had returned from Canada. Wants money to close bargain in land also wants money to buy horses to speculate on received and I wired you I would write particulars.["] As you remember I agreed with Ern [Allie's brother age thirty-six] to help him out with money to get started with and you may sign a note with him and Ern to secure the money.

Make the loan long enough to enable Horace to net some with land if possible. I do not care to have you go into the horse deal. I know nothing about it and cannot see after it. If it is a good thing Uncle Ben [Allie's brother age thirty-eight] can go in with Horace and secure the money. Allie you know I am owing a lot of money and if hard times should come we would get finished. The case against me is also going to be very expensive and we must stop somewhere. I will protect you in signing with Ern for Horace. I enclose you the statement of my account at Smoot Drug Co[mpany] for the year 1903. File it away. I am feeling much better but the weather here is beastly. Hot rainy weather one day and next day cold. It is very trying on people not used to it. Last Monday Frank Cannon, Parley L. Williams,[41] and A[rthur] L. L. Thomas arrived here[42]—Thomas to answer charges filed against him by [Senator Thomas] Kearns. I beleive [sic] he will win and Parley Williams has a case in the Supreme Court but he is never letting an opportunity pass to slander the Mormon people. He is the most bitter man against the Mormons. It is reported Frank J is here to secure a subcommittee to visit Utah but this I cannot confirm as yet so you need say nothing about it . . . Tell Brownie that Papa expects him to be a perfect little Gentleman and never do a thing to hurt the name of Smoot. Tell Anne K Zella & Ern I received their invitations to a party given by them but was to[o] far away to attend. I know they have a jolly good time together . . . I have only attended one reception given by [Thomas] Kearns to the newspaper men. I could not as a gentlemen do anything else. I must not let feelings interfere with the respect I owe them or cause me to be anything but a gentlemen. I was asked last Thursday evening to another reception given by President and Mrs. Roosevelt at the White House but I did not go. I was too tired. I must close and go and learn if possible what the Committee has decided on in my case, how far they will allow evidence and whether it is me they are going to try or the whole Mormon Church. God bless you and the children. I send you all love and kisses. Yours Reed.[43]

Reed declined holding grudges politically or personally; instead, he was always the "gentleman" when interacting with political allies or adversaries. He expected the same from his children, especially his sons. Invitations for Reed to attend Roosevelt's receptions were frequent; missing them would not help his case. For the senator, social occasions were a nuisance, but for Allie, they were a raison d'être. Knowing this about his wife, the senator made it a point to mention the social events he was attending, even providing small details from each event, especially when fellow partygoers made solicitous comments about his wife. Allie likewise kept her husband informed about the social galas she was attending. This dynamic is illustrated by the following letter (letter 4) home, written by Reed in mid-February:

Another Sunday finds me alone at the Raleigh Hotel room 818. I am going to dinner at 3 o'clock to home of Mrs. Watson N. L. Shelling, a Washington lady that belongs to our church. I was lazy this morning and did not get up until nearly nine o'clock. Every morning during the week I get up as soon as the 7:30 whistle blows, have breakfast at 8 o'clock, walk to the office reaching there about 8:45 a.m. I have been exceedingly busy this week; my mail has greatly increased and have had a great many things to attend to in the different departments for people [at] home [in Utah]. Thursday evening I went to a reception given by wife of Secy of Senate Mr. [Charles G.] Bennett to introduce Miss Faulkner, daughter of Ex Senator [Charles J.] Faulkner [of West Virginia], the attorney we wanted to take my case. You remember you met him at the Hotel one evening while you were here. Did not stop but a few minutes. Last evening at 6 o'clock I attended a reception given by Mrs. [Virginia W.] Faulkner and Miss Faulkner at the New Willard Hotel. A large crowd present—I remained only about one half hour. Mrs. Faulkner said she would never forgive Mr. Faulkner for not taking my case and wanted to meet you ever so much for Mr. Faulkner had spoken so nicely about you.[44] She said we had her sympathy and best wishes. Faulkner is my friend and always puts in a good word for me whenever an occasion presents itself. After returning from Faulkner reception I went to a Banquet given by the Patent Bar Association. Had a very pleasant time, called upon for a speech and made one in response to the introduction—"The man from the wild and wooly west." It was well received and I made many friends. Your loving letter of Feby 7/04 came to hand and I appreciated it as I do all your dear letters, not only for the news given about our dear home and children but for the love and confidence they carry for me from the dearest little funny Mama in the world. Some talk that Congress will adjourn during May. I certainly hope so, especially if my case is decided. . . . Your report of Mamie's [Mary Jane's] party done me good and Allie I do think if Ma [Reed's mother-in-law] and Mamie would spend the money for cultivating friends at home, for occasions similar to the one you wrote about, instead of going to other places among total strangers, I beleive [*sic*] they both would enjoy life better. Of course we cannot regulate affairs of this kind nor do I want to but I can tell you what I think. I would so like to see Ma happy and well. I love her and would do most anything for her . . . I was so glad the 6th warders gave you a surprise, Allie, true friends are among the precious gifts of God I assure you I appreciate them . . . Mrs. [Jennie Judge] Kearns left here yesterday for New York and from there she will go home. I understand she is not coming back this winter. Mrs. Kearns is a very sensible and a great lady and I rather like her.[45] She is a much nicer woman than her husband is a man. Considerable talk here about having Jos[eph]. F. [Smith] subpoenaed as a witness and a member of the Quorum of Apostles. From what Jos[eph] F writes me he is ready for it. He has no fear of an investigation. I will attend meeting to-night. L[ewis] W. Shurtleff of Ogden has sent up his card so I will close.[46] This is Valentines day but I have not sent the valentines but I guess they will have enough without. Love and kisses for my little wife. Yours, Reed.[47]

FIGURE 5.4. Allie and Reed's family portrait with five children taken in 1900 in front of their Provo, Utah, home. From left to right: Zella, Allie, Harold, Anne, Harlow, Chloe, and Reed. Courtesy of the Kathryn Smoot Egan, great-granddaughter of Reed Smoot.

Sending Valentine cards to the family was the last item on the beleaguered senator's to-do list, and Carl Badger, his private secretary, was probably grateful his employer did not ask him to perform such a task. Badger was also undertaking a balancing act between law school and his duties as secretary, in addition to the stress of being apart from his young family. In letters to his wife Rose, Badger was occasionally fretful about the topic of polygamy and the national commotion it enflamed. One letter told of his law professor, Justice [John Marshall] Harlan of the Supreme Court, who "came in late" to class one day and "vented his feelings" about the "strange set of conditions that existed out there [in Utah]" and posited his opinion that Congress "might be compelled to amend the constitution to provide against the contingency of a lot of polygamists getting control of western states and making polygamy legal, and wound up by hoping that the sheltering walls of the penitentiary would soon enfold all such."[48] Harlan's unexpected diatribe was an embarrassment at the time for Badger vis-à-vis his classmates, but as the case unfolded, the young secretary adopted his teacher's exasperation with the conditions in Utah.[49]

When Senate hearings started, lawyers and senators quibbled with witnesses over the ambiguity of language within the 1890 Manifesto banning polygamy, and specifically regarding the statutory status of existing plural marriages performed prior

FIGURE 5.5. Allie and Reed's family portrait with six children taken in approximately 1908 by Harris & Ewing in Washington, DC, shortly after his retention in the US Senate. From left to right: Zella, Anne, Reed, Harold, Chloe, Allie, Harlow, and Ernest. Courtesy of the L. Tom Perry Special Collections, Brigham Young University.

to 1890. This created confusion over the legality of polygamous cohabitation—the continued conjugal living of husbands with plural wives—and various Church authorities took license to interpret it how they pleased. This interpretive confusion, however, worked in Smoot's favor, since one of the salient charges made against him was that "all of the first presidency and the twelve apostles encourage, countenance, conceal, and connive at polygamy and polygamous cohabitation."[50]

In his concluding arguments in late January 1905, lead attorney for the opposition, Robert W. Tayler, critiqued the "abstract reasoning" of Smoot's attorney that "the church has no authority to deal with any man who is engaged in the business of polygamous co-habitation . . . because the manifesto of 1890 related alone to the contracting of new plural marriages." Tayler was not swayed and rebutted, "[since] there is no rule of the church against [polygamous cohabitation] . . . then there is no objection to it [by the Church]"; therefore, "the church does encourage it, the church does connive at it, the church does countenance it."[51] Taylor was making a fair point on polygamous cohabitation vis-à-vis the institutional Church; however, associating Smoot with the practice of polygamous cohabitation was tricky business, since the senator had persuasively absolved himself earlier on the witness stand of such polygamous complicity.[52] But unsympathetic voices toward Mormonism did not comprehend that cessation of polygamous relationships altogether would in many cases leave women and children unsupported and destitute.

As his case was argued by fractious lots on both sides, Smoot remained grounded in civility. Allie provided Reed support amidst this firestorm: "I know you will win and I will come out right." In the same letter, she also expressed her frustration about the misbehavior of thirteen-year-old son Brownie, who "is so self-willed and it takes so much patience to talk and then he does things that worry me so. As soon as he is out of the grades he must be put in school of strong discipline."[53] In her correspondence with Reed, Allie was also keen to include family successes, including the news that sixteen-year-old Chloe was working as a teacher and had become a "big, fine young girl."[54]

Following the first round of hearings, the committee adjourned to the end of the year. During this break, Theodore Roosevelt campaigned for and was reelected president. When the Smoot hearings resumed, the prosecution called new witnesses to testify for a period of eight days, with some testimony pertaining to the temple ceremonies, which for Smoot did "not look or sound very nice."[55] Upon completion, the prosecution closed its case, and Smoot departed by train for Provo to spend Christmas with his family to rejuvenate before he would be called to the stand.

Beginning on January 11, 1905, and extending to the end of the month, carefully selected witnesses included prominent non-Mormons living in Utah as well as Mormon experts on Church doctrine such as James E. Talmage. Nine days into this round of testimony Reed Smoot was unexpectedly called to the stand when a scheduled witness failed to appear.[56] Suffering from a bout of indigestion, Smoot summoned the energy to respond to tough questions cautiously yet openly. Several senators had already differentiated Smoot from the LDS Church they despised but hoped to hear Smoot condemn members of the Church hierarchy for illegal polygamous practices. Smoot attempted to walk a tightrope that distanced him from the actions of his fellow apostles while maintaining a respectful tone that retained and salvaged relations.[57] According to historian Milton R. Merrill, Smoot's testimony helped his cause. The press reacted positively, causing a "trend of feeling" to move in his favor.[58]

During this difficult period for Reed, the senator remained attentive to Allie's circumstances. Managing the household alone, Allie struggled to stay on top of her many responsibilities. Lamenting her struggles to find "a wash woman," Allie sardonically labeled herself "the finest little old fat warsh woman you ever seen" and that the children "have [had] a good laugh on me to think a real live Senator's wife is a wash woman."[59] Reed responded by hoping she "could get a good girl to help with the washing and the children in the morning."[60] Allie wanted to be in

Washington with her husband, but Reed rebuffed the idea as a way to protect her from being immersed in a toxic environment where an "awful feeling . . . against the church" existed.[61]

Less than a week later, the senator changed his mind and invited Allie to join him for Roosevelt's inauguration. Not wanting Allie to travel alone to Washington, Reed suggested she bring along her sister Mamie. Allie also invited Harold, then an eighteen-year-old college student at the University of Utah, to join her on the cross-country trip.[62] Chloe, who was a year younger than Harold, had become her mother's confident and was entrusted to watch over the younger children while Allie traveled to Washington. In her faithful weekly letters, Chloe tried to ease her mother's mind but lacked the authoritative means to discipline her siblings.[63] Brownie, age fourteen, was corralled into writing one letter to his mother in which he informed her that he was "trying to be a good boy" and that the bishop ordained him "a deacon [in the Aaronic priesthood] last Thursday."[64]

From all indications, Allie's trip east was a success, without controversy or blight. Allie Smoot made herself at home, even proxy mothering Carl Badger by having him "gargle with Listerine" to salve a sore throat.[65] On inauguration day, Allie took in the day's events, being struck by the elegance of the Roosevelt family.[66] Soon after the inaugural festivities, Allie treated herself to some shopping, where she "bought a number of purses."[67] This respite from single parenthood was wonderful but could not last.

Traveling home soon thereafter, Allie was struck with sadness knowing she would soon be back to the loneliness of refereeing the children's squabbles. Brownie, then thirteen years old, tested the limits of her patience by refusing to help around the house, even throwing "a rock" that "hit Harold yesterday and made a very ugly wound . . . [and took] three stitches in the back of his head" to close.[68] Reed's fight in Washington was taking a toll on his wife and family back home, wounds that would leave indelible scars.

Even though concluding arguments had been made back in January 1905, shortly after Smoot's testimony, hearings were reopened with new witnesses being called to provide additional testimony on subjects related to LDS temple ceremonies. For Smoot the fight seemed to have no end, and rumors swirled on who might be subpoenaed to testify in Washington. During this time of uncertainty, Reed penned the following two letters (together letter 5) to Allie in early 1906:

[Saturday Evening] My Dear Allie, I am going to write you tonight instead of to-morrow night—as I expect to go to [Joseph] Howell's to-morrow night as most of the Utah people will be there for the purpose of holding [a Church] meeting and I feel I should attend . . . Am feeling fairly well and my apetite is good. Do not sleep very much but no bad effects from it. Last evening I was asked to dinner at Mrs. Brandenbergs and accepted as I wrote you . . . The dinner served was pretty good, but not like one of our dinners, and I guess the black cook done the most of the cooking.[69] Mrs. Brandenberg is a very pleasant, wholesome and agreeable lady and makes you feel at home. They have three children, one boy and two girls. No they are not as bright as our children and Brandenberg realizes it. I did not leave until a quarter to eleven oclock. Mrs. B. is so anxious to meet you and made me promise if you came here for only a few days during this session I would have you call . . . We talk religion some little but only on questions asked by them. Mrs. B says she is afraid Mr. B will become a Mormon yet.

I know nothing new to report on my case. You no doubt saw the hearing was to be resumed on Feby 6 instead of Jany 25. [Chairman Julius Caesar] Burrows says [attorney John G.] Carlisle could not come until Feby 6. There is an awful bitter feeling against the church, more so, I believe, than since its organization. I am worrying over adverse legislation more than over my chances to retain my seat. It would not surprise me to see a constitutional amendment adopted embracing or incorporating the Idaho Test oath, which virtually disfranchises every Mormon. This is the result aim to be accomplished by Burrows and [Fred T.] Du Boise and I am afraid [that] most of the Senators will approve of it. They are disgusted with our double dealing and they say they are going to put a stop to it.[70]

[My Dear Allie.] I received your dear letter written January 10, my birthday and reminding me that I was forty-four years old. I used to think a man 44 years old was an old man, but I have changed my ideas regarding that matter. I think I would prefer to have it said I am 44 years young, even if I do feel at times like I am seventy-five as I have so often heard you say. If I ever get settled again and get this everlasting load off my shoulders I am going to take life a little easier or at least I think so now. There is not much new to report here. The papers are full of all manner of reports and sensational stuff and the Senators are receiving stacks of letters demanding that they vote against me but I don't believe I am losing any friends among the Senators and every time I go out I think I make some [new friends]. Burrows and Du Boise are not satisfied with the record and are now going to try and get something against me personally and they think they will get it in the Endowment Oath. I have not learned who the new witness will be, with exception of one and for fear he is not subpoenaed by [the] time you receive this letter I will not name him but you know him well. He is to be their star witness. I have befriended him many times.

Monday evening I went to the reception at Speaker Cannon's home but did not remain but a short time. Met a great many of the Senators and Representatives. There were no ladies present. Last evening I attended a reception given by Mr. Gifford Pinchot his Father and Mother to meet the members and officers of the American Forestry Association. Had a delightful time. A great crowd out but I was certainly surprised at such a large crowd of fashionable ladies with so few good looking ones. Pinchot you will remember was at our home to dinner once and last summer I went up big Cottonwood Canyon with him. He is a very dear friend of President Roosevelt's. They are wealthy people and have an elegant home. I made a number of friends among the ladies and ones that will talk some. Mrs. Wilson, wife of Secy [of Agriculture James] Wilson, wanted me to understand she was always a defender of mine. The wealthy old maid Miss Stevens was very much interested in me and I had to spend more time with her than anyone else. She is a great talker and goes every where and knows every body. We talked about our belief and even polygamy was not so black [and white] to her . . . You remember Miss [Helen Varick] Boswell. She stopped at our house with Miss [Mary Yost] Wood on their way to [the] Portland fair.[71] She called at Senate to day to see me and brought with her Mrs. Adams one of the leading ladies of Baltimore for the purpose of having her meet me. I talked to them about 15 minutes and Mrs. Adams said Miss Boswell had said so much about you and the children our home and my self she did not want to leave Washington this time without meeting me . . .

I have heard but little from home outside your letters . . . Tell Zella [age nine] poor Papa was all alone on his birthday and thought of home many times . . . I just received a telegram saying Prof. Wolfe was subpoenaed so I will say he is the one I have reference to in beginning of this letter. I know he was going to be one week ago. I will have to close for this time. I do hope the children are getting along alright and that they will be men and women while I am away and all the time. I send you all love and kisses. Good night Allie and may success be ours. Yours Reed.[72]

As he braced for additional hearings, Smoot actively corresponded with his ecclesiastical and political colleagues back in Utah. In a letter to Joseph F. Smith, Smoot suggested there be a day of fasting and prayer on the part of Church leaders: "I am sure it can do no harm [the fasting and prayer] . . . and I fully believe it will do some good." For those in the hierarchy who begrudged his political ambition and felt the apostle-senator was responsible for the predicament, Smoot asked President Smith not only to "impress upon them the fact that it is not me that is in danger but the Church," but also that they pray that God forgive him.[73]

Six witnesses for the prosecution testified over four days when the hearings reopened in February 1906. More than a month later, the defense called seven witnesses for two final days. Over this time, Allie lived in Washington alone with Reed. Energized by the break, Allie began making "the [hotel] rooms [Smoot lived in] look very pretty," while also "enjoying herself at the enjoyable feminine occupation of 'buying things.'"[74] She was also active socially, attending a few public events such as the "laying of the cornerstone of the House of Representatives Office Building," where President Roosevelt spoke.[75]

When final arguments were made by Smoot's attorneys on April 13, 1906, Allie for the first time appeared in the committee room "dressed in a light striped-blue-grey gown and becoming hat to match" and "took a seat towards the rear." Her entrance caused a "flutter among the audience," with attendees whispering, "That is Mrs. Smoot."[76] In that moment, Allie personified what had only been alluded to—she was the elegant wife of Apostle Reed Smoot, the one person who could ratify that Reed was not a polygamist and, thus, qualified to be a United States senator. It was surely one of their finest moments together, but Allie did not feel well, writing to her daughter Chloe that she felt pregnant.[77] Reed and Allie Smoot's marriage embodied the Victorian model of Christian marriage, and ironically some Protestant senators believed they were defending this form of Christian marriage by blocking Smoot's entry into the halls of congress. Two months later in early June, the Senate committee voted nonbindingly that Smoot not remain in the Senate. Allie did not remain for this committee action; instead, she reluctantly returned home a couple weeks prior to get home to her children.[78]

Congress adjourned in late June without taking final action on Smoot, thus, leaving Smoot's status in limbo for an additional five months. When it went back in session in late 1906, Allie traveled to Washington to stay with Reed for the case conclusion. This time Allie brought Brownie with her, a move that complicated life since he was a "stubborn" and "headstrong" fifteen-year-old boy. Brownie chafed at being forced to attend high school in Washington because the classes were too advanced, and he also "realize[d] that he is being sent to keep his time occupied." Brownie's recalcitrance was a constant nuisance for Allie over these final months.[79]

Brownie also hated being the only child living in Washington. In an interview with historian Milton Merrill forty years later, Brownie bemoaned the pain his mother felt when not accepted socially in the nation's capital. Allie was diligent to make "the usual social rounds" expected of a senator's wife, which included dropping off "her card" with Washington peers that indicated "Wednesday" as her "home day" to receive visitors. Most Wednesday afternoons when Brownie returned from school, he found his mother in tears because no one had stopped by.[80] Brownie perceived the social ostracism his family encountered was a result of the stigma of polygamy. He felt he and his mother bore the social brunt, which made his school attendance more punishment than opportunity.

In late January 1907, Chairman Burrows proposed that the Senate vote be held on February 20. When the day came, Brownie joined Carl Badger on the Senate floor and "was so excited that he [Brownie] could not stand still." Additionally, Smoot's anxious son "kept interrupting me [Badger] with questions" until "I had to tell him to stop."[81] Senators voted in favor of Smoot,[82] and in the moment victory was sweet. Congratulatory telegrams, letters, and gifts poured into the Smoots' suite at the Highlands Hotel.

The hearings had taken a toll, and Alpha May never recovered the equipoise of her youth. When the family moved to Washington to live in the house Reed built, she never felt comfortable there. The home had been furnished by a professional interior decorator, and for two years, according to daughter Zella, Allie was afraid even to move a picture. She regarded the house as Reed's; hers was in Provo.[83] This dislike of the house is not to suggest any estrangement between the couple; they were loving companions to the end.

After 1920, Allie's health deteriorated to the point that she no longer traveled home to Utah. Suffering from stomach cancer, Allie passed away in 1928. On the couple's wedding anniversary a year prior to Allie's death, Reed, then on a trip to Salt Lake, penned a reflective letter (letter 6) to his dying wife back in Washington:

> I have had you in mind for the last three days as never before ... and what we were doing on the same three days forty three years ago. The memories of them have given me great joy and I have repeatedly thanked our Heavenly Father for giving you to me as you have proven to be a wonderful wife and mother. None better in the world. Remember the high hopes we had of a happy and a successful life and what we were going to do and how it was to be accomplished. Allie dear has it all been realized and now that forty three years have passed are you satisfied? As far as my Allie is concerned I am more than satisfied for she has not only done her part but carried a part of my own load.[84]

After speaking in General Conference in early October 1928, Reed received a telegram from his daughter Chloe informing him that Allie had had convulsions the night before and was unconscious.[85] Soon after the news, Reed boarded a train to Washington so he could "stay with her as much as possible."[86] Allie lingered in misery with Reed nearby for almost a month to the November election. In the early morning hours of November 7, several hours after Republican nominee Hoover was declared the election winner, Reed wrote in his journal, "Mama was near death and did die at 7 A.M." Reflecting that she had been a "long patience sufferer," Reed eulogized that Allie "Died loved by all."[87]

During World War II, with our fathers away at war, my cousins and I lived in the Provo home Reed and Allie built. On the parlor walls hung their portraits, Reed standing tall, almost to the ceiling in a gold frame; Allie seated on the adjacent wall, smiling serenely out at us. The congressional records of the Smoot hearings were encased in the glass bookshelves in the living room. Also in the home were trunks of Allie's beautiful clothes, which I modeled for fashion shows as a teenager in high school. The stories told by my Grandfather Brownie of her kindness, traditions, and lore ingrained in me a sense of how to live graciously.

Over the first few decades of the senator's career, Smoot became the "dominant figure" of Utah's "political and religious landscape." Historian Harvard S. Heath offered his assessment that during this time Reed "almost single-handedly turned around the negative image of Utah and the Mormon church."[88] The difficulties of the Smoot hearings were a shared burden for both Allie and Reed—each spouse relying on the other for emotional support and comfort. Allie and Reed's strength throughout the ordeal reflected the influence of their female pioneer ancestors. Together they modeled the new Victorian paradigm of Mormonism and Mormon sexuality for the twentieth century, where Reed was the patriarch and protector, and Allie the homemaker and primary caretaker of the children. Moreover, these patriarchal Victorian mores, of Allie performing the bulk of domestic responsibilities and Reed shouldering financial matters, connected the Smoots with other similarly situated American families. And even though Reed initially saw the Senate inquiry as an intrusion into his private life and religious commitments, his Senate allies, as it turned out, used the hearings as the vehicle to promote a new image of the LDS Church, one based on the Victorian values displayed by the marriage of Reed and Allie Smoot. This new image would not change the mind of sectarian Protestants who feared continued polygamy and Mormon hierarchal control, but other secularly minded Protestants like President Theodore Roosevelt were impressed and became important allies of Smoot and the Church of Jesus Christ of Latter-day Saints going forward into the twentieth century.

NOTES

1. Harlow Eldredge Smoot was named "Brownie" because he was so small at birth he could be carried on a pillow. His twin, Seth, died at birth. As a result, Allie was very protective of Harlow throughout his life.

2. Milton R. Merrill, *Reed Smoot: Apostle in Politics* (Logan: Utah State University Press, 1990), 39–100.

3. The Provo house, at 183 East First South, is owned now by my cousin Reed Smoot and his wife, Julia. The house is on the National Historic Register.

4. Kathryn Smoot, "The Role of the Newspaper in the Reed Smoot Investigation: 1903–1907" (honors thesis, University of Utah, Salt Lake City, 1964).

5. "Goodnight, Mrs. Smoot," MSS 1187, Reed Smoot Papers, L. Tom Perry Special Collections, Harold B. Lee Library, Brigham Young University (hereafter, Smoot Papers). I recently rediscovered the six letters, still in their original envelopes. To write this essay I also relied on other correspondence found in the Smoot Papers. After spending time reading the senator's notes, letters, and telegrams so beautifully preserved at BYU, I donated my six letters to the collection.

6. "Senator Smoot's Credentials," *Deseret Evening News*, February 23, 1903, 1.

7. Theodore Roosevelt had become president upon the assassination of President William McKinley in 1901.

8. John L. Leilich, superintendent of Missions for the Methodist Church in Utah, falsely accused Smoot in a formal protest of being a secret polygamist. See Smoot Hearings 1:26–30. Smoot biographer, Milton R. Merrill details this unscrupulous assertion. See Merrill, *Reed Smoot*, 13.

9. B. H. Roberts, a Democrat, was elected congressman in 1898 but denied his seat because he was a polygamist. See Davis Bitton, *The Reutilization of Mormon History and Other Essays* (Urbana: University of Illinois Press, 1994): 150–170.

10. Reed Smoot to Allie Smoot, February 26, 1903, Smoot Papers.

11. Smoot family tradition has counted Anne Kirstine as his fourth wife, because his second wife, Sarah Gibbons, divorced A. O. in 1852.

12. My account of Anne Kirstine's life is based primarily on the biographical transcript compiled by her daughter Alice Newell and edited by Loretta Nixon, as found in Loretta D. Nixon and L. Douglas Smoot, *Abraham Owen Smoot: A Testament of His Life* (Provo, UT: Brigham Young University Press, 1994), 193–205.

13. Nixon and Smoot, *Abraham Owen Smoot*, 197. "[Anne] and her lover were devotedly attached to each other, yet she told him if he would not be convinced of Mormonism, he must forget her." She received a letter from her lover just after arriving in Utah. At her request, the letter was buried with her. His name is unknown.

14. In 1853, Brigham Young counseled missionaries in foreign lands to avoid "the mysteries" but instead to focus on the basics of the gospel and the essential ordinances of salvation. If new converts "want to know more, send them home, tell them that Zion is the place for them to receive those teachings which you have not time to teach, and which do not belong to your mission." James R. Clark, comp., *Messages of the First Presidency* (Salt Lake City: Bookcraft Publishers, 1965), 2:117.

15. Nixon and Smoot, *Abraham Owen Smoot*, 199–200. Nelse's losses on the journey to America had been great—a son dead even before they left Liverpool, England; another son dead at sea; his wife dead of cholera that struck Winter Quarters. He no longer wished to be a member of the Church. In Carson City, Nevada, he remarried and had a large family. He and Anne saw each other only a few times afterward.

16. Nixon and Smoot, *Abraham Owen Smoot*, 205.

17. Evidence of her beauty is the portrait of her painted by her son-in-law Lee Greene Richards, a copy of which hangs on the Reed Smoot Wall of the Lee Library at Brigham Young University.

18. For a synopsis of the Edmunds Act, see James B. Allen and Glen M. Leonard, *The Story of the Latter-day Saints* (Salt Lake City: Deseret Book, 1992), 402–407. The Edmunds Act of 1882 made cohabitation and polygamy illegal, punishable by a $500 fine and five years in prison. Those who continued to practice polygamy post January 1, 1883, found themselves outlaws. Horace was among those who were determined to obey the God-given duty to provide for all of their wives and children. In order to give appearance of abiding by the Edmunds Law, they domiciled with one wife, usually the youngest, with the most children—in Horace's case, this was Chloe with her ten.

19. "Goodnight, Mrs. Smoot," Smoot Papers. After 1882, spotting "cohabs" became a cottage industry supported by federal marshals who employed agents dressed as peddlers and census takers to go even into private homes. They would even accost children in their search for polygamists. Allen and Leonard, *The Story of the Latter-day Saints*, 404–405. In my research and writing on this topic, I discovered that some children were taught to lie about their names. See Kathryn Smoot Caldwell, *The Principle* (Salt Lake City: Randall Book, 1983).

20. "Goodnight, Mrs. Smoot," Smoot Papers; "Pedigree Resource File," database, FamilySearch, http://familysearch.org/pal:/MM9.2.1/STBF-G3T (accessed September 14, 2012), entry for Horace Sunderlin/Eldredge/. Chloe's firstborn was Harlow Moroni, who lived only a year and died before Allie was born. "Utah, Deaths and Burials, 1888–1946," index, FamilySearch, https://familysearch.org/pal:/MM9.1.1/F85V-V2Q (accessed 15 Sep 2012), Harlow M. Eldredge, December 12, 1861.

21. The house still stands near where Liberty Park is today in Salt Lake City.

22. Merrill, *Reed Smoot*, 4–5.

23. Allie Smoot to Reed Smoot, February 22, 1903, Smoot Papers.

24. Allie Smoot to Reed Smoot, March 7, 1903, Smoot Papers.

25. Reed Smoot to Carl Badger, October 21, 1903, Smoot Papers. Upon arrival in Washington, Smoot also began to search for a rental home large enough to accommodate his family. Writing to his wife in late November, Smoot explained that he had found a place with three bedrooms, one large reception room, and one bathroom for $160 per month and that "there will be plenty of room for you and some of the children or even for Ma [Chloe] and Mamie [Allie's sister Mary Jane, age twenty-three and unmarried]." Reed Smoot to Allie Smoot, November 19, 1903, Smoot Papers.

26. Merrill, *Reed Smoot*, 42–44.

27. For Smoot's full response, see Proceedings before the Committee on Privileges and Elections of the United States Senate in the Matter of Protests against the Right of Hon. Reed Smoot, a Senator from the State of Utah to Hold His Seat (Washington, DC: US Government Printing Office, 1906) 1:31–40 (hereafter, Smoot Hearings).

28. Allie Smoot to Reed Smoot, January 9, 1904, Smoot Papers. In this letter, Allie also explained, "People are getting pretty tired of Frank Cannon[']s lying. . . . I wish they would go right along with the case but I gess [guess] it will take time. [You] know how ankesh [anxious] I have been over you. I am glad you are eating better. . . . Mr. [Charles Edward] Loose sends his love . . . I went to the six ward party. I had a very nice time . . . I dance[d] more than I have for years. Everyone was so glad to see me and many sent . . . best wishes to you." Loose was a lifelong friend of Smoot's and a mining magnate. His business successes spurred Smoot to become a "man of substance" by the age of thirty-five, when he earned a quarter of a million dollars. See Merrill, *Reed Smoot*, 5. Reed Smoot and Charles Edward Loose are buried in adjoining plots in the Provo City Cemetery.

29. Allie Smoot to Reed Smoot telegram, January 18, 1904, Smoot Papers.

30. Allie Smoot to Reed Smoot telegram, December 12, 1903, Smoot Papers. As Chloe's eldest daughter, Allie was responsible for her mother's care.

31. Allie Smoot to Reed Smoot, January 17, 1904, Smoot Papers. Caring for the children could also be an unpleasant experience for Allie. Sometime after Christmas, young Brownie misbehaved to the point that Allie "did not know what to do with him." Allie was required to shoulder the load of managing the children's disappointments from Reed's absence. After not receiving a letter from Smoot, young Zella declared to the family, "Papa has [tired of] her so he has never written her and she has wrote to [him] so many letters."

32. Carl Badger Diary, in Rodney J. Badger, *Liahona and Iron Rod: A Biography of Carl A. Badger and Rosalia Jenkins Badger* (Bountiful, UT: Family History Publishers, 1985), 210.

33. Frank Cannon was the editor of the skeptical, even antagonistic *Salt Lake Tribune*. For Cannon activities during the Smoot hearings, see Michael Harold Paulos, "Opposing the 'High Ecclesiasts at Washington': Frank J. Cannon's Editorial Fusillades during the Reed Smoot Hearings, 1903–07," *Journal of Mormon History* 37, no 3 (Fall 2011): 1–59.

34. Chloe Antoinette was sixty-two at this time and would spend the rest of her life seeking relief in the spas of the United States and Europe. Samuel P. Smoot, "Goodnight Mrs. Smoot," Smoot Papers.

35. For Smoot, rectitude, honor, and civility were more important values than spirituality.

36. George Brimhall was president of Brigham Young Academy, later Brigham Young University, which A. O. Smoot founded at the insistence of Brigham Young and which bankrupted him at the end of his life. Reed was a member of the first graduating class at age seventeen. He served on the university's executive committee until 1939, when the Church retired him. A few days prior to this letter, Allie had written to Reed, "Brother Brimhall called to see me and I cant tell you how much good it did both Harold and me to be talked so good and spoke so kind of you. I am so [encouraged] about Harold for he has taken right hold of him and it was what he needed so bad." Allie Smoot to Reed Smoot, January 17, 1904, Smoot Papers.

37. Reed wanted his sons to help him the way he had helped his father. But his three sons—Harold, Harlow, and Ernest—lacked financial expertise, and in the end their incompetence and profligacy ruined the senator. See Harvard Heath, "Reed Smoot: First Modern Mormon" (PhD diss., Brigham Young University, Provo, UT, 1990), 1022–1059.

38. Reed Smoot to Allie Smoot, January 19, 1904, Smoot Papers.

39. Allie Smoot to Reed Smoot, January 20, 1904, Smoot Papers.

40. The rancor that developed between Reed Smoot and his brothers-in-law over money issues was legendary even during my time.

41. Parley L. Williams was a non-Mormon attorney living in Salt Lake City who took an active role with Thomas Kearns in forming an anti-Mormon political party—the American Party.

42. A. L. Thomas was the non-Mormon Salt Lake City postmaster at the time of this letter and had previously been the territorial governor of Utah 1889–1893.

43. Reed Smoot to Allie Smoot, January 23, 1904, Smoot Papers.

44. Ex-Democratic senator Faulkner of West Virginia had agreed to take Reed's case for $5,000, but the next day Faulkner, claiming the large business he represented had objected to his taking the case, reluctantly pulled out. See Merrill, *Reed Smoot*, 44. Even though Faulkner refused to take the case, he pledged to Smoot that he, as Smoot wrote, "would do all in his power to help me out in the matter." Reed Smoot to Joseph F. Smith, December 16, 1903, Smoot Papers. Faulkner was true to his promise and within three weeks was sent on assignment by Smoot to work "with the Democrats on the Committee urging them to . . . try me and not the church." Faulkner reported back to Smoot that "he was very successful in this endeavor." See Reed Smoot to Joseph F. Smith, January 9, 1904, Smoot Papers. Two years later, Smoot visited Faulkner and let him know how pleased he had been for "his many kindnesses shown us last year, and in fact ever since the case has been under consideration." See Reed Smoot to Joseph F. Smith, December 12, 1905, Smoot Papers.

45. Reed is perhaps implicitly chiding Allie here because of the following snide remarks she made about Jennie Judge Kearns in a previous letter. "I see Mrs. [Jennie] Kearns is having a gay time [in Washington]; our papers are jest full of her entertainments. I guess it is like everything else they do—a big fuss." Allie Smoot to Reed Smoot, January 17, 1904, Smoot Papers.

46. Personal calling cards announced the arrival of an expected guest. L[ewis]. W. Shurtliff, a Mormon stake president from Ogden, was being considered as a delegate to the Republican National Convention and Reed wanted to make certain of his loyalty. After visiting England in 1870, Shurtliff changed the spelling of his name from Shurtliff to Shurtleff, to match the English spelling. See Paul Miller Hokanson, "Lewis Warren Shurtliff: 'A Great Man of Israel'" (MA Thesis, Brigham Young University, Provo, UT, 1980), 5.

47. Reed Smoot to Allie Smoot, February 14, 1904, Smoot Papers.

48. Badger, *Liahona and Iron Rod*, 214. Before this day in class, Judge Harlan, it seemed to Carl, had not brought up the subject of Utah's "Domestic Relations" because he knew it was a sensitive issue for Badger. Judge Harlan was an associate justice on the Supreme Court and also a professor at the law school Badger attended. See Andrew Novak, "Courtroom to Classroom: Justice Harlan's Lectures at George Washington University Law School," *Journal of Supreme Court History* 30, no. 3 (November 2003): 223–225.

49. For Badger's thinking during the Smoot hearings, see Gary James Bergera's chapter in this volume (chapter 7).

50. Smoot Hearings, 1:44.

51. Smoot Hearings, 3:728, 771–772. Taylor concluded that Smoot's attorneys were conceding the argument on polygamous cohabitation: "Therefore, the church does encourage it, the church does connive it, the church does countenance it. The president of the church and seven of his apostles practice polygamous cohabitation. The president of the church has proclaimed more than once to the thousands of his people that the man who does not thus remain true to his wives will be eternally damned."

52. Smoot Hearings, 3:205.

53. Allie Smoot to Reed Smoot, March 23, 1904, Smoot Papers.

54. Allie Smoot to Reed Smoot, March 27, 1904, Smoot Papers.

55. Reed Smoot to Allie Smoot, December 18, 1904, Smoot Papers. In this letter, Smoot mentioned he met with the president at the White House and that Roosevelt "was very friendly," even though, he contended, "the women are trying to make him take a hand against me."

56. Smoot Hearings, 3:182–83.

57. First Presidency member Anthon Lund congratulated Smoot on his testimony and gave him, as Smoot reported, "strict instruction to take care of my health." Others believed Smoot, as Smoot put it, "went too far when I said if [John W.] Taylor had married since the Manifesto I would not

sustain him." Smoot was nonplussed with this stating, "I did not go as far as Jos[eph] F. [Smith,] for he said he would be excommunicated." Reed Smoot to Allie Smoot, February 8, 1905, Smoot Papers.

58. Merrill, *Reed Smoot*, 69.

59. Allie Smoot to Reed Smoot, January 22, 1905, Smoot Papers; Allie Smoot to Reed Smoot, January 10, 1905, Smoot Papers.

60. Reed Smoot to Allie Smoot, February 11, 1905, Smoot Papers.

61. Smoot longed for Allie's companionship but, as he wrote her, "made up my mind [that] I did not want you placed in a position" of discomfort here in Washington. Reed Smoot to Allie Smoot, February 2, 1905, Smoot Papers.

62. Reed Smoot to Allie Smoot, February 8, 1905, Smoot Papers.

63. For examples of letters, see Chloe Smoot to Allie Smoot, February 22, 1905, Smoot Papers and Chloe Smoot to Allie Smoot, February 28, 1905, Smoot Papers. Allie was well aware of how difficult the children could be and how challenging it was for Chloe to manage the household, while dealing with Miss Cook, the hired help with whom she had no standing with her demanding, cranky grandmother.

64. Harlow Smoot to Allie Smoot, February 28, 1905, Smoot Papers.

65. Carl Badger to Rose Badger, *Liahona and Iron Rod*, 257.

66. Carl Badger to Rose Badger, *Liahona and Iron Rod*, 260–261.

67. Carl Badger to Rose Badger, *Liahona and Iron Rod*, 261.

68. Allie Smoot to Reed Smoot, March 20, 1905, Smoot Papers.

69. Around the turn of the century, many African Americans, both men and women, worked as servants in households where the duties included cooking. For more on this topic see Philip S. Foner and Ronald L. Lewis, eds., *The Black Worker: A Documentary History from Colonial Times to the Present*, Vol. 5: *The Black Worker from 1900 to 1919* (Philadelphia: Temple University Press, 1980).

70. Reed Smoot to Allie Smoot, January 13, 1906, Smoot Papers.

71. Misses Helen Varick Boswell and Mary Yost Wood were chairwomen of the Women's National Republican Association, Washington, DC. They wrote to Allie, June 2, 1905, reminding her they had met at Republican meetings in Chicago and Washington and asked to "renew acquaintance with you [Allie] for a few hours in Provo on June 22." Smoot Papers.

72. Reed Smoot to Allie Smoot, January 17, 1906, Smoot Papers.

73. Reed Smoot to Joseph F. Smith, January 21, 1906, Smoot Papers.

74. Carl Badger to Rose Badger, *Liahona and Iron Rod*, 313. According to Carl Badger, some people told Allie that "there is nothing to buy in Washington" to which she declared, "[I] can find ways to spend money."

75. Carl Badger to Rose Badger, *Liahona and Iron Rod*, 318.

76. "Final Argument in Smoot Case," *Deseret Evening News*, April 13, 1906, 1.

77. Chloe Smoot to Allie Smoot, April 29, 1906, Smoot Papers. Allie was forty-two years old at the time. Her daughter Chloe consoled from Utah writing, "I will take care of it when it comes and I wont have to be married for a few years longer."

78. Carl Badger to Rose Badger, *Liahona and Iron Rod*, 325–326. In a letter Allie, a frazzled Chloe penned the following: "Do not worry about anything home here I will do the best I can and that is all any one can do. I get terrible worry over things and wish I could keep the bills down but I can't. The house cleaning has cost a lot but mother I haven't got a thing we didn't need . . . The bath room is something that could not go any longer. I only hope you will like it. I have worried over it so much and have done all I could do." Chloe Smoot to Allie Smoot, April 25, 1909, Smoot Papers.

79. Carl Badger to Rose Badger, *Liahona and Iron Rod*, 338. According to Carl Badger, one day at the senator's office Brownie "almost made his mother cry."

80. Merrill, *Reed Smoot*, 38–39. Allie did have one notable experience at a social event in early January 1907. While attending a presidential reception with Reed, Roosevelt made a point to single

Allie for recognition, stating as he exited in a pleasant, loud voice, "Good night, Mrs. Smoot." Carl Badger to Rose Badger, *Liahona and Iron Rod*, 347.

81. Carl Badger to Rose Badger, *Liahona and Iron Rod*, 369.

82. "After Four Years' Delay," *Deseret Evening News*, February 20, 1907, 1.

83. "Goodnight, Mrs. Smoot," Smoot Papers. Allie continued to manage the Provo home until 1913.

84. Reed Smoot to Allie Smoot, September 19, 1927, Smoot Papers.

85. Chloe Smoot to Reed Smoot, October 7, 1928, Smoot Papers.

86. Harvard S. Heath, ed., *In the World: The Diaries of Reed Smoot* (Salt Lake City: Signature Books, 1997), 693.

87. Heath, *In the World*, 695.

88. Heath, *In the World*, xv.

6

Under the Gun at the Smoot Hearings

Joseph F. Smith's Testimony

Michael Harold Paulos

Soon after Apostle Reed Smoot's Senate election,[1] the *Salt Lake Tribune* headlined: "Ministers Getting Arguments Ready for Smoot."[2] The ministers in question were Protestant clergymen hoping to influence senators, while Smoot himself was receiving counsel from LDS president Joseph F. Smith and others in the Church hierarchy. The newspaper headline presaged the impending contest of religious ideas beneath a veneer of legal and political issues. Historians Harvard Heath and Kathleen Flake have ably plumbed the circumference of this fascinating controversy, exploring its impact on modern Mormonism.[3] Heath specifically described the Smoot hearings as the Mormon Church's "quest for legitimacy."[4] The quest implied taking certain calculated risks, and the game plan seems to have been executed by the Church president himself after receiving a subpoena to testify on behalf of Senator Smoot and the LDS Church in Washington. The sixty-five-year-old Church president embraced this challenge with pugnacity and gumption, approaching it as an opportunity for him personally to set the record straight about both him and his people. Entering Washington in 1904, Smith had a predetermined strategy of using political obfuscation throughout his testimony to match what he viewed as Washington demagoguery spurred on by a hostile religious and political establishment looking to squelch the rights of religious minorities.

But Smith's appearance in Washington was not merely a game to outflank politicians with cunning testimony, nor was it just an opportunity to proselytize

DOI: 10.7330/9781646421176.c006

the good news of the LDS gospel. His intentions, which undergirded his entire appearance, was to convey to the nation that the Church of Jesus Christ of Latter-day Saints and its people were ready to move beyond the decades of political and legal conflict and become full participants in American democracy. Smith could have pursued a compromise that would have allowed him to submit sworn testimony affidavits rather than appearing in person, but instead he embraced this challenge head-on. After decades of difficult frontier living and government persecution, the LDS president had developed a gruff demeanor when dealing with outsiders, and his brusque retorts to committee members questions, when combined with his uncouth appearance, did not project a fashionable form of progressive modernity. But his physical presence, as well as his willingness to engage with America at the highest levels of government, sent a message of accommodation that rippled across the country, accelerated the normalization of his Church, and paved the way for Smoot's confirmation.

For more than a decade, Progressive Era developments thrust new ideas and other novelties into American life that transformed how citizens viewed the world. For much of the country there was a sense of excitement and optimism about the future, as technological advancements improved the quality of life of many Americans, and progressive ideas about secularism and citizenship offered civic opportunities to a wider berth of individuals. But not everyone in the country received these cultural movements with pleasure, especially those whose position and status within America were threatened by this "progress." To this cohort of citizens, these shifts toward secular progress represented an existential hazard to their vision of America's religious foundation and Christian identity. The Mormon prophet was not ignorant of these progressive shifts within America, nor was he willing to allow the Church's "enemies," as he frequently described them, to derail Smoot's election or his state's constitutional rights, even if it meant creating controversy by rolling around in a political mudhole, as it were. At the same time, President Smith was optimistic about the progress being made within the country, though his primary focus was how to leverage these trends to best benefit the Church of Jesus Christ of Latter-day Saints. Sending an apostle to Washington, and then ardently protecting both Smoot and Utah's constitutional right of representation when Smoot's election was challenged, were strategic decisions made by Smith to optimize his influence to steer the Church toward long-term success.

Those outside the LDS faith in Utah and the Christian majority in American politics detected unprecedented effrontery in the election of Smoot, a member of the Church's second-ranked ecclesiastical quorum. Two weeks after Smoot's election by the Utah legislature in January 1903, achieved with President Smith's blessing,[5] the *Deseret News* reported that Senator Chauncey Depew (R-NY)[6] exploded against what he viewed as Mormon interference into the statehood debates for Arizona and New Mexico. He reported, more or less incorrectly as it turned out, that polygamy was spreading throughout the West and asserted that the Mormon Church's plan in sending Smoot to Congress was to "prevent any amendment which would completely exclude polygamy."[7] Given the level of emotion embodied in Depew's misgivings, Smoot was apprehensive as he prepared to travel East to assume office. He turned to President Smith for a blessing, which the president readily bestowed.[8] Reassured by this support, Smoot boarded a train in late February 1903 for the capitol, where he served as a senator for the next thirty years.

Given this swirling controversy, Smoot was pleasantly startled by the warm reception he received from several fellow Republican senators. Even though formal protests had accumulated to prevent his seating, the Senate swore him in with the proviso that they would then consider the challenges to his election.[9] This small victory must have given the apostle some optimism about the future. Responding to the welcome news, President Smith and his counselors (John R. Winder and Anthon H. Lund) wrote:

> It is of course very gratifying to us to know that you have made so many friends, and especially so that the President [Theodore Roosevelt] is so kindly disposed towards you. We have pleasure in believing that your friends will increase in number, and that their friendships will grow stronger to you, and that your enemies will not only be worsted in the fight they are making against you but that they will be looked upon with contempt by the honorable people of the nation.[10]

Smoot's Church superiors believed that there were many honorable citizens residing in America; fair-minded folks not swayed by hyperbolic caricatures being brandished about Latter-day Saints by jealous businessmen and ministers in Utah. But in retrospect, this optimistic assessment miscalculated the power still held by Protestant traditionalists in America and the storm about to burst over the ambitious attempt to place an apostle in the nation's highest deliberative body. Nor did Smoot himself foresee that in exactly one year, his prophet-president would be sitting next to him in a capitol hearing, under a national spotlight, enduring the slings and arrows of an unfriendly Senate committee. Although Smoot continued to make friends in Washington to some degree, the corollary that his enemies would be worsted was not fulfilled in the short term. Perhaps the most crucial political friend Smoot had in Washington was US president Theodore Roosevelt. Although initially opposed to Smoot's election, Roosevelt made a quick about-face after meeting the obviously moral and ardent Republican Smoot in person, stating, "Mr. Smoot, you are a good enough American, or Gentile, for that matter for me."[11] Smoot had passed the President's litmus test.

Eager to put the best possible face on the precarious situation, Smoot reported to LDS leaders in Salt Lake about the positive interactions he was enjoying with

Senate colleagues. This collegiality would not necessarily translate into favorable votes, as he would learn, but it gave him hope. Senate colleagues Redfield Proctor (R-VT) and Marcus Hanna (R-Ohio) assured Smoot that they personally "took no stock whatever in the charges filed" against his seating. Senator Nelson Aldrich (R-RI) had "received a great many petitions" urging the Utahan's dismissal but "paid no attention to them" and tossed them into the waste paper basket.[12] Similarly warm sentiments of support were expressed by Senator George Hoar (R-MA).[13] In the cloakroom, Senator Eugene Hale (R-ME) joked that Smoot claimed never to have "cohabited with any woman other than [his] wife" and that, if true, he was making the other senators look bad.[14]

These sanguine reports may have given Joseph F. Smith a false impression about the welcome he might expect to find in Washington. Smoot underemphasized the many hostile colleagues he encountered, many of whom dispensed with any facade of friendliness. At the time of Smoot's election, the Republican Party controlled the House, Senate, and presidency; so Smoot, a Republican, should have theoretically enjoyed the majority support of Congress.[15] However, several GOP senators were avowedly adversarial, including some committee members who would hear Smoot's case, that he admitted being "a little afraid" of them and realized that "any serious opposition" would come from members of his own party—Republicans appointed to sit on the committee.[16] In fact, the most strident and powerful of his critics was the committee's unrelentingly hostile chairman, Julius Caesar Burrows (R-MI.).[17] Facing political pressure in his home state and using the sentiment against the Mormon apostle to his advantage, Burrows generated headlines throughout the hearings. Apprising the First Presidency of Burrows's adversarial position, Smoot wrote privately that President Roosevelt was trying his best to "change the course mapped out by Burrows" but that Burrows would not be dissuaded, since he was seeking reelection and was "doubtful" about the success of his electoral chances.[18]

President Smith, a committed Republican, responded soothingly but somewhat unrealistically that Burrows would have no long-term effect and explained that the Michigan senator's actions would besmirch his legacy of public service. Moreover, the LDS prophet grouped Burrows into a "long list of Anti Mormon monomaniacs" who had faded into obscurity both on "earth" and in "Heaven."[19] Smith's message, sent to Smoot after his visit to Washington, reinforced Smoot's perception that the contest being made against him was based on illegitimate bigotry toward Mormonism.

In point of fact, Smith and the LDS First Presidency had expressed a more accurate grasp of the situation a few months earlier when he learned that the hearings would not focus on Smoot's personal qualifications but on the LDS Church itself. In private correspondence to Smoot, the First Presidency mused upon the "gravity of the situation" and surmised that it was "very apparent that a determined effort will be made to arraign the Church" at the hearings.[20] Much to the presidency's chagrin, this prediction proved dismayingly accurate.

Smoot's first year in the Senate passed in a flurry of paperwork but without any public hearings. As the March 1904 opening of the hearings approached, Smoot became uncomfortably aware of the degree of hostility that existed toward Mormons. Newspapers published malicious editorials and cartoons caricaturing Joseph F. Smith and Reed Smoot.[21] Much of the outrage was generated by the erroneous assumption that Smoot was a secret polygamist. This charge was formally presented to the Senate committee who promptly dismissed it, but it continued to haunt the proceedings for the next three and a half years.[22] Better founded was public anger against the Church because of continued rumors of plural marriage. The hearings established post-manifesto polygamist activities by Apostles Matthias Cowley, Heber J. Grant, John Henry Smith, George Teasdale, and John W. Taylor, naturally fueling the suspicion that there were many other undiscovered cases.[23]

In addition to the pressure Smoot was receiving from unfriendly Senate colleagues, he acknowledged that some of his apostolic colleagues found his political ambitions unseemly and dangerous. Smoot had been an apostle since only 1900, called by Lorenzo Snow, who passed away a year later and was succeeded by Joseph F. Smith, who quickly became Smoot's staunchest supporter. In 1903, he was still only forty-one, younger than all of the other apostles except two sons of Church presidents: Abraham O. Woodruff (ordained in 1897 at age twenty-four, making him senior in the quorum to Smoot) and Hyrum Mack Smith (the thirty-one-year-old son of Joseph F. Smith, who was just junior in the quorum to Smoot). Smoot admitted to President Smith that he knew "some of the brethren have taken the position that I was to blame for all this unpleasantness and trouble brought upon the Church." He "never worried one second over myself or what may happen to me in this investigation, but I have laid awake nights thinking how I could protect you and your counselors from being brought into the fight."[24] Heavily involved professionally while residing in Provo, Smoot had not socialized with many of his colleagues in the Twelve prior to his election and was therefore not privy to the surreptitious post-manifesto plural marriages being performed,[25] nor to the brotherly "understandings" that facilitated such arrangements. It is possible that, sensing some duplicity among his colleagues, he intentionally avoiding learning such inconvenient facts. Moreover, he clearly wanted to retain both positions, possibly, giving the edge to keeping his Senate seat. At least three times in writing to President Smith, he offered to resign, either from the apostleship or from the Senate (though he never went as far as announcing that he *would* resign or insisting that he be allowed to resign as apostle).[26] In these ways, Smoot tried to compromise with and placate his detractors. A further complication of the dynamic is that the lack of bonding worked both ways. At least a few apostles did not feel close to Smoot and begrudged him his political ambitions, which appeared more important than his commitment to his apostolic calling.

By early 1904, the press was reporting the wish lists of Smoot's opponents regarding potential witnesses. Most prominent among the suggested names was that of Joseph F. Smith. Smoot well understood that polygamy's sexual details would be a magnet for journalists, eager to purvey prurient information about the private lives and practices of the Mormon leaders to their readers. "Of course," Smoot informed Smith by giving a preview of his hearings tactics, "I can testify that I do not know of any of the First Presidency or Twelve Apostles having sexual intercourse with more than one woman. I can even testify that I do not know that a child has been born to President Joseph F. Smith, or any of the First Presidency, or the Quorum of Twelve Apostles by their plural wives since the manifesto."[27] Smoot was explaining to President Smith in precise terms what he didn't know, which also implicitly informed his leader what he did not want to know, concerning the intimate details of his ecclesiastical colleagues' conjugal lives. Moreover, Smoot was not asking Smith to provide him with answers to these information gaps, since Smoot needed to retain a healthy level of incognizance and plausible deniability for him to maintain truthful authenticity when fielding questions, both formal and informal, from his Senate colleagues.

Smoot, in this regard, was following the shopworn playbook of craftiness and guile developed by the LDS hierarchy during the polygamous raids of the 1880s when federal marshals were gathering evidence to incarcerate polygamists. Kathleen Flake, in her study of the Smoot hearings, explained that during this era, "'Mind your own business' became part of the Latter-day Saint creed" and that Joseph F. Smith "did his best not to know" anything about the "domestic arrangements" of his ecclesiastical colleagues, stating: "My motto is and always has been to protect to the uttermost in my power the rights and secrets . . . of my friends and the friends of the kingdom of God."[28] Smoot's indirect appraisal to Smith of his ignorance not only validated they were working from the same playbook, but it was also a shrewd way to coordinate his testimony with Smith's that ensured no contradictions occurred between them before the committee. Later, when Smith was asked by the Senate committee if Smoot had "ever" advised him "to desist from polygamous cohabitation," he responded using this playbook, stating that he was not sure that Smoot "knows anything about them." At a later time, when Smith was asked about his awareness of his ecclesiastical subordinates' conjugal relationships, he testified to not being "familiar" with the family relations of most of the apostles.[29]

Since his calling to the apostleship, Smoot at a minimum had heard the rumors about illegal polygamous marriages taking place after 1890. However, as his approach reveals here, he was intentionally incurious about the connubial lives of his apostolic brethren. Smoot, when on the stand, would only testify about things he knew absolutely from hands-on experience, which in this case amounted to very little. While Smoot's calculating approach does him credit as a politician and as someone who is loyal to the team, so to speak, it is likely that such testimony would not be found credible by the skeptical members of the Senate committee. Despite these tactics in political contrivance, Smith, sensing some trepidation from Smoot about the challenges ahead, explained that they had nothing to hide and claimed that they would, in fact, welcome such exposure:

> We are and always have been open to investigation with regard to our religion and our religious practices . . . We are pleased to have another opportunity of present-ing the doctrines of the Church of Jesus Christ before the world. This we have been striving to do for the last seventy years. Thousands of our elders have gone forth from nation to nation . . . endeavoring to get the people to understand what "Mor-monism" is, and we have spent hundreds of thousands of dollars in endeavoring to expose it and bring it to the notice of the world. Don't shrink from the issue, tell them to come ahead, invite them to make a most thorough investigation, the more thorough the better in all and everything that belongs to us.[30]

By late February, the *Salt Lake Tribune* reported that twenty-two witnesses had been subpoenaed, with President Smith heading the list.[31] The Church president dutifully took the train to Washington and became the first witness to testify when the hearings opened on March 2, 1904. Reporting from Washington, *Harper's Weekly* explained that "six Methodists, two Congregationalists, two Presbyterians, an Episcopalian, a Baptist, and a Unitarian compose the tribunal before which the Mormon Church is on trial at Washington."[32]

A New York newspaper noticed that President Smith sported a "scraggly beard" that dropped "well down on his chest," also that "in the lapel of his coat is a button an inch in diameter, on which is his own picture." His eyes were "small and shifty," the reporter added, no doubt pandering to the readers' expectations. More informative was the observation that "Smith speaks like a preacher. His voice is sonorous. His words are well chosen. It is evident that he has had much practice in talking to the public. His temper is not well in hand, for at times he flares up and answers questions sharply. He rarely moves when other witnesses are on the stand. He watches each man closely but betrays neither satisfaction at nor disapproval of the testimony. He looks like the solemn personage he is, impressed with his own authority, and evidently given to impressing others so far as he is able."[33] Smith's stoic solemnity displayed on the stand was the embod-iment of the LDS prophet's personal narrative, or "personal myth" as historian Stephen Taysom propounds. This myth was "grounded" in his appropriated "memories of the Missouri and Nauvoo periods," when the Church sustained violent persecution that included the murder of his father, Hyrum Smith, and uncle Joseph Smith. For Church members living during the time of Smoot's election, Joseph F. Smith was the "site of memory" and "living symbol" of the Church's traumatic past. Through his public utterances beginning in the mid-1880s, Smith shaped the "wider Mormon collective memory" on how these events were remembered. This "personal myth" as it were, was also the "useful tool" for how Smith made "sense of the difficulties he faced on the polygamy 'underground,' his conflicted emotions surrounding the Manifesto of 1890, the humiliation of the Reed Smoot hearings." Smith's memories of the past "took the uncertainty out of present trauma by linking it with past," which constructed a schematic that "enabled" the prophet to hold firm the "idea of righteous suffering and living martyrdom."[34] Armed with this memory construction and worldview, Smith was infused with a confidence that both he and the Church would ultimately surmount any external persecution, even if it meant that his church would have to make accommodations.

Nevertheless, President Smith would have been anxious about being grilled under the national spotlight in a forum where all topics had been ruled fair game. Certainly he anticipated that he must meet difficult questions about his domestic situation. However, he seems to have entered the chambers intent on being utterly candid about his personal situation while preserving considerable reticence about the behavior of others. The predictable result of this approach was that his remarks attracted national attention, newspapers running front-page stories as new disclosures came out of each day's testimony. President Smith may have miscalculated the goodwill to be derived by his transparency. To some of his detractors, far from appearing upright and honorable, his answers seemed brazen and flippant, as if he were defying the nation to take action against his continued embrace of plural marriage. An example of this occurred during one exchange in which President Smith was asked by the protestant attorney Tayler about the fitness of him continuing to cohabitate with his five wives and if he considered "it an abandonment of your family to maintain relations with your wives except that of occupying their beds," to which he rebuffed, "I do not wish to be impertinent but I should like the gentleman to ask any women, who is a wife, that question." Smith's shifty answer to this question beclouded the claims of patriarchal prurience, because the manner of his response shifted responsibility for the continued conjugality of his marital relationships from himself to his wives.[35]

President Smith was "under the gun" for six days; his testimony spanned more than sixteen hours and filled a total of 262 published pages.[36] Representative excerpts from his testimony show the breadth of the questions asked him and his openness in responding about himself while deflecting questions involving others. The first exchange occurred in the morning session of the committee's first day of questioning. The committee had first asked about the Church's business dealings, including ownership of the *Deseret News*, and about LDS doctrinal concepts.

FIGURE 6.1. "Shall Reed Smoot, A Mormon, Hold a Seat in the United States Senate?" President Joseph F. Smith was the first witness at the Reed Smoot Hearings, where he testified for sixteen hours over six days. Attorneys, senators, Chaplain E. E. Hale, women from the W[omen's]. C[hristian]. T[emperance]. U[nion]., and Mormon elders looked on as President Smith was "under the gun" answering questions. *Frank Leslie's Illustrated Newspaper*, March 17, 1904. Photo courtesy of the Library of Congress. https://www.loc.gov/item/2002720308/.

Wednesday, March 2, 1904; 11:30 AM[37]

> SENATOR HOAR: Is the doctrine of the inspiration of the head of the church and revelations given to him one of the fundamental or non-fundamental doctrines of Mormonism?
>
> MR. SMITH: The principle of revelation is a fundamental principle to the church.
>
> SENATOR HOAR: I speak of the revelations given to the head of the church. Is that a fundamental doctrine of Mormonism?
>
> MR. SMITH: Yes, sir.
>
> SENATOR HOAR: Does or does not a person who does not believe that a revelation given through the head of the church comes from God reject a fundamental principle of Mormonism?
>
> MR. SMITH: He does; always if the revelation is a divine revelation from God.
>
> SENATOR HOAR: It always is, is it not? It comes through the head of the church?

MR. SMITH: When it is divine, it always is; when it is divine, most decidedly.

THE CHAIRMAN [JULIUS C. BURROWS]: I do not quite understand that—"when it is divine." You have revelations, have you not?

MR. SMITH: I have never pretended to nor do I profess to have received revelations. I never said I had a revelation except so far as God has shown to me that so-called Mormonism is God's divine truth; that is all.[38]

THE CHAIRMAN: You say that was shown to you by God?

MR. SMITH: By inspiration.

THE CHAIRMAN: How by inspiration; does it come in the shape of a vision?

MR. SMITH: "The things of God knoweth no man but the spirit of God;" and I can not tell you any more than that I received that knowledge and that testimony by the spirit of God.

MR. TAYLER:[39] You do not mean that you reached it by any process of reasoning or by any other method by which you reach other conclusions in your mind, do you?

MR. SMITH: When I have reached principles; that is, I have been confirmed in my acceptance and knowledge of principles that have been revealed to me, shown to me, on which I was ignorant before, by reason and facts . . .

SENATOR BAILEY:[40] Before we proceed any further, I assume that all these questions connected with the religious faith of the Mormon Church are to be shown subsequently to have some relation to civil affairs. Unless that is true I myself object to going into the religious opinions of these people. I do not think Congress has anything to do with that unless their religion connects itself in some way with their civil or political affairs . . .

MR. TAYLER: . . . Mr. Smith, in what different ways did Joseph Smith, jr., receive revelations?

MR. SMITH: I do not know, sir; I was not there.

MR. TAYLER: Do you place any faith at all in the account of Joseph Smith, jr., as to how he received those revelations?

MR. SMITH: Yes, sir; I do.

MR. TAYLER: How does he say he got them?

MR. SMITH: He does not say.

MR. TAYLER: He does not?

MR. SMITH: Only by the spirit of God.

MR. TAYLER: Only by the spirit of God?

MR. SMITH: Yes, sir.

MR. TAYLER: Did Joseph Smith ever say that God or an angel appeared to him in fact?

MR. SMITH: He did.

MR. TAYLER: That is what I asked you a moment ago.

MR. SMITH: He did.

MR. TAYLER: Did Joseph Smith contend that always there was a visible appearance of the Almighty or of an angel?

MR. SMITH: No sir; he did not.

MR. TAYLER: How otherwise did he claim to receive revelations?

MR. SMITH: By the spirit of the Lord.

MR. TAYLER: And in that way, such revelations as you have received, you have had them?

MR. SMITH: Yes, sir. . . .

––––––––––––––––––

Despite Joseph F. Smith's claim that he was "pleased to have another opportunity of presenting the doctrines of the Church of Jesus Christ before the world," as this testimony shows, he was actually vague and cursory, sometimes misunderstanding questions—apparently deliberately—and passing up numerous opportunities to deliver short sermons on Mormon doctrine, the First Vision, the nature of revelation, and prophetic authority. And despite the New York Sun's comment on his flashes of "temper," hindsight makes it obvious that Smith was surprisingly equitable, not a trait he was particularly known for in his early life.[41] The fact that he did not vary from impeccably genteel deportment is some measure of his control during this ordeal. Clearly, this testimony required his most concentrated effort and rigorously gentlemanly etiquette.

Of significance, rather than perceiving this line of theological questioning to be a missionary opportunity, Smith made little effort to clarify the misunderstandings. Such misunderstandings would have been inevitable in any case as the attorney and witness tried to communicate the philosophical underpinnings of their differing religious assumptions. This line of questioning concerning the voice of God to both clergy and laity was a familiar concern for many religious communities, particularly Latter-day Saints back home in Utah. Subsequent witnesses questioned on theological points—among them future apostle James E. Talmage—were also uncooperative with the committee.[42] These witnesses seem to have been offended by the prying and somewhat voyeuristic questions into Church teachings, apparently feeling, like Senator Bailey, that these matters had no business in a senatorial hearing.[43] By not overtly missionizing or sermonizing on the distinctiveness of LDS doctrine, while giving some muzzy answers to queries about his faith, Smith was appealing to the secular sensibilities of the section of the country who were becoming less explicitly religious-centric. Approaching his testimony this way, Smith minimized the appearance of religious zealotry, which placed secular space between the LDS Church and the Christian churches opposing Smoot's retention in the Senate.

Using quick-witted instincts developed over years of defending his religious faith, Smith's approach acted to Smoot's benefit. Smith had called the Provo businessman to the Quorum of the Twelve in part because of Smoot's business acumen and political activism—not because of his church experience.[44] When discussions turned to theology, Smoot's training was inadequate, a fact rather painfully evident from Smoot's doctrinally shallow testimony toward the end of the hearings.[45] By making himself a target, Smith allowed the perception of some distance to emerge between the two of them. The utility of Smoot's appointment to the Twelve was that the Church needed someone to represent its interests in the nation's capital, and Smoot was the ideal candidate. Unassuming and likeable, he was deferential to authority, usually allowed insults to pass by without a public response, instead placing his energy into building coalitions.[46] As a result, when issues emerged that were of critical importance to Utah, he was in a position to call in favors.[47] Smoot genuinely liked the opportunities afforded from holding a position of power, which gave him motivation to campaign vigorously and to think in terms of fostering popular approval.

President Smith took a calculated risk, betting he could appeal to the better natures of Smoot's Senate colleagues and the country by showing up and taking tough questions. When Salt Lake stake president Angus M. Cannon testified a month and a half later, he relied on the Fifth Amendment and asked to be exempted from answering questions that he thought might incriminate him. He took this approach, at least in part, because "in the public press . . . my president [Smith] has been caricatured and his family has been caricatured throughout the United States and throughout the world," and Cannon was determined to avoid this outcome.[48] Immediately after this segment of his testimony, the hearings adjourned for a two-hour lunch break, then resumed on the feverishly sensational topic of plural marriage.[49]

Mr. TAYLER: The revelation [1890 Manifesto] which Wilford Woodruff received, in consequence of which the command to take plural wives was suspended, did not, as you understand it, change the divine view of plural marriages, did it?

Mr. SMITH: It did not change our belief at all.

Mr. TAYLER: It did not change your belief at all?

Mr. SMITH: Not at all, sir.

Mr. TAYLER: You continued to believe that plural marriages were right?

MR. SMITH: We do. I do, at least. I do not answer for anybody else. I continue to believe as I did before.

MR. TAYLER: You stated what were the standard inspired works of the church, and we find in the Book of Doctrine and Covenants the revelation made to Joseph Smith in 1843 respecting plural marriages. Where do we find the revelation suspending the operation of that command?

MR. SMITH: Printed in our public works.

MR. TAYLER: Printed in your public works?

MR. SMITH: Printed in pamphlet form. You have a pamphlet of it right there.

MR. TAYLER: It is not printed in your work of Doctrine and Covenants?

MR. SMITH: No, sir; nor a great many other revelations, either.[50]

MR. TAYLER: Nor a great many other revelations?

MR. SMITH: Yes, sir.

MR. TAYLER: How many revelations do you suppose—

MR. SMITH: I could not tell you how many.

MR. TAYLER: But a great many?

MR. SMITH: A great many.

MR. TAYLER: Why have they not been printed in the Book of Doctrine and Covenants?

MR. SMITH: Because it has not been deemed necessary to publish or print them.

MR. TAYLER: Are they matters that have been proclaimed to the people at large?

MR. SMITH: No, sir; not in every instance.

MR. TAYLER: Why not?

MR. SMITH: Well, I don't know why not. It was simply because they have not been.

MR. TAYLER: Is it because they are not of general interest, or that all of the people need to know of?

MR. SMITH: A great many of these revelations are local.

MR. TAYLER: Local?

MR. SMITH: In their nature. They apply to local matters.

MR. TAYLER: Yes, exactly.

MR. SMITH: And these, in many instances, are not incorporated in the general revelations, and in the Book of Doctrine and Covenants.

MR. TAYLER: For instance, what do you mean by local?

MR. SMITH: Matters that pertain to local interests of the church.

MR. TAYLER: Of course the law or revelation suspending polygamy is a matter that does affect everybody in the church.

MR. SMITH: Yes.

MR. TAYLER: And you have sought to inform them all, but not by means of putting it within the covers of one of your inspired books?

MR. SMITH: Yes.

MR. TAYLER: The various revelations that are published in the Book of Doctrine and Covenants covered twenty-five or thirty years, did they not?

MR. SMITH: Yes, sir.

MR. TAYLER: And as new revelations were given they were added to the body of the revelations previously received?

MR. SMITH: From time to time they were, but not all.

MR. TAYLER: No; but I mean those that are published in that book?

MR. SMITH: Yes, sir.

MR. TAYLER: You have, I suppose, published a great many editions of the Book of Doctrine and Covenants?

MR. SMITH: Yes, sir.

MR. TAYLER: And as recently as 1903 you have put out an edition of that book?

MR. SMITH: Well, I can not say that from memory.

MR. TAYLER: No; but within the last year, or two, or three?[51]

MR. SMITH: Yes; I think, likely, it is so.

MR. TAYLER: As the head of the church, have you given any instruction to put within that book of Doctrine and Covenants any expression that the revelation of Joseph Smith has been qualified?

MR. SMITH: No, sir.

MR. TAYLER: The revelation of Joseph Smith respecting plural marriages remains in the book?

MR. SMITH: Yes, sir.

MR. TAYLER: And in the last editions just as it did when first promulgated?

MR. SMITH: Yes, sir.

MR. TAYLER: And it remains now without expurgation or note or anything to show that it is not now a valid law?

MR. SMITH: In the book?

MR. TAYLER: In the book; exactly.

MR. SMITH: Yes, sir.

MR. TAYLER: And in connection with the publication of the revelation itself.

MR. SMITH: But the fact is publicly and universally known by the people.

THE CHAIRMAN [JULIUS C. BURROWS]: There is one thing I do not understand that I want to ask about. This manifesto suspending polygamy, I understand, was a revelation and a direction to the church?

MR. SMITH: I understand it, Mr. Chairman, just as it is stated there by President Woodruff himself. President Woodruff makes his own statement. I can not add to nor take anything from that statement.

THE CHAIRMAN: Do you understand it was a revelation the same as other revelations?

MR. SMITH: I understand personally that President Woodruff was inspired to put forth that manifesto.

THE CHAIRMAN: And in that sense it was a revelation?

MR. SMITH: Well, it was a revelation to me.

THE CHAIRMAN: Yes.

MR. SMITH: Most emphatically.

THE CHAIRMAN: Yes; and upon which you rely. There is another revelation directing plural marriages, I believe, previous to that?

MR. SMITH: Yes.

THE CHAIRMAN: And I understand you to say now that you believe in the former revelation directing plural marriages in spite of this later revelation for a discontinuance?

MR. SMITH: That is simply a matter of belief on my part. I can not help my belief.

THE CHAIRMAN: Yes; you adhere to the original revelation and discard the latter one.

MR. SMITH: I adhere to both. I adhere to the first in my belief. I believe that the principle is as correct a principle to-day as it was then.

THE CHAIRMAN: What principle?

MR. SMITH: The principle of plural marriage. If I had not believed it, Mr. Chairman, I never would have married more than one wife.

THE CHAIRMAN: That is all. . . .

Some senators on the committee perceived a contradiction between belief and action, between stated intent and actual behavior, as well as an implicit suggestion that God through his prophets would succumb to political pressure. These themes were recurring points of emphasis throughout the hearings as the prosecution hammered home its view that Mormon leaders had not acted in good faith. In fact, it appeared to some skeptical outsiders that the LDS hierarchy was blatantly insincere about its belief in revelation,[52] using the doctrine as convenient means of self-justification. Again, President Smith took the higher ground, as he viewed it, by acknowledging the ambiguities in God's laws—gray areas where principles come into conflict. Again, he passed up several opportunities to provide fuller and more nuanced answers, with the result that, the more forthcoming he tried to be, the more contrived his answers appeared to be to the opposition. His answers fell explosively among the skeptical committee members, exploded again on the front pages of the nation's newspapers—and from there settled disturbingly into the public consciousness.

When the day's session closed, President Smith's testimony was the sensation of the capital. Some measure of the public interest is a paragraph in the *Evening Star* the following day commenting that "it was necessary . . . to post a policeman at the door of the room of the committee . . . All persons except those directly interested were kept out of the room, though outside the door it was impossible almost to maintain a passageway through the corridor of the Capitol."[53] On Thursday, March 3, President Smith again took the witness stand to be bombarded by questions about his private life. This testimony was the most controversial testimony yet, remaining problematic among scholars looking at the matter as dispassionately as possible but still disagreeing about what it means or what motivated it. Most think the president's answers fell along a spectrum of possible motives that ranged from technically accurate, to honest misunderstandings of the terms used, to subtly misleading, to outright lies. "Lying for the Lord" is how one historian summed up the president's testimony, while others have labeled it "sensational" and "concealing."[54] Kathleen Flake, a trained historian and attorney, provided a more nuanced view of Smith's testimony based on her experience with "law and how it works." She stated that she does not believe that Joseph F. Smith lied but conceded he was "tough," even to the point of being "a hostile witness" who used "very careful" language. Expanding further, Flake explained, "A good lawyer is trained not to ask any question that she does not already know the answer to. And when you ask your question, you give the witness two choices: You can either make an admission against your interest or you can perjure yourself. That's the only choice a good lawyer will give you on the witness stand—unless you're a very smart witness and you'll split the difference."[55]

Judgment about President Smith's veracity may depend on exactly which elements of his testimony one emphasizes. For much of the proceedings, he appears to have been strictly honest—even willing to be a sacrificial lamb when speaking of himself.[56] In many ways, it was his unexpected candor that led to further misunderstandings. Certainly, he hedged to the point of prevarication about the status of new plural marriages and the consent, sanction, and knowledge of these unions. Even so, it is striking how unflinchingly he admitted that he had fathered eleven children by five wives since the manifesto. This aspect of his testimony was a reflection of his complicated personal character and the weight of his office, and to some extent it was a possible strategy worked out with legal counsel about the degree to which he should cooperate with the committee's probing. However, it is assumed that his preference carried the greatest weight in such a hypothetical discussion, though he would surely have sought inspiration through prayer, but no public statements have been located where he claims inspiration for the approach taken.

The Thursday morning session on March 3, 1904, opened at 10:45 AM. This was one of the most important sections of testimony from any witness. In it, President Smith makes a careful-yet-obscure distinction between his acts as an individual Latter-day Saint and the acts, knowledge, or authorization of "the Church." The opening distinction he made between a "law" and a "rule" of the Church was useful primarily as a time-consuming and attention-diverting quibble to distract the committee, whose frustration at the circular action shows in a couple of places.[57]

———————

MR. TAYLER: Is the law of the church, as well as the law of the land, against the taking of plural wives?

MR. SMITH: Yes, sir; I will say—

MR. TAYLER: Is that the law?

MR. SMITH: I would substitute the word "rule" of the church.

MR. TAYLER: Rule?

MR. SMITH: Instead of law; as you put it.

MR. TAYLER: Very well. Then to take a plural wife would be a violation of a rule of the church?

MR. SMITH: It would.

MR. TAYLER: Would it be such a violation of the rule of the church as would induce the church authorities to take it up like the violation of any other rule would do?

MR. SMITH: It would.

MR. TAYLER: Is the cohabitation with one who is claimed to be a plural wife a violation of the law or rule of the church, as well as of the law of the land?

MR. SMITH: If the committee will permit me, I could not answer the question yes or no . . .

MR. SMITH: That is contrary to the rule of the church and contrary as well to the law of the land for a man to cohabit with his wives. But I was placed in this position. I had a plural family, if you please; that is, my first wife was married to me over thirty-eight years ago, my last wife was married to me over twenty years ago, and with these wives I had children, and I simply took my chances preferring to meet the

consequences of the law rather than to abandon my children and
their mothers; and I have cohabited with my wives—not openly,
that is, not in a manner that I thought would be offensive to my
neighbors—but I have acknowledged them; I have visited them.
They have borne me children since 1890, and I have done it knowing
the responsibility and knowing that I was amenable to the law. Since
the admission of the State there has been a sentiment existing and
prevalent in Utah that these old marriages would be in measure
condoned. They were not looked upon as offensive; as really violative
of law; they were, in other words, regarded as an existing fact, and
if they saw any wrong in it they simply winked. In other words,
Mr. Chairman, the people of Utah, as a rule, as well as the people of
this nation, are broad-minded and liberal-minded people, and they
have rather condoned than otherwise, I presume, my offense against
the law. I have never been disturbed. Nobody has ever called me in
question, that I know of, and if I had, I was there to answer to the
charge; or any charge that might have been made against me, and I
would have been willing to submit to the penalty of the law, whatever
it might have been.[58] . . .

President Smith, despite his imperturbable composure during his startling testimony, apparently realized its negative impact. Smoot's secretary, Carl Badger,
reported that "when President Smith had concluded his testimony," he left mut-
tering, "I am sorry for Reed, I am sorry for Reed."[59] Smith knew that these details
about his personal life would be damaging to Smoot's case, yet he had told the
committee what they wanted to know. The senators were obviously startled,
not only by Smith's confession of cohabitation but especially by his nonchalant
assumption that, once statehood had been achieved, Mormons assumed that all
had been forgiven and forgotten and that those who had previously married more
than one wife could resume living with them. This description flatly contradicted
both what Church president Wilford Woodruff and Smith himself had assured the
master in chancery in 1891.[60] On the other hand, it was not the first time (or would
it be the last) that local "arrangements" in the United States would vary from what
politicians and others promised to a national audience. Smith reiterated several
times throughout his testimony that "the Church," the breathless and inanimate
entity, had not officially permitted any new plural marriages after the manifesto.[61]
Given the incontrovertible evidence that plural marriages were performed after
the manifesto, which included President Smith's personal involvement in new
polygamous marriages, the prophet's disclaimer has been troublesome to some
readers since it appears to be an instance of lying. Flake, using a legalistic and

semantic framework, argues that Smith, "who was sufficiently concerned for his personal integrity and skilled in casuistry to avoid lying," employed the generic term "the Church," which in his mind relayed to the audience "the traditional distinction between the church and its members," which therefore kept his testimony within the bounds of truthfulness.[62] Thus, under this semantic framework, it was impossible for "the Church" to give permission for new plural marriages since permission could only be given by individual Church officials, who were not "the Church," but acting only as an agents of such. In this way, Smith created a demarcation line between "the Church" and the activities of its top officials, which allowed for Smith to cagily deflect telling the truth in actual fact. In this way, Smith was perhaps being wise as a serpent rather than harmless as a dove (Matt. 10:16).[63]

Flake's analysis of Smith's canny use of rhetorical distortion is, for the most part, sound. Smith does appear, however, at one point in his testimony to fudge slightly on this device. During Smith's first disavowal, made on the second day of his testimony, he was elaborate and specific, "there has never been [since the manifesto], to my knowledge, a plural marriage performed in accordance with the understanding, instruction, connivance, counsel, *or permission of the presiding authorities of the church, or of the church*, in any shape or form; and I know whereof I speak, in relation to that matter."[64] Subsequent declarations by Smith did not aver the refutation that no new plural marriages had the "*permission of the presiding authorities of the church*," which was undeniably false, but instead stuck to the generic construction that "the Church" did not give permission. Smith's foregoing words, were taken verbatim from the published version of the hearings, and based upon the shorthand notes of stenographers. This transcript is ambiguous on one important point, that is, whether Smith was using the modifying phrase, set off by a comma in the transcript, "*or of the church*," to replace the mendacious statement that no presiding authorities had given permission to post-manifesto marriages. Or perhaps, he used this modifier "*or of the church*" as a way to add empathic augmentation to his comprehensive denial, making it a veritable falsehood. Smith's inquisitors did not probe him further about his statement regarding the actions of presiding authorities, nor did they later revisit the subject for additional clarification, which suggests that they understood the modifier "*or of the church*," to replace the "*permission of the presiding authorities of the church*" non-sequitur.

Howbeit, it is impossible to know precisely Smith's linguistic intent or the specific words he used on the stand without a recording of the testimony. However, it is relevant to note that six days later Smith added a clarifying caveat that no "official member of the church, in good standing" would violate the promise of the Church to not perform new plural marriages. By adding the qualifier that no Church leader "in good standing" would have performed a new plural marriage, Smith provided an additional escape hatch to maintain truthfulness, since any Church authority, including Joseph F. Smith himself, who performed a plural marriage after the manifesto would not have been considered in good standing at the time the plural marriage was solemnized. This rhetorical device, that of "in good standing," was likewise used by Smith as an amorphous tool to deflect sharp questions on thorny issues. For example, early in his testimony, Smith responded affirmatively to Senator Hoar's theoretical question if a Church member could remain "in good standing" if they lived a "moral" life, but "reject one of your revelations" while "still believe[ing] in the main principles of the church." Conversely, when asked later by Senator Hoar about a different scenario, that is if "an apostle" could remain in "good standing" if he was confronted with a circumstance where "the divine command by revelation enjoined one thing and the human law the contrary," and the apostle "disobeyed God and obeyed man," Smith responded elliptically, "I rather think he would be considered as a little out of harmony with his associates if he did that." From a Church discipline standpoint, the phrase-statuses "out of harmony" or not "in good standing" were toothless, since for most everyone in these categories, no ecclesiastical repercussions were presumptive. This is illustrated by a later witness, Francis M. Lyman, then serving as the president of Quorum of the Twelve Apostles, when he conceded that by continuing to cohabit with his plural wives, he was breaking the "the rule of the church" which he considered to be "the law of God." These violative activities, or similar actions by dozens of other Church leaders, did not bring any adverse ecclesial consequences, such as being released from his high position in the hierarchy.[65]

Smith's time on the stand was exhausting, and using historian Stephen Taysom's construction of Smith's position as the "site of memory," the LDS president would have viewed his proximity as a witness through the prism of persecution. In his letters to Smoot, he framed the hearings existence in victimology upholstery, which would have influenced Smoot to view the event from the same vantage point. For more than seventy years, Mormons had been under attack from the United States, at least in Smith's mind. He knew that Burrows and a few others were gladly exploiting the hearings to push an anti-Mormon populist platform for political gain. It appears probable that as the questioning became more pointed, he engaged in some one-upmanship, matching his opponents' sophistry with his own. Readers of his full testimony will notice that he sometimes seems to be scrapping like a crafty pugilist. When he detected a feint in the opponent's jab, he responded with a swift counterpunch. At other times, he took some lumps after letting down his guard, while in other cases he committed rhetorical mistakes that reverberated adversely with Smoot's Senate colleagues. These moments display the complicated aspects of his personality, situations where he detected genuineness on the part of his inquisitors; however, it may also be that he saw some advantage in the ebb and flow of the testimony, especially when he noticed how his candidness caught his questioners off guard, sparking unplanned moments of silence when his questioners grabbled for appropriate replies. All in all, it was a workmanlike performance, though not a perfect one.

Reflecting on his grueling testimony two years after the fact, President Smith referred to the event as "the crucial test to which I was subjected."[66] His unvarnished truthfulness about himself flabbergasted the country and dismayed Smoot's colleagues. After being initially stymied by the disclosures, those who were so inclined made use of the new information to Smoot's disadvantage with the result that, as Smoot wrote to Smith in early April 1904, it had been difficult "to keep some of my former friends from deserting me."[67] They told him privately that they had been "shocked more over the admission made by" President Smith that he had continued to cohabitate with his plural wives than by the prior assumption that some Church leaders had broken the law. This was because some of Smoot's adversaries felt Smith had all but bragged about having disregarded not only the "law of the land," but the "law of God" as well (meaning the manifesto), leading them to believe he was "insincere and untruthful."[68]

Eventually the Senate voted to confirm Smoot, and he served concurrently as an apostle and senator for five six-year senate terms. Joseph F. Smith's testimony had been instrumental in the cascade of effects that ultimately distanced the Church from polygamy. Motivated by the pressure from Washington, President Smith issued the so-called Second Manifesto at April 1904 General Conference, only a month after his ordeal in Washington. This official statement warned that excommunication would be the punishment of "any officer or member of the Church" who "assume[d] to solemnize or enter into . . . [plural] marriage."[69] It may be that Joseph F. Smith went to Washington to school the US Senate in the ways of righteousness and ended up feeling the sting of their reasonable criticism, leading him to finally take serious action to put an end to polygamy once and for all. Bound by the Second Manifesto, Apostles John W. Taylor and Matthias F. Cowley resigned from the Quorum of Twelve Apostles for their noncompliance with contracting post-manifesto marriages and later refusal to testify in Washington. Other Church leaders, who likewise violated the conditions of the manifesto, could have been punished by Church action but were not, because their activities did not become a political issue. Taylor and Cowley, because they refused to comply with the subpoena to testify in Washington, were seen as poster children for Mormon malfeasance in the national consciousness, and the Church, under the weight of political pressure, had to sacrifice these popular personalities to save Smoot.[70]

In addition to these effects on President Smith and Mormonism, the Smoot hearings provided the scaffolding for the nation to finally solve the Mormon conundrum, a problem the country had been dealing with for more than forty years. When the hearings concluded, intolerance and prejudice toward the LDS Church did not vanish, and flashes of intolerance would persist over the ensuing decade. However, this opposition did not express itself in federal intervention or punitive legislation aimed at the Church nor its membership. Flake suggests that the hearings were the factory where a "forge" was developed that allowed for "Latter-day Saints, the Protestants and their senators" to hammer "out a twentieth-century model for church-state relations."[71] The integrity of this arrangement was tested seven years later in 1911, when Smith, under subpoena, traveled again to Washington to testify before a special House committee investigating the relationship between the national Sugar Trust and the Church-owned Utah-Idaho Sugar Company. Smith's testimony at these hearings generated fewer headlines, despite Utah-Idaho's company executives, comprising mostly LDS leaders, being reprimanded by the Hardwick Committee for having an improper relationship with the Sugar Trust and for engaging in "unseemly" business practices.[72] Had these Hardwick hearings been held in 1904, rather than in 1911, one could easily imagine the Hardwick committee aggressively investigating the Church and its leaders for criminal practices, similar to how the Church was probed at the Smoot hearings. But as it happened, the Hardwick hearings did not scrutinize the LDS Church like the government had in 1904, providing evidence that the country no longer felt the LDS Church was an acutely dangerous threat, nor were there the same political benefits available from attacking the Church. Progressive Era shifts impacted wide swaths of American life, offering new opportunities to those who had previously been on the margins. The Smoot hearings addressed an important part of these margins, and for members of the Church of Jesus Christ of Latter-day Saints, the future held many new possibilities of national inclusion and belonging.

Smith's testimony at the Smoot hearings was a crucible. In important ways he proved his mettle, while in other ways he learned useful lessons that would help the Church in the future. Smoot would soon become a fixture in Washington, and the Church would have more personal contact with the Eastern establishment whom he and others had for so long dismissed in sermons and writings as the "Great Babylon." Moreover, it was this testimony, more than any other event during Smith's presidency that most directly, and profoundly, contributed to the LDS Church's abandonment of polygamy and its transformation into the modern era. It was at this moment, Smith's self-described "crucial test," where he took substantial risk by matching wits with some of the country most prestigious leaders, that set the stage for Mormonism's acceptance into America's religious pantheon, where it would start the process of assimilation into American society at large.

NOTES

1. "Smoot Is Now a Real Senator," *Deseret News*, January 20, 1903. Articles cited from the Salt Lake papers appear in the Journal History of the Church of Jesus Christ of Latter-day Saints (chronological scrapbook of typed entries and newspaper clippings, 1830–present), LDS Church History Library.

2. "Ministers Getting Arguments Ready for Smoot," *Salt Lake Tribune*, January 20, 1903.

3. Harvard S. Heath, "Reed Smoot: First Modern Mormon" (PhD diss., Brigham Young University, Provo, UT, 1990); Kathleen Flake, *The Politics of American Religious Identity: The Seating of Senator Reed Smoot, Mormon Apostle* (Chapel Hill: University of North Carolina Press, 2004).

4. Heath, "Reed Smoot," 84.

5. President Smith provided Smoot with unwavering support before and after his successful election to the US Senate. Four years later, President Smith and Presiding Bishop Charles W. Nibley privately discussed Smoot's political future. When Nibley commented that it would not be wise for Smoot to run for reelection in 1908, President Smith listened "with some impatience." As Nibley described Smith's actions, "Finally, bringing his fist down on the railing between us he stated in these emphatic terms: 'If I have ever had the inspiration of the spirit of the Lord given to me forcefully and clearly it has been on this one point concerning Reed Smoot, and that is, instead of his being retired, he should be continued in the United States Senate.'" Charles W. Nibley, "Reminiscences of Charles W. Nibley," holograph, LDS Church History Library, 85–86, as qtd. in Thomas G. Alexander, *Mormonism in Transition: A History of the Latter-day Saints, 1890–1930* (Urbana: University of Illinois Press, 1986), 30.

6. Depew was elected to two terms, 1899–1911, and served on the Privileges and Elections Committee during the entire Smoot hearings.

7. "Rawlings Replies to Depew," *Deseret News*, February 13, 1903.

8. "Meeting of the First Presidency and Apostles," Journal History of the Church of Jesus Christ of Latter-day Saints (chronological scrapbook of typed entries and newspaper clippings, 1830–present), February 12, 1903, LDS Church History Library, Salt Lake City.

9. "Mr. Smoot's Seat in the Senate," *Deseret News*, March 4, 1903. Approximately five years previously, B. H. Roberts was blocked from taking his seat in the House of Representatives after being elected to that office. Roberts, however, was a polygamist, while Smoot was a monogamist. Gary James Bergera, *The Autobiography of B. H. Roberts* (Salt Lake City: Signature Books, 1990), 199–219.

10. First Presidency, letter to Smoot, March 9, 1903, Reed Smoot Papers, L. Tom Perry Special Collections, Harold B. Lee Library, Brigham Young University, Provo, UT. Unless otherwise noted, all correspondence cited in this chapter is from the Smoot Papers.

11. Reed Smoot, letter to Joseph F. Smith, November 10, 1903.

12. Smoot, letter to Joseph F. Smith, November 10, 1903. Proctor served three terms, 1891–1908, and died in office. Hanna served two terms, 1897–1904, and died in office. Aldrich served five terms, 1881–1911. None of the three served on the committee investigating Smoot.

13. Hoar was elected to five terms, 1877–1904, and died in office. He served on the Committee on Privileges and Elections until his death. For Smoot's report of Hoar's support, see Smoot, letter to Joseph F. Smith, November 14, 1903.

14. Smoot, letter to Joseph F. Smith, January 11, 1904. Hale served five terms, 1881–1911; he did not serve on the Senate committee investigating Smoot.

15. At Smoot's election, there were fifty-eight Republicans (including Smoot) and thirty-two Democrats in the US Senate.

16. Smoot, letter to Joseph F. Smith, November 18, 1903.

17. Burrows was elected to three terms as senator, 1895–1911, and served as chairman of the Committee on Privileges and Elections.

18. Smoot, letter to Joseph F. Smith, February 5, 1904.

19. Smith, letter to Smoot, April 20, 1904.

20. First Presidency, letter to Smoot, November 17, 1903.

21. "'Horribly Caricatured and Made Hideous in Cartoons': Political Cartooning and the Reed Smoot Hearings," in *Mormons and American Popular Culture*, vol. 2 (Praeger Publishers, 2012): 121–43; Michael H. Paulos, "Political Cartooning and the Reed Smoot Hearings," *Sunstone* (December 2006): 36–40.

22. Proceedings before the Committee on Privileges and Elections of the United States Senate in the Matter of the Protests against the Right of Hon. Reed Smoot, a Senator from the State of Utah, to Hold His Seat (Washington, DC: US Government Printing Office, 1906), 1:27 (hereafter, Smoot Hearings).

23. Kathleen Flake, *The Politics of American Religious Identity: The Seating of Senator Reed Smoot, Mormon Apostle* (Chapel Hill: University of North Carolina Press, 2004); Victor W. Jorgensen and B. Carmon Hardy, "The Taylor-Cowley Affair and the Watershed of Mormon History," *Utah Historical Quarterly* 48 (Winter 1980): 4–36; B. Carmon Hardy, *Solemn Covenant: The Mormon Polygamous Passage* (Urbana: University of Illinois Press, 1992); D. Michael Quinn, "LDS Church Authority and New Plural Marriage, 1890–1904," *Dialogue: A Journal of Mormon Thought* 18, no. 1 (Spring 1985): 1–105; Kenneth L Cannon II, "After the Manifesto: Mormon Polygamy, 1890–1906," *Sunstone* (January–April 1983): 27–35.

24. Smoot, letter to Joseph F. Smith, February 5, 1904.

25. D. Michael Quinn, "LDS Church Authority and New Plural Marriage," and B. Carmon Hardy, *Solemn Covenant*, have documented at least 220 of these new clandestine marriages.

26. Smoot, letter to Joseph F. Smith, February 5, 1903; Carl Badger, Journal, March 22, 1904, in Rodney J. Badger, *Liahona and Iron Rod: A Biography of Carl A. Badger and Rosalia Jenkins Badger* (Bountiful, UT: Family History Publishers, 1985), 210; Smoot, letter to Joseph F. Smith & Counselors, December 8, 1905.

27. Smoot, letter to Joseph F. Smith, January 26, 1904.

28. Flake, *The Politics of American Religious Identity*, 66, 76,

29. Smoot Hearings, 1:136–145.

30. Smith, letter to Smoot, January 28, 1904.

31. "Subpoenas for Smoot Witnesses," *Salt Lake Tribune*, February 25, 1904.

32. Philip Loring Allen, "The Mormon Church on Trial," *Harper's Weekly*, March 26, 1904, 469–471.

33. *New York Sun*, March 9, 1904.

34. Stephen C. Taysom, "The Last Memory: Joseph F. Smith and *Lieux de Mémoire* in Late Nineteenth Century Mormonism," *Dialogue: A Journal of Mormon Thought* 48, no. 3 (Fall 2015): 1–20.

35. Smoot Hearings, 1:131.

36. He testified Wednesday through Saturday, March 2–5, Monday, March 7, and Wednesday, March 9.

37. Smoot Hearings, 1:98–100. I have standardized the formatting of the quoted testimony.

38. Smith later clarified that "while he had never received from God a revelation on some new doctrine or commandment, to be written and preserved and handed down as a law to the Church, he had been guided, from the day of his baptism to the present, by divine influence, and had been aided time and again by the spirit of God in his work in the ministry, and strongly expressed the wish that if, in his day, some new revelation should be needed by the Church, he might be worthy to receive it." Salt Lake High Council Minutes, March 19, 1905, excerpt in my possession.

39. Robert Walker Tayler (1852–1910) was elected to four terms as a representative from Ohio (1895–1902). He had led Congress's successful resistance against seating B. H. Roberts. In Smoot's case, he served as lead counsel for the Protestants. He should not be confused with Apostle John W. Taylor.

40. Joseph Weldon Bailey (1862–1929), a Democrat from Texas, was elected to two terms as US senator (1901–1913) and served on the Committee on Privileges and Elections investigating Smoot.

41. Bruce A. Van Orden, "Joseph F. Smith," *Encyclopedia of Mormonism* (New York: Macmillan, 1992), 3:1350. Scott Kenney, "Before the Beard: Trials of the Young Joseph F. Smith," *Sunstone* (November 2001): 20–42.

42. For Talmage's lengthy testimony, see Smoot Hearings, 3:4–129, 400–436.

43. After the Smoot hearings, Smoot's friend Senator Albert Jeremiah Beveridge (R-IN) expressed a similar negative reaction on the Senate floor: The hearings, he said, had been held "at enormous expense to the American people . . . over $26,000 of the people's money has been spent on the attempt to ruin this man." Congressional Record, February 20, 1907, 3410.

44. Heath, "Reed Smoot," 70–73.

45. After the first day of Smoot testimony, Talmage confided in his diary, "Senator Smoot himself took his place in the witness chair . . . It is the general feeling that Bro. Smoot did his case much good by his own testimony. His greatest uncertainty was manifest in connection with questions on the doctrinal and theology of the church. This we all regret, because in view of the testimony long ago made part of the record in this case, that the First Presidency and Twelve are to the people 'prophets, seers, and revelators,' any statement from one of these officials on doctrinal points would appear to the Committee in the nature of an authoritative exposition, so that any variation expressed by a layman would be of little worth to them, except to show conflict of opinion and confusion in evidence. An early adjournment was taken this afternoon owing to Bro. Smoot's indisposition." Talmage, Diary, January 20, 1905, Talmage Papers, Perry Special Collections. Smoot testified for ten hours (128 published pages) on three different days. Smoot Hearings, 3:182–309.

46. Smoot biographer Milton R. Merrill, *Reed Smoot: Apostle in Politics* (Logan: Utah State University Press, 1990), 400–401, stated that Smoot "was not an architect, he was a builder. To this kind of building process he brought inhuman physical energy, a colossal industry, personal honesty and integrity, a prodigious memory, a remarkable eclecticism in the accumulation of statistical facts, and a fabulous loyalty to those at the head of the enterprise."

47. Merrill, *Reed Smoot*, 105–176. Smoot can best be explained as the opposite of his father, Abraham Owen Smoot, who was a polygamist, slave owner, Democrat, and fully committed Mormon. Smoot was one of the territory's first Republicans, monogamous, pro-Union, and more or less secular. He followed his father's example in business but otherwise seemed to have different views from him. George D. Smith, "Nauvoo Roots of Mormon Polygamy, 1841–46: A Preliminary Demographic Report," *Dialogue: A Journal of Mormon Thought* 27, no. 1 (Spring 1994): 21, 29–30; Lester E. Bush Jr. and Armand L. Mauss, *Neither White nor Black: Mormon Scholars Confront the Race Issue in a Universal Church* (Midvale, UT: Signature Books, 1984), 34.

48. Although Cannon copped a plea, he proceeded to admit that he maintained conjugal relations with his plural wives after the Manifesto, had fathered three children since then, and agreed that he had thus violated "the law of [my] church and the law of the land." The committee and press appear to have soft-pedaled his admissions in part because Cannon meekly noted that he was "only mortal." Smoot Hearings, 1:775–94.

49. Smoot Hearings, 1:107–9.

50. The manifesto was issued as a press release and subsequently published in newspapers, including the *Deseret News*. It first appeared in the Doctrine and Covenants in 1908. Robert J. Woodford, "The Historical Development of the Doctrine and Covenants" (PhD diss., Brigham Young University, Provo, UT, 1974), 3:1825–1833.

51. Woodford, "The Historical Development of the Doctrine and Covenants," 1:92, specifies that between 1882 and 1920 there were "no less than 28 printings," but he does not identify them by year. Woodruff's 1890 Manifesto was added to the 1921 edition, not as a section but as an "official declaration." This action was taken three years after President Smith's death, under the presidency of his successor, Heber J. Grant.

52. For a spirited discussion of these topics, see Smoot Hearings, 1:312–19.

53. "Now Has Five Wives," *Evening Star*, March 3, 1904, clipping in Journal History, LDS Church History Library.

54. First quote: Hardy, *Solemn Covenant*, 363–80; second quote: Merrill, *Reed Smoot*, 47, 50–51; third quote: Quinn, "LDS Church Authority," 97–98.

55. Kathleen Flake, response during question-and-answer session after her paper, "Does It Matter How We Remember the Abandonment of Plural Marriage?" Salt Lake Sunstone symposium, August 2004, SL-0426, transcribed from mp3 in my possession.

56. My conclusion is based on Flake's assessment: "A close reading of the [Smoot Hearings] record permits the conclusion that Joseph F. Smith was sufficiently concerned for his personal integrity and skilled in casuistry to avoid lying outright." Flake, *The Politics of American Religious Identity*, 75.

57. Smoot Hearings, 1:128–33.

58. More than a month following this testimony, President Smith clarified these comments in a letter to Smoot, "You may tell Senator Hoar for me, if you chose, that I have never broken a law of God to my knowledge in my life, and that I did not testify that I had. And I never to my knowledge broke but one law of my country. And that law is against my conscience and against good morals, so far as I am concerned. That is the law against living with my family, whom I took before the law was enacted. I never said in my testimony that for disregarding that law I expected to ask for or receive mercy. I plainly said that I would rather face the penalties of that law than the more dreadful consequences of abandoning my children and their mothers." Smith, letter to Smoot, April 9, 1904.

59. Badger, qtd. in Badger, *Liahona and Iron Rod*, 213.

60. On October 19–20, 1891, President Woodruff testified the following before the master in chancery: "Q. Did you intend to confine this declaration [the manifesto] solely to the forming of new relations by entering new marriages?—A. I don't know that I understand the question.—Q. Did you intend to confine your declaration and advice to the church solely to the forming of new marriages, without reference to those that were existing—plural marriages?—A. The intention of the proclamation was to obey the law myself—all the laws of the land—on that subject, and expecting the church would do the same.—Q. Let me read the language, and you will understand me, perhaps, better: 'Inasmuch as laws have been enacted by Congress forbidding plural marriages, I hereby declare,' etc. Did you intend by that general statement of intention to make the application to existing conditions where the plural marriages already existed?—A. Yes, sir.—Q. As to living in the state of plural marriage?—A. Yes, sir; that is, to the obeying of the law.—Q. In the concluding portion of your statement you say: 'I now publicly declare that my advice to the Latter Day Saints is to refrain from contracting any marriage forbidden by the law of the land.' Do you understand that that language was to be expanded and to include the further statement of living or associating in plural marriage by those already in the status?—A. Yes, sir; I intended the proclamation to cover the ground—to keep the laws—to obey the law myself, and expected the people to obey the law ... Q. Your attention was called to the fact that nothing was said in the manifesto about the dissolution of existing polygamous relations. I want to ask you, President Woodruff, whether, in your advice to the church officials and the people of the church, you have advised them that your intention was and that the requirement of the church was that polygamous relations already formed before that should not be continued—that is, there should be no association with plural wives—in other words, that unlawful cohabitation, as it is named and spoken of, should also stop, as well as future polygamous marriages?—A. Yes, sir; that has been my view." Also testifying before the master in chancery was Joseph F. Smith, "Q. Do you understand that the manifesto applies to cohabitation of men and women in plural marriage where it had already existed?—A. I can not say whether it does or not.—Q. It does not in terms say so, does it?—A. No. I think, however, the effect of it is so. I don't see how the effect of it can be otherwise." Smoot Hearings, 1:22.

61. Smith made this or a similar assertion five times. Smoot Hearings, 1:129–130, 143, 177, 360, 485.

62. Flake, *The Politics of American Religious Identity*, 76.

63. One month after his testimony, President Smith explained to a group of priesthood holders, "The press reports are such that it shows that lies and misr[e]presentation are abroad and they are doing all they can to injure us as a people therefore we should be discreet in our utterances and

be as wise as serpents but harmless as doves." Thomas A. Clawson, Diary, April 5, 1904, Utah State Historical Society, Salt Lake City.

64. Smoot Hearings, 1:129–130; emphasis mine.

65. Smoot Hearings, 1:98, 317, 429, 485.

66. Joseph F. Smith, qtd. in Joseph Heinerman, "Reed Smoot's 'Secret Code,'" *Utah Historical Quarterly* 3 (Summer 1989): 263.

67. Smoot, letter to Smith, April 9, 1904.

68. Smoot, qtd. in Heath, "Reed Smoot," 125; Smoot, letter to E. H. Callister, March 22, 1904.

69. James R. Clark, ed., *Messages of the First Presidency of the Church of Jesus Christ of Latter-day Saints*, 6 vols. (Salt Lake City: Bookcraft, 1970), 4:84.

70. Taylor and Cowley were later excommunicated and disfellowshipped respectively. Victor W. Jorgensen and B. Carmon Hardy, "The Taylor-Cowley Affair and the Watershed of Mormon History," *Utah Historical Quarterly* 48 (Winter 1980): 16–36.

71. Kathleen Flake, "Mr. Smoot Goes to Washington: The Politics of American Religious Identity, 1900–1920" (PhD diss., University of Chicago, 2000), 3–4.

72. Matthew C. Godfrey, *Religion, Politics, and Sugar: The Mormon Church, the Federal Government, and the Utah-Idaho Sugar Company, 1907–1921* (Logan: Utah State University Press, 2007): 51–92.

7

"Some Divine Purpose"

Carl A. Badger and the Reed Smoot Hearings

Gary James Bergera

I am thoroughly convinced that this investigation answers some divine
purpose—that we need it and therefore it has come.
—CARL A. BADGER, 1905

LDS Church apostle Reed Smoot (1862–1941) was sworn in as a member of the
US Senate on March 5, 1903, amid a whirlwind of criticism regarding his fitness
to serve in national office.[1] Almost immediately, Senate hearings were convened
to investigate charges against Smoot, allegations that centered on his status as a
member of the ruling hierarchy of the Church of Jesus Christ of Latter-day Saints.[2]
The ensuing four-year controversy affected few people more intimately than
Smoot's twenty-five-year-old personal secretary, Carl Ashby Badger.[3] "I believe,"
Badger wrote in early 1904, "that we all feel that the case is much more serious
than it was ever thought it would be."[4] As Badger's experience shows, more was at
stake than Smoot's service or his Church's reputation. For Badger, the revelations
that followed in the wake of the Senate's investigations significantly affected the
nature of his relationship to his church and its teachings.

The degree to which Badger was representative of his generation speaks to
the impact of the Smoot hearings and of the revelations they produced on those
young Latter-day Saints who, like Badger, straddled the nineteenth and twentieth
centuries. Living in Washington, Badger was experiencing eastern culture and
education based on the moralistic religion of the Protestant establishment, which
came into sharp contrast with some of the practices of his childhood religion,
including temple rites and plural marriage. This was a period of immense transition for the LDS Church, when Utah entered statehood and the Church began
to move away from its isolationist pioneer heritage to a more active engagement

DOI: 10.7330/9781646421176.c007

FIGURE 7.1. Portrait Carl A. Badger around 1920. Carl was a law student in Washington, DC, while also serving as Senator Smoot's personal secretary during the Senate hearings. Courtesy of the Utah State Historical Society.

with American values, culture, and polity. For Badger, and other young intellectually oriented Saints, the Smoot hearings not only bared to the world some of their church's more nontraditional teachings and practices but exposed to a bewildered, sometimes aghast American public the Church's occasionally convoluted accommodations to modernity. Badger was especially shocked to learn of the extent of the past perfidy of some senior members of his church's hierarchy, but remained hopeful throughout the drawn-out proceedings that the exposure might produce reform that would accrue to his church's long-term benefit.

Carl Badger's career as secretary to Utah's new senator was initially a fluke—the fortuitous afterthought of a precocious twenty-three-year-old political neophyte. Badger belatedly applied for the position in January 1903, after having several months earlier learned that he was too young to run for the Utah legislature. Taking the news stoically, he wrote in mid-1902, "Though it is not a crime to a young man it debars me from trying my wings. But then who knows but that in itself is a blessing."[5] Less than six months later, Badger confidently mused, "I am in politics... very much. [I] started by threatening to run for the legislature but withdrew when I found that I am not old enough by a year. I then determined to try to Reed Smoot[']s secretaryship if he be elected Senator. This purpose I have held to."[6] Two days after Smoot's election to the Senate by a majority of the Republican members of the Utah legislature, Badger explained to the man he hoped would be his employer: "I wish I could offer you the wisdom, the experience, the ability that comes only with years; as it is, all that I have is the enthusiasm, the determination of youth. I feel that this is the chance of a life time and if I am your choice, I am resolved to make the most of my opportunity."[7]

Badger was not the only up-and-comer intent on being Smoot's secretary. J. Reuben Clark Jr. (1871–1961) applied for the secretaryship in late November 1902, two full months before Badger and was endorsed by several prominent Utahns, including LDS Church president Joseph F. Smith (1838–1918). Smith went so far as to note his recommendation of Clark in a brief handwritten postscript to Clark's letter of application. Despite Smith's endorsement, Smoot decided (perhaps because Badger had actively campaigned for him) to hire Badger.[8]

Badger's reasons for seeking employment with Smoot were unapologetically self-serving. Once chosen, he tried to exploit as fully as possible the many opportunities—the close ties with the powerful and influential—his privileged association with a US senator afforded. He knew, and accepted, that as secretary he was fully at Smoot's beck and call. He regularly took dictation, and typed speeches, correspondence, and anything else Smoot needed. He undertook various research projects, helped to prepare witnesses, and served, at least initially, as a sounding board for Smoot. However, as time passed, Badger came to dislike, even resent, the seemingly endless demands and mind-numbing minutia, convinced he was ready for bigger tasks. He also was increasingly put off by Smoot's aloofness. Badger enrolled in Columbian College's law school (later George Washington University) and served as senior class president in 1906, which brought him into contact with the ethical principles of the modernist wing of the Protestant establishment. Yet however ambitious and opportunistic he was, Badger also possessed a strong sense of individual integrity and family obligation. His criticism could be cutting, his affection deep. He was frank and blunt and did not willingly tolerate duplicity, hypocrisy, or deceit.

Badger, reflecting the views of some other Washington, DC, observers, did not believe that hearings into the allegations regarding Smoot's qualifications would open that spring of 1904. "There's every disposition," he wrote, "on the part of the Committee on Privileges and elections not to take the case up, and there are weighty political reasons why it should not be done at this time." He believed—wrongly—that Smoot's own Republican Party would see to it that "all these charges [will not be aired] at the present time." "For this reason," he wrote, "I do not believe that the Committee will go into the Senator's case at this session, nor next summer, but next winter when the campaign is behind us, they will go into the situation thoroughly." Smoot, however, did not share his youthful secretary's views. Badger informed his brother-in-law, "[The Senator] believes that the case will be gone into right away, but everything points the other way to me."[9] Official hearings opened two weeks later, on March 2, 1904.

As testimony commenced with President Joseph F. Smith, Badger seemed hopeful, but as sequent witnesses were called to testify such as president of the Church's Quorum of Twelve Apostles, Francis M. Lyman (1840–1916),[10] Badger's attitude became less positive. Later, he skipped entire sessions, explaining he felt better emotionally when he did not witness the testimony at "the hearings" in person.[11] His exposure to members of his church's upper echelon led him to conclude that several of the men whom he had dutifully sustained as "Prophets, Seers, and Revelators" had not been entirely sincere in their earlier promises to the US government. The force of Badger's feelings is apparent in the following three excerpts from his correspondence:

> (1) It was with humiliation that I heard the brethren acknowledge that the[y] had broken the law of God and of their country. I know that it is folly to condemn individuals when we are all in the same muddle. Public sentiment, the sentiment that you and I have helped create, has sustained them in what they have done. The great wrong is in an attempt to continue what we have promised to give up.[12]

> (2) I do not think that the brethren realize what they say when the[y] declare that they have broken the law of God,—they make him out a very easy "Boss." The truth of the matter is that very few of our people have been willing to admit that the [1890] Manifesto was a revelation and that the leading authorities have not encouraged this view, but rather that the necessities of the case compelled that we openly give up what we secretly clung to.[13]

> (3) I hope our people will look at this matter in its true light; we have got to learn our lessons, and instead of shouting about the opportunity which we have had of teaching our faith to the world, we ought to dot down the unpleasant but obvious fact, that the lesson which the world is learning from the testimony thus far given is, that we have failed to keep our word.[14]

Although of polygamous heritage himself, Badger had little sympathy for the Church's "celestial law [i.e., plural marriage]." "I am afraid," he confided to his diary, "I believe more in the inspiration of the [1890] Manifesto than of the selection of the D[octrine] & C[ovenants] which say we 'must' practice that principle."[15]

Badger was particularly critical of LDS apostles John W. Taylor (1858–1916) and Matthias F. Cowley (1858–1940), two prominent leaders whose continuing advocacy of polygamy was widely suspected, if not openly acknowledged. "Apostles Taylor and Cowley must come to Washington," Badger insisted, "or everything that the protestants may desire to impute to them will be taken as confessed."[16] "I want to see Brother Taylor compelled to make this admission," Badger pushed. "I think we are greatly indebted to him for all this 'unpleasantness',—if you can refer to a national scandal as such."[17] Strongly urged to appear before the Senate investigating committee, both apostles declined. "In the event of their [i.e., Taylor's and Cowley's] having performed new marriages," Badger wrote on March 22, "the Senator said to-day that he volunteered, 'if the President [i.e., Joseph F. Smith] thought best,' to resign his seat in the senate, rather than ~~humilate~~ place the sorrow on the apostles, the wrongly married people and the Church. Apostle [Francis M.] Lyman wrote Richard [Lyman's son] 'that they were at their wits ends to know what to answer.' Dick wrote back that any guilty man would be."[18]

"If these men [i.e., Taylor and Cowley] do not come," Badger lamented two days later,

> and from all that I can learn they do not want to come, we are in a bad place . . . I
> do not know whether I can convey to you the serious[ness of] that nothing that
> they can say can hurt us as their refusal to come will hurt us. They are the ones
> against whom the charges that the Apostles have been teaching polygamy is made,
> and for them to stay away will be to admit all that can be charged against them. I
> do not hesitate to say that it will be a shame and a disgrace if they do not come.[19]

Badger, in this instance, underestimates the adverse political consequences that Taylor's and Cowley's testimony would have had on Smoot's case had they testified of the sub-rosa continuation of plural marriage. Instead, Badger believed that only through full cooperation could the Church maintain integrity and advance its interests.

In early April 1904, several weeks after his return to Salt Lake City, Joseph F. Smith issued what has since been termed the "Second Manifesto." Smith's own politically tuned sense of the need for stronger reassurances to skeptical Americans coincided with the advice of his closest associates. When Smith's announcement appeared in Washington, DC, newspapers, Badger could not have been more elated. "I almost tumbled out of my chair," he wrote, "when the boy brought the paper this morning and I read the heading,—'*Yield to the Law*'— 'Polygamy Renounced by Conference of Mormons.' I was very glad to read the statement made by President Smith . . . I wish it had come ten years ago, but in this world we are not changed in the twinkling of an eye, we grow more and more unto the perfect day."[20]

Some of Badger's confidantes, particularly his wife, worried about his more heated rhetoric, especially his criticisms of polygamy. "About my talking against polygamy," Badger later wrote to Rose, ". . . I believe that polygamy is not the ideal system of marriage, that is all I have said; and I cannot say any less . . . Now is the time, if there is ever to be a time, when something should be said about it." Badger's attitude here was similar to that of antipolygamy Protestants in the East, and he continued, "We cannot tamper with fire, and that is what we are doing when we preached that polygamy is divine; the next step is: 'Then it is not too hard for me'. I am against the practice of polygamy, and I will fight it, now and always."[21]

The first round of committee testimony concluded on May 2, 1904, in anticipation of the Senate's summer recess. Hearings were not to open again until December 12. Testimony then proved to be fast-paced, intense, and often just as sensational as earlier. The protesters presented twenty-one witnesses in the space of eight days before hearings adjourned on December 20 for the Christmas break. The bulk of this second round centered on the Church's sacred temple ceremonies. Various witnesses testified, occasionally in detail, of Mormonism's secret rituals. Photographs of a man sporting a large, white wig and beard, demonstrating ritualistic gestures, appeared on the front pages of the *New York Herald* and the *Washington Times*. Excerpts from the hearings, as well as from previously published exposés, tantalized readers with their intimations of esoteric rites. Counsel was particularly intent on establishing the existence of an "oath of vengeance" administered to all LDS temple patrons, who pledged their unceasing prayers to avenge, by violence, if necessary, the blood of the latter-day martyred LDS prophets.[22]

As Smoot's secretary, Badger was frequently asked by classmates about the investigation. Badger informed his wife that "the boys here at school were much interested in the testimony given before the Committee" and that he was discussing the case with them. This became awkward for Badger, as he found himself torn between loyalty to his church and expressing his true feelings and moral sentiments about the actions of some Church leaders. Ultimately, Badger concluded that he may be spreading too much negative information and that it "would be wise for me to hold my tongue." Badger also found himself in a quandary when discussing the Smoot case with fellow Church members. After openly criticizing "the course pursued by some of the leading brethren" with Church members on the East Coast, Badger began to hear rumblings that some local Church leaders were not pleased, causing Badger to conclude he needed to be more "wise in his words."[23]

Although testimony was equivocal, it was evident to almost all observers that a nerve had been exposed. Badger was informed that Joseph F. Smith believed "in the event of the divulgence of the temple ceremony, 'if there was anything in the Church which the Lord desired removed [from the ritual], he hoped he would remove it.'"[24] Another president—US President Theodore Roosevelt (1858–1919)—"told Senator Smoot to have the temple ceremonies abolished, they were 'foolishness.'"[25] Badger feared that the temple rituals and especially their oaths of secrecy and penalties for divulging them might adversely influence the investigating committee.

"If the Senate comes to the conclusion," he wrote to Rose, "that the obligations [for secrecy] taken in the Temple are merely archaical, academical, and that they

FIGURE 7.2. Portrait of Rose Bader (1901). Rose had indirect influence on the hearings from Utah by her frequent correspondence with her husband, Carl, then serving as Senator Smoot's personal secretary in Washington. Courtesy of the Smith-Pettit Foundation, Salt Lake City, Utah.

do not bind the conscience and the conduct of those who take them, I suppose that they will not be sufficient to unseat the Senator; but if these ceremonies are thought to mean just what they say [i.e., that traitors will be put to death], I do not see how the judgment that they are against 'public policy' will be avoided."[26] Although references to retribution were not dropped from the temple covenants until 1927, and the penalties until 1990, such "foolishness," however embarrassing at the time, was passed over by the committee as among the lesser of the Church's crimes.

Finally, on December 20, the protesters called Charles Mostyn Owen (1859–1941), Mormon baiter and provocateur par excellence, to the stand. Owen cited the names of additional Latter-day Saints believed to have secretly entered plural marriage since the 1890 Manifesto. He also admitted that it was he behind the white wig and beard publicly exposing the LDS temple oaths on the front pages of the *Herald* and *Times*.[27]

As hearings were winding down in December 1904, the weight of testimony began to take a heavier-than-expected toll. Badger told Smoot that he "was discouraged with the Church leaders, and that unless something was done I did not know what the effect would be upon the young people—that is, something must be done with those who have violated the pledge against the taking of new wives." Smoot's reply did little to ease his secretary's anxiety: "Nothing will be done; I [i.e., Smoot] believe they were authorized to take the wives."[28] "I am sick and tired of all this hypocrisy that we have been practicing," Badger lamented.[29] He was disheartened as well to learn that Smoot had been instructed by the Church to drop any suggestion that polygamous cohabitation should be "given up."[30]

During this difficult time, Badger found himself gaining a more nuanced appreciation of Smoot. "The Senator is a very practical man," he told Rose, "he is not spiritually minded. He is not well educated, has done comparatively little reading . . . The Senator is not a brave man in a moral sense, but we all shrink when it comes to the test . . . I do not say this in a light mood. I am thoroughly convinced that this investigation answers some divine purpose—that we need it and therefore it has come . . . The Senator has been under a very severe strain, and deserves our sympathy."[31] In a later letter, he added: "I feel sorry for him [i.e., Smoot] . . . He is tormented if he does not have something to occupy his time, and I am punished generally along with him, for he comes back to the dictation of letters like a homing pigeon; and I sink into the depths of despair, for the Senator's letters are long as he has nothing else to do."[32]

Toward the end of December 1904, Badger met privately with Franklin S. Richards, the fifty-five-year-old legal advisor to the First Presidency and one of the most influential behind-the-scenes men in LDS history. Their discussion proved to be something of a turning point for Badger. Here was a man whose own experiences with the LDS hierarchy paralleled in important ways those Badger was then encountering. Attentive, sympathetic, and loyal, Richards was, in Badger's eyes, a model of integrity, faith, and the sometimes uncomfortable union that binds the two. Why, Badger asked, should he not leave the Church if he disbelieved the things that "all orthodox Mormons considered essential." Richards answered that in 1877 he convinced Apostle Joseph F. Smith, over Smith's objections, to testify publicly that "polygamy was not manditory [sic] upon the church." When Richards returned to Salt Lake City, he continued, "he came near to loosing [sic] his fellowship" in the Church. Then in 1904, he heard now-president Smith voluntarily tell the Smoot investigating committee that "the doctrine never had been manditory [sic]." Why not remain in the Church, Richards told Badger; "there is good here, and truth, and noble men and women. I have done more for those whom I love by staying with them than I could have fighting what I considered their faults."[33]

Whatever Badger was looking for—consolation, understanding, reassurance—he seemed to find it in Richards's counsel. Apparently, more than any other single event, their late-night conversation gave Badger the foothold for which he had been searching. The Church had disappointed Badger, and he was embarrassed by the revelations generated through this external scrutiny. Richards's remarks became something of a beacon guiding Badger throughout the coming months and years.

Shortly after testimony ended for the Christmas 1904 holidays, Badger wrote to LDS apostle George Albert Smith (1870–1951), expressing his disappointment with the Church's past actions and especially present leniency toward those whose absence on the witness stand did much more than simply compromise themselves. Although Church members who entered plural marriage after the 1890 Manifesto did so believing that such obedience was a requirement for their exaltation, Badger could not sanction such devotion, particularly when duplicitous. Six weeks later, Smith responded, sympathetic but unconvinced:

> To take hasty action with reference to some men whose names have figured prominently in the investigation, would only add fuel to the flame and would gratify the sensation-monger unnecessarily. The church will not do anything simply to curry favor, but will handle its affairs in its own way and not at the dictation of the rabble . . . consequently it will take its own time in its own affairs.[34]

"I, for one, do not feel like asking for any hasty action," Badger replied,

> but I am sure that something must be done, and the question is when and what shall be done. I want all the people, Mormon and non-Mormon, to know what we intend to do. We can go back to the practice of polygamy with honor, if we openly avow our determination, but if we lie or deceive, we can neither look man or God in the face; and I have no patience with declarations which can mean two or a dozen things and which convey only half of the truth.[35]

"There has been something done that has caused many people to censure the Church," Smith quickly answered, "but the facts have not been forthcoming up to the present, and the position of the Presidency of the Church may have been misunderstood . . . Don't be mislead [*sic*] into believing that the Church or its President has gone wrong: This is only a trick of the Devil to lead some of our young people astray. The lie is always a weapon for the unrighteous."[36]

Badger may have understood Smith's intentions, but he found little peace in ignoring the facts of the situation. "This is a contemptible attitude for us to be in," he had written home some weeks earlier.

> We are occupying a cowardly, hypocritical attitude in this matter, and cannot but reap a harvest of humiliation and shame . . . no one doubts but what the country, which had been fighting us on this issue for a quarter of a century, understood that polygamy had gone, and we allowed them to have such an impression,— encouraged them in it for our own ends, and we are now estopped to say that we

made no agreement. Where is our honor on this matter[?] It makes me angry. Well, the end is not yet.[37]

"I hope, dear, that you will try to see the situation through my eyes," he later added to Rose.

> I believe that down in the heart of the people there is a distrust of men who will not keep their word, and that there is a loyalty to the promises which we have made to the Government, and that time will bring these sentiments to the surface. For one I can give up my belief in prophets when it comes to choosing between them and honest men . . . We have the duty placed upon us to see that we keep our promises and we are going to do it.[38]

By the end of the year, Badger again tried to explain himself more fully to Rose, though ultimately decided to keep his views to himself. "Darling, I cannot decide for you," he wrote in a letter he did not send,

> but I must and will decide for myself. You say that the leaders of the Church are the greatest men on the earth to-day. I say they are not. They are neither the greatest teachers, greatest lawgivers, greatest discoverers in science, nor are they the best re-ligiously and morally. They are good men, but their goodness is the same goodness that other good men have. You know as well as I do that I do not want to be wrong. I have nothing to gain in a wrong conclusion in these matters, but I will not hold my peace when I think I am right and there seems necessity for speech; and I will not skulk in the dark when I should act in the light. I want to be honest and free, and I am going to be. I do not want to hurt you or mother, and I believe that you are the only people that I think deserve any consideration when it comes to taking a painful course that appears to be right; and I have my doubts as to whether principle should be sacrificed for you. I know it should not. The question is, what should I do; when I know that, I hope I will be honest enough to do it.[39]

Senate hearings reopened on January 11, 1905. The defendants at last presented their case, charging the protesters with hearsay, inconsistency, irrelevance, and inaccuracy. Some forty-plus witnesses were called to testify in defense of Smoot and the Church during the next two and a half weeks until the committee adjourned. The following October, Apostles Taylor and Cowley resigned from the Quorum of the Twelve in an attempt to defuse criticisms against Smoot.[40] However, Smoot's and the Church's critics, claiming new information, pushed for a reconsideration of the case, and hearings reopened four months later on February 7, 1906. "The whole course of the Church in the history of this investi-gation by the Senate," Badger wrote a month before hearings resumed, "has been one of folly. If the Church had taken a firm, honorable stand at the beginning of the disclosures, it would be high in public confidence and respect; but it has slowly but surely forfeited both, and stands to-day before the people of the United States discredited and dishonored; and this by its own conduct, conduct which violated its solemn pledge to the people of the United States."[41]

Badger also took the opportunity again to address Rose's concerns regarding the nature of his faith:

> I want you to be with me in all that I do, and I would not lead you astray for worlds, but I would be equally recreant to my high trust if I were to falter when I think your happiness and mine in all time to come depends upon my taking a course that may bring present unpleasantness. I love the right and the truth and am ready to give my service to their promotion. I am not consistent, but if I were to wait for consistency before trying to do what I know to be right, I would never do anything. I would like to make the name of "apostate" respected in the land of the Mormon, either in myself or in someone more worthy. This may seem a hard task. I hope it is not a necessary one. I believe there is a larger, broader, better truth than our people have, what kind of a man would I be if I did not acknowledge my convictions?[42]

Smoot's defense rebutted this second wave of testimony, and seven witnesses were rushed through the investigative machinery in one day. Final arguments and closing statements were made in mid-April 1906, at which time the committee took the case under advisement. Fewer than two months later, in early June, they voted 7 to 5 that Smoot was not entitled to a seat in the Senate. It was not until eight months later that the full Senate voted officially on a resolution calling for Smoot's removal. The motion failed to pass, and Utah's apostle-senator miraculously retained both his political office and his religious calling.

Following the issuance of the committee's findings in mid-1906, Badger took the time to explain his feelings, as intensely felt and complex as they were, at length in a letter. His missive reveals a man maturing in his beliefs, whose renewing commitments suggest a tempering perhaps not unknown to others whose own faith travels a path similar to Badger's.

> If we wish to convert the world to the truths of polygamy, let us first be honest. If as a people we had strictly observed the [1890] Manifesto, I believe that our example would have challenged the admiration of the world; but we have thought that there is something higher than honesty, and behold our confusion. I resent anyone saying that I am not as loyal to my people as those who deny conditions which they know exist; and I affirm my determination to try to tell the truth about everything. I wish it could have been said to the Senate committee: Come, gentlemen, bring your searchlights; go into every corner; we will hide nothing; our record is like the saying of the Almighty, one jot or one tit[t]le of the world that has proceeded from our mouth has not remained unfulfilled. How proud we would be today if this were so, though it had caused the blood to flow from many

hearts. One man at the head of the American nation has done more in five years for reform because he has been honest, than has been accomplished in any twenty years before. Simple honesty, the facts, publicity, is his sovereign remedy; a remedy from which we shrink—but I pray for the last time. I wish it were possible for me to hurl in the teeth of the world the accusation and the boast: while you have been cruel, we have been honest.[43]

He addressed similar sentiments to his mother:

My head may be a poor one, but it was given me for use, and if I am conscientious in my judgments, ready to learn, and willing to right a wrong, I am not afraid to be called to account for using it. If this is the pledge you wish, dear mother, I gladly give it; but I cannot surrender what little reason I have to the guidance of those who you may think have a divine right to lead me—or to anybody else for that matter. I am willing to pray that I may be shown the light, but I am not willing to pray that this or that be shown me as the light. If you want me to investigate, I will try to follow the light as I see it; but if you want me to take someone's opinion of what is light, when my own judgment says it is not, I cannot give you my pledge.[44]

Facing the new year, 1907, Badger worried privately about the personal price Smoot had paid for his role in the hearings:

I see no peace for the Senator in the Church or civil life, as a leader. He is disliked by many of his coreligionists; many of them think him poorly grounded in his faith and unlearned in its doctrines. He has the unalloyed dislike of those who sympathize with polygamy. In the political world he is thought to be narrow; his public service is limited by his looking at duty as a personal consideration—he is disposed to reward his friends, even unjustly, and punishes his enemies dispropor-tionately . . . a public man must learn that he is the instrument of the people for the carrying on of government, and that the people elect him to do their bidding, with their machinery, and for their benefit.[45]

Regarding his church, Badger hoped that it might "see faithfulness to our prom-ises in regard to polygamy, and thus prevention of a constitutional amendment for my State, great pride in greater participation in the life of our union."[46] Little won-der, not quite two months later, Badger should express outrage at the intimation, unfounded as it turned out, that the Church might continue the sub-rosa practice of plural marriage. "I must confess that the situation is beyond me," Badger wrote to his wife. "The Senator has just said that he intends to tell the brethren when he gets home that if they want to continue this 'polygamy business' they must leave the United States." "I asked," Badger elaborated,

if he meant unlawful cohabitation, and he said no. Well, I am dumbfounded that there should be the least suggestion of the possibility of the Church attempting to establish polygamy . . . I cannot entertain the thought that such a thing is possible. To think of it as being possible is to make the Church out a hypocritical fraud; but here is the Senator talking about the calamity as though it were a possibility.[47]

Badger returned to Salt Lake City in 1907. His juris doctorate in hand, he entered private practice and eventually became senior partner in the firm of Badger, Rich, and Rich. Also active in Republican politics, he served in the Utah State Senate in 1909 and in 1911, ran unsuccessfully for Utah governor in 1920, and was a popular public speaker locally on patriotic, civic, and religious topics. He was a member of the Sunday School Board of the LDS Church's Salt Lake Stake, a member of the Mutual Improvement Association Board of the LDS Liberty Stake, and was active in LDS-sponsored Boy Scouts units. He attended the Citizens' Military Training Camp at Fort Douglas (Salt Lake City) and later was appointed a captain in the judge advocate staff corps of the Utah National Guard. In early 1937, he was appointed brigadier general of the Sixty-Fifth Field Artillery Brigade. That same year, Rose, age sixty, passed away following a series of increasingly painful cerebral hemorrhages. Badger quickly remarried but never fully recovered from the devastation of Rose's death. Over the ensuing months, he grew more and more anxiety-ridden and depressed. On Sunday, October 22, 1939, just nine days shy of his sixty-first birthday, Badger drove to his "summer estate" at the mouth of Big Cottonwood Canyon, a few miles southeast of Salt Lake City, held a loaded pistol against the roof of his mouth, and fired. Five days later, following his funeral in the LeGrand Ward Chapel, his body was laid to rest next to Rose's in the Salt Lake City Cemetery.[48] "The passing of Carl A. Badger," the *Salt Lake Tribune* editorialized, "leaves a void in various circles that will be noticeable for a long time."[49]

Both Carl and Rose Badger remained practicing members of the LDS Church. According to family members, Rose tended to be the more orthodox and unquestioning, Carl the more intellectually inclined and skeptical of false spirituality. Rose "believed that one could never receive the same conviction from intellectual study and experience that one could by the Spirit. To question scripture or pronouncements of Church leaders was not only wicked but a waste of time." Carl believed otherwise: "He saw flaws, and often he was right. Carl did not question promptings of the Spirit. He prayed often and very sincerely. He had, however, heard testimonies, perhaps under emotional stress, which he knew to be fallacies; and he did not trust others for information he could determine for himself."[50] To one of his sons, Carl wrote three years before his death, "It is a fine thing to think things over. This is akin to prayer—soul communication with the invisible parent. I am glad you are thinking seriously."[51] Whatever loss of religious innocence he experienced during the Smoot hearings, Badger maintained throughout his life a tempered belief in the core values and doctrines of the Church he had served and would continue to serve.

It is not known to what extent other Church members, especially among Badger's own peers, shared the same or similar struggles that Badger underwent as a result of the Smoot hearings. There are hints that older Latter-day Saints may have been somewhat more forgiving of their leaders' duplicity, whereas younger members may have been less tolerant and more harsh in their judgements. Certainly, Badger was proved correct when high-ranking LDS officials began in 1909 to hold formal disciplinary hearings—with rulings that sometimes imposed expulsion from the Church on transgressors—into the continuing polygamous activities of some of the Church's more fundamentalist-oriented members.[52] Among the most high-profile LDS leaders called to account for their advocacy of continued polygamy, former apostles John W. Taylor and Matthias W. Cowley were both publicly "handled" when, in 1911, Taylor was expelled from the Church and Cowley's priesthood authority was revoked (meaning he could not perform any priesthood-related functions).[53] In fact, Badger lived to see his Church adopt a much more aggressive approach to post-manifesto polygamy than he probably would have thought possible.

Badger's experiences during the Smoot hearings highlight the personal agony that sometimes arises when connivance is thought necessary to defend the truth. The experience left him bruised for a time, but the insights he gained into himself, his relationship to his church, the nature of faith, and to the men he continued to sustain as—fallible—leaders left him, he believed, a better person. Badger's experience stands today, in part, as a reminder of the immense personal responsibility all who believe must bear.

NOTES

1. For a biography of Smoot, see Milton R. Merrill, *Reed Smoot: Apostle in Politics* (Logan: Utah State University Press, 1990).

2. For studies of the investigation, see Harvard S. Heath, "The Reed Smoot Hearings: A Quest for Legitimacy," *Journal of Mormon History* 33 (Summer 2007): 1–80; and especially Michael Harold Paulos, ed., *The Mormon Church on Trial: Transcripts of the Reed Smoot Hearings* (Salt Lake City: Signature Books, 2008).

3. Born on October 31, 1878, in Salt Lake City to Rodney Carlos Badger (1848–1923) and Louisa Adeline Ashby (Noble) Badger (1849–1944, m. 1877), Badger was christened Carlos but preferred Carl. He attended the Weber Academy in Ogden, Utah, and graduated from LDS College in Salt Lake City. From 1897 to 1899 (except for a brief period in early 1899 when he returned to Salt Lake City), he served a full-time proselytizing mission for the LDS Church in Colorado. Following his mission, he married Rosalia (Rose) Jenkins on June 26, 1901. Rose had been born in Salt Lake City on April 20, 1877, to Thomas Jenkins (1829–1905) and Mahala Elmer (1847–1934, m. 1870). For a biography, see Rodney J. Badger, *Liahona and Iron Rod: The Biography of Carl A. and Rose J. Badger* (N.p.: Family History Publishers, 1985; copyright 1986). (In popular LDS parlance, "Liahona," a term in the *Book of Mormon*, may refer to Church members whose faith is of a questioning nature, and "Iron Rod," also in the *Book of Mormon*, to members whose faith is of an unquestioning nature. According to their son and family biographer Rodney Badger, Carl was a "Liahona," Rose an "Iron Rod.")

4. Badger, letter to Ed Jenkins, March 8, 1904, in Carl A. Badger Collection, L. Tom Perry Special Collections, Harold B. Lee Library, Brigham Young University, Provo, UT. Unless otherwise noted, all manuscript materials cited in this essay may be found in the Badger Collection. Edward Elmer Jenkins (1873–1944) was Badger's brother-in-law.

5. Carl A. Badger, Diary, July 9, 1902.

6. Carl A. Badger, Diary, December 31, 1902.

7. Qtd. in Carl A. Badger, Diary, January 23, 1903.

8. See J. Reuben Clark Jr., letter to Reed Smoot, November 22, 1902, in Reed Smoot Collection, Perry Special Collections. One of Clark's biographers wrote that "for reasons unexplained, Smoot gave [Clark's] application exceedingly short shrift." Frank W. Fox, *J. Reuben Clark, Jr.: The Public Years* (Provo, UT: Brigham Young University Press / Salt Lake City: Deseret Book Co., 1908), 21. Another biographer added that Clark "would never forget nor forgive the indifferent coolness with which [Smoot] ignored [Clark's] church-endorsed application." D. Michael Quinn, *Elder Statesman: A Biography of J. Reuben Clark* (Salt Lake City: Signature Books, 2002), 13. As with Badger's rebound from his frustrated bid for the Utah legislature, Clark, too, would bounce back to become far more influential in both politics and religion than either man probably ever thought possible.

9. Badger, letter to Ed Jenkins, February 18, 1904.

10. See Paulos, *The Mormon Church on Trial*, 154–176.

11. Badger, letter to Rose Badger, December 18, 1904.

12. Badger, letter to Ed Jenkins, March 16, 1904. "Not sent" is written at the top of the letter. On this same day, Badger confided to his diary that Smoot "said to-night if 'these things' did not stop he would go out of the Church." Badger, Diary, March 16, 1904.

13. Badger, letter to Ed Jenkins, March 18, 1904.

14. Badger, letter to R. S. Collett, March 21, 1904 (marked "Not sent").

15. Badger, Diary, March 22, 1904. The Doctrine and Covenants is a collection of early revelations, most of which were received by LDS Church founder Joseph Smith (1805–1844). The revelation authorizing polygamy, to which Badger refers, is found in section 132 (LDS edition). When section 132 was read aloud to the Senate investigating committee, Badger complained that it was "a horrible experience . . .—it sounded terrible" Diary, March 5, 1904.

16. Badger, letter to Ed Jenkins, March 16, 1904 (marked "Not sent").

17. Badger, letter to Ed Jenkins, March 18, 1904.

18. Badger, Diary, March 22, 1904.

19. Badger, letter to Ed Jenkins, March 24, 1904. "The Senator says Bro. [Joseph F.] Smith writes that he cannot find [or] get any word from the 'absented' [i.e., John W. Taylor and Matthais F. Cowley]—like a mother brandishing a stick at her flock hid in the willows asking them if they want to come and interview a neighbor who has called to see about some windows who have been broken by stray stones, of course not." Badger, Diary, March 26, 1904.

20. Badger, letter to Ed Jenkins, April 7, 1904.

21. Badger, letter to Rose Badger, November 10, 1904.

22. For discussion of the relevant Smoot hearings testimony on LDS temple oaths, see Michael Harold Paulos, "Senator George Sutherland: Reed Smoot's Defender," *Journal of Mormon History* 33 (Summer 2007): 103–108.

23. Badger, letter to Rose Badger, April 23, 1905.

24. Badger, letter to Ed Jenkins, December 21, 1904. Badger also recorded a story he had heard from a fellow Latter-day Saint that in Badger's view, "for strangeness to moral straightness is a prize one. It began by my observing that these new cases of polygamy should be tried. [This acquaintance] says that . . . [t]he law of the Church, which is the law of God, is not against polygamy, and the Church will not punish polygamy. If you are forced to do wrong, it is not you who do wrong, but the one who forces you." Badger, Diary, December 22, 1904.

25. Badger, Diary, February 12, 1905. When Badger, who was "an ardent admirer of Roosevelt," met the president for the first time in early 1907, weeks before the vote on Smoot, Roosevelt explained to him that he initially opposed Smoot's candidacy because "I foresaw this whole trouble; . . . and I thought the people of Utah ought not to bring it down on them . . . But when Senator Smoot came here as the duly elected representative of the State of Utah, that was another thing. The people of Maryland have a constitutional and a legal right to send Archbishop [John] Ireland to the Senate; it would not be wise for them to do so, but if they were to do it, he would have every right to a seat in the Senate." Badger, letter to Rose Badger, January 28–30, 1907.

26. Badger, letter to Rose Badger, December 17, 1904.

27. For Owen's testimony, see Paulos, *Mormon Church on Trial*, 383–389. A year later, Badger almost bumped into Owen. "I do not like to do a mean thing," he told Rose, "but I have often thought that he was one fellow I would like an introduction to just for the opportunity to refuse my hand." Badger, letter to Rose Badger, December 14, 1905.

28. Badger, Diary, December 18, 1904.

29. Badger, letter to Rose Badger, December 19, 1904.

30. Badger, Diary, December 22, 1904.

31. Badger, letter to Rose Badger, January 27, 1905.

32. Badger, letter to Rose Badger, January 28, 1906.

33. Badger, Diary, December 21, 1904.

34. George Albert Smith, letter to Carl A. Badger, February 8, 1905.

35. Badger, letter to George Albert Smith, March 22, 1905.

36. George Albert Smith, letter to Badger, March 31, 1905.

37. Badger, letter to Rose Badger, February 12, 1905.

38. Badger, letter to Rose Badger, April 23, 1905.

39. Badger, letter to Rose Badger, December 8, 1905 (marked "Not Sent").

40. Badger viewed Taylor's and Cowley's resignations cynically. "The truth of the matter," he told Rose, "is that they were put out for the sole purpose of allaying prejudice and shielding the Church . . . not to punish their wrong. That in itself is not bad, but there is something so darkly dishonorable about claiming that they were given to punish the new cases of polygamy, that I should think it impossible that a Church could put forth any such false claim." Badger, Letter to Rose Badger, April 29, 1906. The next month, Smoot told Badger that "it was hoped some day to forgive them [i.e., Taylor and Cowley] and take them back into the quorum." Badger, Diary, May 24, 1906. "To think of it as being possible," Badger subsequently wrote to Rose, "is to make the Church out a hypocritical fraud; but here is the Senator talking about the calamity as though it were a possibility." Badger, letter to Rose Badger, February 21, 1907. Such fears would prove to be unfounded; see later in this chapter.

41. Badger, letter to Rose Badger, January 11, 1906. "I, for one," he stressed to Smoot a few months later, "have long since come to the conclusion that to retain our self-respect and to make it possible for our friends to stand by us, it would be necessary for us to repudiate all responsibility for the new polygamist marriages which have taken part and to punish those who are guilty." Badger, letter to Reed Smoot, April 8, 1906.

42. Badger, letter to "My darlings," January 26, 1906.

43. Badger, letter to "My dear Clarlie [Charlie?]," June 22, 1906. I have been unable to identify the recipient.

44. Badger, letter to Louisa Badger, June 16, 1906.

45. Badger, letter to Rose Badger, December 30, 1906.

46. Badger, Diary, December 31, 1906. Some congressmen believed that the only way the Latter-day Saints could be trusted was to amend the US Constitution to define marriage explicitly as the union of one man and one woman. The proposed amendment failed to gain momentum.

47. Badger, letter to Rose Badger, February 21, 1907.

48. See Badger, *Liahona and Iron Rod*, 441–454. Rodney Badger's account of his parents' deaths, especially of his father's, is as courageous as it is painful. (It was Rodney who found his father's body.) Civil authorities tried to ease the family's suffering by officially finding the death to have been accidental. For Badger's death certificate, see Carl Ashby Badger, Death certificate, at https://axaemarchives.utah.gov/cgi-bin/indexesresults.cgi?RUNWHAT=IDXFILES&KEYPATH=IDX208420174890, retrieved December 16, 2020.

49. "Passing of Carl A. Badger Accidental Death in Canyon," *Salt Lake Tribune*, October 25, 1939, 6.

50. Badger, *Liahona and Iron Rod*, iii.

51. Qtd. in Badger, *Liahona and Iron Rod*, 387.

52. Given Badger's distaste for polygamy, the post-1890 Manifesto plural marriage of his younger sister Elizabeth (1883–1945) to Alpha J. Higgs (1864–1952) on February 1, 1909, was a particularly bitter pill. "This matter is too painful and too personal for me to discuss," Badger told the media at the time. "I shall do everything in my power to right the wrong which I feel has been done, not only [to] my family and the state of Utah, but [to] my church." Qtd. in Badger, *Liahona and Iron Rod*, 408.

53. Taylor died outside the Church (and only decades later was readmitted by proxy rebaptism); Cowley was restored to full membership in 1936 but never again held high Church office.

8

"A Systematic, Orderly, and Unusually Intelligent Fight"

Senator Fred T. Dubois and Reed Smoot

John Brumbaugh

Idaho politician Fred T. Dubois gained national prominence by demanding the expulsion of Mormon apostle Reed Smoot from the US Senate. Among the "chief strategist for the protestors," Dubois's argument for this action was unambiguous: removing Smoot from Washington would protect the home, the family, and the American way of life.[1] Persuaded by the cause, religious groups and women's organizations throughout the country rallied behind Dubois's call. These groups praised the junior senator from Idaho for his stance against Smoot and propelled him to popularity on the tidal wave of anti-Mormonism sweeping the nation.[2] Dubois's fight against the Mormon Church during the Reed Smoot investigations (1903–1907) marked a high point, in terms of visibility and notoriety, of his public career.

Exploring Dubois's political career provides insight into the Smoot hearings. First serving as a Gentile politician in the "Mormon Corridor" during the paradoxical polygamy years of 1882 to late 1902, Dubois developed a grievance with Mormonism. When understood, this grievance explains his later activism at the Smoot hearings. Second, Idaho's election campaign during 1902 will be considered in the context of why Dubois invested himself so completely at the Smoot hearings. During these elections, Mormon voting patterns abruptly changed to the detriment of Dubois's political party. Third, Dubois's activities over the months prior to the Smoot hearings will be explored, including his collaborative efforts with the popular women's group the National Congress of Mothers. With significant help

DOI: 10.7330/9781646421176.c008

FIGURE 8.1. Portrait of Fred Dubois in 1890, when he served as a territorial delegate for Idaho and the year it became a state. Photo courtesy of the Church History Library collection.

from Dubois, national grassroots opposition to Smoot flourished and millions of petitions flooded the nation's capital demanding the removal of Senator Smoot.

Examining the collaboration between Dubois and the National Congress of Mothers reveals how the antipolygamy crusade aligned with the United States Women's Movement. Dubois claimed his conflict with Reed Smoot and Mormonism was a "systematic . . . orderly and unusually intelligent fight."[3] Furthermore, Dubois's reaction to the Reed Smoot election provides an interesting case study of Mormon "Orientalism" and the racialization of Mormonism in the early twentieth century, where Mormons continued to be seen as backward, foreign, uncivilized, and potentially dangerous to American civil order.

Dubois used deliberate strategies to confirm nineteenth-century caricatures of Mormonism and the social differences between Mormonism and the greater society of the United States. Often these differences were cast along racial lines. Although most members of the Church of Jesus Christ of Latter-day Saints were white, the practice of polygamy and leanings toward theocratic rule disqualified their whiteness. It was not biology, but Dubois's social construction of Mormon difference that created the racial reality of Mormonism.[4]

Dubois sought to differentiate the peculiar aspects of Mormonism with the socially acceptable mores of the United States. Specifically, Dubois confirmed the otherness of Mormonism as a religious tradition and dangers it posed for civilized people within the country.[5] For Dubois and his constituency, adherents of Mormonism were more than ignorant dupes and morally deficient pariahs; they represented the vilest of evils whose stratagem was to corrupt all of society. As historian W. Paul Reeve notes in his work on ninetieth-century Mormon otherness, Mormonism was a prime example of "backward racial descent,"[6] which in turn was a clear danger to American democracy.

LIFE IN IDAHO 1882–1902

Fred T. Dubois was a mediocre politician with important connections, including Abraham Lincoln's son Robert Lincoln and three-time presidential candidate William Jennings Bryan, who helped him establish a political career. His public service was confined to the western state of Idaho, where he served in various capacities, as a territorial marshal, a territorial representative, and a two-term (nonconsecutive) United States senator (1892–1898 and 1900–1906). Dubois was also enigmatic and erratic, dubbed by historian Rufus Cook a political "chameleon" for his expedient changes of positions.[7] However, contrary to Cook's assertion, there was one issue that consistently motivated Dubois throughout his career—the political threat of the Mormon Church.

A troubled personal history with Mormonism provided Fred Dubois a unique perspective on the election of Reed Smoot. In his childhood years in Illinois, Dubois was a neighbor and friend to Robert Lincoln, who later made possible his entrance into Idaho politics in 1882. As a nationally prominent Republican, Lincoln's influence brought Dubois the appointment of federal marshal over the Idaho Territory, and it was during this time that Mormonism entered Dubois's purview.[8]

Around the time of this 1882 appointment, the federal government passed onerous legislation, known as the Edmunds Anti-Polygamy Act, to punish Mormons for upholding the peculiar crime of polygamy. As a new appointee, Dubois claimed he was "absolutely obsessed with the Mormon problem" and consumed with the desire to eradicate polygamy and the Church's power in politics. Reflecting on the situation, Dubois wrote that Idaho "had within its borders probably more criminals than the State of Illinois . . . every member of the Mormon Church was a criminal either in practice or as an accessory."[9] Distrustful of the intentions of federal officials, Mormon communities closed themselves off to federal influence, complicating the job for federal marshals. This led some state officials, including Dubois, to enforce polygamy laws unscrupulously and with a heavy hand. Dubois spearheaded night raids into Mormon settlements, and in 1885, the Idaho territorial legislature passed the infamous Test Oath law to disqualify Mormons from voting in Idaho. Historian Leonard J. Arrington explained that Dubois's motivation to enforce the Test Oath law was based on his desire to eliminate the influence of Mormon bloc voting.[10] In 1886, Dubois resigned his territorial position to run for political office as a Republican candidate for territorial delegate. Dubois defeated incumbent John Hailey by arguing against the annexation of northern Idaho into Washington and in favor of the "Test Oath" law.[11]

Beginning in the late 1880s and extending into the 1890s, Dubois began to soften his approach to Mormonism. This dynamic resulted from the confluence of three events: first, the LDS Church's 1890 "Manifesto" announcement ending polygamy; second, the dissolving of the Mormon People's Party in the Utah; third, the disbanding of the Church's political party and distribution of Mormon voters in Utah into both the Republican and Democratic Parties.[12] Dubois's letters during this time struck a different tone, including a letter sent to the chairman of the Idaho Republican State Central Committee, Edgar Wilson, arguing against the Test Oath law. In this letter, Dubois provided two criteria for deliverance, first that the LDS Church "abandon polygamy" and second, "their leaders no longer attempt . . . to use their positions to influence the judgment of their followers in political matters."[13] Later in 1895, the Idaho legislature, with three political parties in a competition of the Mormon vote, ended the Test Oath law.[14]

From the Test Oath vote in 1895 up to 1902, Dubois said little of Mormonism and was preoccupied by significant changes to his career. Like many western politicians in the 1890s, Bryan-style populism was the biggest concern of the day. During exploratory period, Dubois switched from Republican to Silver Republican and finally landed in William Jennings Bryan's Democratic Party.[15] Therefore, by favoring key elements of the Populist movement of the West, Dubois not only gained the support of many Idaho citizens but also cemented his alliance with the nationally popular William Jennings Bryan.[16]

1902 IDAHO ELECTION RESULT AND THE MORMON FACTOR

The common axiom "All politics are local" has specific application to Senator Dubois and the Smoot hearings. His involvement in the hearings can be traced to the local Idaho elections of 1902, when Idaho voters shifted away en masse from Democrats to William Borah's Progressive Republicans, which reignited his anti-Mormon fervor. Prior to these elections, Dubois believed local government offices would be won by Republicans but that Idaho's state legislature would stay Democratic. On Election Day, the "Party of Lincoln" swept Idaho's elections, stunning Dubois and frustrating Bryan, who quizzically asked, "I would like to know what [causes] in your judgment contributed to the republican majority? I thought that we were going to carry the legislature, even though we lost the state."[17]

Dubois's biographer, Leo Graff, retrospectively provided three answers to Bryan's question. First, Idaho Democrats were connected by association to the unpopular and corrupt Democratic Idaho governor, Frank Steunenberg. Second, Republicans nationally were surging due to the strong leadership of Theodore Roosevelt, who was also well regarded in the state. Third, Mormon bloc voters shifted support to the Republican Party after direction from Church leaders. Stung by the unexpected defeats, Dubois blamed the losses entirely on the Mormon Church.[18]

Church influence on Idaho elections was not a topic of suspicion for Dubois in 1896 or 1898, when Idaho voted overwhelmingly Democrat. Two years later, slight shifts in voting patterns occurred, with returns in some areas starting to lean Republican. Dubois suspected Church influence was at play but refrained from making public accusations since he was ostensibly a Republican.[19] By 1902, however, Democratic strongholds with large Mormon populations flipped Republican, which impelled Dubois to end his brief anti-Mormon hiatus. What incensed Dubois most about these electoral reversals was that Mormon voters in these regions abandoned Democrats shortly after Mormon apostle and Republican Party advocate John Henry Smith visited the area, giving the impression he was sent from Church headquarters to influence voting patterns in these Mormon regions. Smith's journal validates Dubois's concerns, with one entry documenting the apostle's visit to Rexburg, Idaho, to gain support for the Republican Party.[20]

Some local Church members were likewise concerned over their Church's heavy influence in politics. An ally of Dubois's, Dr. J. M. Woodburn of Rexburg, reported, "Many Democratic Mormons say that the people are disgusted with apostolic" interference. Woodburn relayed his opinion that the "handwriting" was already "on the wall" for Democrats, and the party was on the cusp of defeat.[21] More than a week later, another Idaho Democrat, R. E. Lockwood, provided additional details of how the apostle's trip decimated Democrats. Assigning the blame to local Democrats, Lockwood argued that Democrats should have acted more swiftly to expose Smith's political meddling.[22]

Frustrated by the presumed vulnerability of Democrats to Mormon influence, Dubois considered other political options. To his chagrin, he was unable to devise a plan that allowed him to attack Mormon leaders in Utah while maintaining a viable political position back home. Dubois's quandary was the result of two dynamics, the historical sea-change occurring in Mormon voting patterns and his personal distrust of Church leaders. For the latter half of the nineteenth century, when Utah was a territory, Mormon voters sided with Democrats because of their position on state's rights as well as the Republicans campaign to end polygamy. Mormon leanings toward the Democratic Party created uncomfortable bedfellows. Southern Democrats, energized over the issue of states' rights vis-à-vis slavery and understanding polygamy as a states' rights issue, shied away from legislation detrimental to the LDS Church. At the same time Democrats had to distance themselves from the moral issue of polygamy.[23] Mormons affinity toward Democrats was not permanent, and by the turn of the century and for many years thereafter, Utahans voted mostly for Republicans in national elections.[24] Dubois was certainly aware of these Mormon voting patterns, but his compunction with polygamy and aversion to Church influence created indecision that prevented him from creating a stratagem that courted Mormon voters back to the Democratic fold. Instead, he took a laissez-faire approach in which he hoped Mormon voters would naturally drift back.[25]

The election of Mormon apostle Reed Smoot to the US Senate in early 1903 provided a new avenue for Dubois to exploit the Mormon issue. Historical precedent suggested that a Mormon apostle was not welcome in Washington. Apostle Moses Thatcher, in 1896, circulated Smoot's name as a potential Democratic candidate for the Utah Senate seat, but President Grover Cleveland advised he withdraw based on concerns that he was an ecclesiastical authority in the LDS Church.[26] With an open Senate seat in 1900, Reed Smoot vied for the position but was advised to withdraw by President William McKinley in favor of Catholic mining magnate Thomas Kearns.[27] Two years later, Smoot desired another bite at the apple, quickly becoming the odds-on favorite to win the seat. President Theodore Roosevelt, following historical precedent, inserted himself into the election, telling the *New York Times* he felt it unwise to send a Mormon apostle to Washington, expressing his concern that "the selection of any apostle would arouse bitter feelings and do irretrievable injury to the best interests of Utah."[28]

In the months following Smoot's election, Dubois worked to undermine the influence of the Mormon Church locally by quietly organizing in each county "anti-Mormon delegations" in preparation for the Idaho Democratic Convention. These delegations were expected to not only attack Idaho Republicans for supporting Smoot's candidacy, but also push for a reenactment of the Test Oath law.[29] A shrewd politician, Dubois juxtaposed these efforts with supportive but disingenuous statements about Smoot's election in the national press. Dubois could have gained national traction with an overt anti-Mormon platform but instead played a double game that tiptoed around direct attacks, which would have jeopardized his political standing in Idaho.

Two days after President Theodore Roosevelt's aforementioned remarks in the *New York Times* arguing against Smoot's election, Dubois criticized Republicans in the same newspaper for interfering in Utah politics. "There is no reason," argued Dubois, "why Reid [*sic*] Smoot should not be elected to the Senate . . . You can as logically claim that a Methodist Bishop or an Episcopalian would not be allowed to take his seat as a Senator if elected by a Legislature of any state, as to say that a Mormon apostle would not be accorded the same right."[30]

Dubois's attack on Roosevelt was political theater at its finest and served two intended purposes. First, by appearing reasonable in his criticisms of the GOP's titular head, Dubois damaged his political counterparts. Second, his ostensible support of Smoot curried favor with Mormon voters out West. Reporting on the favorable press received, Utah newspaper editor and close personal friend Frank J. Cannon, relayed back to Dubois that his comments "made a very fine impression" on Mormon leaders, which positioned Democrats to potentially gain support of Mormon voters in the future.[31] In the end, Dubois chose not to build upon this as a way to forge regional Mormon-Democrat alliance but instead focused exclusively on politics in Idaho. Summarizing his aspirations, Dubois wrote a friend, "I shall always insist, that the Church leaders in Utah keep their hands out of our politics, and I am ready and will be ready at all times to defend this position."[32]

Early in 1903, Dubois remarked on the Senate floor that he did not need political support from the Mormon Church. The context for these comments was the statehood debate in Congress for New Mexico and Arizona. Because these two territories housed significant LDS populations, the topic of Mormonism was broached by Dubois, who warned, "If the Mormon people should openly, through their First Presidency, interfere in the politics of Idaho, he would guarantee to take the stump and disfranchise every Mormon in one campaign."[33] Two weeks later, a friend apprised Dubois of the seriousness of the Mormon Church's political involvement in Idaho, writing, "The Mormon Church is gaining ground in your home County the fact can not [sic] be ignored and . . . other counties of our Fair state are being invaded."[34] Frustrated by these developments, Dubois expressed, "there can be no successful politics for the Democracy in Idaho or the republicans either . . . unless the power of the Mormon hierarchy is broken."[35]

As the summer approached, Dubois positioned himself to lead the crusade against Mormonism in what eventuated in his final political battle against the Utah Church. Since Dubois had heretofore been unsuccessful in ending what he viewed as Mormon interference in Idaho politics, he would now take more drastic measures at disenfranchising all Mormon voters in the United States. Taking this dogged stand, Dubois "boxed himself into a corner," leaving his political survival dependent upon defeating Smoot and the Mormon Church.

BECOMING A CENTRAL FIGURE IN THE MORMON OPPOSITION

Dubois wrote in his autobiography, "Those of us who understand the situation were not nearly so much opposed to polygamy as we were to the political domination of the Church." But for Dubois, explaining to outsiders the detrimental impact of political domination, as opposed to obvious evils of polygamy, was difficult because to fully "understand what this political domination meant," a person must come in direct "contact with it." To overcome this impediment, Dubois "made use of polygamy . . . as our great weapon of offense and to *gain recruits* to our standard."[36] Therefore, Dubois shifted the emphasis to the specter of polygamy, using it as a foil to quell Church interference.[37]

Smoot's case was referred to the little-used Senate Committee on Privileges and Elections, a committee that Dubois had been appointed to serve on two years previously. This serendipitous assignment afforded Dubois great influence on the Smoot question.[38] Commenting on the effectiveness these protests had on the country, Dubois explained, "[Smoot's] opponents have succeeded in cheating out . . . a sentiment against the Mormons throughout the East."[39] He also expressed optimism that these protests would benefit Idaho Democrats, "If the people out there get a *correct report* of this fight . . . it certainly ought to make matters better for us and our friends."[40] Dubois expected that the bad press would help Idaho Democrats by discouraging Republicans leaders from courting Mormon voters. In addition, Dubois anticipated that the opposition to polygamy and Smoot would be bipartisan: "It looks very much as though the republicans will line up solidly against the mormans [*sic*] and in fact they have done so."[41] As these many pieces of the prosecution began to fall in place, good fortune seemed to be on the Idaho senator's side, and Dubois had good reason to be optimistic.

Formal hearings did not convene immediately,[42] which proved a boon for Dubois since it provided extra time to research the case, establish a prosecution strategy, and cultivate important allies. During the summer of 1903, Dubois set out on a fact-finding trip through southeastern Idaho and into Utah as a way to dredge up information on post-manifesto polygamous marriages and other topics incriminating to Smoot.[43] By the end of this investigative trip, Dubois was convinced the Church was guilty of political malfeasance. Soon, he was contacting religious groups and women's organizations throughout the country looking for allies to prosecute the Mormon Church.

Once back in Washington, Dubois began teasing out a case against Smoot based broadly on the following points: (1) Apostle Smoot made an oath requiring him to obey the Church in all things, (2) all Mormons who've gone through the endowment ceremony in Mormon temples have taken additional oaths that disqualify for civic office, and (3) the Mormon Church is actively promoting and practicing polygamy. Aligned with the formal protests made against Smoot, Dubois believed he could transition opposition for Smoot into opposition to the entire Utah-based Church. Dubois felt that when America learned of these three items, it would be "easy to pass any needed [anti-Mormon] legislation which we desire," including an antipolygamy amendment that disenfranchised Mormon voters.[44] Evidence to support each of these charges was garnered by Dubois in the months leading up to the hearings.

Dubois's first charge that Smoot had taken a special oath of unquestioned loyalty to the prophet of the Church when he became an apostle was based on a suggestion from a Salt Lake weekly newspaper publisher, Charles Carroll Goodwin. Goodwin shared his view that "Smoot can be kept out if you but press the point that his [apostolic] . . . oaths have virtually alienated him. That by [them] he has practically expatriated himself; That no oath he may take as senator can release him from the higher oath he has taken to obey the head of the Church in all things."[45] The second charge that Mormons were disloyal citizens because of an oath taken in LDS temples was bolstered by sworn affidavits of former Mormons who had participated in the sacred rites. One affidavit suggested that "anyone who has gone through the Temple and has taken his endowments therein, can not be a loyal citizen of the United States" because "Mormons [are] taught . . . that all Governments were corrupt, and had to be overthrown."[46] Each of these charges reinforced the perception many American held of Mormon secrecy and sedition.

On the third charge of post-manifesto marriages, Dubois possessed damaging information collected during the aforementioned fact-finding trip.[47] Many of Dubois's associates were enlisted to assist with this junket, including J. M. Woodburn, a Rexburg physician and member of the Rexburg City Council, who had been described by a state politician as the "most rabid Anti Mormon I have ever met."[48] Using his position as a physician, privy to some private information of patients' lives and the region's birthing records, Woodburn gained insight into the perpetuation of polygamy in the region, which he summarized in a six-page letter with "data . . . as to polygamous practices among the Mormon people in this vicinity."[49] Surprising for Dubois, the trip's findings had minimal impact on actual testimony since the first witness, President Joseph F. Smith, stunned the nation by confessing to his continued practice of polygamous cohabitation.[50] But all was not lost—some of this information was used as a tool to generate support of women's groups and religious organizations. Working "in concert" with these two groups, Dubois also leveraged the information to lobby senators and raise funds to defray attorney fees incurred by Smoot's opposition.[51]

After consideration of these three points, Dubois determined to deemphasize the first two since they focused too much on Reed Smoot and not enough on the politically potent issue of the Mormon Church. Writing to Mormon detractor E. B. Critchlow, the Idaho senator concluded that the investigation needed "to be entirely outside of the question as to whether or not Reed Smoot is a polygamist, or . . . has taken an oath as an apostle."[52] Rather, the investigation should center on "the relation which the Mormon Church sustains to the Government, and whether its leaders are encouraging polygamy by their open polygamous practices, and . . . whether the leaders of the Mormon Church exercise control politically and otherwise over their followers."[53] Polygamy would be used as a political weapon but only in the context of authoritarian control of Mormon leadership.

Just months before the start of the hearings, Dubois established himself as the ringleader of the anti-Mormon protest in two important ways. First, as a prominent member of the committee with ready access and influence with Chairman Burrows, Dubois had a national megaphone to prosecute Smoot. Signatories of the original protest, men such as John L. Leilich of the Salt Lake Ministerial

Association, found Dubois a key ally in the anti-Mormon fight. Leilich sent Dubois numerous pieces of information to aid the prosecution, including sworn affidavits about the endowment oaths made in Mormon temples, names of potential witnesses to testify at the Smoot hearings, and statistical evidence that implied Church involvement in the 1900 presidential campaign. On this last point, Dubois communicated to Leilich he needed clear evidence to "prove that the republican politicians made a trade with Mormon leaders" for votes in Mormon-populated states.[54] Leilich responded by supplying election results in Utah for the previous two presidential cycles showing radical shifts in voting patterns.[55]

The second way Dubois engineered the protest was his role as the preeminent middleman disseminating anti-Mormon information. Perhaps more important than his role on the committee, Senator Dubois used his influence to organize a national grassroots campaign against Smoot. Focusing on protecting the sanctity of marriage and the American home, Dubois fostered a bipartisan groundswell to oust Smoot from the Senate. Receiving numerous letters from individuals eager to help, Dubois mobilized volunteers and organized protests. His goal was to have the American public "write as many letters as possible, to various Senators," demanding the removal of Smoot.[56] For instance, Dubois instructed Reverend A. K. Wright of the Boise Church of Christ, "that you have as many individual letter[s] as possible sent from the State to Senator Heyburn [a Republican senator from Idaho who favored Smoot staying in the Senate], as well as any other senators whom individual members of the various churches known to you may be personally acquainted with."[57] Dubois similarly advised Wright, "Secure the co-operation of all Church people possible and all women's associations, and concentrate your efforts upon Senators. If you have friends in other states, or if your friends have, get them to direct their [efforts] towards the sympathy of the Senators of those states."[58] Dubois challenged like-minded citizens to deploy their full energy and networking force to excite their neighborhoods against the apostle-senator and his church.

Working in tandem with his wife, Edna Dubois, the senator successfully collaborated with the National Congress of Mothers (NCM), an organization whose stated goal was to protect American families and homes throughout the nation. The politically active Edna Dubois advocated for a number of social causes, particularly those that benefited families, children, and women. Educated and involved, she rose to office treasurer within the NCM, and even though she was bedridden from pregnancy over the months prior to the hearings, Edna Dubois introduced her husband to the leaders of the NCM as her contribution to the fight.[59]

Persuading the NCM to join the cause against Smoot was one of Dubois's most salient accomplishments, since the NCM had strong relationships with newspaper outlets, in addition to a membership of over a million women nationwide.[60] Dubois held initial meetings at his home in Washington with NCM leaders during

FIGURE 8.2. Portrait of
Edna Maxfield Dubois,
with children Elizabeth
M. Dubois (*left*) and
Margaret (Toussaint)
Dubois (*right*). Circa
1907. Image reproduced
from the Register of
the Edna M. Dubois
Collection, 1902–1931.
(Pocatello, Idaho: Eli M.
Oboler Library, Idaho
State University, 1985), 3.

November of 1903, though this was not the first time its leadership was informed of polygamous life in Utah. Just five months previous, Utah chapter head of NCM and strong opponent of polygamy, Corinne Allen, cautioned NCM members of the dangers of polygamy at a meeting held in Detroit.[61] But it was Dubois, at this November meeting, who closed the sale and convinced the group to full throatily join him in opposing Smoot. If the case against Reed Smoot was "well presented," wrote NCM president Hannah K. Schoff from her home in Philadelphia, than she promised to deploy the organizations full influence across the country and with "many organizations."[62] Excited about the next steps, Schoff abruptly returned home to Philadelphia to go "to work at once."[63] By coordinating with the NCM, Dubois influenced the agitation of women against Smoot and the Mormon Church. He did more than just call these groups to action; he systematically directed them toward what he considered to be an "orderly and unusually intelligent fight."[64] In a postmeeting letter to Dubois, Schoff expressed her commitment to the cause, stating she was "strongly in favor of following out the plan outlined by you [Fred Dubois]."[65] Schoff was ready to go to work, and soon convened a meeting with local NCM leaders to plot an "educative campaign" aimed to both "arouse the country to a realization of the facts" on Mormonism,[66] and "protect the country against the menace of Mormonism in its treasonable and polygamous practices."[67] A subcommittee then "formed a plan and worded [an] appeal" that served as the template for the flood of petitions sent to Washington demanding Smoot's removal.

Using the networking structure outlined by Dubois, Schoff sent materials to each NCM "State President" informing them of the actions and decisions of the executive board. Within this communication, Schoff implored the presidents to appeal for support at every club and church within each respective state, while also including information on a protest rally to be held at the nation's capital in early December.[68] But before sending, Schoff made sure to send a draft copy to Dubois for approval, which he swiftly and heartily provided. Poised for a fight, the NCM's executive sent out approximately 20,000 copies to the various branches around the country.[69]

By mid-December 1903, the NCM had organized protests in New York, Philadelphia, Wilmington, and Washington. Anti-Mormon lecturers were dispatched to various states, including North Carolina and Alabama. Relationships with reporters and newspaper editors were rekindled as a way to parlay damaging information on Mormonism into the public domain.[70] Newspapers represented an important front for Schoff and Dubois to wage battle. The dynamics of the early twentieth century were flavored by the publishing influence of newspaper magnate William Randolph Hearst. Hearst, then gearing up to run for president in November 1904, was seeking Dubois's endorsement and offered in exchange his support "to join with you in an earnest effort to carry Idaho . . . and . . . make a vigorous fight against the Mormons."[71] Only a few years prior, Hearst had provocatively used the pages of his newspaper, the *New York Herald*, to launch a national moral crusade against polygamist B. H. Roberts's entrance into the US House of Representatives.[72] Hearst's proposal was attractive to Dubois since one of his newspapers, the *San Francisco Examiner*, had wide readership in the mining camps throughout the Rocky Mountains. Hearst also carried influence with a number of labor organizations. But Hearst's quixotic presidential candidacy was too volatile, and the Idaho senator believed that Hearst's association with organized labor would weaken the Democratic Party's push for "equal rights to all and special privileges to none" and elected not to provide his endorsement.[73]

Additionally, the NCM sought to combine efforts with other women's groups, including the National Union of Women's Organizations (NUWO). This would ensure that every US senator would receive letters from constituents. Furthermore, this collaboration was instrumental to persuading the National Union to retain Robert W. Tayler, a former representative who successfully led the political effort in to block the aforementioned B. H. Roberts from taking his elected House seat, as the chief attorney "to take charge of the case against Smoot."[74] Consulting with Tayler and attorney John Carlisle, Dubois worked to determine "the line of attack and . . . who we summon as witnesses" for the hearings.[75]

Schoff's vision for this fight against Mormonism expanded beyond the unseating of Smoot. She desired a full disclosure of every alleged evil in Mormonism as well as a call for complete reform of the Church. For many years prior to the Smoot hearings, national women's groups lobbied the federal government to pass legislation that would reform Mormonism. But for Schoff, these efforts had not sufficiently brought Mormonism into modernity, and the Smoot hearings were a prime opportunity to finish the job. "Our work will not end with the unseating of Smoot," explained Schoff, "unless Mormonism is shown in its true colors and pursued persistently and fearlessly . . . There will be another civil war in our country, for the conditions will be worse even than slavery. Those who look ahead know that such practices will not be tolerated peaceably."[76] By the end of 1903, Schoff was touting her organization's successes, including the distribution of thousands of petitions and circular letters, the enlistment of newspapers willing to support the cause, and the completion of a number of protest meetings. Overall, Schoff was pleased with the "campaign for the sacredness of marriage and the purity of the home" and assured Dubois that he could "rely on us to continue the avalanche of petitions."[77]

Dubois also reveled in the "splendid effort which the women's clubs are making [and it] is having its effect and must bring results."[78] Collectively, these protests represented an important voice in the Smoot imbroglio, for these women sincerely felt they were working to preserve the American home. Schoff's activities were advantageous for her career, and she was promoted to become the president of the National League of Women's Organization. This organization had stewardship over a consortium of women's groups all opposed to Smoot, including the Interdenominational Council, Women's Christian Temperance Union, Christian League for Social Purity, National Congress of Mothers, and Daughters of the American Revolution.[79] Thus the antipolygamy/anti-Mormon crusade embraced by Hannah Schoff was carried to the highest levels of the US women's movement.

THE REED SMOOT HEARINGS AND THE AFTERMATH

The groundwork laid by women's organizations under the leadership of Hannah Schoff formed a key opposition group to Reed Smoot during his Senate hearings. With the foundation laid, Dubois hoped to "unseat Mr. Smoot in a hurry."[80] But this was not to be. The Smoot hearings evolved into a prolonged political fight that

FIGURE 8.3. "Thanksgiving Day Is Coming—But Will Senator Dubois Get His Turkey?" Cartoonist William Morris of the *Idaho Spokesman-Review* satirically sketches out Senator Dubois's efforts to sack Senator Smoot's political career. *Idaho Spokesman-Review* as reprinted in the *Salt Lake Herald*, November 26, 1906. Courtesy of the Brigham Young University Family History Center.

extended three years, eventually backfiring on Dubois's career. The Senate committee investigating Smoot, consisting of eight Republicans and five Democrats, met for the first time to hear testimony on March 2, 1904.[81] Historian Paul M. Holsinger, in his essay on Smoot's opposition, noted that a quick ouster was only possible had the vote on Smoot been taken in the summer of 1904, when public outrage was at its height. "But," Holsinger concluded, the "hearings trudged into a second year, much of the sensationalism and stoked excitement had worn off."[82] Formal hearings ended in 1906, with a majority of the committee recommending that Smoot be removed. Six months later, however, the full Senate voted to allow Smoot to keep his seat.

Following the drawn-out affair, Dubois's career in national politics took a markedly different course. All of the anti-Mormon legislative proposals he advocated for, including the efforts to disenfranchise Mormon voters and an antipolygamy constitutional amendment, failed to gain traction. Back in Idaho, Dubois's situation was even bleaker. His four-year effort to oust Smoot alienated Republicans and Democrats, leading to a reelection loss that signaled the end of Idaho's anti-Mormon movement. Reeling from these disappointments, Dubois bid a self-aggrandized farewell to the Senate, when he declared he was "the last representative of the American citizenship of the Rocky Mountain country opposed to the domination of the Mormon hierarchy in our politics."[83] It was a major fall from grace for the man who carefully directed many women's organizations in the fight against Mormonism.

Idaho's state elections in 1902 provided a catalyst for Dubois to return to the provincial anti-Mormon politics of his past, and this local campaign parlayed into a national protest after the election of Apostle Reed Smoot. By linking his crusade with the strength of the antipolygamy plank of the Women's Movement, Dubois sagaciously organized a fight that catapulted him into national fame. Ironically, the popularity and prestige he gained at the Smoot hearings failed to yield him anything more than a moral victory, and he was summarily voted out of office by a chagrined legislature that felt his anti-Mormon obsession distracted him away from his responsibilities to Idaho.[84]

The Reed Smoot hearings had long-term consequences for the image of the Mormon Church. Dubois, with the assistance of several national women's organizations, was able to generate an enthusiastic campaign to expose the evils of Mormonism. Through the publicity of the Reed Smoot hearings, the story of Mormonism's otherness was broadcast around the world over, not only impacting US policies in favor of the Church, but also influencing international perceptions of the Mormon Church.[85] In sum, Fred T. Dubois's systematic, orderly, and unusually intelligent fight succeeded in perpetuating Mormonism otherness to early twentieth-century Americans. Mormon status within this stratum of US society was further relegated to characteristics of nonwhite communities.

NOTES

1. Kathleen Flake, *The Politics of American Religious Identity: The Seating of Senator Reed Smoot, Mormon Apostle* (Chapel Hill: University of North Carolina Press, 2004), 49.

2. Willis K. Crosby to Senator DuBois, November 20, 1903, Frederick T. Dubois Collection, Special Collections, Eli M. Oboler Library, Idaho State University, Pocatello, ID (hereafter, FD Collection). Throughout this essay, I use the term "anti-Mormon" or "anti-Mormonism" to describe the actions of Fred Dubois. Use of this term has not been to degrade Dubois in any way but is meant to describe Dubois's actions in the simplest words. He was in opposition to Mormonism.

3. Fred T. Dubois to H. K. Schoff, November 14, 1903, Book 03, Mar 6, 1903–Mar 12, 1904, book 29, letter Books, FD Collection.

4. W. Paul Reeve, *Religion of a Different Color: Race and the Mormon Struggle for Whiteness* (New York: Oxford University Press, 2015), 4.

5. Terryl L. Giverns, *The Viper on the Hearth* (New York: Oxford University Press, 2013), 2–6.

6. Reeve, *Religion of a Different Color*, 8.

7. Rufus G. Cook, "The Political Suicide of Senator Fred T. Dubois of Idaho," *Pacific Northwest Quarterly* (October 1969): 193–198.

8. Cook, "The Political Suicide," 195; Leo W. Graff, *The Senatorial Career of Fred T. Dubois* (New York: Garland Publishing, 1988), 5.

9. Frederick T. Dubois, "Autobiography," 14–15, 21, FD Collection. There seems to be no specific reason for Dubois comparing Idaho and Illinois except that they were the two states he knew best and the contrast in population. According to the 1880 US Census Idaho had just over 40,000 residents. In the same census, Illinois neared 3 million residents.

10. Leonard J. Arrington, *History of Idaho*, vol. 1 (Moscow: University of Idaho Press, 1994), 371. For the most complete discussion of the anti-Mormonism movement in Idaho, see Merle W. Wells, *Anti-Mormonism in Idaho, 1872–92* (Provo, UT: Brigham Young University Press, 1978).

11. Graff, *The Senatorial Career*, 5.

12. Arrington, *History of Idaho*, 429–431.

13. Fred Dubois to Edgar Wilson, July 24, 1892, FD Collection. See also Dubois, "Autobiography," 163, FD Collection.

14. Merle W. Wells, "The Idaho Anti-Mormon Test Oath, 1884–1892," *Pacific Historical Review* 24, no.3 (August 1955): 251.

15. Cook, "The Political Suicide," 197; Bradley J. Young, "Silver, Discontent, and Conspiracy: The Ideology of the Western Republican Revolt of 1890–1901," *Pacific Historical Review* 64, no. 2 (May 1995): 244; Young, "Silver, Discontent, and Conspiracy," 243. For the most complete overview of Fred Dubois during this period, see Graff, *The Senatorial Career*, 180–210.

16. Graff, *The Senatorial Career*, 285–322.

17. William J. Bryan to Fred T. Dubois, December 15, 1902, FD Collection.

18. Graff, *The Senatorial Career*, 362.

19. R. E. Lockwood to Fred T. Dubois, November 11, 1902, FD Collection.

20. Graff, *The Senatorial Career*, 360–361. Also see J. M. Woodburn to Fred T. Dubois, November 1, 1902, FD Collection. On October 26, 1902, John Henry Smith wrote the following entry in his journal, "I was at four [political] meeting[s] today." Jean Bickmore White, ed., *Church, State, and Politics: The Diaries of John Henry Smith* (Salt Lake City: Signature Books, Inc, 1990), 511. Another Mormon apostle accompanied John Henry Smith to southeastern Idaho, but his identity remains a mystery. Smith does not make mention of the man in his journal.

21. J. M. Woodburn to Fred T. Dubois, November 1, 1902, FD Collection.

22. Lockwood was a newspaper publisher in Idaho. R. E. Lockwood to Fred T. Dubois, November 11, 1902, FD Collection.

23. Sarah Barringer Gordon, *The Mormon Question: Polygamy and Constitutional Conflict in Nineteenth-Century America* (Chapel Hill: University of North Carolina Press, 2002), 57.

24. Reasons for this Mormon shift to the GOP are manifold and beyond the purview of this essay. See historian Jonathan H. Moyer's recently finished "Dancing with the Devil: The Making of the Mormon-Republican Pact" (PhD diss., University of Utah, Salt Lake City, UT, 2009).

25. The *New York Times* reported approximately 15,000 of Idaho's residents were members of the Mormon Church. *New York Times*, February 10, 1903. Leonard Arrington estimated the number was closer to 20,000, which represented about 20 percent of the total state population. Arrington, *History of Idaho*, 530.

26. Jonathan H. Moyer, "Dancing with the Devil," 294.

27. Moyer, "Dancing with the Devil," 270.

28. "President Does Not Want Mormon Apostle in Senate," *New York Times*, January 10, 1903, 1.

29. Ramsay M. Walker to Fred T. Dubois, January 13, 1903, FD Collection.

30. "Action of President Severely Criticised," *New York Times*, January 12, 1903, 1.

31. Frank J. Cannon to Fred Dubois, January 26, 1903, FD Collection.

32. Fred T. Dubois to J. M. Woodburn, January 22, 1903, FD Collection.

33. "Debate on the Bill," *New York Times*, February 6, 1903, 3.

34. N. A. Just to Senator F. T. Dubois, February 19, 1903, FD Collection.

35. Fred T. Dubois to the Capital News, November 17, 1903, FD Collection.

36. Emphasis mine. Dubois, "Autobiography," 25, FD Collection.

37. In his recent treatise on anti-Mormonism in the nineteenth century, Spencer Fluhman explains that during an earlier time period, critics of the Church similarly used polygamy as "the most effective entrée for addressing other anti-Mormon concerns," including "theocracy or some other perceived evil." J. Spencer Fluhman, *"A Peculiar People": Anti-Mormonism and the Making of Religion in Nineteenth-Century America* (Chapel Hill: University of North Carolina Press, 2012), 13.

38. Fred T. Dubois, "The Mormon Question," speech delivered at the Democratic State Convention at Lewiston, Idaho August 16, 1904, FD Collection.

39. Fred T. Dubois to W. Jones, March 2, 1903, FD Collection.

40. Emphasis added. Fred T. Dubois to C. B. Wheeler, February 23, 1903, FD Collection.

41. Fred T. Dubois to C. B. Wheeler, February 23, 1903, FD Collection.

42. Graff, *The Senatorial Career*, 392 and 394.

43. Reed Smoot to Ben E. Rich, November 12, 1903, Smoot Papers, L. Tom Perry Special Collection, Harold B. Lee Library, Brigham Young University, Provo, UT; Heath, "The Reed Smoot Hearings," 20.

44. Fred T. Dubois to H. K. Schoff, February 3, 1903, FD Collection.

45. C. C. Goodwin to Fred T. Dubois, February 9, 1903, FD Collection; "Why," *Goodwin's Weekly*, December 12, 1903, 2.

46. F. A. Sakuth, "Endowment House Oath Taken in the Temple," May 8, 1903, FD Collection.

47. Reed Smoot to Ben E. Rich, November 12, 1903, Reed Smoot Papers, L. Tom Perry Special Collections, Harold B. Lee Library, Brigham Young University, Provo, UT (hereafter, Smoot Papers); Harvard S. Heath, "The Reed Smoot Hearings: A Quest for Legitimacy," *Journal of Mormon History* 33, no. 2 (Summer 2007), 1–80.

48. This description was made by Idaho state senator Harry Heitfeld. Harry Heitfeld to Charlie E. Arney, November 5, 1903, box 1, folder 6, Charles E. Arney Collection, Special Collections, Eli M. Oboler Library, Idaho State University, Pocatello.

49. J. M. Woodburn to Fred T. Dubois, July 8, 1903, FD Collection.

50. Smith disclosed that after the manifesto he maintained conjugal relationships with his wives. See Michael Harold Paulos, "Under the Gun at the Smoot Hearings: Joseph F. Smith's Testimony," *Journal of Mormon History* 34, no. 4 (Fall 2008): 181–225.

51. Fred T. Dubois to Rev. D. J. Mc Millan, November 14, 1903, FD Collection.

52. Fred T. Dubois to E. B. Critchlow, February 7, 1904, FD Collection.

53. Fred T. Dubois to H. P. Henderson, February 7, 1904, FD Collection.

54. Fred T. Dubois to Rev. J. E. Leilich, November 17, 1903, FD Collection.

55. John L. Leilich to Fred T. Dubois, November 7, 1903, FD Collection; John L. Leilich to Fred T. Dubois, November 12, 1903, FD Collection; John L. Leilich to Fred T. Dubois, November 23, 1903, FD Collection. In 1896, Democratic candidate William Jennings Bryan won Utah over Republican William McKinley by more than 50,000 votes. Four years later McKinley won the state by just over 2,100, a suspicious shift of more than 53,000 votes.

56. Fred T. Dubois to S. E. Wishard, November 24, 1903, FD Collection.

57. Fred T. Dubois to Rev. A. K. Wright, November 11, 1903, FD Collection.

58. Ibid. See also A. K. Wright to Fred T. Dubois, October 30, 1903, FD Collection.

59. Mrs. Frederic Schoff to Fred T. Dubois, November 12, 1903, FD Collection.

60. Hannah K. Schoff to Fred T. Dubois, November 16, 1903, FD Collection.

61. Joan Smyth Iverson, *Anti-polygamy Controversy in U.S. Women's Movements, 1880–1925: A Debate on the American Home* (New York: Garland, 1997), 216–217.

62. Mrs. Frederic Schoff to Fred T. Dubois, November 12, 1903, FD Collection. Hannah Schoff is a difficult person to track. She signed her name as Mrs. Frederic Schoff, Hannah K. Schoff, and

H. K. Schoff. Letters addressed to her and newspaper articles about her include spellings Shoff, Schaff, and Shaff.

63. H. K. Schoff to Senator Dubois, November 21, 1903, FD Collection. Also attending this meeting held at Dubois's home was Alice McLellan Birney, the founder and former president of the NCM.

64. Fred T. Dubois to H. K. Schoff, November 14, 1903, FD Collection.

65. H. K. Schoff to Senator Dubois, November 21, 1903, FD Collection. In her important study on the matter, historian Joan Iverson traces the origins of the antipolygamy crusade made by women's groups to the latter part of the nineteenth century, well before Dubois came on the scene. However, Senator Dubois proved to be a key congressional ally who also played a central role in directing and organizing the crusade during the Smoot hearings iteration. See Iverson, *Anti-polygamy Controversy*, 217–218, 223.

66. H. K. Schoff to Senator Dubois, December 22, 1903, FD Collection.

67. H. K. Schoff to Senator Dubois, December 10, 1903, FD Collection.

68. "To Protest against Smoot," *New York Times*, November 22, 1903, 3; H. K. Schoff to Fred T. Dubois, November 21, 1903, FD Collection.

69. H. K. Schoff to Fred T. Dubois, November 22, 1903, FD Collection.

70. H. K. Schoff to Senator Dubois, December 7, 1903, FD Collection; H. K. Schoff to Senator Dubois, December 22, 1903, FD Collection. The NCM also met with representatives of the Associated Press.

71. R. F. Pettigrew to F. T. Dubois, March 14, 1904, FD Collection; R. F. Pettigrew to F. P. Dubois, March 17, 1904, FD Collection; R. F. Pettigrew to F. T. Dubois, March 18, 1904, FD Collection.

72. See R. Douglas Brackenridge, "'About the Worst Man in Utah': William R. Campbell and the Crusade against Brigham H. Roberts, 1898–1900," *Journal of Mormon History* 39, no. 4 (Winter 2013): 112–113, 115–117, 137–140.

73. H. G. Redwine to Fred T. Dubois, March 26, 1904, FD Collection.

74. H. K. Schoff to Fred T. Dubois, December 7, 1903, FD Collection; Davis Bitton, *The Reutilization of Mormon History and Other Essays* (Urbana: University of Illinois Press, 1994), 150–170.

75. Fred T. Dubois to H. K. Schoff, December 9, 1903, FD Collection.

76. H. K. Schoff to Fred T. Dubois, December 10, 1903, FD Collection.

77. Hannah K. Schoff to Senator Dubois, December 29, 1903, FD Collection. One senator received in the mail more than a thousand petitions per day. Flake, *The Politics of American Religious Identity*, 5. Historian M. Paul Holsinger estimated that between 2 and 4 million letters were sent to Washington demanding Smoot's removal. M. Paul Holsinger, "J. C. Burrows and the fight against Mormonism: 1903–1907," *Michigan History* (Fall 1968): 185.

78. Fred T. Dubois to H. K. Schoff, December 9, 1903, FD Collection.

79. Iverson, *Anti-polygamy Controversy*, 217.

80. Fred T. Dubois to J. M. Woodburn, December 7, 1903, Book 03, "Letter Book #9 March 6, 1903–March 12, 1904," box 29, Letter Books, FD Collection.

81. Michael Harold Paulos, ed., *The Mormon Church on Trial: Transcripts of the Reed Smoot Hearings* (Salt Lake City: Signature Books, 2008), 19.

82. M. Paul Holsinger, "For God and the American Home: The Attempt to Unseat Senator Reed Smoot, 1903–1907," *Pacific Northwest Quarterly* (July 1969): 157.

83. "Speech of Hon. Fred T. Dubois of Idaho: In the Senate of the United States, Wednesday, February 20, 1907" (Washington, DC: US Government Printing Office, 1907).

84. Graff, *The Senatorial Career*, 503–504.

85. Malcolm R. Thorp, "'The Mormon Peril': The Crusade against the Saints in Britain, 1910–1914," *Journal of Mormon History* (1975): 72.

LDS Officials Involved with New Plural Marriages from September 1890 to February 1907

D. Michael Quinn

Loathing for "Mormon polygamy" was the real reason that the US Senate investigated the Church of Jesus Christ of Latter-day Saints from 1904 to 1907. Although most opponents of Utah's recently elected Senator Reed Smoot acknowledged that he had remained a monogamist, they wanted to demonstrate violations of the "manifesto" signed by LDS President Wilford Woodruff on September 24, 1890 "to refrain from contracting any marriage forbidden by the law of the land." This "Smoot Case" finalized half a century of nationwide hysteria about Mormonism as a threat to every American's traditional, monogamous marriage.

The Senate and its attorney demonstrated special interest in alleged breaches of the manifesto involving three levels of LDS leadership. First, "General Authorities" (or the central hierarchy) who had jurisdiction over the entire Church: that is, the Church president and his two counselors (who constituted a three-man First Presidency), the Quorum of the Twelve Apostles (which included Smoot), the Twelve's two counselors (who served only to March and October 1891 respectively), the patriarch to the Church (who presided over all local patriarchs), the seven presidents of Seventy or First Council of the Seventy (who presided over all Mormons who held the proselytizing office of Seventy), and the presiding bishop with his two counselors (who instructed all bishops of local "ward" congregations and presidents of smaller "branch" congregations). Second, officials who were commissioned ("called") by the First Presidency to be general board members at LDS headquarters over the Church's Sunday Schools and programs

245

DOI: 10.7330/9781646421176.c009

for youths, as well as those men called to preside over the Church's weekday universities, colleges, and academies. The third level comprised local officers who were directly commissioned by general authorities, that is, First Presidency's secretaries, mission presidents (who supervised proselytizing beyond the geographic limits of LDS "stakes"—which were similar to Catholic/Episcopalian dioceses), temple presidents and their counselors (who supervised sacredly secret ordinances), stake presidents and their counselors (who presided over several wards within a stake), stake patriarchs (who gave Mormons predictive blessings that were recorded and furnished to the recipient), local Seventy's presidents (who supervised proselytizing within stakes), local bishops with their counselors, and branch presidents with their counselors.

This appendix identifies only officials within those levels of leadership who promoted, or specifically authorized, or performed, or entered into new polygamous marriages after the 1890 Manifesto. This includes relationships (1) that were technically legal marriages solemnized civilly for a man (whose legal wife had died or divorced), where the man also had a continuing marital relationship with a living woman regarded as his wife by the LDS Church, (2) that began as a mutual agreement between the man and woman without an officiator, or (3) that were solemnized in LDS temples by subterfuge.

Such polygamous relationships are excluded from this appendix if they are not known to involve at least one official within the three specified levels of leadership. On the other hand, post-1890 polygamous proposals (without consummation) by such men are included in the chronology. The names of polygamous husbands and proposers of polygamy are in ALL CAPS, while the names and titles of general authorities are underlined. A child's birth is usually given only to estimate the month of an undated marriage, while other significant results of a marriage listed here are often omitted to save space. Where documents and contextual evidence disagree with traditional understanding by current descendants, priority is given here to documents and context.

Those three levels of LDS leadership were involved in at least 258 polygamous marriages that occurred under varying circumstances from the published announcement of abandoning polygamy on September 25, 1890, to the beginning of sworn testimony in the US Senate on March 2, 1904. Nearly fifty of the husbands were named in publications by the federal government. Remarkably, at least thirty-one more polygamous marriages involving those levels of leadership occurred from the start of testimony until the end of the Smoot Case in February 1907. By then, twenty-five LDS officials had knowingly performed post-manifesto polygamy.[1]

---

1. Involving the specified LDS officials, the number of polygamous marriages listed here includes all the kinds of conjugal relationships explained in this introduction. At least fifty-five additional marriages involved *only* subordinate LDS officials or *only* rank-and-file Mormons from September 1890 to February 1907, so those are not listed here.

30 September 1890—Apostle JOHN W. TAYLOR, at the Quorum of Twelve's first meeting since the Church President's declaration: "Said that when he had read the Manifesto[,] he felt 'damn it' [—] He said that he remembered the Revelation that Prest. Woodruff had had from the Lord [on 24 November 1889,] which was read to us some time ago[,] in which He told us that He would sustain us in carrying out the law of plural marriage. He also remembered finding among his father's (i.e., deceased Church President John Taylor's) papers the word of the Lord to him [on 27 September 1886] in which the Lord said that plural marriage was one of His eternal laws and that He had established it, that man had not done so and that He would sustain and uphold his saints in carrying it out. He said that this was given to his father in answer to prayer in which he had asked the Lord if it would not be right under the circumstances to discontinue plural marriages."

"I know that the Lord has given this manifesto to Prest. Woodruff[,] and He can take it away when the time comes or he can give it again. I feel all right now and am glad that I do." (Apostle HEBER J. GRANT's "Journal Book B," 443–444, LDS Church History Library; compare with variations of wording in Apostle ABRAHAM H. CANNON's published diary for this date)

1 October 1890 (not "10 October 1889")—Apostle JOHN W. TAYLOR (age 32) and third wife, JANETTE MARIA WOOLLEY (age 20), were married in Salt Lake City by Apostle Francis M. Lyman (see 21 June 1894 and 8 April 1906). The next day, TAYLOR and Lyman joined with fellow apostles in voting privately to "sustain" the recently published manifesto. A "general conference" of Mormons did so publicly on October 6.

17 October 1890—CHRISTIAN F. OLSEN (age 31) and second wife, MARY ANN UNSWORTH (age 23), were married near Las Palomas, Chihuahua, by the Mexican Mission's acting-president Alexander F. Macdonald. By October 6, Church President WILFORD WOODRUFF had signed authorizations for this and the six other post-manifesto marriages performed by Macdonald before 1891. Married civilly in Utah on 26 June 1891, after first wife's divorce.

The number of LDS officiators totaled in this introduction excludes those who performed only licensed marriages (even if bigamous). In such cases, the officiator might not have realized that the marriages were polygamous in fact for the husband.

According to the date they knowingly performed their first post-manifesto polygamous ceremony from September 1890 to February 1907, the LDS officiators were Francis M. Lyman, Alexander F. Macdonald, Moses Thatcher, George Teasdale, Daniel H. Wells, Charles O. Card, Marriner W. Merrill, Brigham Young Jr., Joseph F. Smith, Heber J. Grant, Anthony W. Ivins, L. John Nuttall, Anthon H. Lund, John W. Taylor, Matthias F. Cowley, Franklin D. Richards, John William Hyde, Abraham Owen Woodruff, Seymour B. Young, Rudger Clawson, John A. Woolf II, James Kirkham, Dan Muir, Joseph W. Summerhays, and Judson A. Tolman.

22 October 1890—Ward bishop JAMES C. PETERSEN (age 32) and second wife, AUGUSTA PERSSON (age 26), were married near Las Palomas by the Mexican Mission's acting-president Alexander F. Macdonald.

22 October 1890—BENJAMIN J. JOHNSON (age 33) and second wife, HARRIET JANE HAKES (age 21), were married near Las Palomas by acting-president Alexander F. Macdonald.

25 October 1890—CALVERT L. ALLRED (age 26) and second wife, ANDREA JENSEN (age 18), were married in La Ascención, Chihuahua, by the Mexican Mission's presidency counselor Alexander F. Macdonald, despite arrival of Apostle GEORGE TEASDALE as the new president.

25 October 1890—ERASTUS BECK (age 37) and second wife, NANCY ELIZABETH ACORD (age 21), were married in La Ascención by presidency counselor Alexander F. Macdonald.

5 November 1890—US district attorney filed a lawsuit to confiscate Salt Lake City's "Temple Block." As a result, Church President WILFORD WOODRUFF signed no more authorizations this year for plural marriages. Federal government seized the unfinished temple for five months.

8 November 1890—Quorum of the Twelve's counselor Daniel H. Wells indicated willingness to perform the polygamous ceremony, when forwarding a written request from Utah resident TIMOTHY JONES to First Presidency's First Counselor George Q. Cannon, who declined it. See 6 February 1895.

20 November 1890—Apostle Moses Thatcher unsuccessfully sought permission from Church President WILFORD WOODRUFF for Mexican resident JOSEPH C. BENTLEY to marry polygamously. See "Mid-December 1890," 6 February 1891, and 22 January 1895.

21 November 1890—Formerly ward bishopric counselor BYRON H. ALLRED SR. (age 43) and third wife, MARY ELIZA TRACY (age 16), were married near Las Palomas, Chihuahua, by the Mexican Mission's presidency counselor Alexander F. Macdonald, with authorization-letter signed by Church President WILFORD WOODRUFF on October 4.

5 December 1890—JAMES MADSEN JENSEN (age 38) and third wife, SUSANNA ELIZABETH ROPER (CASE—age 27), were married with civil license (under his partial pseudonym of "Jens Madsen" and her falsified age) in Lawrence, Emery Co., Utah, by ward bishop Calvin W. Moore while JENSEN (legally a widower) cohabited with his pre-1890 plural wife.

11 December 1890—Local Seventy's president ANSON BOWEN CALL (age 27) and second wife, HARRIET CAZIER (age 20), were married in Colonia Juárez, Chihuahua, by the Mexican Mission's presidency counselor Alexander F. Macdonald, "to whom my note of recognition from President Wilford Woodruff was addressed" and signed by October 6.

Mid-December 1890—Apostle Franklin D. Richards unsuccessfully sought permission from Church President WILFORD WOODRUFF to authorize a polygamous marriage for Mexican resident JOSEPH C. BENTLEY. See 20 November 1890, 22 January 1895, and 31 August 1898.

13 January 1891—Deseret Evening News printed Apostle BRIGHAM YOUNG JR.'s statement: "The Mormons are a law-abiding people; they have found stringent laws in Mexico, prohibiting the practice of polygamy, which laws they have respected and obeyed in every particular." The previous June, he married a plural wife in Mexico, performed by Alexander F. Macdonald.

6 February 1891—GEORGE M. BROWN (age 48) and third wife, PEARL MELISSA WILSON (age 19), were married as residents in Colonia Díaz, Chihuahua, Mexico, by Apostle Moses Thatcher, witnessed by resident Apostle GEORGE TEASDALE. Two months earlier, Seventy's President George Reynolds (serving as the First Presidency's assistant secretary) notified TEASDALE that an official would visit about BROWN's request for a plural wife. See 14 July 1900 and 8 August 1900.

12 February 1891—ROBERT O. GRUWELL (age 22) and second wife, JULIA DELCENA JOHNSON (age 20), were married as residents in Colonia Díaz by resident Apostle GEORGE TEASDALE.

19 March 1891 or thereabout (not "April 1890")—Seventy's President BRIGHAM H. ("B. H.") ROBERTS (age 34) and third wife, MARGARET CURTIS (SHIPP—age 41), were married in Salt Lake City by Quorum of Twelve's counselor Daniel H. Wells, who died on March 24. ROBERTS said he didn't ask permission from First Presidency. See 19 February 1893, 20 February 1897, and 23 January 1900.

1 April 1891—SAMUEL JOHN ("S. J.") ROBINSON (age 27) and second wife, ANNIE ELIZABETH WALSER (age 20), were married as residents in Colonia Juárez, Chihuahua, Mexico, by resident Apostle GEORGE TEASDALE.

2 April 1891—Church President WILFORD WOODRUFF told apostles and his counselors: "The principle of plural marriage will yet be restored to this Church, but how or when I cannot say."

14 May 1891—First Presidency ruled that "the apostles are at liberty to perform marriages for such persons as are unable for any reason to go to the temple for the time being."

20 August 1891 (when Apostle HEBER J. GRANT asked if the Manifesto was "a revelation")—First Presidency's Second Counselor Joseph F. Smith "answered emphatically no." See 10 August 1892, 24 October 1894, 6 July 1895, 17 June 1896, 25 February 1898, 10 May 1898, "By July 1899," 6 August 1900, 8–9 August 1900, 21 October 1900, 8 November 1900, 18 January 1901, 29 August 1901, 15 November 1901, 9 March 1902, 17 April 1902, 27 May 1902, 7 April 1903, 6 September 1903, 6 April 1904, 11 April 1904, 24 May 1904, 3 August 1904, 16 September 1905, 8 December 1905, 21 February 1906, and "After 2 September 1906."

23 September 1891—First Presidency's secretary LEONARD JOHN (L. JOHN) NUTTALL (age 57) and third wife, CATHERINE ANN CONOVER (HUNT—age 50), married "in the sealing room" of Manti Temple, Sanpete Co., Utah, when "we confirmed our covenant with each other" without an officiator (see 5 April 1894). Two months later, he "copied revelation given to Prest John Taylor into my book for private use" (see 30 September 1890). She had herself officially sealed by proxy to NUTTALL in Manti Temple on 20 October 1905, eight months after his death. See 19 September 1897.

23 September 1891—Formerly mission president JOHN U. STUCKI (age 54) and third wife, ANNA CLARA SPORI (age 32), were married as residents of Idaho in Logan Temple, Cache Co., Utah (according to descendants).

19–20 October 1891—Church President WILFORD WOODRUFF, First Counselor George Q. Cannon, Second Counselor Joseph F. Smith, Senior Apostle Lorenzo Snow, and junior Apostle Anthon H. Lund testified in court that the manifesto prohibits new plural marriages anywhere in the world. They promised that violators of the manifesto will be excommunicated. Beginning the evening of October 20, the Deseret News published those statements in its daily issue, its semiweekly issue, and its weekly issue. See 6 April 1904 and 25 March 1905.

20 January 1892—JAMES S. EMMETT (age 41) and second wife, MILLICENT JANE GRUWELL (age 19), were married as nonresidents in Colonia Díaz, Chihuahua, Mexico, by resident Apostle GEORGE TEASDALE, as authorized in letter "dictated" by First Presidency's First Counselor George Q. Cannon on January 13.

14 February 1892 (not "30 April 1892")—PHILLIP HURST (age 55) and fourth wife, SARAH EMMA GIBSON (age 41), were married as residents in Colonia Dublán by Apostle GEORGE TEASDALE.

By May 1892—Recently rejected by his congregation "for good and sufficient cause," formerly ward bishop JAMES YORGASON (JOHANSON/JORANSON/JORGENSON—age 44) and seventh wife, ANNA LOUISA SVEDERUS (age 27—his "hired girl" from late 1880s until this year), married each other in Fountain Green, Sanpete Co., Utah, by verbal agreement (without an officiator—see 23 September 1891 and 5 April 1894). Child on 14 February 1893; arrested in March.

2 August 1892—Ward bishopric counselor DAVID W. RAINEY (age 34) and second wife, JANETTA HANSON (age 21), were married as nonresidents in Cardston, Northwest Territory (later Alberta Province), Canada, by the settlement's LDS president Charles O. Card, with letter from WILFORD WOODRUFF—probably in April—the last signed by a serving Church President. See 16 July 1894.

10 August 1892—RASMUS LARSEN (age 53) and second wife, ANNIE SOPHIA CHRISTENSEN (age 35), were married as nonresidents in Colonia Juárez, Chihuahua, Mexico, by resident Apostle GEORGE TEASDALE, as "quite satisfac-

tory to all of us [including Second Counselor Joseph F. Smith]." in authorization letter signed by First Presidency's First Counselor George Q. Cannon on July 18.

1 September 1892—WILLIAM B. PARKINSON (age 40) and fourth wife, MARGARET WALLACE SLOAN (age 30), were married with civil license in Manti Temple, Sanpete Co., Utah, by its president's counselor John B. Maiben. PARKINSON (divorced only eight days earlier) cohabited with pre-manifesto plural wives and regularly "visited" his "divorced" wife.

30 November 1892—DAVID C. CAZIER (age 58) and third wife, SARAH ANN WARRILOW (ANDREWS—age 44), were married with civil license in Manti Temple, Sanpete Co., Utah, by its president—Apostle Anthon H. Lund. Juab Stake's president William Paxman and its high council had approved on 14 October 1892 CAZIER's plan to give his living wife what he called "a sham divorce" in order to legally marry SARAH ANN as a plural wife.

21 December 1892—Stake presidency counselor JOSEPH HYRUM GRANT (age 39) and second wife, LOUISA WINEGAR (COLTRIN—age 41), were married by subterfuge (as proxy sealing to her dead husband) in Logan Temple, Cache Co., Utah, by its president—Apostle MARRINER W. MERRILL. Received "second anointing" as couple in Salt Lake Temple on 29 March 1895, with required recommend signed by Church President WILFORD WOODRUFF. See 24 October 1894 and 17 June 1896.

19 February 1893—Seventy's President BRIGHAM H. ("B.H") ROBERTS preached in Colonia Díaz, Chihuahua, Mexico, that plural marriage "is a correct principle and will remain on the earth somewhere[,] and the sun will shine on it forever." See 19 March 1891 and 20 February 1897.

25 May 1893—JOHN A. BAGLEY (age 31) and third wife, LYDIA ESTELLA AUSTIN (age 29), were married as nonresidents in Colonia Díaz by resident Apostle GEORGE TEASDALE.

21 August 1893—WILLARD CARROLL (age 45) and second wife, ELIZABETH EMMA SLADE (McCONKIE—age 22), were married as residents in Colonia Juárez, Chihuahua, by resident Apostle GEORGE TEASDALE.

8 December 1893—WILLIAM P. A. McDERMOTT (age 40) and second wife, SARAH JANE SMEDLEY (MARLER—age 33), were married bigamously as Idaho residents with civil license in Logan Temple, Cache Co., Utah, by its president—Apostle MARRINER W. MERRILL.

24 December 1893—First Presidency secretary L. JOHN NUTTALL preached in Colonia Díaz, Chihuahua, Mexico: "The Order of Celestial Marriage is not done away with by any means. It will be commanded when the saints will live it right. Prest. Woodruff has not went [*sic*] back on the principle in the least." See 23 September 1891 and 19 September 1897.

5 April 1894 (during meeting of First Presidency and apostles)—First Counselor George Q. Cannon announced: "I believe in concubinage, or some plan whereby men and women can live together under sacred ordinances and vows until they can be married." In response, Church President WILFORD WOODRUFF "said that he did not believe there would be any harm or wrong in a man raising children by another woman, if his wife were barren, provided he did so upon proper principles." See 23 September 1891, 4 March 1897, and 16 August 1900.

19 May 1894—Formerly ward bishop JAMES F. JOHNSON (age 38) and second wife, CLARA MABEL BANYARD (age 16), were married as nonresidents in Colonia Juárez, Chihuahua, Mexico, by Apostle BRIGHAM YOUNG JR. First post-1890 polygamous entry by First Presidency secretary George Reynolds, a Seventy's President in "Book B, Out of Temple Sealings." See 6 February 1891 and 11 March 1898.

2 June 1894—Stake presidency counselor ISAAC SMITH (age 36) and third wife, ELIZABETH FUHRIMAN (age 22), were married as nonresidents in Cardston, Northwest Territory (later Alberta Province), Canada, by the settlement's LDS president Charles O. Card, his last-known plural ceremony.

4 June 1894—AMOS COX (age 37) and third wife, GRACE ELLEN CHESTNUT (age 22), were married as residents in Colonia Juárez, Chihuahua, Mexico, by Apostle BRIGHAM YOUNG JR. Recorded by First Presidency secretary in "Book B, Out of Temple Sealings." See 6 February 1891 and 19 May 1894.

10 June 1894—FRANKLIN S. BRAMWELL (age 35) and second wife, MARTHA ADELGUNDA HINCKLEY (age 28), were married as nonresidents in Colonia Juárez by Apostle BRIGHAM YOUNG JR. Ditto.

14 June 1894—JAMES W. MEMMOTT (age 53) and third wife, MARY ANN MELLOR, (HALES—age 29), were married as residents in Colonia Juárez by Apostle BRIGHAM YOUNG JR. Ditto.

21 June 1894—Stake president JESSE W. CROSBY JR. (age 45) and third wife, SARAH ANN MEEKS (age 33), were married with civil license in Salt Lake Temple by Apostle Francis M. Lyman—while CROSBY (legally a widower) cohabited with his pre-manifesto plural wife, whose permission for the civil marriage Lyman had required.

16 July 1894—JOHN W. BARNETT (age 33) and second wife, HATTIE LOENZA MERRILL (age 21), were married in Franklin, Oneida (later Franklin) Co., Idaho, by Apostle MARRINER W. MERRILL. Her recommend was initialed by "W. W. per G. Q. C." See 2 August 1892, 1 April 1895, 11 July 1899, 27 August 1903, and 5 August 1905.

24 October 1894—First Presidency's First Counselor George Q. Cannon told his son, Apostle ABRAHAM H. CANNON (who had three wives), that Church

President WILFORD WOODRUFF and Second Counselor Joseph F. Smith approved ABRAHAM's polygamously marrying the apostle's first cousin ANN MOUSLEY CANNON (age 25) as part of a proxy ceremony uniting her to his deceased brother for eternity—"if done in Mexico, and Pres. Woodruff promised the Lord's blessing to follow such an act." This was endorsed by her father, stake president Angus M. Cannon, but she declined the proposal. See 17 June 1896 and 23 October 1903.

22 January 1895—JOSEPH C. BENTLEY (age 35, resident) and second wife, GLADYS ELIZABETH WOODMANSEE (age 29, former resident), were married in Colonia Juárez, Chihuahua, Mexico, by Apostle GEORGE TEASDALE. See 20 November 1890 and "Mid-December 1890."

6 February 1895—TIMOTHY JONES (age 45) and second wife, ELIZABETH ANN DONE (REYNOLDS—age 40), were married as nonresidents in Colonia Juárez by Apostle GEORGE TEASDALE. See 8 November 1890.

22 February 1895—WILLIAM E. ROWBOTHAM (age 44) and third wife, LUCY ANN VICTORIA LINDQUIST-FENN (age 16), were married in Colonia Díaz by Apostle GEORGE TEASDALE.

23 February 1895—Branch president ORSON O. RICHINS (age 32) and third wife, SARAH AMANDA SHURTLIFF (HARPER—age 30), were married in Colonia Díaz by resident Apostle GEORGE TEASDALE.

4 March 1895—CARL E. NIELSEN (age 34) and fourth wife, EMMA JANE STEVENS (BURNHAM—age 27), were married in Colonia Juárez by Apostle GEORGE TEASDALE.

1 April 1895—CHARLES E. MERRILL (age 29) and third wife, ANN VICTORIA STODDARD (age 25), were married in Richmond, Cache Co., Utah, by Apostle MARRINER W. MERRILL. See 16 July 1894, 11 July 1899, 27 August 1903, and 5 August 1905.

8 April 1895—Apostle ABRAHAM H. CANNON (with three wives) wrote: "Susa Y. Gates talked with me in the evening about her daughter Leah [Dunford], and said she would like her to find a good husband. She would have been pleased for me to marry her, if it were possible. She would also like her husband [Jacob F. Gates] to get another wife, so as to fulfill the law of God." See 29 December 1895, 20 February 1897, and 19 September 1897.

14 June 1895 (according to descendants)—Ward bishopric counselor ALONZO H. COOK (age 39) and third wife, JOHANNE KIRSTINE (HANNAH CHRISTINE) JENSEN (age 26), were married. This was the day after she presented a recommend to the Salt Lake Temple.

30 June 1895—Formerly branch president DAVID A. STEVENS (age 36) and second wife, MARY ALMIRA BOICE (SPRAGUE—age 19), were married near Las

Palomas, Chihuahua, Mexico, by Apostle BRIGHAM YOUNG JR. Recorded by First Presidency secretary in "Book B, Out of Temple Sealings." See 6 February 1891 and 19 May 1894.

30 June 1895—Formerly ward bishopric counselor DAVID J. WILSON (age 52) and second wife, MIRIAM ADELIA COX (age 16), were married near Las Palomas by Apostle BRIGHAM YOUNG JR. Ditto.

6 July 1895 or thereabout—Local Seventy's president ENOCH B. TRIPP (age 72) and sixth wife, MARY ZILPA HARRIS (NEIMAYER—age 38), married in Salt Lake County by "a covenant" (without an officiator—see 5 April 1894). "Cut off" in 1898, TRIPP was twice refused baptism by stake president, so Church President Joseph F. Smith ordered his total reinstatement in 1903.

15 September 1895 (at meeting of First Presidency with apostles), Apostle HEBER J. GRANT "was told to warn Bishop O. F. Whitney . . . not to become too intimate with Miss Babcock . . ." Two years earlier, ward bishop ORSON F. WHITNEY (then, age 38, with two wives then living) had written to MAUD MAY BABCOCK (then age 26): "My sister, my sweet sister, if a name dearer and sweeter were, it should be thine." See 18 March 1897, 11 July 1900, and 3 July 1903.

15 October 1895—CHARLES R. SAVAGE (age 63) and fourth wife, ANNA LEONA SMITH (CLOWES—age 48), were married with civil license in Salt Lake Temple by First Presidency's secretary GEORGE F. GIBBS—while SAVAGE (a widower and divorced from one plural wife) cohabited with a pre-manifesto plural wife. See 17 May 1900 and 6 October 1903.

27 October 1895, recently released mission president Karl G. Maeser wrote: "When a few of the select were in the [Logan] temple in their temple robes[,] it was prophesied that polygamy would again be restored again on earth in our day but only the worthy could enter it." Apostle MARRINER W. MERRILL, the temple's president, was probably the speaker.

29 December 1895—Apostle ABRAHAM H. CANNON (age 36) had been polygamously courting LEAH EUDORA DUNFORD (age 21) for eight months. She and his other polygamous fiancée LILLIAN HAMLIN (age 25) met with him on this day at the home of LEAH's mother, Susa Young (Dunford, Gates). He died before marrying LEAH. See 8 April 1895, 17 June 1896, 20 February 1897, and 19 September 1897.

1 January 1896—JAMES UDY (age 75) and fourth wife, HOLLY ANN MURPHY (McRAE, BAXTER—age 61), were married with civil license in the Salt Lake Temple by its president's counselor—the Presiding Bishopric's Second Counselor John R. Winder—while UDY (legally a widower) cohabited with his pre-manifesto plural wife. In 1900, HOLLY died.

1 April 1896—Senior Apostle Lorenzo Snow told the Twelve "that the principle [of plural marriage] was just as true today as it ever was, and bore his testimony to the

effect that it will again be practiced by this people." See 20 October 1898, 7 October 1899, 17 May 1900, and 26 May 1901.

18 April (not "15 April") 1896—Local Seventy's president PARLEY P. BINGHAM (age 36) and second wife, ISABELLA McFARLAND (age 24), were married as nonresidents in Colonia Díaz, Chihuahua, Mexico, by resident Apostle GEORGE TEASDALE.

18 April 1896—ALBERT D. THURBER (age 41) and second wife, AGNES CRAIG GARDNER (age 31), were married in Colonia Díaz by resident Apostle GEORGE TEASDALE.

17 June 1896—Apostle ABRAHAM H. CANNON (age 37) and fourth wife, LILLIAN HAMLIN (age 25), were married by subterfuge (as part of proxy sealing to his deceased brother) in the Salt Lake Temple by the First Presidency's Second Counselor Joseph F. Smith. CANNON died unexpectedly on 19 July 1896, and their child was born posthumously on 22 March 1897. See 21 December 1892, 24 October 1894, 29 December 1895, and 24 December 1901.

18 February 1897—JOHN W. S. SMITH (age 56) and second wife, MARGARET JOSEPHINE WILSON (BROWN—age 42), were married bigamously with civil license in St. George Temple, Washington Co., Utah, by its president David H. Cannon. They lived in Utah, while first wife remained with children in Arizona, where she died as "wife of J. W. Smith."

20 February 1897 (in New York City)—Seventy's President BRIGHAM H. ("B.H.") ROBERTS (age 39) was courting LEAH EUDORA DUNFORD (age 22) for fourth wife. Susa Young (Dunford, Gates) advised her daughter that "your whole soul would be satisfied in time and eternity with such a man for a leader and companion," but LEAH married someone else. See 19 March 1891, 19 February 1893, 8 April 1895, 29 December 1895, 19 September 1897, and 23 January 1900.

22 February 1897—Ward bishopric counselor MILES P. ROMNEY (age 53) and fifth wife, EMILY HENRIETTA EYRING (SNOW—age 26), were married in Colonia Juárez, Chihuahua, Mexico, by Apostle HEBER J. GRANT. Stake president Anthony W. Ivins had refused ROMNEY, and GRANT reluctantly officiated after "my protest" to Apostle JOHN HENRY SMITH—whose diary recorded GRANT as officiator. See 28 February 1897, 5 March 1898, 25 April 1899, 9 January 1900, 26 May 1901, 18 January 1902, 6 October 1903, and 9 December 1906.

28 February 1897—ORSON P. BROWN (age 33) and second wife, JANE BODILY GALBRAITH (age 17), were married in Colonia Díaz, Chihuahua, by Apostle HEBER J. GRANT. Ditto.

4 March 1897 (during First Presidency's meeting with apostles)—First Counselor George Q. Cannon again recommended "some plan" for "men [who] had wives that were barren ... [and for such a man] to take a wife that will bear him children." He proposed that the two make a "solemn covenant"—without an

officiator—that would be followed by a "connection which could be looked upon as illicit with the other sex," but Cannon affirmed that "there would be no sin, under our circumstances." See 23 September 1891, 5 April 1894, and 16 August 1900.

18 March 1897 (at meeting of First Presidency with apostles)—Senior Apostle Lorenzo Snow reported that ward bishop ORSON F. WHITNEY no longer thought "it was the will of the Lord that he should take May Babcock" as a plural wife (see 15 September 1895), but that she (age 29) now wanted to polygamously marry the recently released mission president CHARLES W. STAYNER (age 56). He died in 1899, and MAUD MAY BABCOCK married no one else.

By 11 June 1897 (when released as a set-apart temple ordinance-worker by Apostle MARRINER W. MERRILL for this "unwise course")—THOMAS MOORE (age 69) was courting "Sister Wood" as his intended second wife in Logan, Cache Co., Utah. See 1 April 1895 and 29 July 1899.

22 June 1897—WALTER W. STEED (age 39) and second wife, SUSAN ALICE BELL CLARK (age 28), were married in Ciudad Juárez, Chihuahua, Mexico, by stake president Anthony W. Ivins as the first polygamous ceremony he performed for nonresidents, authorized now in writing by First Presidency's First Counselor George Q. Cannon.

22 June 1897—Local Seventy's president BRIANT STRINGHAM JR. (age 44) and second wife, SABINA SMITH (age 22), were married as nonresidents in Ciudad Juárez by stake president Anthony W. Ivins.

22 June 1897—DANIEL H. SNARR (age 37) and second wife, PHOEBUS McCARROLL (age 22), were married as nonresidents in Ciudad Juárez by stake president Anthony W. Ivins.

16 September 1897—ARTHUR RILEY (age 44) and second wife, SARAH LYDIA DAVIS (age 32), were married in Ciudad Juárez as nonresidents by stake president Anthony W. Ivins.

16 September 1897—SAMUEL F. BALL (age 48) and third wife, MARGARET OSBORN BROWN (age 30), were married in Ciudad Juárez as nonresidents by stake president Anthony W. Ivins.

19–20 September 1897 (not "Aug."—as carelessly misstated in Quinn's 1997 Extensions of Power)—Church President WILFORD WOODRUFF (age 90) and 11th wife, LYDIA MARY OLIVE MAMREOFF VON FINKELSTEIN (MOUNTFORD—age 42), were married by his secretary L. JOHN NUTTALL aboard a "steamer" (the "Sausalito Ferry") crossing San Francisco Bay, California. The next day, the men boarded steamship Columbia, on route to Portland, Oregon. Apostle Anthon H. Lund wrote on December 1: "President Woodruff took me to one side and spoke to me concerning Mrs. Mountfert [sic]. I was rather astonished." WOODRUFF's journal concealed his overnight visit with her in Ogden, Utah on 27–28 December

1897, but NUTTALL wrote MOUNTFORD on 19 June 1901: "I have not forgotten the Ogden & other days with our Mutual friend." MATTHIAS F. COWLEY (his grandnephew by marriage) told other apostles on 10 May 1911 that "President Woodruff married a wife a year before he died, Madam Mountford." In Salt Lake Temple on 23 November 1920, Lund (then serving as First Presidency's first counselor) performed the vicarious sealing for WOODRUFF and MOUNTFORD. An advocate of post-manifesto polygamy, Susa Young (Dunford, Gates), was her proxy. See 2 April 1891, 23 September 1891, 8 April 1895, 29 December 1895, 20 February 1897, 25 October 1897, and 3 August 1904.

25 October 1897—Apostle GEORGE TEASDALE (age 65—a widower of three wives, with his legal wife still living) and fifth wife, MARION ELIZA SCOLES (age 32), were married aboard the steamship Columbia near Portland, Oregon, by Apostle Anthon H. Lund, as authorized verbally by Church President WILFORD WOODRUFF (see 1 January 1898). Recorded by First Presidency secretary in "Book B, Out of Temple Sealings" (see 6 February 1891, 19 May 1894). She died in childbirth on 17 December 1898.

By mid-November 1897—Local Seventy's president SAMUEL T. WHITAKER (age 37—a nonresident) and second wife, AVALINA EMILY MILLS (SAVILLE—age 38—recently arrived resident), were married in Colonia Juárez, Chihuahua, Mexico, by stake president Anthony W. Ivins. After SAMUEL's telegraphed request on November 5, the letter authorizing this ceremony from First Presidency's First Counselor George Q. Cannon was forwarded to him in El Paso, Texas, by the First Council of Seventy's secretary John M. Whitaker (his brother), but the ceremony is missing from the incomplete transcription of Ivins' "Marriage Record" (see 10 May 1898). Descendants haven't acknowledged the marriage, but the First Presidency granted AVALINA in 1904 a "divorce" (cancellation of their polygamous sealing). See 15 November 1899.

After 19 November 1897 (when she was endowed in the Salt Lake Temple)—Ward bishop LOREN H. HARMER (age 43) and third wife, MARY ELLEN ANDERSON (age 22), were married in Colonia Juárez by stake president Anthony W. Ivins. HARMER was not present at his Utah ward's Sunday meetings from 21 November until 5 December 1897, but the ceremony is missing from the incomplete transcription of Ivins's "Marriage Record" (see 10 May 1898). Child on 30 October 1898. First Presidency's First Counselor George Q. Cannon (who had sent the letters of authorization to Ivins since June 1897) wrote on 13 March 1900 that MARY ELLEN "is really a plural wife" but that HARMER "confessed to adultery [in court] rather than to expose any person [i.e., Cannon himself and Ivins] . . . [or to] expose the Church in any way . . ."

23 November 1897—Formerly branch president THOMAS TIDWELL (age 71) and fourth wife, MARY ABBIE EAKLE (age 39), were married with license in

American Fork, Utah Co., by John McNeil, justice of the peace—while TIDWELL (legally divorced) cohabited with a pre-1890 plural wife.

29 November 1897—A faithfully LDS monogamist complained to the First Presidency's First Counselor George Q. Cannon that Apostle BRIGHAM YOUNG JR. (nearly 61) had asked the man's eldest daughter, AMANDA INEZ KNIGHT (age 21), to become the apostle's seventh wife. When confronted with this complaint on 7 January 1898, YOUNG said he "would do what he could to repair the effect of what he had said by seeing Brother [Jesse] Knight himself and talking with him." She was set apart as a full-time missionary to Britain on 1 April 1898.

3 December 1897—Formerly stake president WILLIAM D. HENDRICKS (age 68, nonresident) and fifth wife, ELEANORE ANNA MAYBIN (GREENWELL—age 26, resident), were married in Ciudad Juárez, Chihuahua, Mexico, by stake president Anthony W. Ivins.

1 January 1898—Local Seventy's president FERDINAND F. HINTZE (age 43) and fourth wife, NORA MIKKELSEN (age 25), were married aboard "a ferry boat between U.S. and Canada" (after leaving Chicago, Illinois, on route to Detroit, Michigan—i.e., on Lake Huron) by Apostle Anthon H. Lund, as authorized by Church President WILFORD WOODRUFF. See 25 October 1897.

24 January 1898—Local Seventy's president JOSEPH A. SILVER (age 40) and second wife, ELIZABETH FARNES (age 27), were married as nonresidents in Colonia Dublán, Chihuahua, Mexico, by stake president Anthony W. Ivins.

25 February 1898—General board member JOSEPH W. SUMMERHAYS met with the First Presidency's Second Counselor Joseph F. Smith in Chicago to discuss his hope to marry a plural wife: "I told him some of the brethren were getting wives[,] and I asked him if it would be alright if I took one. He said it would under certain conditions." See 25 September 1903.

5 March 1898—FRED W. HEATON (age 31) and second wife, ABIGAIL COX (age 25), were married in Colonia Juárez, Chihuahua, Mexico, by Apostle JOHN W. TAYLOR. Recorded by Apostle JOHN HENRY SMITH. In 1893, Apostle Francis M. Lyman had forbidden their marriage.

6 March 1898—CHARLES WHIPPLE (age 34) and second wife, MARY LOUISE WALSER (age 20), were married in Colonia Juárez by Apostle JOHN W. TAYLOR. Recorded by Apostle JOHN HENRY SMITH.

8 March 1898—LUCIAN M. MECHAM (age 36) and second wife, MARY ANN HARDY (age 36), were married in Colonia Pacheco, Chihuahua, by Apostle JOHN W. TAYLOR. Ditto.

8 March 1898—Ward bishop GEORGE W. HARDY (age 34) and second wife, EMMA SYLVANIA ROWLEY (age 19), were married in Colonia Pacheco by Apostle JOHN W. TAYLOR. Ditto.

10 March 1898—BRIGHAM STOWELL (age 43) and third wife, ELLEN MARIE SKOUSEN (age 26), were married in Colonia Juárez by Apostle JOHN W. TAYLOR. Ditto.

11 March 1898—Local Seventy's president, ANSON BOWEN CALL (age 34) and third wife, DORA PRATT (age 19), were married in Colonia Dublán by Apostle JOHN W. TAYLOR. Ditto; last polygamous entry in "Book B, Out of Temple Sealings" by First Presidency secretary George Reynolds, a President of Seventy. See 19 May 1894 and 25 October 1897.

13 April 1898—Local Seventy's president BENJAMIN E. RICH (age 42) and fourth wife, LAURA BOWRING (age 39), were married in Salt Lake City by Apostle MATTHIAS F. COWLEY, following instructions by the First Presidency's First Counselor George Q. Cannon: "There was no laying on of hands, but he gave the authority personally." See 20 October 1898.

10 May 1898 (according to his diary)—Local Seventy's president JOSEPH H. DEAN (age 42) and third wife, AMANDA WILHELMINA PETERSSON (ANDERSON—age 38), were married as nonresidents in Colonia Juárez, Chihuahua, Mexico, by stake president Anthony W. Ivins. Ceremony is missing from incomplete transcription of Ivins's "Marriage Record" as excerpted by his son. First Presidency's Second Counselor Joseph F. Smith had verbally counseled DEAN on 21 April 1898 about this marriage, and First Counselor George Q. Cannon wrote authorization for Ivins on May 3.

1 June 1898—Ward bishop HASKELL S. JOLLEY (age 37) and second wife, ELLEN ELIZA HARRISON (age 26), were married in Colonia Juárez as nonresidents by stake president Anthony W. Ivins.

14 July 1898—Stake presidency counselor HELAMAN PRATT (age 52) and third wife, BERTHA CHRISTINA WILCKEN (STEWART—age 35), were married in Ciudad Juárez by stake president Anthony W. Ivins—the first he performed for a resident-husband.

31 July 1898—ALBERT MINNERLY (age 61) and second wife, HENRIETTA PEARCE (HALL, STEERS—age 46), were married in Colonia Juárez by stake president Anthony W. Ivins.

10 August 1898—JAMES HOOD (age 35) and second wife, JEMIMA JOHNSTON RUSSELL (age 27), were married in Colonia Juárez as nonresidents by stake president Anthony W. Ivins.

31 August 1898—DAVID ECCLES (age 49) and third wife, MARGARET FERGUSON CULLEN (GEDDES—age 33), were married in Baker City, Oregon, by Apostle Franklin D. Richards (not by Apostle MARRINER W. MERRILL in Ogden, Utah). This was the only-known polygamous ceremony that Richards performed after manifesto. Child on 21 May 1899. See 17 May 1900.

14 September 1898—WILLIAM C. OCKEY (age 48) and third wife, OVENA ANDREA JORGENSEN (age 24), were married as nonresidents in Colonia Dublán, Chihuahua, Mexico by stake president Anthony W. Ivins.

29 September 1898 or thereabout (when she was endowed in Salt Lake Temple)— Local Seventy's president HUGH WATSON (age 44) and fifth wife, ELIZABETH ANTOINETTE CHAPUIS (age 33), were married. First Presidency granted her a "divorce" in 1903.

20 October 1898—Local Seventy's president and recently appointed mission president BENJAMIN E. RICH (age 42) and fifth wife, MADORA CATHERINE LODEMA JACKMAN (CLEGG—age 43), were married in Preston, Oneida (later Franklin) Co., Idaho, by Apostle MATTHIAS F. COWLEY. Years later, COWLEY told the Twelve that new Church President Lorenzo Snow "simply told me that he would not interfere with Brother Woodruff's and Cannon's work." See 1 April 1896, 13 April 1898, 7 October 1899, 17 May 1900, and 26 May 1901.

23 October 1898—Stake presidency counselor JOSEPH MORRELL (age 42) and second wife, MARY ANN DAINES (age 29), were married in Preston by Apostle MATTHIAS F. COWLEY.

23 October 1898—MILES A. ROMNEY (age 28) and second wife, LILY BURRELL (age 21), were married in Colonia Juárez, Chihuahua, Mexico, by stake president Anthony W. Ivins.

23 October 1898—HEBER M. CLUFF (age 34) and second wife, SUSAN CAROLINE SIMS (age 23), were married in Colonia Juárez as nonresidents by stake president Anthony W. Ivins.

18 November 1898 or thereabout (after stake president said "he could not get a woman sealed to him")—Stake patriarch WILLIAM C. MOODY (age 79) and sixth wife, CHARLOTTE ALBERTINA LUNDSTEDT (DESPAIN—age 41), married in Thatcher, Graham Co., Arizona, by verbal agreement (without an officiator). He was excommunicated on 13 January 1901; baptized again on 29 April 1902. See 23 September 1891, 5 April 1894, and 4 March 1897.

10 December 1898—WILLIAM J. STONE (age 32) and second wife, EMMA BROWN (WILLIAMS—age 33), were married bigamously with civil license in Tooele, Utah, by stake president Hugh S. Gowans. STONE was imprisoned for this on 12 May 1899.

10 January 1899—Ward bishop WINSLOW FARR JR. (age 61) and fourth wife, SARAH ANN MITCHELL (GRAHAM—age 47), were married in Colonia Dublán, Chihuahua, Mexico, by stake president Anthony W. Ivins.

11 January 1899 or thereabout (when she was endowed in Salt Lake Temple) to "about 1901" (according to descendants)—Stake patriarch JOSEPH D. SMITH (age 52 in 1899) and third wife, ELIZA JANE STEPHENSON (age 25 in 1899), were married.

4 February 1899 (when published in <u>New York Herald</u> before being reprinted in Utah)—<u>First Presidency's First Counselor George Q. Cannon</u> told a Mormon reporter (son of <u>Apostle BRIGHAM YOUNG JR.</u>): "A man might go to Canada and marry another wife. He would not be violating our laws, and would not be in danger of prosecution [in Canada] unless the first wife should follow him there from Utah and prefer a charge of bigamy against him. He might go to Mexico and have a religious ceremony uniting him to another. That would not violate our law."

Early March 1899—PIERRE (PETER) A. DROUBAY III (age 43) and second wife, MARTHA JANE DUNN (BRAMMETT—age 27), were married as nonresidents in Mexico by advice of <u>Apostle JOHN W. TAYLOR</u> (on February 22 in Denver, Colorado). She and DROUBAY were excommunicated in October. Child "John W." on 21 December 1899 in Tooele, Utah.

25 April 1899 (speaking to LDS missionaries in California)—<u>Apostle HEBER J. GRANT</u> "talked much on polygamy, & intimated that he would perform the ceremony in Mexico for any man who did not have any children, though he said that President would not consent to it"—probably referring to their mission president. At this time, married men often served as full-time LDS missionaries. <u>See</u> 22 February 1897, 26 May 1901, 18 January 1902, 6 October 1903, and 26 January 1907.

3 May 1899 (<u>not</u> "5 March 1891")—Formerly mission president, ward bishop, and stake patriarch JOHN THEODORE BRANDLEY (age 47) and third wife, ELIZA ROSINA ZAUGG (age 31), were married in Butte, Silver Bow Co., Montana, by <u>Apostle JOHN W. TAYLOR</u>, who traveled from Denver, Colorado, to meet the couple on their way from Utah to a new residence in Canada.

22 May 1899—Ricks College president DOUGLAS M. TODD SR. (age 38) and third wife, HANNAH MATILDA McMURRAY (age 28), were married in Salt Lake City by <u>Apostle MATTHIAS F. COWLEY</u>. <u>Apostle MARRINER W. MERRILL</u> had advised TODD to do this.

15 June 1899 (according to descendants)—Local Seventy's president JAREN TOLMAN (age 46) and fourth wife, MARY ALICE BYBEE (PATTERSON—age 36), were married polygamously in Bountiful, Davis Co., Utah. <u>See</u> February 1906 for his father's verified role in post-1890 marriages.

By July 1899—EZRA T. HYDE (age 33) and second wife, CAROLINE VICTORIA KILGORE (age 27), were married in Logan, Cache Co., Utah, by his brother John William Hyde (whose wife was a niece of then-<u>Second Counselor Joseph F. Smith</u>'s wife Alice). With births on 29 April 1900 and in August 1901, she married another man in 1903. <u>Salt Lake Tribune</u> said on 25 December 1904 that EZRA had "forged [a] letter" of authorization supposedly written by <u>Smith</u>. In April 1905, she told LDS leaders that "Will Hyde" had officiated with "written authority from one of the apostles." On 2 September 1905, <u>Tribune</u> printed EZRA's claim that "the Mormon church is not at all to blame in my affair, and that whatever responsibility there is rests upon my shoulders," yet he still affirmed: "Whatever authority I ever claimed to possess[,] I did actually possess."

11 July 1899—Apostle MARRINER W. MERRILL told the Twelve's quarterly meeting that "the Manifesto was Not a revelation from God, and that Plural Children would always be Born in the Church from year to year for all time to come." See 20 August 1891, 21 December 1892, 16 July 1894, 1 April 1895, 9 January 1900, 7 April 1901, 27 August 1903, and 5 August 1905.

19 July 1899—Apostle MATTHIAS F. COWLEY (age 40) and third wife, HARRIET BENNION (HARKER—age 40), were married "for time only" in Logan Temple, Cache Co., Utah, by its president—Apostle MARRINER W. MERRILL, who sealed them (without explanation) "for time and all Eternity" on 1 June 1900. See 16 September 1905.

23 July 1899—Ward bishop GEORGE C. NAEGLE (age 38) and third wife, MARGARET ROMNEY (age 19), were married in Colonia Juárez, Chihuahua, Mexico by stake president Anthony W. Ivins—the last plural marriage that President Lorenzo Snow allowed him to perform.

29 July 1899—Ward bishop THOMAS BLACKBURN (age 41) admitted proposing polygamous marriage in Loa, Wayne Co., Utah, for which he was released a week later. See 11 June 1897.

7 September 1899—JOHN T. DAVIS (age 21) and second wife, MARY ANN GLEDHILL (age 39), were married bigamously with license (under pseudonym "David J. Davis," with falsified age) in Manti, Sanpete Co., Utah, by ward bishop William T. Reid. DAVIS was imprisoned in 1901.

29 September 1899—Apostle HEBER J. GRANT told the Davis Stake high council that "there were many Latterday Saints that really hoped Poligamy [sic] was done away with." See 4 February 1905.

7 October 1899—Mission president LOUIS A. KELSCH (age 42) and second wife, MARY LUCRETIA LYERLA (age 26), were married in Salt Lake City by Apostle MATTHIAS F. COWLEY. Church President Lorenzo Snow again accepted COWLEY's previous authorization.

14 October 1899—Mission president BENJAMIN E. RICH (age 43) and sixth wife, ALICE CAROLINE McLACHLAN (age 30), were married in Salt Lake City by Apostle MATTHIAS F. COWLEY. Ditto.

15 November 1899—Local Seventy's president SAMUEL T. WHITAKER (age 39—legally a widower) and third wife, MARGARET ANN THOMAS (age 32), were married with civil license in Salt Lake Temple by its president's counselor—the Presiding Bishopric's Second Counselor John R. Winder—while WHITAKER's post-manifesto wife remained undivorced until 1904, when the First Presidency cancelled her polygamous sealing. See "By mid-November 1897."

26 November 1899 (<u>not</u> "12 October")—ROBERT L. McCALL (age 30) and second wife, CHRISTINA SOUTHEIMER (age 24), were married as nonresidents in Colonia Juárez, Chihuahua, Mexico, by <u>Apostle ABRAHAM OWEN WOODRUFF</u> (who wrote "R. M. & C. S." in his diary). McCALL had been refused by stake president Anthony W. Ivins, but <u>Church President Lorenzo Snow</u> had given WOODRUFF permission in November 1898 to seal marriages for "young people" residing distant from temples. <u>See</u> 23 July 1899.

26 November 1899—Local Seventy's president EDWARD W. PAYNE (age 32) and second wife, LUCY ALICE FARR (age 19), were married in Colonia Juárez by <u>Apostle ABRAHAM OWEN WOODRUFF</u>. Recorded by stake president Anthony W. Ivins.

12 December 1899 (<u>not</u> "1895")—Formerly ward bishopric counselor HEBER KIMBALL MAXHAM (age 50) and second wife, CAROLINE DELCINA JOHNSON (age 25), were married in Colonia Oaxaca, Sonora, Mexico, by <u>Apostle ABRAHAM OWEN WOODRUFF</u>, after MAXHAM had been refused by stake president Anthony W. Ivins.

14 December 1899—Ward bishopric counselor and general board member RODNEY C. BADGER (age 51) and third wife, ELIZABETH HARRISON (age 34), were married in Salt Lake City by <u>Apostle MATTHIAS F. COWLEY</u>.

By 31 December 1899 (according to some descendants)—Ward bishop APOLLOS G. DRIGGS (age 58) and fourth wife, EDITH FLORENCE ROBINSON (age 45), were married in Salt Lake City. Released as bishop on 17 June 1900—two months after local newspaper claimed that he had a new wife. Civilly married by set-apart temple ordinance-worker Royal B. Young on 10 May 1902—following first wife's death—while DRIGGS cohabited with two pre-1890 plural wives.

By January 1900—DAVID P. FELT (age 39) and second wife, ANNA MATTSON (APELGREN—age 31), married in Salt Lake City with "a covenant" and "written contract" (by consent of ward bishop George R. Jones). Child on 14 October 1900, raised by first wife. <u>See</u> 5 April 1894.

9 January 1900 (during the Quorum of Twelve's quarterly meeting)—<u>Apostle MARRINER W. MERRILL</u>, while "speaking of the principle of plural marriage, said it had come to stay in some form or another." Rather than challenging his subordinate's statement, <u>Apostle JOHN HENRY SMITH</u> emphasized caution: "I think we should be secretive and not give ourselves away."

23 January 1900—US House of Representatives officially excluded polygamist <u>Seventy's President BRIGHAM H. ("B. H.") ROBERTS</u> despite his election by Utah's voters. <u>See</u> 19 March 1891, 19 February 1893, 20 February 1897, and 16 January 1904.

17 May 1900 (as advised by <u>Apostle JOHN HENRY SMITH</u> and by First Presidency's secretary GEORGE F. GIBBS)—<u>Church President Lorenzo Snow</u> and his <u>First</u>

Counselor George Q. Cannon instructed a ward bishop to stop investigating post-manifesto marriage of MARGARET CULLEN (GEDDES, ECCLES). See 1 April 1896, 31 August 1898, and 20 October 1898.

17 May 1900—Apostle GEORGE TEASDALE (age 68—widower of four wives, plus divorced from one) and sixth wife, DOLLIE LETITIA THOMAS (age 23), were married with license in Logan Temple, Cache Co., Utah, by its president—Apostle MARRINER W. MERRILL. But TEASDALE continued to overnight with "divorced" wife whenever he was in Salt Lake City, while LETITIA remained at his main residence in Nephi, Juab Co. See 25 October 1897 and 9 April 1904.

11 July 1900—As Apostle GEORGE TEASDALE left the Salt Lake Temple with ORSON F. WHITNEY, he advised this ward bishop to seek a plural wife. See 18 July 1900 and 3 July 1903.

14 July 1900—Acting president of Brigham Young Academy in Provo GEORGE H. BRIMHALL (age 47) and third wife, ALICE LOUISE REYNOLDS (age 26—daughter of Seventy's President George Reynolds), were married in Price, Emery Co., Utah, by Apostle JOHN W. TAYLOR. See 6 February 1891, 19 May 1894, 25 October 1897, 11 March 1898, and 8 August 1900.

18 July 1900—JOHN M. CANNON (age 34) and second wife, MARGARET PEART (CARDALL—age 31), were married in Salt Lake City by Apostle MATTHIAS F. COWLEY.

18 July 1900—Local Seventy's president HUGH J. CANNON (age 30) and second wife, VILATE GRAY PEART (age 29), were married in Salt Lake City by Apostle MATTHIAS F. COWLEY. Ward bishop ORSON F. WHITNEY (age 45) had proposed to her four days earlier.

18 July 1900—Ward bishop ROBERT MORRIS (age 56) and fourth wife, SARAH ELLEN DUNCAN (age 32), were married with civil license in Manti Temple, Sanpete Co., Utah, by its president John D. T. McAllister—while MORRIS (a widower) cohabited with pre-manifesto plural wives.

6 August 1900—Stake patriarch THOMAS CHAMBERLAIN JR. (age 46) and sixth wife, MARY ELIZABETH WOOLLEY (age 30), were married in Salt Lake City by Apostle MATTHIAS F. COWLEY. She gave birth on 3 February 1902 in the otherwise-empty house of Julina Lambson (Smith), who was residing in Beehive House with then-President Joseph F. Smith. Julina nursed her after postbirth surgery, and MARY ELIZABETH remained in Julina's house until 1904.

8 August 1900 (not "1894," not "1898")—Brigham Young Academy's president BENJAMIN CLUFF JR. (age 42) and third wife, FLORENCE MARY REYNOLDS (age 26—daughter of Seventy's President George Reynolds), were married in Colonia Díaz, Chihuahua, Mexico, by Seventy's President Seymour B. Young, as instructed by First Presidency's Second Counselor Joseph F. Smith (despite in-

person refusals of CLUFF by stake president Anthony W. Ivins in September 1899 and by <u>Church President Lorenzo Snow</u> on 13 October 1899). <u>See</u> 14 July 1900.

9 August 1900—JOSEPH I. CLAWSON (age 44) and second wife, CELESTIA JANE DURFEE (age 22), were married in Colonia Dublán, Chihuahua, by <u>Seventy's President Seymour B. Young</u>, as instructed by <u>First Presidency's Second Counselor Joseph F. Smith</u>. <u>See</u> 21 October 1900

16 August 1900 (during meeting of First Presidency with apostles in Salt Lake Temple)—<u>First Counselor George Q. Cannon</u> said to <u>Lorenzo Snow</u>: "President, I ask that I not be excommunicated if I fall in love without your approval, if I have no children and take a woman and have one by her." <u>See</u> 23 September 1891, 5 April 1894, and 4 March 1897.

23 August 1900—Ward bishop JAMES L. WRATHALL (age 39) and second wife, CHARLOTTE ELIZABETH ROWBERRY (age 27), were married in Salt Lake City by <u>Apostle MATTHIAS F. COWLEY</u>. WRATHALL had received "second anointing" with first wife on May 17.

25 August 1900—Branch president HARRY E. BAKER (age 45) and third wife, CHARLOTTE ANN MILLS (age 34), were married in Salt Lake City by <u>Apostle MATTHIAS F. COWLEY</u>.

25 August 1900—HARRY E. BAKER (age 45) and fourth wife, REBECCA GERTRUDE LORDEN (age 23), were married in Salt Lake City by <u>Apostle MATTHIAS F. COWLEY</u>.

24 September 1900—Ward bishop WILLIAM H. LEWIS (age 62) and fourth wife, MARY KIRSTINE LARSEN (JENSEN—age 47), were married in Lewiston, Cache Co., Utah, by <u>Apostle MATTHIAS F. COWLEY</u>.

7 October 1900—Local Seventy's president CHARLES A. WELCH (age 40) and second wife, EMMA ROSETTA BULL (WHITE—age 38), were married in Salt Lake City by <u>Apostle MATTHIAS F. COWLEY</u>.

13 October 1900—DAVID O. WILLEY (age 51) and second wife, ANN ELIZABETH COWLEY (age 36), were married in Salt Lake City by <u>Apostle MATTHIAS F. COWLEY</u>.

21 October 1900—Ward bishop JOHN T. WHETTEN (age 38) and third wife, LORANIA NELSON (FOUTZ—age 41), were married in Colonia García, Chihuahua, Mexico, by Juárez Stake's patriarch Alexander F. Macdonald. This ceremony was secretly authorized by <u>First Presidency's Second Counselor Joseph F. Smith</u>, even though <u>Church President Lorenzo Snow</u> had told Macdonald in person on 13 August 1900 <u>not</u> to perform this requested marriage. WHETTEN'S original letter of request and <u>Counselor Smith</u>'s letter to Macdonald accompanied the certificate that the patriarch prepared for this marriage. Six months after the ceremony, <u>President Snow</u> threatened to excommunicate Macdonald for per-

forming such marriages. Upon receiving those certificates eleven years after being sustained in October 1901 as Snow's successor, President Smith said: "All of this work that Brother Macdonald performed [from 1900 to his death in 1903] was duly authorized by me." See 8 August 1900, 9 August 1900, and 8 November 1900.

3 November 1900—Stake president FRANK Y. TAYLOR (age 38) and second wife, ALICE MAY NEFF (age 23), were married in Salt Lake City by Apostle MATTHIAS F. COWLEY.

3 November 1900—JOHN M. CANNON (age 35) and third wife, HARRIET SEYMOUR NEFF (age 35), were married in Salt Lake City by Apostle MATTHIAS F. COWLEY.

6 November 1900—Mission president FRANKLIN S. BRAMWELL (age 41) and third wife, MARY ANN MARTIN (age 32), were married in Salt Lake City by Apostle MATTHIAS F. COWLEY.

8 November 1900—JOHN ECHOLS (age 40) and fourth wife, SARAH ELIZABETH ANGLE (age 19), were married in Colonia Juárez, Chihuahua, Mexico, by Apostle ABRAHAM OWEN WOODRUFF, with verbal authorization from First Presidency's Second Counselor Joseph F. Smith (despite Church President Lorenzo Snow's repeated refusal to allow new polygamous marriages in Mexico, even for residents). See 8 August 1900 and 21 October 1900.

14 November 1900—Ward bishop GEORGE M. HAWS (age 41) and third wife, MARTHA HENRIETTA WALL (age 22), were married in Colonia Juárez by patriarch Alexander F. Macdonald.

18 November 1900—At Juárez Stake conference, Apostle ABRAHAM OWEN WOODRUFF wrote that he "felt the spirit of prophecy and prophecied [sic] that 'no year should pass until the coming of the Son of Man in which there should be no poligamist [sic] children born.['] All present said Amen." Among those present were First Presidency's Second Counselor Joseph F. Smith and Seventy's President Seymour B. Young. See 8 August 1900 and 8 November 1900.

18 November 1900—ABRAHAM DONE (age 47) and second wife, LOUISA MATILDA WILHELMINA HAAG (ABEGG—age 31), were married in Colonia Juárez by stake patriarch Alexander F. Macdonald, with recommends signed by stake president Anthony W. Ivins.

18 November 1900—MORLEY L. BLACK (age 25) and second wife, RACHEL ANN LUNT (age 17), were married in Colonia Juárez by stake patriarch Alexander F. Macdonald. Ditto.

19 November 1900—NEWEL K. YOUNG (age 23) and second wife, GENEVA COOLEY (age 17), were married in Colonia Juárez by stake patriarch Alexander F. Macdonald. Ditto.

19 November 1900—WILLARD R. GUYMON (age 36) and third wife, ELLEN GOWER LUNT (age 20), were married in Colonia Juárez by stake patriarch Alexander F. Macdonald. Ditto.

20 November 1900—ERNEST GUY TAYLOR (age 28) and second wife, GERTRUDE MARTINEAU (age 30), were married in Colonia Juárez by stake patriarch Alexander F. Macdonald.

25 November 1900—Ward bishopric counselor DAVID P. BLACK (age 26) and second wife, ALZADA KARTCHNER (age 15), were married in Colonia García, Chihuahua, by stake patriarch Alexander F. Macdonald.

29 November 1900—WALTER JOSHUA STEVENS (age 43) and second wife, SARAH ELLIS HAWLEY (PEARSON—age 40), were married in Colonia García by stake patriarch Alexander F. Macdonald, with recommends signed by stake president Anthony W. Ivins.

6 January 1901—EDWARD F. TURLEY (age 31) and second wife, ANNIE SARIAH MARTINEAU (WALSER—age 25), were married in Colonia Juárez by patriarch Alexander F. Macdonald. Ditto.

6 January 1901—Local Seventy's president HENRY S. TANNER (age 31) and second wife, MARY ISABEL RICHARDS (age 22), were married in Salt Lake City by Apostle MATTHIAS F. COWLEY.

16 January 1901—Formerly ward bishopric counselor and county sheriff HUGH L. ADAMS (age 49) and second wife, HANNAH MARIA BAYLES (age 39), were married in Salt Lake City by Apostle MATTHIAS F. COWLEY.

18 January 1901—Apostle ABRAHAM OWEN WOODRUFF (age 28) and second wife, ELIZA AVERY CLARK (age 18), were married in Preston, Oneida (later Franklin) Co., Idaho, by Apostle MATTHIAS F. COWLEY. OWEN's diary shows that he received permission to court her from First Presidency's Second Counselor Joseph F. Smith on 30 August 1900 ("he counsiled [*sic*] me to follow the impression I have had") and from First Counselor George Q. Cannon on 11 October 1900 ("Spoke to Prest. C about E."). See 17 April 1902 and 26 May 1904.

22 January 1901 (not "1900")—SAMUEL S. NEWTON (age 42) and second wife, AMY SUSAN JOHNSON (age 31), were married bigamously as residents of Utah with civil license in Evanston, Uinta Co., Wyoming, by ward bishop James Brown.

10 February 1901—Mission president JOSEPH E. ROBINSON wrote: "I received the information and encouragement I wanted from Bro. G." This referred to Apostle HEBER J. GRANT's approval of his marrying polygamously, which occurred two months later in Utah. See 7 April 1901.

21 February 1901—MOSES M. SANDERS JR. (age 48) and third wife, LILLIAN MAY JACKSON (age 22), were married in Colonia Juárez, Chihuahua, Mexico, by stake patriarch Alexander F. Macdonald, with recommends signed by stake president Anthony W. Ivins.

22 February 1901—ORSON P. BROWN (age 37) and third wife, ELIZABETH GRAHAM MACDONALD (WEBB—age 26), were married in Colonia Juárez by stake patriarch Alexander F. Macdonald. Ditto.

22 February 1901—LOUIS PAUL CARDON (age 32) and second wife, EDITH JEMIMA DONE (age 21), were married in Colonia Juárez by stake patriarch Alexander F. Macdonald. Ditto.

2 March 1901—WILLIAM L. YOUNG (age 25) and second wife, LAURA PHOEBE HAWS (age 16), were married in Colonia Pacheco, Chihuahua, by patriarch Alexander F. Macdonald: "Approved [by] A. W. Ivins[—]Prest. of Stake."

8 March 1901—Stake patriarch LORIN FARR (age 80) and sixth wife, CLARA JANE BATES (McPHEETERS—age 42), were married with civil license in Salt Lake Temple by its president's counselor—the Presiding Bishopric's Second Counselor John R. Winder—while FARR (legally a widower) cohabited with two of his pre-manifesto plural wives.

12 March 1901—JABEZ E. DURFEE (age 46) and fourth wife, NANCY DUELLA MURPHY (HUMPHREY—age 43), were married in Colonia Dublán, Chihuahua, Mexico, by stake patriarch Alexander F. Macdonald.

5 April 1901—Stake president OLIVER C. HOSKINS (age 73) and third wife, PHILENE HALL (ZUNDELL—age 37), were married in Salt Lake City by Apostle MATTHIAS F. COWLEY.

6 April 1901—Formerly local Seventy's president ERASTUS BECK (age 48) and third wife, PEARL VERONA WHITING (age 24), were married in Colonia Díaz, Chihuahua, Mexico, by stake patriarch Alexander F. Macdonald, with recommends signed by Juárez Stake president Anthony W. Ivins.

7 April 1901—Apostle MARRINER W. MERRILL (age 68) and eighth wife, HILDA MARIE ERICKSON (age 31), were married in Salt Lake City by Apostle MATTHIAS F. COWLEY.

7 April 1901—Mission president JOSEPH E. ROBINSON (age 33) and second wife, WILLMIA BROWN (age 23), were married in Salt Lake City by Apostle MATTHIAS F. COWLEY. See 3 October 1901, 11 April 1904, 3 August 1904, and 10 April 1906.

10 April 1901—Ward bishop HEBER BENNION (age 42) and second wife, EMMA JANE WEBSTER (age 27), were married in Salt Lake City by Apostle MATTHIAS F. COWLEY.

16 May 1901—GEORGE A. McCLELLAN (age 28) and second wife, NELLIE ALLAN (age 19), were married in Colonia Juárez, Chihuahua, Mexico, by stake patriarch Alexander F. Macdonald, with recommends signed by stake president Anthony W. Ivins.

23 May 1901—Branch president HEBER F. JOHNSON (age 40) and second wife, ELLEN HODGSON (SENIOR—age 61—his widowed mother-in-law), were married in Colonia Juárez by stake patriarch Alexander F. Macdonald. Ditto.

24 May 1901—Stake patriarch ALEXANDER JAMESON JR. (age 42) and second wife, MARY AMELIA LARSEN (age 31), were married in Colonia Juárez by patriarch Alexander F. Macdonald: "A. W. Ivins verbally approved this."

26 May 1901—Church President Lorenzo Snow allowed Apostle HEBER J. GRANT to seek a plural wife (according to GRANT's diary and his 1906 letter to next Church President Joseph F. Smith). Snow withdrew permission on July 11th, even though GRANT (age 44) was courting FANNIE WOOLLEY (age 36). See 17–18 January 1902 and 6 October 1903.

17 June 1901—General board member GEORGE M. CANNON (age 39) and second wife, ELLEN CHRISTINA STEFFENSON (age 24), were married in Salt Lake City by Apostle MATTHIAS F. COWLEY.

27 July 1901—Deseret News published Apostle MATTHIAS F. COWLEY's talk, in part: "His [God's] hand will not be stayed until every principle revealed to the Prophet Joseph Smith will be established in power upon this earth and carried out by the sons and daughters of God." This was post-1890 code for new polygamy.

7 August 1901—GEORGE M. CANNON (age 39) and third wife, KATHERINE VAUGHAN MORRIS (age 25), were married in Salt Lake City by Apostle MATTHIAS F. COWLEY.

8 August 1901—Apostle and President of Quorum of the Twelve BRIGHAM YOUNG JR. (age 64) and seventh wife, KISTY/KIRSTY MARIA WILLARDSEN (age 33), were married in Sugarhouse District, Salt Lake City by Apostle MATTHIAS F. COWLEY. On 11 April 1903, YOUNG died. She married no one else.

27 August 1901—Ward bishopric counselor ROBERT SHERWOOD (age 43) and third wife, ALICE TERESA SCHOENFELD (age 27), were married in Salt Lake City by Apostle MATTHIAS F. COWLEY.

29 August 1901—Apostle JOHN W. TAYLOR (age 43) and fourth wife, ELIZA ROXIE WELLING (age 21), were married in Farmington, Davis Co., Utah, by Apostle MATTHIAS F. COWLEY, after TAYLOR received permission "in parables" from First Presidency's Second Counselor Joseph F. Smith. See 1 October 1890 and February/March 1903.

29 August 1901—JOHN W. TAYLOR (age 43) and fifth wife, RHODA WELLING (age 20), were married in Farmington, Utah, by Apostle MATTHIAS F. COWLEY. Ditto.

22 September 1901—Ward bishop JOSEPH C. BENTLEY (age 41) and third wife, MAUD MARY TAYLOR (age 16), were married in Colonia Juárez, Chihuahua, Mexico, by Apostle MATTHIAS F. COWLEY.

24 September 1901—DANIEL SKOUSEN (age 36) and second wife, SARAH ANN SPILSBURY (age 18), were married in El Paso, Texas, by Apostle MATTHIAS F. COWLEY.

25 September 1901—MILES A. ROMNEY (age 31) and third wife, ELIZABETH BURRELL (age 19), were married in Colonia García, Chihuahua, Mexico, by stake patriarch Alexander F. Macdonald.

3 October 1901—Mission president JOSEPH E. ROBINSON (age 33) and third wife, HARRIET SPENCER (age 24), were married in Salt Lake City by Apostle MATTHIAS F. COWLEY. See 7 April 1901, 11 April 1904, 3 August 1904, and 10 April 1906.

9 November 1901—JAMES N. SKOUSEN JR. (age 29) and second wife, EMMA FREDRIKA MORTENSEN (age 24), were married in Colonia Juárez, Chihuahua, Mexico, by stake patriarch Alexander F. Macdonald.

9 November 1901—ABEL W. HARDY (age 24) and second wife, CYNTHIA JANE PORTER (age 16), were married in Colonia García, Chihuahua, by stake patriarch Alexander F. Macdonald.

10 November 1901—Formerly ward bishop ARTHUR B. CLARK (age 47) and third wife, MARY POULSON (ANDERSON—age 65), were married in Salt Lake City by Apostle MATTHIAS F. COWLEY.

11 November 1901 (not "1898")—NEILS/NIELS FREDERICKSEN (age 53) and second wife, HANNAH MARIA FREDERICKSEN (JORGENSEN—age 41), were married in Colonia Dublán, Chihuahua, Mexico, by stake patriarch Alexander F. Macdonald.

15 November 1901—JOHN F. BURTON (age 29) and second wife, FLORENCE ADORA PORTER (age 25), were married in Salt Lake City by Apostle MATTHIAS F. COWLEY, by instructions from new Church President Joseph F. Smith (BURTON's first cousin once-removed).

19 November 1901—Díaz Academy's principal CHARLES R. FILLERUP (age 28) and second wife, MARY EVALYN JOHNSON (age 17), were married in Colonia Díaz, Chihuahua, Mexico, by stake patriarch Alexander F. Macdonald.

19 November 1901—ABIA E. JOHNSON (age 36) and second wife, VIVIAN LEMMON (age 18), were married in Colonia Díaz by stake patriarch Alexander F. Macdonald.

17 December 1901—Local Seventy's president and new municipal judge HENRY S. TANNER (age 32) and third wife, CLARICE THATCHER (age 22), were married in Salt Lake City by Apostle MATTHIAS F. COWLEY. Her father, ex-Apostle Moses Thatcher, disinherited her for it.

24 December 1901—Ward bishop LEWIS M. CANNON (age 35) and second wife, LILLIAN HAMLIN (CANNON—age 31—widow of Apostle ABRAHAM H.

CANNON), were married in Salt Lake City by Apostle MATTHIAS F. COWLEY. See 17 June 1896.

27 December 1901—General Superintendent of Church Schools JOSEPH M. TANNER (age 42) and fourth wife, CARRIE AMELIA PETERSON (age 31, sister-in-law of First Presidency's Second Counselor Anthon H. Lund), were married in Salt Lake City by Apostle MATTHIAS F. COWLEY.

29 December 1901—JOHN J. WALSER III (age 29) and second wife, MAY ADELIA ROBINSON (age 21), were married in Colonia Juárez, Chihuahua, Mexico, by stake patriarch Alexander F. Macdonald.

2 January 1902—Formerly ward bishop JAMES H. NEWTON (age 38) and second wife, ADA KAY (age 25), were married in Salt Lake City. He was excommunicated for this on 3 April 1903.

3 January 1902—GEORGE FRANCIS HICKMAN (age 32) and second wife, CHLOE PALMER (age 23), were married in Salt Lake City by Apostle MATTHIAS F. COWLEY.

7 January 1902—Apostle Reed Smoot (a monogamist) referred "to the principle of plural marriage" during the Quorum of Twelve's quarterly meeting, then said: "this order of marriage, if universally practiced, would save the world much sorrow and distress;—looked for its restoration . . ." See 20 January 1903, 16 January 1904, 26 May 1904, 8 December 1905, "After 2 September 1906," and 21 February 1907.

8 January 1902—Ward bishop ANGUS J. CANNON (age 34) and second wife, ANNIE RAUWERDA (ROWERDA) BOCKHOLT (age 23), were married in Salt Lake City by Apostle MATTHIAS F. COWLEY.

15 January 1902—JOSIAH E. HICKMAN (age 39) and third wife, HELEN JOSEPHINE HANSEN (age 21), were married in Salt Lake City by Apostle MATTHIAS F. COWLEY. In 1905, HICKMAN was wrongly rumored as advocate of a polygamist schism in Provo, Utah.

17 January 1902—Stake president GEORGE C. PARKINSON (age 44) and second wife, FANNIE WOOLLEY (age 37), were married in Colorado Springs, Colorado, by Apostle MATTHIAS F. COWLEY.

18 January 1902—Apostle HEBER J. GRANT (having no living sons, and with two pre-manifesto wives in their mid-forties) wrote from Japan to an Arizona stake president: "I want a wife or two—so that my name will not be wiped off the earth . . ." GRANT mailed a copy of this letter to Apostle JOHN HENRY SMITH. See 25 April 1899, 26 May 1901, and 6 October 1903.

27 January 1902—Formerly stake presidency counselor; now Oneida Academy's principal EDWIN CUTLER (age 33) and second wife, CAROLINE ERICKSON (age 26), were married in Preston, Oneida (later Franklin) Co., Idaho, by Apostle MATTHIAS F. COWLEY.

3 February 1902—Ward bishopric counselor JAMES HENDRY (age 40) and second wife, ELIZA STOLL (HAYES—age 39), were married in Salt Lake City by Apostle MATTHIAS F. COWLEY.

Mid-February 1902—Local Seventy's president BENJAMIN F. LeBARON (age 41) and his intended second wife (unnamed) were about to be married in Colonia Dublán, Chihuahua, Mexico, when "the young lady" suddenly returned to Arizona, "and the ceremony was not consummated."

4 March 1902 or thereabout—Formerly mission president; now Salt Lake City's police chief THOMAS H. HILTON (age 31) and second wife, JOSEPHINE McMURRIN (age 15, sister of Seventy's President Joseph W. McMurrin), were married in Colonia Dublán ("by an Apostle" according to HILTON'S descendants). Child on 15 June 1903.

6 or 7 March 1902—HARRY A. BRAMWELL (age 35) and third wife (first plural), SOPHRONIA TUCKER (SMITH—age 27), were married in Great Falls, Cascade Co., Montana, by Apostle ABRAHAM OWEN WOODRUFF, who asked his own wife, Helen, on August 5 to contact "Sophronia Tucker . . . Tell her I have no authority to release them from any covenant they have made with the Lord." Child on 9 January 1903.

9 March 1902—CHARLES F. GARDNER (age 43) and second wife, SARAH ELLEN COX (age 16), were married as residents in Colonia Juárez, Chihuahua, Mexico, by stake president Anthony W. Ivins. This is the first-known polygamous marriage that recently sustained Church President Joseph F. Smith allowed Ivins to perform. See 23 July 1899.

12 March 1902—THOMAS CHAMBERLAIN III (age 25) and second wife, CHRISTINA MARIE LARSEN (age 19), residents of Kane Co., Utah, were married bigamously with civil license in Logan Temple, Cache Co. by the temple president's counselor Thomas Morgan.

13 March 1902—Formerly local Seventy's president JOSEPH W. MUSSER (age 30) and second wife, MARY CAROLINE HILL (age 28), were married in Salt Lake City by Apostle MATTHIAS F. COWLEY.

13 March 1902—Stake presidency counselor and Juárez Academy's president GUY C. WILSON (age 37) and second wife, AGNES MELISSA STEVENS (age 18), were married in Colonia Juárez, Chihuahua, Mexico, by stake president Anthony W. Ivins.

2 April 1902—Ward bishop HEBER BENNION (age 43) and third wife, MARY BRINGHURST (age 21), were married in Salt Lake City by Apostle MATTHIAS F. COWLEY.

6 April 1902—Stake president WILLIAM H. SMART (age 40) and second wife, MARY ELIZABETH WALLACE (GARRETT—age 44), were married in Salt Lake City by Apostle MATTHIAS F. COWLEY.

13 April 1902—General board member HORACE H. CUMMINGS (age 43) and second wife, MATILDA SOPHIA WILCOX (BLISS—age 42), were married in Salt Lake City by Apostle MATTHIAS F. COWLEY.

17 April 1902—Apostle ABRAHAM OWEN WOODRUFF (age 29) discussed with Church President Joseph F. Smith his hope to marry Ogden schoolteacher CLARA PRATT ELDREDGE (age 25) as third wife: "In refer[r]ing to the Ogden case[,] he [JFS] said while I can not advise you to do this[,] I will not advise you not to do it.'" See 18 January 1901 and 26 May 1904.

Before 27 May 1902 (when he became a full-time missionary, and not on "20 May 1904")—Local Seventy's president RICHARD D. BROWN JR. (age 55) and fourth wife, EMMA EMILY SCHOFIELD (age 19), married in Harrisville, Weber Co., Utah, by verbal agreement (without officiator—see 5 April 1894). By pseudonym "Mrs. Farnsworth," she admitted this to ward bishopric on 14 July 1902, causing BROWN to return from British Mission on August 27. EMMA retracted her previous statement on September 8, after which bishop exonerated BROWN, who remained Seventy's president. After third wife's legal divorce on 18 March 1904, he and EMMA were married with civil license on April 26 in Layton, Davis Co., Utah, by ward bishop Daniel B. Harris.

27 May 1902 (not "17 May")—WALTER B. LEWIS (age 35) and second wife, ESTHER DELCINA WILSON (age 23), were married in Colonia Juárez, Chihuahua, Mexico, by stake president Anthony W. Ivins—the first known that President Joseph F. Smith let him perform for a non-resident.

17 June 1902 or thereabout—ADELBERT CAZIER (age 42) and second wife, ELIZABETH GRACE McCUNE (age 38), were authorized by Apostle GEORGE TEASDALE (undoubtedly with a ceremony) to resume their sexual relationship in Salt Lake City, for which CAZIER and GRACE had been excommunicated on 19 October 1890 in Nephi, Juab Co., Utah. They had been approved on 15 January 1892 for baptism—on the condition of ending their sexual cohabitation, which requirement they had delayed accepting until April 1892. CAZIER told Seventy's President BRIGHAM H. ("B. H.") ROBERTS on 29 September 1903: "Sister Grace McCune is my God given Wife." Child on 23 October 1904.

24 July 1902—MAHONRI M. STEELE JR. (age 32) and second wife, MARTHA JANE LeFEVER (age 29), were married as nonresidents in Northwest Territory (later Alberta Province), Canada, by Apostle MATTHIAS F. COWLEY.

3 August 1902—Local Seventy's president SAMUEL G. SPENCER (age 38, brother-in-law of Apostle RUDGER CLAWSON) and third wife, ELIZABETH ANNIE CABLE (age 27), were married in Preston, Oneida (later Franklin) Co., Idaho.

12 August 1902—Mission president JAMES G. DUFFIN (age 42) and second wife, AMELIA BARBARA CARLING (age 25), were married as nonresidents in Ciudad Juárez, Chihuahua, Mexico, by Apostle MATTHIAS F. COWLEY.

16 August 1902—JOEL S. EAGER (age 44) and third wife, EMILY JANE LEE (age 28), were married in Colonia Juárez, Chihuahua, by <u>Apostle MATTHIAS F. COWLEY</u>, witnessed by stake president Anthony W. Ivins.

16 August 1902—ORIN E. BARNEY (age 34) and second wife, SARAH ELIZABETH FENN (age 17), were married in Colonia Juárez by <u>Apostle MATTHIAS F. COWLEY</u>. Ditto.

16 August 1902—ISAAC ALLDREDGE III (age 31) and second wife, MARIA DELILA VanLEUVEN (age 19), were married in Colonia Juárez by <u>Apostle MATTHIAS F. COWLEY</u>.

16 August 1902—JOHN J. HUBER JR. (age 31) and second wife, PERCIS LULU MAXHAM (age 21), were married in Colonia Juárez by <u>Apostle MATTHIAS F. COWLEY</u>, witnessed by stake president Anthony W. Ivins.

16 August 1902—CHARLES W. LILLYWHITE (age 27) and second wife, ABIGAIL ESTELLA LEE (age 25), were married in Colonia Juárez by <u>Apostle MATTHIAS F. COWLEY</u>. Ditto.

16 August 1902—JABEZ E. DURFEE (age 48) and fifth wife, MARY FRANCES ADAMS (MERRILL—age 38), were married in Colonia Juárez by stake patriarch Alexander F. Macdonald.

17 August 1902—Ward bishop GEORGE W. HARDY (age 38) and third wife, BETSY JANE BUTLER (age 21), were married in Colonia Juárez by stake patriarch Alexander F. Macdonald.

17 August 1902—Formerly ward bishopric counselor WILLARD CALL (age 36) and second wife, LEAH PRATT (age 22), were married in Colonia Juárez by <u>Apostle MATTHIAS F. COWLEY</u>, witnessed by stake president Anthony W. Ivins.

7 September 1902—Ward bishop ORSON P. BROWN (age 39) and fourth wife, ELIZA SKOUSEN (age 20), were married in Colonia Juárez by stake president Anthony W. Ivins.

20 October 1902—THOMAS M. CARROLL (age 27) and second wife, EFFIE VILATE PORTER (ROWLEY—age 25), were married in Colonia García by patriarch Alexander F. Macdonald.

28 October 1902—SAMUEL W. JARVIS (age 47) and second wife, PEARLEY DEAN TAYLOR (age 21), were married in Colonia Juárez by stake president Anthony W. Ivins.

27 November 1902—Formerly mission president HENRY E. BOWMAN (age 43) and second wife, WILHELMINA WALSER (age 22), were married in Colonia Juárez by Anthony W. Ivins.

2 December 1902 (according to descendants)—JOSEPH JACKSON (age 49) and third wife, MARY ANN JONES (RAY—age 30), were married in Colonia Juárez by

stake president Anthony W. Ivins. Ceremony is missing from incomplete transcription of Ivins' "Marriage Record." (See 10 May 1898.)

8 December 1902 (while visiting Mexican colonies with Apostle Hyrum M. Smith, son of Church President Joseph F. Smith)—Seventy's President J. GOLDEN KIMBALL wrote: "Polygamous marriages are very frequent and common in this country. One man asked me to propose to a young lady living in SL City[,] asking her to have him. I think I shall undertake it."

24 December 1902—Formerly ward bishopric counselor PHILLIP H. HURST (age 42) and third wife, GEORGEANNA JONES (HURST—age 24), were married in Colonia Dublán, Chihuahua, Mexico.

19 January 1903—JOHN J. WALSER JR. (age 53) and third wife, ELIZABETH BRAITHWAITE (BURRELL, COON—age 44, his widowed mother-in-law), were married in Colonia Juárez, Chihuahua, by stake president Anthony W. Ivins.

19 January 1903—JAMES F. CARROLL (age 32) and second wife, ANNIE ELIZA BURRELL (age 22), were married in Colonia Juárez by stake president Anthony W. Ivins.

20 January 1903—Local Seventy's president JENS C. L. BREINHOLT (age 61) and fourth wife, MARGRETHA LISETTE HANSEN (ARNDT—age 43), were married in Colonia Juárez by stake president Anthony W. Ivins.

20 January 1903—Apostle Reed Smoot was elected to US Senate. See 23 January 1900, 16 January 1904, and 20 February 1907.

21 January 1903—Ward bishopric counselor ANSON BOWEN CALL (age 39) and fourth wife, JULIA SARAH ABEGG (age 17), were married in Colonia Juárez, Chihuahua, Mexico.

21 January 1903—Ward bishop ELAM W. McBRIDE (age 48) and second wife, OLIVE BLACKBURN CHAMBERS (GRAVES—age 34), were married bigamously with civil license in Salt Lake Temple by its president's counselor—First Presidency's First Counselor John R. Winder—while McBRIDE's first wife in Idaho "separated, this time more or less by mutual consent, that Elam might live what was then considered a higher law of the Gospel which our Church had been forced to suspend."

8 February 1903—HYRUM A. CLUFF (age 36) and second wife, DELIA FLORETTA HUMPHREY (age 18), were married in Colonia García, Chihuahua, Mexico, by stake patriarch Alexander F. Macdonald.

12 February 1903—JOHN A. BAGLEY (age 40) and fourth wife, MARY MATILDA PETERSON (age 26), were married in Preston, Oneida (later Franklin) Co., Idaho, by Apostle MATTHIAS F. COWLEY.

After 12 February 1903—Ward bishop WILFORD W. CLARK (age 40) and second wife, PERNECY MAE BAGLEY (age 26), were married by Apostle MATTHIAS

F. COWLEY. Reported eight years later by <u>Apostle Francis M. Lyman</u> (without ceremony's date/place or wife's name).

By 15 February 1903—Ward bishop PHILO W. AUSTIN (age 36) and his intended second wife, MARY WOODRUFF (age 35), were preparing to marry polygamously when she unexpectedly died. She was sealed by proxy four days later to AUSTIN by <u>Apostle ABRAHAM OWEN WOODRUFF.</u>

23 February 1903—JOHN C. BEECROFT (age 31) and second wife, ARLETTA AMELIA FARNSWORTH (age 16), were married in Colonia García, Chihuahua, Mexico, by stake patriarch Alexander F. Macdonald.

23 February 1903—JOHN A. WHETTEN (age 23) and second wife, MARTHA ELIZABETH CARLING (age 18), were married in Colonia García by stake patriarch Alexander F. Macdonald.

February/March 1903—<u>Apostle JOHN W. TAYLOR</u> (age 44) proposed twice (weeks apart) to FLORENCE IVINS (age 17) in Colonia Juárez, Chihuahua, to become his sixth wife. She said the proposals were "perfectly honorable," and her father, stake president Anthony W. Ivins, advised her to accept <u>TAYLOR</u>—but only if she really wanted to. She didn't, but her sister soon became another man's plural wife. <u>See</u> 1 October 1890, 29 August 1901, and 13 May 1903.

1 March 1903—Local Seventy's president EDWARD W. PAYNE (age 35) and third wife, ROSALIA TENNEY (age 18), were married in Colonia Dublán by stake president Anthony W. Ivins.

1 March 1903—Local Seventy's president FREDERICK W. JONES JR. (age 29) and third wife, LAURA ANN MOFFETT (age 17), were married in Colonia Dublán by stake president Anthony W. Ivins.

5 March 1903—Ward bishop JOHN T. WHETTEN (age 40) and fourth wife, SARAH LOUISA ELLIS (HASSELL—age 28), were married in Colonia Juárez by stake patriarch Alexander F. Macdonald.

10 March 1903—Formerly local Seventy's president DANIEL B. JONES (age 45) and second wife, RHODA ANN MERRELL (age 19), were married as nonresidents in Colonia Juárez by stake president Anthony W. Ivins.

12 March 1903 (<u>not</u> "October 1902")—Formerly ward bishop ARTHUR B. CLARK (age 49) and fourth wife, MARINDA ELIZABETH GRIFFITH (HOBSON, McCOMBER—age 46), were married in Preston, Oneida (later Franklin) Co., Idaho, by <u>Apostle MATTHIAS F. COWLEY.</u>

By 18 March 1903—Ward bishop DANIEL CONNELLY (age 41) was polygamously courting "Miss" HENRIETTA PEARCE (age 21) as his intended second wife in Eureka, Juab Co., Utah. Stake president James W. Paxman advised first wife on July 9 to be "forgiving," and he allowed CONNELLY to remain bishop for five more years.

7 April 1903—As a grand jury prepared to investigate new polygamy in Salt Lake City, Church President Joseph F. Smith told LDS leaders: "I would be willing to lay down my life to protect your liberty." Its July report found no evidence that any resident had married a new plural wife.

9 April 1903—Stake president DAVID K. UDALL (age 51) and third wife, MARY ANN LINTON (MORGAN—age 38), were married in Preston, Oneida (later Franklin) Co., Idaho, by Apostle MATTHIAS F. COWLEY. In 1905, UDALL was arrested in Arizona for unlawful cohabitation.

24 April 1903—Local Seventy's president and general board member LOUIS A. KELSCH (age 46) and third wife, JULIA MATILDA GUTKE (BRIXEN—age 43), were married in Preston by Apostle MATTHIAS F. COWLEY.

2 May 1903—Formerly ward bishopric counselor LUMAN E. SHURTLIFF (age 47) and third wife, MARY JANE ROUNDY (age 21), obtained a license in Lincoln Co., Nevada, for what would have been a bigamous marriage. With no civil record of a ceremony, some descendants claim that it occurred in Utah, but it was not on 10 June 1902 (as claimed).

13 May 1903—Stake presidency counselor GUY C. WILSON (age 47) and third wife, ANNA LOWRIE IVINS (age 20), were married in Colonia Juárez, Chihuahua, Mexico, by stake president Anthony W. Ivins. See 13 March 1902 and February/ March 1903.

5 June 1903 (not "1902")—ABRAHAM DONE (age 50) and third wife, ELLEN PRECINDA MOFFETT (age 20), were married in Colonia García by stake president Anthony W. Ivins.

9 June 1903—Seventy's President J. GOLDEN KIMBALL (age 50) wrote: "I am at present troubled regarding the principle of plural marriage . . . and cannot free myself from the thought that I should in some inconceivable way obey the same." He began courting "Miss Gillespie."

13 June 1903—WILLIAM A. MORTON (age 37) and third wife, JOSEPHINE ERICKSON (age 30), were married in Colonia Juárez, Chihuahua, Mexico, by stake president Anthony W. Ivins. She died on 28 June 1904.

22 June 1903 or thereabout (not "4 October 1903," when all of Mexico's polygamy officiators were in Salt Lake City)—Formerly ward bishopric counselor MARIUS (MORRIS) MICKELSON (age 37) and second wife, KATHERINE MATILDE (MATILDA) MARGRETHA SORENSEN (age 25), were married in Colonia Dublán, Chihuahua, as newly arrived residents.

25 June 1903—Stake president REUBEN G. MILLER (age 41, son-in-law of First Presidency's First Counselor John R. Winder) and second wife, MARTHA NELSON (age 33), were married in Preston, Oneida (later Franklin) Co., Idaho, by Apostle MATTHIAS F. COWLEY.

25 June 1903—Formerly ward bishop MATHONI W. PRATT (age 46) and second wife, AGNES JONES URE (age 32), were married in Salt Lake City.

3 July 1903—Ward bishop ORSON F. WHITNEY (age 48) and third wife, MIRINDA ANNA TORGESON (age 34), were married in Logan, Cache Co., Utah—according to a coded entry in his diary, which referred ten days later to himself as "Mohammed" (who allowed Muslims to marry "two or three or four" wives). On 24 May 1905, WHITNEY wrote: "Spent the evening at M. A.'s," and still mentioned "M. A. T." six years later. <u>See</u> 15 September 1895, 11 July 1900, and 18 July 1900.

15 July 1903—WARREN LONGHURST (age 35) and second wife, HELEN MARGARET CLARK (age 22), were married as nonresidents in Colonia Juárez, Chihuahua, Mexico, by stake president Anthony W. Ivins.

15 July 1903—Recently released as ward bishopric counselor BYRON HARVEY ALLRED JR. (age 33) and second wife, MARY EVELYN CLARK (age 18), were married as nonresidents in Colonia Juárez by stake president Anthony W. Ivins.

22 July 1903—Formerly stake presidency counselor JOSEPH F. THOMAS (age 45) and second wife, ETHEL GERTRUDE MICKELSON (age 19), were married in Salt Lake City by <u>Apostle GEORGE TEASDALE</u>. He had been "asked by Matthias Cowley to take a second wife."

1 August 1903 or thereabout—Stake presidency counselor ISAAC H. GRACE (age 45) and second wife, KATHRYN SORENSEN (age 33), were married. Child on 20 September 1904.

21 August 1903—ARTHUR W. HART (age 33) and second wife, EVADYNA HENDERSON (age 17), were married in Preston, Oneida (later Franklin) Co., Idaho, by <u>Apostle MATTHIAS F. COWLEY</u>.

26 August 1903—Formerly ward bishop BENJAMIN B. BROWN (age 36) and second wife, MARY VILATE HANSEN (age 30), were married as nonresidents in Colonia Juárez, Chihuahua, Mexico, by stake president Anthony W. Ivins.

27 August 1903—ALBERT M. MERRILL (age 31) and second wife, MAUD AUSTIN (age 27), were married in Salt Lake City by <u>Apostle MARRINER W. MERRILL</u>. <u>See</u> 16 July 1894.

29 August 1903—Stake president Anthony W. Ivins first mentioned in his diary the visit by <u>RUDGER CLAWSON</u> to Colonia Juárez, Chihuahua, Mexico. A son later wrote that the apostle "commanded Father in the name of the Lord to take another wife." He remained a monogamist. <u>See</u> 3 August 1904.

31 August 1903—JOHN C. NAEGLE JR. (age 39) and second wife, MILLICENT DOROTHY JAMESON (age 19), were married in Colonia Juárez by <u>Apostle RUDGER CLAWSON</u>.

6 September 1903—<u>Church President Joseph F. Smith</u> told Alberta Stake's priesthood meeting in Cardston, Northwest Territory (later Alberta Province), Canada: "No man ought to occupy a prominent position in the Church unless he is converted to every principle thereof." Post-manifesto code for polygamy.

6 September 1903—JOHN W. WOOLF (age 33) and second wife, MARTHA QUINA AUSTIN (LARSON—age 30), were married in Cardston, Northwest Territory (later Alberta Province), Canada, by Apostle MATTHIAS F. COWLEY.

11 September 1903 (according to descendants)—Ward bishop FRANKLIN D. LEAVITT (age 33) and second wife, JANE STEWART GLENN (age 20), were married in Cardston by stake patriarch John A. Woolf II, as authorized by Church President Joseph F. Smith, and conveyed to Woolf by resident Apostle JOHN W. TAYLOR (who acknowledged it).

14 September 1903—Stake president BYRON SESSIONS (age 51) and second wife, JANET EASTON (age 20), were married in Byron, Big Horn Co., Wyoming, by Apostle MATTHIAS F. COWLEY.

19 September 1903—Stake president HEBER S. ALLEN (age 38) and second wife, ELIZABETH SKIDMORE HARDY (age 18), were married in Cardston by stake patriarch John A. Woolf II (according to Apostle MATTHIAS F. COWLEY, not by Apostle JOHN W. TAYLOR).

25 September 1903—General board member JOSEPH W. SUMMERHAYS (age 54) and fifth wife, JANNA ANDREA FERNANDA ENHOLM (age 27), were married in Chicago, Illinois, by Apostle MATTHIAS F. COWLEY. See 25 February 1898 and 16 September 1905.

29 September 1903—Formerly ward bishop ARTHUR B. CLARK (age 49) and fifth wife, ETHEL ADOLPHIA SHIRLEY (age 27), were married as nonresidents in Ciudad Juárez, Chihuahua, Mexico, by stake president Anthony W. Ivins.

2 October 1903—Ward bishop NEWTON WOODRUFF (age 39) and second wife, ELIZABETH SUSAN WEEKES (age 37), were married in Salt Lake City by Apostle MATTHIAS F. COWLEY.

6 October 1903 or thereabout—First Presidency's secretary GEORGE F. GIBBS advised Apostle HEBER J. GRANT to enter plural marriage before leaving Utah to preside over the European Mission, saying, "that I was a fool, having no sons and with the great city of Liverpool in which to hide a wife, if I did not get one." This year, GIBBS (age 56) polygamously courted OLEA SHIPP (age 26), who declined him. Before GRANT left, Apostle MATTHIAS F. COWLEY told him, "if he could get a wife[,] he, Cowley, would go with him to Canada or Mexico and help him out." GRANT wrote that Apostle ABRAHAM OWEN WOODRUFF "tried his level best to get me to take a plural wife before I went to Europe, claiming that President Smith approved of it." On 5 January 1906, GRANT's letter asked Church President Joseph F. Smith NOT to drop COWLEY and JOHN W. TAYLOR from the Twelve: "What they have done I also have done or intended to do, and in so doing I would have done what I thought had the approval of my brethren." See 22 February 1897, 25 April 1899, 26 May 1901, 18 January 1902, and 26 January 1907.

22 October 1903—Apostle <u>JOHN HENRY SMITH</u> advised First Presidency that the polygamous cohabitation (renewed after a decade of Church-required celibacy) by GRACE McCUNE with ADELBERT CAZIER should "be passed over"—despite first wife's complaints to LDS leaders.

23 October 1903—Apostle <u>JOHN HENRY SMITH</u> (age 55) proposed to ANN MOUSLEY CANNON (age 34) as his intended third wife, assuring her that "a man [—] situated as I am [—] is allowed to marry again, by going beyond Uncle Sams [*sic*, Sam's] limits to do so." She politely declined his offer, which he unsuccessfully repeated on October 31. By contrast, in a meeting of the apostles nearly six years later, <u>SMITH</u> claimed that he ended his post-manifesto courtship of an unnamed woman "upon the advice of the Pres. of Church." See 24 October 1894.

3 November 1903—EDWARD C. EYRING (age 35) and second wife, EMMA ROMNEY (age 19), were married in Colonia Juárez, Chihuahua, Mexico, by <u>ABRAHAM OWEN WOODRUFF</u>. Stake president Anthony W. Ivins recorded it.

11 November 1903—LOUIS PAUL CARDON (age 35) and third wife, MARY IRENA PRATT (age 21), were married in Colonia Dublán, Chihuahua, by <u>Apostle ABRAHAM OWEN WOODRUFF</u>. Ditto.

18 November 1903—Ward bishop GEORGE C. NAEGLE (age 43) and fourth wife, PHILINDA KEELER (age 25), were married in Colonia Oaxaca, Sonora, by <u>Apostle ABRAHAM OWEN WOODRUFF</u>. Ditto.

18 November 1903—GEORGE C. NAEGLE (age 43) and fifth wife, JENNIE DORA JAMESON (age 17), were married in Colonia Oaxaca by <u>Apostle ABRAHAM OWEN WOODRUFF</u>. Ditto.

25 November 1903—JORGEN S. JORGENSEN (age 55) and third wife, JOHANNA LOVISE CHARLOTTE IBORG (age 35), were married in Colonia Juárez by stake president Anthony W. Ivins.

26 December 1903—Local Seventy's president WILEY G. CRAGUN (age 43) and second wife, HILDA SOPHIA LARSON (age 28), were married in Salt Lake City by <u>Apostle RUDGER CLAWSON</u>.

27 December 1903—HYRUM D. C. CLARK (age 47, secret father-in-law of <u>Apostle ABRAHAM OWEN WOODRUFF</u>) and second wife, MARY ALICE ROBINSON (age 25), were married in Salt Lake City, probably by an apostle.

5 January 1904—Formerly ward bishopric counselor JESSE M. SMITH (age 45) and second wife, PRISCILLA SMITH (GIBBONS—age 26), were married in Salt Lake City by <u>Apostle MATTHIAS F. COWLEY</u>, witnessed by "two Apostles" (unnamed by SMITH's family).

16 January 1904—US Senate began Smoot Case inquiry due to a formal protest that "the supreme authorities in the [LDS] church, of whom Senator-elect Reed Smoot is one . . . connive at and encourage the practice of polygamy . . ." See 23 January 1900, 7 January 1902, 20 January 1903, 8 December 1905, and 20 February 1907.

31 January 1904—Formerly local Seventy's president JOHN A. SILVER (age 48) and second wife, NELL YOUNG CLAWSON (BROWN—age 31), were married as nonresidents in Colonia Juárez, Chihuahua, Mexico, by stake president Anthony W. Ivins.

1 February 1904 (<u>not</u> "15 June 1899")—Stake president EDWARD J. WOOD (age 37) and second wife, ADALAID SOLOMON (age 32), were married in Cardston, Northwest Territory (later Alberta Province), Canada, by stake patriarch John A. Woolf II (according to <u>Apostle MATTHIAS F. COWLEY</u>). <u>See</u> 11 September 1903.

23 February 1904—Formerly mission president OLONZO D. MERRILL (age 36) and second wife, MARY LAURA HANSEN (age 23), were married in Preston, Oneida (later Franklin) Co., Idaho, by <u>Apostle MATTHIAS F. COWLEY</u>, "with Angels as our witnesses."

3 March 1904—JAMES THOMPSON (age 55) and fourth wife, BERTHA JENSINE NIELSEN (age 24), were married in Colonia Juárez, Chihuahua, Mexico, by stake president Anthony W. Ivins.

11 March 1904—BRIGHAM H. PIERCE (age 39) and third wife, SARAH ELLEN HARRIS (age 22), were married in Colonia Juárez by stake president Anthony W. Ivins.

13 March 1904—CHARLES E. RICHARDSON (age 45) and fourth wife, DAISIE STOUT (age 19), were married in Colonia Juárez by stake president Anthony W. Ivins.

29 March 1904—HEBER E. FARR (age 28) and second wife, ROSEMILDA RANGHILDA BLUTH (age 21), were married in Colonia Juárez by stake president Anthony W. Ivins.

6 April 1904—In response to the first month of testimony in the Smoot Case, General Conference adopted an "OFFICIAL STATEMENT" (nicknamed "The Second Manifesto"), which stated: "I, Joseph F. Smith, President of the Church of Jesus Christ of Latter-day Saints, hereby affirm and declare that no such [polygamous] marriages have been solemnized [since September 1890] with the sanction, consent or knowledge of the Church of Jesus Christ of Latter-day Saints, and I hereby announce that all such marriages are prohibited, and if any officer or member of the Church shall assume to solemnize or enter into such marriage[,] he will be deemed in transgression against the Church, and will be liable to be dealt with, according to the rules and regulations thereof, and excommunicated therefrom." <u>See</u> 24 May 1904, "By 1 August 1904," 3 August 1904, 16 September 1905, 21 February 1906, "After 2 September 1906," and 26 January 1907.

9 April 1904 or thereabout—WILLIAM D. CUMMINGS (age 42) and second wife, ZINA DORTHIE THAYNE (age 17), were married in Colonia Dublán, Chihuahua, by Mexico's newly resident <u>Apostle GEORGE TEASDALE</u>. This apostle's 1900

divorce and publicly attested ill health during the Smoot Case avoided any need to release TEASDALE from the Twelve on 8 April 1906. Allowed by First Presidency to return to Utah in August 1906, he died on 9 June 1907. See 25 October 1897, 17 May 1900, 11 July 1900, 17 June 1902, and 22 July 1903.

10 April 1904 or thereabout—General Superintendent of Church Schools JOSEPH M. TANNER (age 45) and fifth wife, SARAH TAYLOR (EVANS—age 45), were married in Northwest Territory (later Alberta Province), Canada, by Apostle MATTHIAS F. COWLEY.

11 April 1904—Church President Joseph F. Smith "advised" mission president JOSEPH E. ROBINSON "to locate the girls [his post-manifesto wives] in Mexico." See 3 October 1901.

1 or 2 May 1904—VICTOR C. HEGSTED (age 39) and third wife, HANNAH GROVER (age 33), were married. If (as claimed by descendants) in Salt Lake City on May 1, then not performed (as claimed) by Apostle MATTHIAS F. COWLEY, who was in Canada from April 10 to at least 4 June 1904. If the ceremony was not in Canada by COWLEY on the 1st, then Apostle RUDGER CLAWSON arrived in Salt Lake City the early morning of May 2 and emphasized "a very important appointment at 10 a.m. . . . on Ensign Peak."

24 May 1904—Hawaiian Mission's monogamist president SAMUEL E. WOOLLEY (age 44) wrote his wife, who had returned to Utah in 1902, about his interest in marrying a woman whom she knew: "I believe you are so thoroughly converted that[,] if the priesthood should command[,] you would be willing to obey." His next letter added that "we will be patient and let the Presidency [of Joseph F. Smith] say when it will be." A First Presidency secretary performed the polygamous ceremony two months after the Smoot Case ended. The apostles exonerated WOOLLEY in 1915 for his 1907 polygamous marriage, and he remained mission president until 1919.

26 May 1904—Apostle Reed Smoot complained to First Presidency that Apostle ABRAHAM OWEN WOODRUFF (age 31) had proposed polygamously to CLARA PRATT ELDREDGE (age 27), a niece of Smoot's only wife. OWEN died in Mexico on 20 June 1904, after visiting his plural wife AVERY and newborn. See 18 January 1901, 17 April 1902, and 8 December 1905.

4 July 1904 (month/day claimed by some for wrong year)—Ward bishopric counselor DON MORONI LeBARON (age 46) and third wife, MARY JANE PEARCE (STOWELL, STATEN—age 30), married in Burnham, San Juan Co., New Mexico, by verbal agreement (without an officiator). Married bigamously with civil license (as "Marona Lebron") on 25 November 1904 in Marfa, Presidio Co., Texas, by William A. Wells, justice of peace. Child on 30 May 1905.

9 July 1904—Apostle Francis M. Lyman wrote to Apostle GEORGE TEASDALE in Mexico: "What has already been done [regarding new plural marriages] is shaking

the confidence of Latter-day Saints. We are considered as two-faced and insincere." See 4 February 1905.

By 1 August 1904—Ward bishop LOUIS G. HOAGLAND (age 34) was polygamously courting "a young lady" in Salt Lake City and "has thought of taking up his residence in Mexico, in order to be able to enter the practice of plural marriage." Because he restated this intent in the Fall, the First Presidency prevented the marriage by calling him as mission president for New Zealand.

3 August 1904—Apostle RUDGER CLAWSON (age 47) and third wife, PEARL UDALL (age 24), were married in Grand Junction, Mesa Co., Colorado, by Apostle MATTHIAS F. COWLEY. In October, then-Second Counselor Anthon H. Lund began acting as a go-between for her letters to RUDGER. In May and November 1908, mission president JOSEPH E. ROBINSON "located him and Pearl in adjoining rooms" of California hotels. They began cohabiting in Liverpool on 17 October 1912, after his legal wife returned to the United States from British Mission. By the time PEARL left England on 7 January 1913, RUDGER "had released her from the marriage." Church President Joseph F. Smith granted them a divorce in June 1913. See 20 August 1891, 25 October 1897, 1 January 1898, 3 October 1901, 26 December 1903, 11 April 1904, and 10 April 1906.

11 August 1904—Stake presidency counselor JOHN THEODORE BRANDLEY (age 52) and fourth wife, EMMA MAGDALENE (MAGDALENA) BIEFER (age 35), were married in Stirling, Northwest Territory (later Alberta Province) by Canada's resident Apostle JOHN W. TAYLOR

20 September 1904 (not "1903")—Stake presidency counselor EDWIN T. BENNION (age 36) and second wife, AGNES STEWART CAMPBELL (age 43), were married in Lethbridge, Northwest Territory, "by an apostle." See today's second ceremony.

20 September 1904 (not "1903")—EDWIN T. BENNION (age 36) and third wife, MARY MINERVA CLARK (age 20), were married in Lethbridge "by an apostle." Her sister wrote seven months earlier about BENNION courting MARY with assistance of stake president FRANK Y. TAYLOR. A different writer on 24 February 1904 said that MARY's "friend" planned to travel "up north next summer" with "Prest. T." See today's third ceremony.

20 September 1904 (not "1903")—Stake president and general board member FRANK Y. TAYLOR (age 42, half-brother of Apostle JOHN W. TAYLOR) and third wife, ANNA STEWART CAMPBELL (age 43), were married in Lethbridge "by an apostle." See today's second ceremony.

26 September 1904—GEORGE H. BUDD (age 27) and second wife, MARY JANE DUKE (age 20), were married in Raymond, Northwest Territory (Alberta Province as of 1905), by Canada's resident Apostle JOHN W. TAYLOR.

30 September 1904—Stake president WALTER C. LYMAN (age 40) and third wife, LUCY HALLS (age 24), were married in Northwest Territory after Apostle MATTHIAS F. COWLEY declined to officiate in the United States, but "told him he could go to Mexico or Canada" for another officiator.

8 October 1904—Carl A. Badger, Apostle Reed Smoot's secretary in Washington, DC, wrote: "A B Irvine told me that Apostle [Abraham Owen] Woodruff told him that a certain number of worthy people had been commissioned to keep alive the principle of plural marriage. This was in reference to the new marriages about which gossip was rife." See 10 April 1906.

12 October 1904—Stake presidency counselor ANSON V. CALL II (age 49) and fourth wife, MARGARET ANN HEPWORTH (age 19), were married. She was endowed in Salt Lake Temple today, when he was proxy in a sealing. Required on November 20 to resign as counselor.

19 October 1904—DAVID W. RAINEY (age 46) and third wife, MARGARET BURTON (BARLOW—age 39), were married in Afton, Lincoln Co., Wyoming, with license by stake president George Osmond—while RAINEY (a widower) had a post-manifesto wife and infant living nearby.

1 January 1905—Church President Joseph F. Smith told a meeting of Salt Lake Temple's ordinance-workers that "the ordinances of God [are] more seriously threatened than ever before since the days of Nauvoo [Illinois in 1840s]. We have not only the hatred of outsiders, but of men and women professing to be Mormons."

4 February 1905—Post-Manifesto polygamist JOSIAH E. HICKMAN wrote: "O, but our people are howling over the supposed marriages since the Manifesto. It is principally those who never believed or entered plural marriage. It seems that a large % of our people are joining hands with our enemies to fight those who have entered this principle. There is a division between or among the leaders of the church. I am fearful of the threatened consequences."

25 March 1905—Apostle George Albert Smith told stake presidency counselor Sylvester Q. Cannon (whose three brothers married polygamously from 1896 to 1902 in Salt Lake City) that Church President Joseph F. Smith "does not wish to bring up [ecclesiastical charges against] those men who have entered this state of marriage since the Manifesto, [but] if complaint should be made about them or against them, he feels that he would have to have the case tried." See 19–20 October 1891 and 6 April 1904.

19 April 1905 or thereabout (when she was endowed in Salt Lake Temple)— Ward bishopric counselor PETER ANDERSON (age 52) and third wife, JULIA ANTONIA CHRISTENSEN (age 22), were married. Apostle MATTHIAS F. COWLEY later denied performing this marriage.

9 July 1905—OSCAR "RAY" KNIGHT (age 33) and second wife, CHARLOTTE MAUD HENINGER (age 28), were married in Magrath, now Alberta, Canada, by stake patriarch James Kirkham.

3 August 1905—JOHN T. SMELLIE (age 42) and second wife, ESTHER RUTH KIRKHAM (age 20), were married in Raymond, Alberta, by her father James Kirkham or (less likely) by Apostle MATTHIAS F. COWLEY.

5 August 1905—FRED W. MERRILL (age 27) and second wife, AGNES ELIZABETH CALDERWOOD (age 26), were married in Logan Temple, Cache Co., Utah, by Apostle MARRINER W. MERRILL, who died on 6 February 1906. See 16 July 1894.

6 September 1905 or thereabout (according to diary of stake president EDWARD J. WOOD)—General Superintendent of Church Schools JOSEPH M. TANNER (age 46) and sixth wife, LYDIA MATILDA HOLMGREN (age 30), were married in Cardston, Alberta, Canada.

16 September 1905—Apostle MATTHIAS F. COWLEY (age 47) and fourth wife, MARY LENORA TAYLOR (age 20), were married in Cardston by stake patriarch John A. Woolf II, as arranged by resident Apostle JOHN W. TAYLOR. In late 1910, as urged by then-Apostle Anthony W. Ivins, Church President Joseph F. Smith granted her a formal divorce.

16 September 1905—ERNEST GUY TAYLOR (age 32) and third wife, LILLIE SUSANNA HICKS (age 25), were married in Cardston by stake patriarch John A. Woolf II. See 11 September 1903.

16 September 1905—Church President Joseph F. Smith publicly announced in Colonia Juárez, Chihuahua: "There are no plural marriages being performed at present in the Church, in Mexico or any where else." Hours later, in the home of stake president Anthony W. Ivins, President Smith authorized formerly mission president WILLIAM G. SEARS to marry polygamously, then instructed general board member JOSEPH W. SUMMERHAYS (Smith's traveling companion on this trip) to perform the ceremony in Mexico. See 25 February 1898 and 21 February 1906.

28 October 1905—Apostles JOHN W. TAYLOR and MATTHIAS F. COWLEY signed prewritten resignations with an understanding that those would come into effect only to avoid an anti-Mormon amendment to US Constitution or the expulsion of Apostle Reed Smoot from US Senate. See 8 April 1906.

8 December 1905 (months after she moved from Mexico to Utah)—Apostle Reed Smoot asked Church President Joseph F. Smith "to have Owen Woodruff's [plural] wife removed some place safe." Apostle George Albert Smith then sent ELIZA AVERY CLARK (WOODRUFF) and her child to Wyoming. See 18 January 1901, 7 January 1902, 16 January 1904, and 26 May 1904.

1 January 1906—ALONZO L. TAYLOR (age 27) and second wife, KATE PEARL SPILSBURY (age 24), were married in Colonia Dublán, Chihuahua, Mexico, by Apostle MATTHIAS F. COWLEY.

By 31 January 1906 (according to letter by First Presidency secretary GEORGE F. GIBBS)—Formerly bishopric counselor WILLIAM PANTER JR. (age 64) was polygamously courting ALBERTINA VICTORIA NILSSON (PAXTON—age 45) as his intended third wife in Taylorsville, Salt Lake County, Utah. First wife divorced him within months.

February 1906 (not "1904" and probably on the 14th)—Stake patriarch JUDSON A. TOLMAN (age 79) and fifth wife, ELEANOR MAUDE ODD (WILLIAMS—age 43), were married in Bountiful, Davis Co., Utah (at residence of stake patriarch Samuel Bryson), by ward bishop DAN MUIR. When asked: "Did any member of the Twelve or First Presidency give you authority to do this thing," TOLMAN answered: "No sir." His polygamous marriages began a movement later called "Fundamentalist Mormonism," and TOLMAN was excommunicated on 3 October 1910. There is a huge drop in the number of TOLMAN's blessings recorded at LDS Church History Library (at least as it acknowledged to his descendant-biographer): from 25 in 1905, to only two in 1906, only one in 1907, none in 1908, only one in 1909 (on April 8), and none in 1910. Descendants have one of TOLMAN's blessings that their post-manifesto polygamist ancestor received on 5 March 1909, which was unreported by CHL to the biographer in early 1990s.

21 February 1906—Formerly mission president WILLIAM G. SEARS (age 33) and second wife, ATHELIA VIOLA CALL (age 18), were married in Ciudad Juárez, Chihuahua, Mexico, by JOSEPH W. SUMMERHAYS (see 16 September 1905). Church President Joseph F. Smith "was vexed" that SUMMERHAYS delayed the ceremony until she was endowed. If not before today, this marriage shows the overlapping of authorized violations of the "Second Manifesto" with UNauthorized ceremonies by "Fundamentalist Mormons." The apostles exonerated SEARS and SUMMERHAYS in 1910. Two years later, President Smith told mission president JOSEPH E. ROBINSON (whom he allowed to begin polygamous courtship in September 1907): "It is hard to make some people see the difference between cases [of new plural marriage from 1906 to 1912]—that you will permit this one but won't or can't that one."

8 April 1906—Apostle Francis M. Lyman publicly announced the resignations of JOHN W. TAYLOR and MATTHIAS F. COWLEY from the Quorum of the Twelve Apostles for being "out of harmony with the Presidency of the Church and the quorum to which they belonged." See 28 October 1905.

10 April 1906—JOSEPH E. ROBINSON told the eight apostles who were meeting with mission presidents: "Pres. Taylor died in exile for this principle [in 1887,] and

he gave men authority to perform the ceremony of marriage[,] which authority [—] I have been told [—] was never revoked." See 7 April 1901, 3 October 1901, 11 April 1904, 3 August 1904, and 8 October 1904.

14 June 1906—Stake patriarch JUDSON A. TOLMAN (age 79) and sixth wife, MARIE MARGARET FORSMAN (LAXMAN—age 53), were married at stake patriarch Israel Barlow Jr.'s residence in Bountiful, Davis Co., Utah, by ward bishop DAN MUIR. See "February 1906."

14 June 1906 (not "1905")—Ward bishop DAN MUIR (age 40) and second wife, GEORGINA BARLOW (age 28), were married in Bountiful by stake patriarch JUDSON A. TOLMAN. He consistently claimed that his marriage to WILLIAMS (actually in February 1906) was first time he and MUIR participated in post-manifesto polygamy, and not until 1906 did GEORGINA receive her temple endowment (which TOLMAN expected brides to already have).

After 2 September 1906 (when he returned from trip)—Stake presidency counselor JAMES A. ELDREDGE (age 49—Apostle Reed Smoot's brother-in-law) and second wife, LUCRETIA MAY COOLEY (age 29), were married in Bountiful by stake patriarch JUDSON A. TOLMAN. President Joseph F. Smith in July 1911 dissuaded the apostles from punishing ELDREDGE, who remained counselor until 1915.

9 December 1906 (while meeting with post-manifesto plural wives who had lived in Mexico for nearly three years to avoid subpoenas to testify in the Smoot Case)— Apostle JOHN HENRY SMITH told them: "Sometimes I have to swear (in courts etc)[,] and it doesn't matter what I think [—] so [long] that I can say I don't know." See 22 February 1897 and 23 October 1903.

26 January 1907—Visiting Apostle HEBER J. GRANT spared NATHAN CLAYSON (age 59) from being disfellowshipped or excommunicated when the Juárez Stake presidency dropped him from the high council for having married a plural wife "within the last year." See 6 October 1903.

20 February 1907—US Senate (by a vote of 42 to 28) allowed Apostle Reed Smoot to remain.

21 February 1907—Carl A. Badger, Apostle Reed Smoot's secretary in Washington, DC, confided to his wife: "The Senator has just said that he intends to tell the brethren when he gets home that if they want to continue this 'polygamy business' [—] they must leave the United States. I asked if he meant unlawful cohabitation, and he said no. Well, I am dumbfounded [sic] that there should be the least suggestion of the possibility of the Church attempting to establish polygamy [at the present time]; that it should be thought of for a moment."

21 February 1907 or thereabout (when she received a patriarchal blessing from polygamy advocate Harrison Sperry)—Ward bishop and set-apart temple ordinance-worker THEODORE McKEAN JR. (age 51) and third wife, MAUD ELLEN

BAGGARLEY (age 27), were married in Salt Lake City. Child on 23 October 1908, blessed by ex-Apostle MATTHIAS F. COWLEY.

5 April 1907—General Conference adopted an "Address To the World," which stated in part:

From that time [September 1890] until now, the Church has been true to its pledge respecting the abandonment of the practice of plural marriage. . . . When all the circumstances are weighed, the wonder is, not that there have been sporadic cases of plural marriage, but that such cases have been so few. It should be remembered that a religious conviction existed among the [LDS] people, holding this order of marriage to be divinely sanctioned. Little wonder then that there should appear, in a community as large as ours, and as sincere, a few over-zealous individuals who refused to submit even to the action of the Church in such a matter, or that these few should find others who sympathized with their views; the number, however, is small. . . .

    JOSEPH F. SMITH,
    JOHN R. WINDER,
    ANTHON H. LUND,

In behalf of the Church of Jesus Christ of Latter-day Saints, March 26, 1907. Adopted by vote of the Church in General Conference, April 5, 1907.

Contributors

Gary James Bergera, Smith-Pettit Foundation

John Brumbaugh, Utah State University

Kenneth L. Cannon II, Durham Jones & Pinegar

Byron W. Daynes, Brigham Young University

Kathryn M. Daynes, Brigham Young University

Kathryn Smoot Egan, University of Utah

Konden Smith Hansen, University of Arizona

Michael Harold Paulos, Independent

D. Michael Quinn, Independent

Index

Page numbers in italics indicate illustrations.